HUDSON TAYLOR
&
CHINA'S OPEN CENTURY

Book One: Barbarians at the Gates

HUDSON TAYLOR
&
CHINA'S OPEN CENTURY

BOOK ONE
Barbarians at the Gates

A. J. Broomhall

HODDER AND STOUGHTON
and
THE OVERSEAS MISSIONARY FELLOWSHIP

Chinese calligraphy by Michael Wang. Cover design by Melvyn Gill based on the insignia of a Qing (Ch'ing) dynasty viceroy or provincial governor (courtesy of the Victoria and Albert Museum, Crown copyright).

British Library Cataloguing in Publication Data
Broomhall, A.J.
 Hudson Taylor & China's open century.
 Book One: Barbarians at the gates.
 1. Missions—China—History—19th century
 I. Title
 266'.00951   BV3415.2

ISBN 0 340 52241 0

Foreword to the Series

China appears to be re-opening its doors to the Western world. The future of Christianity in that vast country is known only to God. It is, however, important that we in the West should be alert to the present situation, and be enabled to see it in the perspective of the long history of missionary enterprise there. It is one of the merits of these six remarkable volumes that they provide us with just such a perspective.

These books are much more than just the story of the life and work of Hudson Taylor told in great detail. If they were that alone, they would be a worthwhile enterprise, for, as the *Preface* reminds us, he has been called by no less a Church historian than Professor K. S. Latourette 'one of the greatest missionaries of all time'. He was a man of total devotion to Christ and to the missionary cause, a man of ecumenical spirit, a man of originality in initiating new attitudes to mission, a doctor, a translator, an evangelist, an heroic figure of the Church.

The historian — whether his interests be primarily military, missionary, or social — will find much to interest him here. The heinous opium traffic which led to two wars with China is described. The relationship of 'the man in the field' to the society which sent him is set before us in all its complexity and (often) painfulness. And the story of Biblical translation and dissemination will be full of interest to those experts who work under the banner of the United Bible Societies and to that great fellowship of men and women who support them across the length and breadth of the world.

Dr Broomhall is to be congratulated on writing a major

...k which, while being of interest *primarily* to students
...mission, deserves a far wider readership. We owe our
...ks to Messrs. Hodder and Stoughton for their boldness
...printing so large a series of volumes in days when all
...lishers have financial problems. I believe that author
...d publisher will be rewarded, for we have here a
...cinating galaxy of men and women who faced the
...allenge of the evangelisation of China with daring and
...votion, and none more so than the central figure of that
...laxy, Hudson Taylor himself. The secret of his persev-
...rance, of his achievement, and of his significance in
...ssionary history is to be found in some words which he
...rote to his favourite sister, Amelia:

'If I had a thousand pounds, China should have it. If I
had a thousand lives, China should have them. No! not
China, but *Christ*. Can we do too much for Him?'

Sissinghurst, Kent   Donald Coggan

A MATTER OF PERSPECTIVE

James Hudson Taylor is significant today for two main reasons. His influence in the world of Christian missions continues to be as great as, or greater than in his own day; and that influence extends far beyond China and the world of missions. To examine his role is the purpose of these books.

After centuries in which China remained in almost impenetrable isolation from the rest of the world, her gates swung slowly open in the mid-nineteenth century – and a mere century later slammed shut again. Leading up to that time and during that 'open century', the pressure of the West on a protesting China gave rise to changes undreamed of by the Chinese, Europeans or the Christian Church.

China's 'open century' is not a neatly-packaged period of ten decades. In earlier times tribute-bearing foreigners. were admitted, but only as vassals, never as equals. By the first opium war of 1840–42 and the Treaty of Nanking (Nanjing), concessions were wrested from an unwilling emperor and the summary execution of foreigners in the interior ceased. During the next decade or so of uneasy peace James Hudson Taylor and a few kindred spirits daringly began to test the continuing resistance, penetrating forbidden territory beyond the limits of safety and endurance. Then, in 1860 by the Treaty of Tientsin (Tianjin) and the Peking (Beijing) Convention after the second opium war, of 1858–60, freedom to travel and reside in any part of the empire was granted, though still at some risk to life. At last, after the Chefoo (Yantai)

Convention in 1876, imperial protection became a reality and foreign diplomatic, commercial and religious missions to China multiplied.

For seventy-five more years China suffered successive indignities imposed upon her by the West. The once powerful but increasingly obscurantist Manchu dynasty and its system of government were weakened and exploited until they finally disintegrated. In the process, however, the people were educated and 'enlightened', with the result that the republic inaugurated in 1912 was largely pro-Western and made the most of Western skills and patronage. Then with dramatic suddenness Mao Tse-tung (Mao Ze-dong) seized power in 1949–50 and the 'open century' abruptly ended.

In such unpromising soil 'the Church that will not die'[1] was planted and grew until 'its branches run over the wall'. The story of the missionary movement 'is inextricably bound up with the whole history of the Western invasion of China',[2] and because the opium wars still colour relations between China and the West, the truth about Britain's infamous opium traffic needs to be better known. Hudson Taylor and his associates did much to expose it. As for the criticism that Christian missions entered China 'hand in glove' with imperialism and opium, the facts recorded in this book speak for themselves.

Hudson Taylor was personally caught up in some of those events to the extent of being at the centre of more than one furore, occupying many pages of Parliamentary Papers[3] and debates, and columns in the press. Aged only twenty-one when he landed in Shanghai in 1854 but equipped by character and training to find his niche and gain the experience needed, he founded the China Inland Mission eleven years later, the stock from which a number of other missions trace their origins. Giving over fifty years to the service of China, he lived to see the beginning of a second half-century of even greater missionary achievement.

He attributed his inspiration under God to Charles

Gutzlaff, as he chose to be known after beginning life as Karl Friedrich August Gützlaff of Pomerania, (1803–51).[4] A man much maligned, Gutzlaff set his sights on attaining the unattainable, no less than to reach the remotest corners of the fast-closed empire with the gospel of Christ and in every province to plant a Christian Church — aims which Hudson Taylor was to see fulfilled. As a means to that end Gutzlaff initiated several European and British missionary societies,[5] including the Chinese Evangelisation Society, and Hudson Taylor's epithet for him was 'the grandfather of the China Inland Mission'.[6] In turn Hudson Taylor himself became the initiator of more British, Scandinavian, Continental and North American societies.[7] Any biography of Hudson Taylor must therefore take due account of this visionary prophet, Charles Gutzlaff. Perhaps here too the facts will restore the balance between Gutzlaff's true significance and the mistakes by which he tends to be known. By the same token a few false impressions of Hudson Taylor may fade as he also is seen in a new light.

To account for such an extensive treatment of Hudson Taylor's life and work, the views of an impartial historian may be recalled. The late Kenneth Scott Latourette, Yale University Professor of Missions and Oriental History, wrote in his *History of Christian Missions in China*,[8]

> Hudson Taylor was, if measured by the movement which he called into being, one of the greatest missionaries of all time, and was certainly, judged by the results of his efforts, one of the four or five most influential foreigners who came to China in the nineteenth century for any purpose, religious or secular.[9]

So categorical an assessment from an authority of the calibre of Latourette measures Hudson Taylor's significance by the stature of Robert Morrison, Charles Gutzlaff, Peter Parker, William Jardine, Lord Elgin, Sir Rutherford Alcock, Sir Robert Hart, John Livingston Nevius, General Gordon, Griffith John, William A. P. Martin, Timothy

Richard and other outstanding men who will be introduced as these books progress.

In his Tipple Lectures in 1950 Latourette said of Hudson Taylor that 'the repercussions of his daring faith were to be felt not only in the vast country to which he gave himself, but also in many other lands.'[10] Those repercussions were political and social as well as religious, affecting developments in India, in part through the abolition of the opium trade, and in Africa through the new missions which trace their origins to Hudson Taylor. Without question he would have been the first to disclaim such accolades, attributing all success to God whose servant he was. Such recognition as he deserves does stem from that relationship and lies in his being available at precisely this period of history. Only by knowing something of East-West relations and of Christian missions in China before Hudson Taylor's arrival there can we rightly understand him. The parallel strands of the story to be woven together include:

> Chinese and Western secular history as they bear on this subject;
> Catholic and Protestant missions to China through the centuries;
> Western trade and diplomacy in China as they affected missions;
> Personalities involved in the unfolding drama; and
> Hudson Taylor's own story, to show the sources of his innovations—at some risk of bathos where his private life intrudes upon the tapestry of international events.

Thomas Carlyle in his *Scottish and Other Miscellanies*[11] examined the essentials of a good biography, saying it should show the effects of society on an individual, his effect on society and how in each case they were produced. He cited Hudson Taylor's good friend William C. Burns as one of the few individuals deserving such a study. The standard biography of James Hudson Taylor in two volumes (1911 and 1918), by his son and daughter-in-law Dr and Mrs Howard Taylor, and in the one-volume abridgment (1965), has appeared in eighteen editions and numerous European and other languages and is still in demand. Its success is established. Then why another?

As indicated by its sub-titles, 'The Growth of a Soul' and 'The Growth of a Work of God', that biography, some anthologies and other books based on them have focused on the devotional side of Hudson Taylor's life and mission. They present the man of God. Apart from filial respect, Howard and Geraldine Taylor's generation believed in being generous, emphasising the strengths and passing over the weaknesses, so understandably few detrimental references appear in their books or remain in the archives. Hudson Taylor, however, was also thoroughly human. Feeling deeply, thinking intensely and with catholic generosity, yet dogmatic and authoritarian, he was emotionally his own greatest handicap and goad to greater endeavour. Mastering this, he survived an unusually eventful life as a servant of all, never nursing unhealed wounds. He was a great lover and potentially a greater sinner. His letters to his wife, even late in life, are love-letters, the intimacies often veiled in a minor Chinese vernacular interspersed among purely business matters.

In addition, much other unpublished material exists. Such books as show Hudson Taylor and the China Inland Mission (CIM) in the perspective of history and of other societies (as Marshall Broomhall's *The Chinese Empire*, Eugene Stock's *The History of the Church Missionary Society* and Latourette's histories), are more academic than for general reading. In justice to the older societies and to Hudson Taylor himself a fuller account had sooner or later to be written. Pollock did not set out to bridge this gap.

Hudson Taylor & China's Open Century falls naturally into two halves; the first in three books, beginning with the essential prelude to the story of his eventful first years in China, and to the period in which Hudson Taylor was led on inexorably to the unprecedented ventures for which he is best known. In the second half then follow for four decades the fortunes of the man and his Mission, in which thousands have now served for well over a century.

Apologia

The inordinate length of this biography needs explanation. When the China Inland Mission (CIM) withdrew from China in 1951 and the International Headquarters in Shanghai were taken over by Communist authorities, few Mission papers survived. But bound volumes of the CES *Gleaner*,[12] the CIM *Occasional Paper* (1865–75), *China's Millions, Field Bulletin* and annual reports (1875 to the present day) preserve a good deal of information. For the rest, Dr and Mrs Howard Taylor worked for years in the early part of this century, collecting and verifying documents and data on Hudson Taylor. They themselves were also his constant companions in his last years and made notes of what he said. Some of this was submitted with their queries and reconstructions to his sister Amelia and bears her annotations. Both she and his mother had preserved his letters and journals from his childhood. After the 1951 exodus, the members of the CIM were deployed in most other East Asian countries under the more appropriate name Overseas Missionary Fellowship (OMF) and all this collection is now in the OMF archives. There is no lack of source material.

Over the years I have read and re-read the Howard Taylor and Marshall Broomhall biographies, and twenty years ago learned from John Pollock of the existence of unused archive documents. My own research intended for a short biography unearthed so much of historical value and human interest that I correlated it chronologically for use as a source-book. To my surprise Messrs Hodder & Stoughton judged that many readers would welcome the full story, so, with an attempt to make it readable, here it is, an abridged but unexpurgated, unembellished collection of facts. In order to come freshly to the subject I have deliberately avoided using the classic biographies and

Pollock's imaginative *Hudson Taylor and Maria*. I hope my prosaic approach is justifiable as a complement to them.

Inevitably selection and some editing have been necessary. During the nineteenth century various attempts were made to standardise the roman spelling of Chinese words, and around the mid-twentieth century the Wade-Giles system was in common use, but the *pinyin* system of transliteration is becoming standard. In a history of the nineteenth century this mutation poses problems. The need to be intelligible tends to conflict with the need to be consistent and up-to-date. The People's Republic themselves use names and words made familiar by long usage (e.g. Mao Tse-tung and Peking rather than the *pinyin* Mao Ze-dong and Beijing), so I also have compromised by retaining them and some dialect variations. Other words look so different in the old and new systems, although the same in pronunciation, as to confuse the average reader, so I introduce the old in parenthesis. Many are identical, or so alike, or unfamiliar anyway, that the *pinyin* form is adopted. For the frustrated, Appendices 1 and 2 offer some consolation. With few exceptions the spelling used in quotations is unchanged.

Cumbersome English names and titles such as the Honourable East India Company and the American Board of Commissioners for Foreign Missions have been simplified, with occasional aids to memory, to forms like 'the Company' and 'the American Board', or simply 'LMS' and 'CMS' for London Missionary Society and Church Missionary Society.

Finally, the Acknowledgments and Bibliography set out other main sources from which the substance of this first book is drawn.

AJB

ACKNOWLEDGMENTS

The preparation of this series of books has involved too many people for justice to be done to each in a brief tribute, but I hope all will take the will for the deed. I am honoured and delighted by Lord Coggan's kindness in writing the foreword, the heart-warming mark of a long friendship, and am grateful beyond adequate expression to numerous longsuffering friends without whose painstaking support this work could have foundered. Edward England, Esq, formerly religious director of Messrs Hodder & Stoughton, has amazed and encouraged me by his willingness to publish at such length. Miss L. Longson typed from imperfect audio-recordings, and Miss M. E. Robertson, with Mrs D. de B. Robertson, won the publishers' acclaim for her exemplary transcription from much-edited first drafts. I am grateful also to Miss V. Kay for the expert line-drawings and maps, and to the Home Director and Editorial Secretary of the OMF for unlimited access to the Hudson Taylor archives. While I personally take responsibility for what I have written, and particularly for any opinions I have expressed, such quality as the final form possesses owes much to my kind, because frank, advisers: Colonel P. C. Harvey, Mrs P. J. F. Lenon, L. T. Lyall, Esq, Mrs J. E. G. McIldowie, the Rt Rev S. C. Neill, Rev R. H. Peskett and Dr J. H. Taylor.

For information and access to records and in some cases to rare books and manuscripts I am indebted to the directors, secretaries, librarians and archivists, variously, of the Bank of England Reference Library, the Banking Information Service, Lombard Street, the British and Foreign Bible Society, the British Library, the Church

Missionary Society, the Evangelical Library, the Foreign Office Records Library, the Museum of London Information Service, the National Maritime Museum and the Royal College of Surgeons. No history of this nature could but depend to a large extent upon the researches of scholars who have specialised in this field, and I have leaned upon some for information not readily found elsewhere. For years I have used *A History of Christian Missions*, (Pelican History of the Church: 6, © Stephen Neill, 1964) so when generous permission to quote him (from pp 137, 179, 443, 409, reprinted by permission of Penguin Books Ltd) was received from Dr Neill, I was as pleased as I am honoured by his critical reading of my typescript. He has corrected and challenged me on many points and taken great trouble to help me ensure accuracy. His *Colonialism and Christian Missions* has also served me well. Another indispensable source was Eugene Stock's *The History of the Church Missionary Society*, and for permission to use several quotations I am beholden to Rev H. W. Moore, Home Secretary. For more detail on early Roman Catholic history in China I drew upon Columba Cary-Elwes's *China and the Cross* and gratefully acknowledge permission from the publishers, Longman Group Limited, to quote freely.

Inspiration in the first place came partly from Brian Inglis: *The Opium War*, Hodder & Stoughton; from Dr George Woodcock: *The British in the Far East*, Wiedenfeld & Nicholson; and in the same area of secular history from Professor John King Fairbank: *Trade and Diplomacy on the China Coast*, Harvard University Press. To these copyright holders and their representatives I return sincere thanks for generous replies and permission to use quotations, as also to Franklin Mint Limited for permission to quote from Sir Arthur Bryant's *A Thousand Years of the British Monarchy*, Collins Publishers. The same courtesy and approval have come from the Trustees of the estate of the late Professor Kenneth Scott Latourette, the First New Haven National Bank, represented by Ms Sheilah B. Rostow, from Harry B. Adams, Associate Dean, Yale

University Divinity School, and from The Macmillan Company, New York, for quotations and other material from *A History of Christian Missions in China*. To Harper & Row, Publishers, Inc through Ms Linda S. Rogers I am also indebted for permission to quote from K. S. Latourette's *A History of the Expansion of Christianity*, Vol 6, *The Great Century: North Africa and Asia*, published in the United Kingdom by Eyre & Spottiswoode (Associated Book Publishers Ltd), for whose assistance I am grateful. The Tipple Lectures, under the title *These Sought a Country*, were also published by Harpers. If it is not too invidious to single out one more leading source, Hosea Ballou Morse's *The International Relations of the Chinese Empire*, 1910 (9 vols) must receive special mention. My bibliography and notes specify these and other sources, not only of facts and figures but of incomparable enjoyment during my first months of retirement.

AJB

BOOK ONE   BARBARIANS AT THE GATES

CONTENTS

MAPS

ILLUSTRATIONS

PART I

THE CAULDRON OF HISTORY

GUTZLAFF AND HUDSON TAYLOR

Charles Gutzlaff

Any biography of James Hudson Taylor must do more than pay tribute to the remarkable Charles Gutzlaff (1803–51), it must do him full justice. In September 1849 the Honourable Charles Gutzlaff, Secretary for Chinese Affairs to the governor and government of Hong Kong, sailed for Europe. Knowledge of his coming preceded him and on his arrival in Great Britain he found himself the focal point of a growing excitement. Since the publication in 1833 of his book on three voyages up the coast of China, in the days when only smugglers and adventurers dared attempt it, the name of Gutzlaff had been a household word in Britain and on the continent of Europe.

China was a land of mystery to most people. A few early travellers had written, unreliably, but the impression given of an all-but-inaccessible, hostile country was undoubtedly correct. Roman Catholic missionaries for many decades past had reported persecution, imprisonments and death under imperial edicts banning Christianity in the empire, but in more recent years events leading up to the first opium war and following from it had captured the interest of the public. They knew that Charles Gutzlaff, primarily a Christian missionary, and so fluent in Chinese that some mandarins would not believe he was a foreigner, was one of the leading interpreters and negotiators in the Treaty of Nanking (Nanjing), 1842, the treaty which opened five ports on the coast of China to European trade.

After serving as chief magistrate and governor on Chusan Island during its occupation by the British, Gutzlaff became Chinese Secretary in Hong Kong, and out of daily meetings for prayer and study of the Bible in his government offices, he set up a quickly-growing organisation called the Chinese Christian Union for the distribution and teaching of the Scriptures in mainland China. Good reports of this venture were coming in and now Charles Gutzlaff himself arrived in Europe to organise Chinese Associations to support and send European missionaries to join in the work. British businessmen impressed by his success launched a magazine, *The Gleaner in the Missionary Field*, to promote overseas missions, and soon the enthusiasm was spreading.

One family among many who took the *Gleaner* from the start, in March 1850, was James Taylor's. An apothecary of Barnsley, Yorkshire, he was a wide reader and a man of many interests. Fascinated by China as he was, even before reading Gutzlaff's *Voyages* some fifteen years previously, his concern for Christian missions was of even longer standing. Working with him as his apprentice was his seventeen-year-old son, James Hudson Taylor. Hudson vaguely shared his father's interest in China but was preoccupied with his own adolescent turmoils — until December 2, 1849, while Charles Gutzlaff was on the way home. On that day Hudson reached a decision which was to shape not only his life but that of thousands whom he influenced, and even of China itself.

He believed from that moment that God himself had told him to go to China, and began immediately to gather all the information he could find. Four years previously he had read and re-read Peter Parley's *China and the Chinese*. Now he borrowed Medhurst's *China: Its State and Prospects*, and immersed himself in it. He was not to know that this veteran, Walter H. Medhurst, was to be his friend and adviser when he reached China. With the famous Gutzlaff in Europe, an even greater influence came to bear on Hudson Taylor.

Gutzlaff's China

The first issue of the *Gleaner* reported that there were no more than about two hundred Chinese Protestant Christians altogether, forty-two years after the first Protestant missionary went to East Asia. And most of them were not in China but in the Straits Settlements (Penang, Malacca and Singapore) and in Java, Bangkok and Hong Kong. In all these areas and the new treaty ports on the China coast there were only about fifty missionaries and their wives. But the population of China proper was at the time believed to be 368 million, with many more millions in her dependencies and as immigrants in other countries of South-East Asia.[1] (The Statesman's Yearbook for 1907 cited a Chinese government census giving 426 million, but in 1937 the population was 450 million, so the 1850 figure would seem excessive.)

Apart from political restrictions, the very size of China posed an immense problem to would-be missionaries. The coastline stretched for two thousand miles from the border of Manchuria with Russia to the meeting with what we now call Vietnam. And Indo-China was more than nominally a tributary state. It responded briskly to the Chinese emperor's edicts. By land, the northern border extended between Russia and Manchuria, homeland of the ruling Manchu dynasty of all China, and then away to the west through the steppes and deserts of Mongolia and Turkestan for three and a half thousand miles. Within three hundred miles of Russia's Lake Balkash it then turned southward to where China, Russia and Afghanistan now meet at a single marker stone, with the Pakistan and Kashmir markers only forty miles away. Tibet was a tributary dependency. So were Nepal and Bhutan. Again the long border continued, turning eastward and skirting India and Burma, another tributary state (under Qian Long and for a hundred years), until it met the northern boundaries of Indo-China again. Even at this, China was a shrunken empire in comparison with what she had once been. Yet that was not all. Formosa, now called Taiwan, was a part of China proper; and Korea and the Kuriles, a chain of islands between Japan and Alaska, were tributary.

This immense area was ruled by the emperor's decree from the capital, Peking. It contained every variety of terrain, from the drifting sand-dunes of Gobi and the endless grassy steppes and snowy wastes of Tibet, to the forest-clad mountains of the far west and south and the seemingly endless alluvial plains of the northern and central provinces. Great rivers springing from sources high in the Tibetan plateau diverged to flow northward, eastward and southward. The northward one was the Yellow River, 'China's Sorrow' because of the repeated devastation from her flooding. The Yangzi River (more properly the Chang Jiang), navigable for eighteen hundred miles from its mouth near Shanghai, divided China roughly in two from west to east. And the great Mekong of Indo-China and the Salween in its steep gorges, flowed one into the South China Sea and the other through Burma into the Indian Ocean. But that was not all. A thousand-mile man-made waterway, the Grand Canal, linked north to south from the Tientsin (Tianjin) River near Peking (Beijing) to the Hangchow (Hangzhou) Bay south of Shanghai, crossing the Yellow and Yangzi Rivers.

So extensive a territory knew every kind of climate, from the steamy tropical and sub-tropical ricebowl of the south to the biting wind and deep snows of the far north. Everywhere along the coast was vulnerable to the lashings of Pacific hurricanes (typhoons), and the dusty wheatlands of the north and centre from time to time would suffer as greatly from drought and famine as from flood. The north-western plateau of Gansu (Kansu) and the south-western plateau of Yunnan, Guizhou (Kweichow) and southern Sichuan, both five thousand and more feet high, enjoyed blue skies and a mild climate, while between them in the

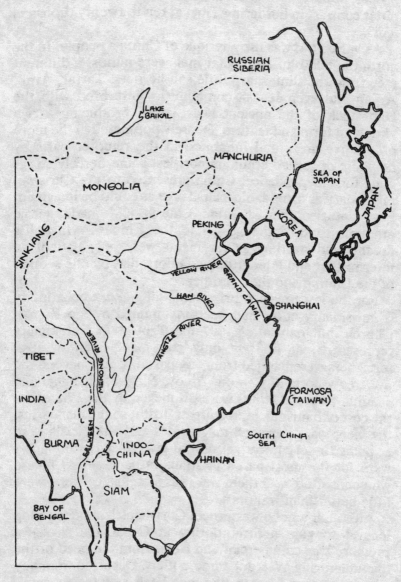

CHINA'S BORDERS AND GREAT RIVERS

deep market garden of the Four Rivers depression, Sichuan proper, hothouse summers and sheltered winters belied the bitter contrast in bordering Tibet at ten to twenty thousand feet.

As varied too was the physique of China's people. In the north the tall, bluff, muscular men were almost a different race from the slim, sharp little southerners. Tartar, Arab, Aryan and even Jewish communities interbred with the Han stock of the ancient heart-lands, producing a rich variety of form and feature. Densely populated in the more productive areas and inhabited in the remoter parts by nomadic or settled ethnic minorities, some fiercely struggling for independence, China presented to the Christian missionary as formidable a challenge as could be imagined. For centuries the Christian Church had made heroic attempts to take the gospel to the Chinese. Gutzlaff's dreams and startling achievements were only part of an intermittent and later sustained effort, first by one section of the Church and then another.

For the last four centuries something akin to continuity of missionary effort had been maintained by the Roman Church, but only after 1807 was Protestant Christianity represented, at first by only one man. Even in 1849 foreigners were banned from any part of China beyond the five treaty ports of Canton, Amoy, Ningbo, Shanghai and Tianjin. Imperial edicts were disobeyed by the Chinese at the cost of banishment, torture or death; so the mandarins, the viceroys, governors, magistrates and all officials were at pains to act always within the law. Because foreigners were for the most part Christians in name, any Chinese who consorted with them were suspect, and converts were little better than traitors.

Although among westerners Christians had been trying longest to gain a firm footing in China, the strongest pressure was commercial and came from the need of the manufacturing West for trade outlets. Debarred from any port other than Canton, the merchants resorted to smuggling, in strongly-armed ships, and the Chinese authorities were at their wits' end to stop the growing spate of the main stock in trade, opium.[2] Involuntarily but inevitably the missionary cause and the commercial cause became intertwined. And when Western governments came to the 'defence' of their commerce in terms of overpowering aggression, the missionaries were swept up and involved.

How then was the great nation of China to be evangelised when account is taken of such a vast area, such a great and diverse population and such determined resistance? From the beginning of their work at the end of the thirteenth century, the Roman Catholic missionaries headed away from the confining coast into the deep interior, into the very capital of the empire and the confidence of emperors. But their fortunes fluctuated, and the Catholic Church itself fell upon evil days in Europe. In the eighteenth century the Jesuits were banned, the papacy itself crumbled. In China a handful of intrepid men barely held on to life, let alone to their purpose. Most of the first Protestant missionaries saw sense only in doing what could be done in and from Canton and Macao and later the 'Five Ports', by translating the Bible, printing Christian literature and teaching such local Chinese as would listen.

Charles Gutzlaff, however, was a visionary. Long before it was permissible or even possible to reside in inland China he was propounding ways of reaching the remotest corners of the empire with the gospel, and succeeded in placing four German missionaries on the mainland, away from the treaty ports, quietly at work under the eyes of the authorities. His grand concept, the Chinese Christian Union, held the germs of success, and the principles he propounded were taken up by several societies. Most notable among individuals impressed by his ideas was James Hudson Taylor who tried them out, and founded a mission which applied them extensively.

CHAPTER ONE

THE ALCHEMY OF EVENTS
1800 BC–AD 1700

Cradle days of the empire   *1800 BC – AD 500*

An understanding of the events of nineteenth-century China and of the action and characters in the long drama leading up to Hudson Taylor's arrival there, depends on a knowledge of the evolution of the empire of that time. That empire was thrown up by the alchemy of long centuries of history. From a languid beginning, a stirring in a cradle-land that by its harsh climate bred strong, hardy men, some of the greatest empires the world has seen eventually developed, only to sink and die. Into this seething, everchanging scene, the coming of Christianity was little more than the coming of a few vulnerable men. Some were more able than others, and some more wise. The most powerful influence they wielded was the message of the gospel. As in the history of the Key Figure of that gospel, success came only through suffering and apparent defeat. If his chief success was imperceptible because spiritual, this is true also of theirs.

Like other peoples the Chinese have their colourful mythology, but the earliest history of China, the legendary part, is reliably in advance of the merely mythological. The very substantial and beautiful red earthenware of the earliest period of the Five Rulers and Xia (Hsia) dynasty in the Yellow River basin, tells of advanced civilisations contemporary with Abraham and Moses. There is equivalent substance in their oral traditions, but the oldest reliable written records of China's history are from the time of the Han dynasties, roughly two hundred years before and after Christ. The history they record goes back to the Shang dynasty, 1766–1122 BC, which ruled the heartland of China at the time of Israel's occupation of Palestine, and of the presiding judges.[3] Its powerful bronzes, flagons and ritual food vessels, clearly indicate the personality of their makers, highly skilled, perceptive people using impressionism and symbolism full of meaning. The stylistic *taotie* (*t'ao-t'ieh*) monster mask is an example. The earliest form of Chinese calligraphy, engraved on bones, comes from the same Shang period. The Shang emperors ruled over the cradle area of the Chinese people in the plains and surrounding hills of what are now the Yellow River provinces of Hebei (Hopeh), Henan, Jiangsu, Shanxi and Shaanxi. All beyond their boundaries were considered to be barbarians, savages by comparison. At the time of Moses the first Chinese clash with the Tartars occurred in 1292 BC.

The Zhou (Chou) dynasty which followed from 1122–255 BC spanned the time of David and Solomon, right through to Nebuchadnezzar, the Captivity, and Cyrus of Persia. The Zhou rulers added the Yangzi valley, the great fertile basin of Sichuan in the west, and some of Manchuria to their kingdom. By driving back the barbarian tribes they dominated China as far south as Hangzhou. Aristotle wrote of silk exports from China. The Chou were still supreme when Old Testament history ended, at the time of Alexander the Great, in the fourth century BC, and of Hannibal in the third century. It was during this time that the Buddha lived and died in India, c 488 BC, and two great indigenous religions of China came into being.

Taoism, later linked with the name of Laozi (Laotzu), was allegedly born at the time of the Babylonian captivity, fifty years before Confucius. It was little related to Laotzu's nobler philosophies of metaphysical quietism, familiar now as 'yoga'. As a religion of the Chinese peasantry, it became little more than a hotchpotch of spiritism, exorcism, magic, geomancy, divination and the rest. Its influence on the people was profound, however, and we shall meet from time to time the serious implications of *feng-shui*, literally 'wind and water', and the way belief in *feng-shui* provoked violent action from the people. The ethics of Taoism were concerned with self-negation and tranquillity of spirit, but were opposed to ethical *codes* of any kind. Taoism in practice degenerated into superstition, a search for the elixir of life, and under the influence of Buddhism acquired a pantheistic system of temples and priestcraft.

Confucianism was a development from a different kind of beginning. Confucius himself, living from 550–479 BC, about the time of Socrates, Plato, Ezra and the end of Old Testament history, was not so much irreligious as un-religious, concerned with social welfare and government. His philosophies propounded a code of conduct for every man, from emperor to slave, with special application of the principles of propriety, justice, loyalty and filial piety to the cultured gentleman official. The result was a highly ethical civic code but a casual attitude to religion except as a system of protocol. It predisposed the Chinese to agnosticism and materialism. Confucius observed ancestor worship as a mark of respect for his forebears, but his followers invested it with the age-old animistic beliefs. They made up for the lack of images and tangible objects of worship by incorporating nature worship, a confused concept of the deities of the hills, rivers and trees, and veneration of Confucius himself as the great sage.

Among all these codes and superstitions there was belief in an overruling power called *Tian* or 'Heaven', and sometimes *Shangdi*, the Supreme Ruler or Lord Above. This deity was good. He loved righteousness, cared com-passionately for the welfare of his people and could be approached through sacrifices and prayer. The emperor's authority as Son of Heaven was derived from *Tian*.

Buddhism did not enter China until about five hundred years after Confucius died (page 39); not the conservative

Teaching of the Elders, Theravada Buddhism, with its Four Truths and Eightfold Path, but the more liberal, accommodating Mahayana form. With their innate genius for absorbing whatever came along and making it their own, the Chinese took up each philosophy as it appeared and adapted it to their purposes. In course of time attempts were made to treat Christianity in the same way, but with very different results.

In 220 BC Qin Shi Huangdi (Ch'in Shih Huang-ti), the 'Napoleon of China', came to power. He built the Great Wall as a defence against the nomad tribes in the great northern wastes beyond, and unified the nation; but in megalomaniac perversity he tried to destroy all historic records from before his time. His special hate was against the Zhou dynasty, and that included Confucius and his writings. He intended himself to be known as the founder-father of the Chinese people. The name 'China' comes in fact from his dynastic title Qin (Ch'in). Fortunately he did not succeed in his aim. The Book of Changes, its contents (mostly charms and spells preserved by oral tradition) now three thousand years old, and Confucius's *Shu Jing* (*Ching*), the Book of History, and *Shi Jing* (*Shih Ching*), the Book of Poetry, survived, as well as the Book of Odes containing customs of the ancients, and the Book of Rites, giving detailed directions for public and private conduct.

The early and late Han dynasties followed, from 206 BC–AD 220. While Carthage was destroyed and Julius Caesar invaded the British Isles, during the rise and spread of Christianity round the Mediterranean shores and east-ward to India, the Han emperors extended their control over Indo-China and part of Korea, and far across the western wilds to Kashgar. Contacts with the Roman empire were made and the *Pax Sinica* saw unprecedented progress. As early as AD 132 China received tribute from a place called Jawa, believed to be the Java of today.

This strong centrifugal pressure from the Han race forced the aboriginal peoples of China, the 'barbarians', farther and farther into the south-west mountains and the

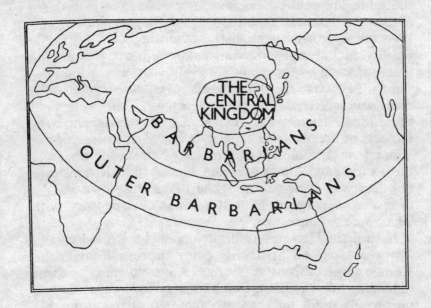

EARLY CHINA'S VIEW OF THE WORLD

jungles of South-East Asia. Far from being a point of passing interest, this is the nub of the whole matter, of China's attitude to foreigners before and during her 'open century'. To understand China's relations with other peoples of the world, all down through history, it is essential to grasp this 'barbarian principle'. Small or large, China was the 'Central Kingdom'. All others were 'out there', fit only to be subject people. As late as the nineteenth century there was little information available even to the Chinese literati — even less than the scant information about China obtainable in the West. Travellers' tales of the Marco Polo type did nothing to encourage mutual respect. On the contrary, distorted imaginings and fictions simply fed the fires of misunderstanding.

New contacts with India led to Mahayana Buddhism coming to China and before long taking firm root. Unlike the more self-centred Theravada or Hinayana Buddhism of Burma, Thailand and Indo-China, Mahayana Buddhism's message was pantheistic, admitting of a Supreme Reality, and also propounding a way of peace and escape from suffering by the elimination of desire. It glorified the saintly *bodhisattvas* who refused to enter Nirvana until every soul was freed from pain and sorrow. China welcomed these ideas. There was a revival of learning and the arts. Objects of beauty were expertly made. The finesse of the Han mirrors of polished bronze, for example, to be seen in the Victoria and Albert Museum, is enough to demonstrate the degree of their culture while Britons used woad, two thousand years before the bitter-sweet 'open century' with which we are concerned.

In time the Han empire broke up and for a hundred and fifty years, while Christianity enjoyed prestige under the Roman emperor Constantine, and Augustine of Hippo was defending the true faith, China suffered from disunion and unrest. Then for another two hundred years, from AD 420–618, separate northern and southern kingdoms brought back law and order. This was the time of the other Augustine, first archbishop of Canterbury, of the Saxon invasion of Britain and the birth of Mohammed at Mecca in AD 569. During the same period events took shape which led to the first appearance of Christianity in China, probably in AD 505. The fact that more than one thousand four hundred years had still to elapse before the 'open century' of this book arrived, emphasises the difficulties involved. It also puts into sobering perspective the whole issue of the evangelisation of the world. The crowded events of the 'open century' fill but a brief half-hour in the time-span of history and in 'the patience and longsuffering of God' to whom a thousand years are but a day.

First Christians in China   *AD 500–800*

The early Church in the Mediterranean lands was concerned to understand the Bible and its doctrines correctly, without deviation or addition. Over the years statements by one bishop or teacher after another were examined and judged by the yardstick of the collected canonical writings which form the Bible, and anything that could not stand up to that scrutiny was rejected. Nestorius, bishop of Constantinople for the past three years, was taken to task by the Council of Ephesus in AD 431 for so stressing the humanity of Jesus as to make him out to be a dual personality, one human and one divine, in one person. According to his exposition of the incarnation, Mary was the mother of the human son, Jesus, but not of the divine. The Council disapproved of this, and when he declined to change his position, they deposed him.

The Syrian Church continued to support Nestorius, who turned his attention eastwards, to the Tigris and Euphrates valleys, and Nestorianism spread to Persia, India, Central and East Asia. Baghdad was its centre, in the heyday of the eighth to thirteenth centuries. More zealous until the thirteenth century than any other Christian communion, the Nestorian Church followed the great trade routes and established Christian communities in the commercial centres from Mesopotamia to Peking, and from South India to Mongolia. This great extension was in part due to persecution by the Zoroastrians in Persia and the rising anti-Christian religion of Islam. In fact the Muslim expansion following the death of Mohammed drove the Nestorians into closer dealings with the Chinese.

In a breviary of the Syrian Church of the thirteenth century there is a statement that St Thomas went to China. It is generally believed that he went as a missionary to South India and there is nothing inherently impossible in the idea of his sailing in a Chinese junk from there, but as Columba Cary-Elwes says in this connection, 'possibilities do not make history'.[4] An old Malabar liturgy (of the south-western coastal region of India) reads, 'Through St Thomas the Kingdom of heaven took wings and sped its flight to the Chinese'; but the *Acts of St Thomas* makes no mention of China and some who might have been expected to refer to the fact, if it were a fact, remained silent. John of Monte Corvino, first Christian bishop in Peking, spent more than a year at Mylapore in South India where the tomb of St Thomas is, and stated that no apostle or disciple of one went to China.[5] The discrepancy, in Professor K. S. Latourette's view, may have arisen from the metropolitan of the Malabar Church including China in his title. The truth remains a matter of conjecture.

Forty-six years after the first, unverified, entry to China by Nestorians in AD 505, some Nestorian monks arrived at Constantinople with silk-worm eggs which they claimed to have brought from China. Certainly in AD 635, the year Aidan of Iona reached Northumbria, a Syrian Christian named A-lo-pen was welcomed by the Tai Zong (T'ai Tsung) emperor, who had Turkish blood in his veins. One of the greatest of all Chinese monarchs, and strongest of all his Tang dynasty, under him the empire extended to include all Manchuria, Korea, and South China, Tibet and Central Asia down to the Hindu Kush, Annam and Tongking. It was probably the largest, wealthiest and most civilised empire in the contemporary world. The Tangs recovered Turkestan westward as far as the Caspian Sea for a century or so and had a common border with the Muslims.

There were twenty-two Tang rulers between AD 618, seven years after Mohammed declared himself a prophet, and AD 907. Under them creative art flourished again. The familiar powerful figures of horses, so muscular and full of vitality that even in porcelain they almost look alive, are typical of the Chinese nation as it then was. Through Chinese and Arab merchant adventurers the Tangs traded with the Indian Ocean regions, and by the eighth century had a Superintendent of Merchant Shipping at Canton to prevent smuggling and to collect duties. In fact, in AD

1000 all overseas trading was nationalised and private dealings with foreigners were banned. Seaborne commerce with 'barbarians' was limited to Canton, Ningbo, Hangzhou, Shanghai and a few other coastal cities, but the ancient caravan routes through Central Asia remained open. Curiously enough in 851 and 878, when King Alfred was defeating the Danes, two Arab travellers discussed the Old and New Testaments with the emperor of China.[6] By then the *Court Gazette* had been begun—the earliest known newspaper.

History is precise at this stage, for the imperial edicts of AD 638, 745 and 845 contain references to the Nestorians. In the first was this commendation: 'We find this religion excellent and separate from the world . . . beneficial to the human race and worthy of being spread all over the Celestial Empire.'[7] But unfortunately for the Nestorians, this was also the time of greatest prosperity for Buddhism in China, and Buddhism with its attractive temples and images and public celebrations gained rapidly over Nestorian Christianity with its monasteries, seclusion and other trappings of Graeco-Roman Christianity. They resorted to compromise and compromise was foredoomed to fail.

Three hundred years before the Chinese developed the art of printing (and seven centuries before John Gutenberg) the Nestorians translated the New Testament into Chinese (see page 51). Long afterwards, in the nineteenth century, a pagan Chinese priest found a hoard of Christian manuscripts in one of the famous cave temples at Dunhuang. (They were seen by Sir Aurel Stein and Professor Pelliot in 1908 and samples brought to Europe.) There was a list of three hundred and fifty books used by Christians in Tang dynasty China, including the Psalms of David, the Gloria in Excelsis in seven-character verse, and a hymn to the Trinity. It is impossible to know how much was achieved, how many Chinese became true Christians before the Nestorian Church disappeared. Nor are we in a position to condemn the Nestorians for failure on the ground of such evidence as is available.

First period of suppression *841–907*

In 841 the Tang emperor Wu Zong (Tsung), an ardent Taoist, issued a vindictive edict and severe persecutions began. Occurring first at Buddhist, then at Taoist instigation, the suppression of not only Christian but also Buddhist and Taoist monasteries seems at first perplexing. The explanation is that the emperor regarded all monastic seclusion as an unhealthy aberration. As many as 44,600 Buddhist monasteries were destroyed. When the enlightened Qing (Ch'ing) dynasty emperor Kang Xi published a collection of historic edicts in 1685, with his own editorial comments, it included the Wu Zong edict:

> As to the religions of foreign nations, let the men who teach them, as well as those of Da Qin (the Nestorians) and Mu Hu Bi (the Parsees), amounting to 3000 persons, be required to resume the ways of ordinary life . . .[8]

The Nestorians withdrew to the border lands and succeeded in converting the Uighur Tartars – incidentally giving them their present Mongol alphabet.

Some workmen, digging foundations in 1625, some thirty miles from the great imperial city of Xi'an (Sian), in Shaanxi, came upon an inscribed slab of black marble. They informed the mandarin. He read that the monument had been erected in the days of the Tang emperors, in 781. It was probably buried by Christians when Wu Zong's edict was promulgated. A rubbing was taken by a secret Christian serving as an inferior mandarin when the monument was unearthed, and sent to Roman Catholic priests in hiding at Hangzhou near the coast.

The stone, nine feet by three feet, stands now in the Forest of Tablets at Xi'an. It is impressive. At the top is a cross and a decorative motif; below, a long statement in 1,700 Chinese characters and also in Syriac. It summarises the essentials of Christian doctrine, but omits any but veiled references to the death and resurrection of Christ:

> . . . the Illustrious and adorable Messiah, veiling His true

majesty, appeared in the world as a man. Angels proclaimed the glad tidings. A virgin brought forth the Holy One in Da Qin (Judea). A bright star announced the felicitous event. Persians saw its splendour and came with tribute. He fulfilled the Old Law . . . He appointed His new doctrines . . . purging away the dust (of defilement) and, perfecting the truth (in men) . . . He ascended to His true (place) . . .'

Mention of 'twenty-seven books' and 'the Old Law of the Twenty-Four Sages' Discourses' implicitly refers to the New and Old Testaments as 'the true Scriptures'. There then follow a history of the Nestorian movement in China, many names which are taken to be those of foreigners, and a hymn extolling God and the Tang emperors.

Exactly a hundred years later, in 1725, during one of the periodical persecutions, a Syriac manuscript with characters the same as those found on the Xi'an monument, was found in the possession of a Muslim in China who claimed descent from either a Christian or Jewish ancestor. It contained part of the Old Testament and some hymns.

This first suppression of the Nestorians was tragically thorough. After the Tang dynasty they almost completely disappeared from China. They had been there continuously for two and a half centuries and had established churches in many towns and cities. Why then did they not survive? No certain answer can be given. It was partly because the adherents were foreign travellers and merchants, but not entirely. With Buddhism at the height of its vigour, the Nestorians apparently tried to adapt to Buddhist forms, and their lack of distinctiveness as Christians appears to have led to their annihilation. But more than that, when James Legge, Professor of Chinese at Oxford after thirty years as a missionary to China, asked 'one of the most zealous living missionaries' what he attributed the Nestorian démarche to, his reply was, 'How could it succeed? There was no gospel in it!', meaning that the message of the Church is no gospel unless it is that 'Christ died for our sins, as written in the scriptures; that he was buried, and that he was raised to life three days later, as written in the scriptures.' The nearest reference to the crucifixion in surviving Nestorian records in China seems to be, 'He hung up the shining Sun in order to triumph over the empire of darkness.'[10]

A possible explanation of this obscurity may be considered. The Chinese mastery of imagery in poetry and prose to convey the sense unfailingly must be remembered, and while this quotation may seem cryptic and obscure to the Western mind, its meaning could have been apparent to readers at that time. When Chairman Mao said, 'Let all the flowers bloom', for example, it elicited frank expression of opinions from the nation. The Nestorians' success in getting inside the Chinese mind may have been greater than is customarily granted to them in the West. Under persecution they may have had to use veiled language as John did in the Revelation, while the message was plain to those they taught by word of mouth. On the other hand, as Bishop Stephen Neill thinks more likely, Nestorianism may have 'failed because it remained monastic and did not penetrate the life of ordinary people. The concealment of the Cross . . . was on the principle of hiding from unbelievers the mysteries, especially those which they would be liable to hold in contempt.' Whatever the case, the Xi'an monument remains as clear proof to China of Christianity as a worldwide faith, not a late Western introduction, and of the fact of its acceptance in China more than a thousand years ago.

Golden horde and golden opportunity   907–1368

The Tang dynasty went down in chaos and after a few decades under the Five Rulers China found order for two hundred years during the Song dynasty, 907–1127. While King Knut (Canute) ruled Britain, Norway and Denmark, through the Norman conquest to the time of the Magna Carta and during the Crusades (from the early eleventh century to mid-thirteenth century), the wonderfully aesthetic Song dynasty restored stability and peace in China.

Increasingly however, they faced, feared and resisted the constant pressure of Tartar hordes from the steppes of Mongolia and Manchuria. For a time the Great Wall, already a thousand years old, kept the aggressors out. But the Tartars went on battering at the Chinese defences until they yielded. Then the invaders persisted in pursuit until they drove the Songs far south beyond the Yangzi. Because the Nestorians were influential among the Tartars, opposition to them continued under the Song emperors until Christianity in China was not only suppressed but forgotten.

Any stability in China during the Song dynasty was little more than a lull before one of the world's most stupendous storms — the terrifying conquest not only of Asia but of Eastern Europe by the Mongols. When the eruption took place, about the time of the Magna Carta in 1215, and the first English parliament, the mounted men of the steppes overran everything in their path. Born and bred in the saddle, they were accurate with their bows at any angle, shooting forward, sideways or backward at full gallop. The 'Golden Horde' was, strictly, the camp of the Batu Khan with his tent of gold, but came to be used of the armies of the great Khans. When Genghis Khan marched, all males marched with him, with Genghis at the head. Like a scourge over the territories doomed to conquest, they slaughtered and devastated as they went. They were victorious from the China Seas to Poland and Hungary and up the Danube to the gates of Vienna. From Burma to the Amur River in Siberia north of Manchuria and from Karachi and all Persia to north-west of Moscow they cast their net of chain-mail.

Genghis Khan, one of the greatest military geniuses of history, was also an administrator and law-giver of Napoleonic quality. Under Genghis the whole population of the inner empire was organised on a basis of heads of tens being answerable to heads of hundreds, heads of hundreds to *khans* of thousands, and every *khan* to the Khan of Khans. This system, known as *bao-jia* (*pao-chia*) had been used in the Zhou dynasty and history repeated itself after the Taiping rebellion. Mao Tse-tung used the same technique to clamp down instantaneous control upon the China he overran with his minority forces in 1949–50.

The area of Genghis Khan's conquests was too vast to remain a unit for long, but his empire did stand as a world power for two hundred years. It gave dynasties to China and Persia, and controlled most of Asia, Russia and Eastern Europe. Babur, founder of the Mogul empire of India, 1526, claimed descent from Genghis Khan and Tamerlane. Remotest Western Europe knew of fabulous 'Cathay', and its glories, and Genghis Khan's contacts with Christianity had far-reaching repercussions for China.

After two sons of Genghis succeeded him, his grandson Mengku Khan, 'the Great Khan', became the supreme ruler, in 1251, destroying Baghdad in 1258 and Damascus two years later in a war against Islam. He was followed by Kublai, who ruled for thirty-five years, 1259–94. The Polo brothers, Matteo and Nicolo, made use of the caravan routes, at long last safe from marauding Muslims, to reach China in 1260, and on their second journey took young Marco with them. He arrived in Peking in 1275 and chronicled the splendours of Kublai's court and kingdom, which surpassed anything he knew of in Europe, never having been to Byzantium.

Marco Polo is the source of information we shall return to as we pick up the threads of history about the second Nestorian enterprise in China. But first we must go back again to mention the Tartar tribal rivalries in the vast expanses of Central Asia, from Lake Balkash in the west, across the Gobi Desert to the Ordos Desert within the great northward loop of the Yellow River and the Great Wall. Part of the Chinese Empire at the time of its greatest enlargement, they were outside the weakened empire of the Tangs and Songs. Some of them accepted Nestorian teachers and in a manner reminiscent of the Old Testament supported family priests. Often these priests were no more Christian than the tribesmen they served, and were frequently debauched. There is no way of distinguishing true Christian from false at this distance in time. All we know is that in spite of decadence there nevertheless were devout followers of the Nestorian missionaries, even in the princely families. The name Cathay comes from one of these tribes, the Khitan, and the Russians still refer to China as Kitay, but not until the early seventeenth century was the identity of Cathay and China established by the heroic journey of Benedict of Goes, a lay Jesuit, across Central Asia in 1602–05.

Intermarriage brought Christian women into the Khan families, and Kublai Khan's own mother was in fact a Christian Kerait princess from south-east of Lake Baikal. Nestorian Keraits became high-ranking officials of the Mongol princes. Two of Mengku Khan's chief ministers were Nestorians and had a chapel at his court. And Christian Uighurs were sent as emissaries to Rome and Paris. So all through Central Asia there came to be at least nominally Christian communities, with supervising bishops. Ongut Nestorian crosses of the eleventh to four-teenth centuries have often been excavated, especially from graves in the Ordos country.

Kublai Khan completed the subjugation of China and established the Yuan dynasty. It lasted a hundred and ten years, with the 'sons of Han', the true Chinese, tolerating their alien rulers. Under the Tartars the Chinese thrived, but when the opportunity arose, they threw the aliens out.

Once again the Nestorians were caught on the wrong foot. Under the Mongol Yuans they enjoyed imperial favour, like the priests of Buddhism and Islam who were also subsidised, and a Nestorian metropolitan or archbishop had his seat in Peking, Marco Polo's Cambaluc (Khanba-lik), in 1275. If they leant on the Yuan staff, however, they must fall when it broke. Nestorian communities sprang up in many parts of China and in 1289 Kublai Khan had a government ministry to supervise some thirty thousand members. In Zhenjiang (Chinkiang), on the intersection of the Yangzi and Grand Canal, a Christian governor built

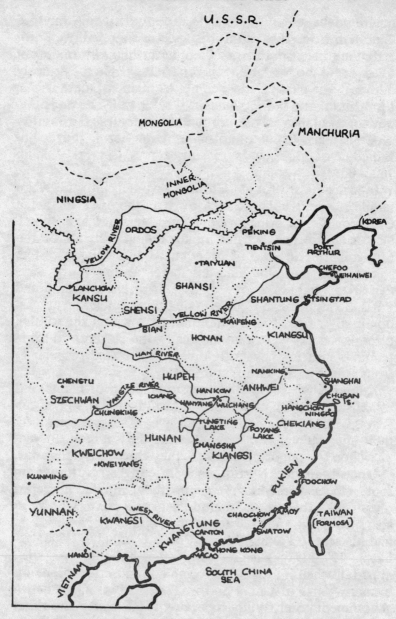

CHINA'S PROVINCES AND MAIN CITIES (see Appendix 2)

seven monasteries, and in Yangzhou there were three Nestorian churches used by foreign merchants, in the fourteenth century. These were two of the cities in which Hudson Taylor was later to suffer most from the hands of the Chinese. There were churches also as far apart as Hangzhou near the eastern coast, Yunnan in the far south-west, and Gansu in the north-west, as well as around the capital. Interestingly enough, on January 22, 1952, when some demolition work on the walls of Yangzhou was being done, an inscription in Latin was found. It read, 'Here lies Catherine of Viljours who died in the year of the Lord 1342, in the month of June'[11] — when Marco Polo was governor of Yangzhou. She was the wife of a merchant. Marco Polo had a story of seven hundred thousand families of a secret sect who came out into the open when religious liberty was announced. They were probably not old Nestorians but descendants of Manicheans, whose religion was a syncretism between Buddhism, Zoroastrianism and Christianity.

It happened that the Mongol conquests coincided with the beginnings of the Renaissance in Western Europe. The so-called Dark Ages which followed the collapse of the Roman empire were ending, and intense activity of thought and expansion of effort had begun. A Franciscan friar, John of Plano Carpina, though sixty-three and stout, reached the court of Mengku Khan in 1253 and described Nestorian services which he attended. He said that they had both New and Old Testaments in Chinese characters and

> they worship one God. They adore and reverence Jesus Christ our Lord, and believe the article of eternal life, but are not baptized. They . . . esteem and reverence our Scriptures. They love Christians.[12]

Another traveller, William of Rubruck, a year or two later described the court of Mengku in Mongolia as a rendezvous for the whole world, with even an Englishman and a

Frenchman there, but he found drunken, immoral 'Nestorians' alienating the Mongols by their behaviour.

So when the Polo brothers returned from their first epic
journey with letters from Kublai Khan to the Pope, asking
for a hundred teachers of science and religion, 'wise in the
Christian law and acquainted with the seven arts',[13] interest
was aroused, but not enough. The papacy was preoccupied
with the Albigensian heresy and with increasing its tem-
poral power. It was the age of the Crusades, from 1096 to
the mid-thirteenth century, and spiritual issues were subordinate. The saintly Ramón Lull (1238–1315) advocated
a Chair in the University of Paris for the study of Tartar
languages,

> that our learned men, by preaching to them and teaching
> them, may by the sword of Truth overcome their falsehood
> and restore to God a people as an acceptable offering, and
> may convert our foes and His to friends.[14]

> Missionaries will convert the world by preaching, but also
> through the shedding of tears and blood and with great
> labour, and through a bitter death.[15]

At the age of eighty Lull himself died of injuries received
during his fourth period in North Africa. Only two
Dominicans set off with the Polos in November 1271, and
they gave up and returned. Seven years later the Pope sent
five Franciscans, when he heard incorrectly that Kublai
Khan had been baptised, but they also went no farther
than Persia.

At last in 1294 the first missionary from the Roman
Church arrived at Peking shortly before Kublai Khan died,
the Franciscan John of Monte Corvino. He had travelled
by Chinese junk from South India. For five years he was
vigorously opposed by the Nestorians, but the Court
received him. By 1300 he had built a church with three
bells. In January 1305 he wrote a letter reporting that he
had bought a hundred and fifty boys, baptised them and
was teaching them Greek and Latin and to sing.[16] All told

he had baptised six thousand, and for good measure had translated the New Testament and Psalter into the Tartar language. For twelve years he worked without a colleague or even news from Europe, and after thirty years in Peking he died, the archbishop of Cambaluc, and was mourned by the city. Latourette accords him this eulogy,

> ... for single-hearted devotion and quiet persistence he deserves to be ranked with the foremost princes of all faiths and times.[17]

Farthest from home of any missionary of any religion, he established the Roman Catholic Church in the capital of the mightiest empire of his time — and not only there in Peking but in other cities also.

A peripatetic Franciscan friar, Odoric, who went to China via Ceylon and South China and returned to Europe by the Central Asian route, between 1322 and 1328, found Franciscan Christians in Fujian province, Hangzhou and Yangzhou. How widely the Tartar New Testament was read will never be known. And what kind of gospel old John of Monte Corvino taught can only be surmised. What is known is that the Yuan dynasty began to break up and with it Christianity in China, even more than after the demise of the Tang dynasty.

A Chinese philosopher of 200 BC said,

> The prince is a dish and the people are the water;
> if the dish is round the water will be round,
> if the dish is square the water will be also.

Kublai's people followed his lead, but when the dynasty crumbled away, the Nestorian and Catholic communities crumbled too. Persecution began even before Kublai died, because a kinsman who attacked him used a cross on his banners. Kublai rebuked the persecutors, saying the cross had not helped his enemies so it could not be on their side; but a second period of suppression of Christianity in China had begun. As the routes through Central Asia were less well policed, so missionaries lost their lives trying to get through.[18] Muslims dominated the Indian Ocean, and Europeans, whether missionary or merchant, were unable to travel that way either. Several attempts were made to replace the archbishop of Cambaluc but each appointee was either imprisoned or died on the way, or was never heard of again. In 1338 a papal envoy, John of Marignolli, was well received by the Great Khan Timur-i-leng, but within twenty years 'Tamerlane' emulated Genghis Khan in spreading destruction and terror as far west and south as to the Middle East and India. For a century and a half China was virtually cut off. No travellers and no news reached the West. Even tribute-bearing ambassadors from other countries were taken in closed carts under escort, to prevent them seeing anything of the Celestial Kingdom. Those priests already in China received no support or reinforcement.

In 1368 a Buddhist monk, turned bandit and then warlord, led the revolution which toppled the Yuans and set up the Ming dynasty with himself as first emperor. Once again a truly Chinese revolt had worsted the foreign rulers. In the flow and counter-flow of Chinese history the whole process was to be repeated in 1644, when the Mings succumbed to the Manchurian Tartars, and again two and a half centuries later when their dynasty, the Qing (Ch'ing), fell to the Chinese with much bloodshed at the revolution in 1911–12. Meanwhile, under the Ming emperors Christianity almost disappeared from China for two long centuries.

Age of exploration   1368–1580

The Ming dynasty, 1368–1644, is renowned for its superb art. No one admiring its exquisite porcelains, paintings or lacquer work could doubt the advanced degree of civilisation attained in this direction. It paralleled the Reformation and Renaissance in Europe. The Ming were outstanding in other ways too. Kublai Khan's fleet had swept the waters of Java and Malaya, and now Ming admirals sailed the Indian Ocean, between 1403 and 1433, long before Bartholomew Dias, 1488. They made seven expeditions under the famous eunuch Zhong Hu. With sixty ships and twenty-seven thousand men he traded with Malaya, Sumatra, Ceylon, India, Aden, Arabia, the Persian Gulf and Mogadishu on the East African Coast. A party from one expedition saw the sights of Mecca.[19] According to the Mings, vassal states sent tribute every ten years, apart from trade with Chinese ships. China had a way of labelling every relationship with other people in these terms, but it is recorded that they claimed to have chastened some insubordinate rulers in Ceylon and Palembang, Sumatra. The Chinese dominance hastened the decline of the Hindu Majapahit establishment in Java and Sumatra and so contributed to the rise of Muslim power in the Malayan archipelago. The sultans of the archipelago which was to become the Philippines paid tribute in this way, and to this day Ming porcelains and other artefacts are found even in remote islands.

European ships were venturing farther afield too, and before long the epic adventures and discoveries of the great sailors began. The overseas expansion of Renaissance Europe had started, and to the end of this story China felt the impact. In Latourette's view four major factors were involved: the circumnavigation of the world, the fermentation of ideas arising from the Renaissance, the Reformation and revival of a living faith in Europe, and the resulting reaction within the Roman Church. In 1492 Columbus was carrying a letter from Ferdinand and Isabella of Spain to the Great Khan in Cathay when he discovered the American continent. He thought he had found East Asia.[20] The Portuguese Vasco da Gama rounded the Cape of Good Hope in the same year. The major drama of East-West relations was about to begin.

Vasco da Gama sailed on across the Indian Ocean to India. In 1511 the Portuguese took Malacca on the Malayan peninsula and four years later their ships attempted to trade at Chinese ports. In 1520 they sent an embassy to the Ming court, but Japanese pirates had been ravaging the coast from north to south and China wanted nothing to do with 'outer barbarians'. So the Portuguese were escorted back to Canton — a riposte which over the years was to be repeated *ad nauseam*.

This was the time of papal supremacy, when the oceans were allocated to the Spanish westward of Brazil, and to Portugal eastward. When Magellan, a Portuguese in the service of Spain, rounded Cape Horn, crossed the Pacific Ocean and landed on Leyte in the Philippines, the fat was in the fire, for Portugal claimed exclusive right to the Orient. Magellan had already been to the East Indies for his own country. He died in the Philippines, but his ship sailed on, the first ever to circumnavigate the globe. Spain and Portugal struggled for supremacy in South-East Asia, and the Dutch and English joined in for good measure. After 1558 the Reformation became well established and British seafarers challenged the papal maritime powers at their own game.

The arrogance and aggressiveness of the Portuguese appalled the Chinese with their Confucian decorum. By 1550 they allowed them only to touch at the island of Shangchuan (Ch'üan), at the mouth of the Canton estuary, and to erect temporary huts. Seven years later, in return for tribute which they continued to pay until 1848, they were permitted to use the small peninsula on Xiangshang island, and two islets, at Macao, and began to build.

A sixteenth-century Chinese author described the beginning of troubles. In the Sinologue W. A. P. Martin's translation, the story ran,

In the days of the Ming dynasty, a ship of the red-haired barbarians came to one of our southern seaports and requested permission to trade. This being refused, the strangers begged to be allowed the use of so much ground as they could cover with a carpet, for the purpose of drying their goods. Their petition was granted; and taking the carpet by the corners, they stretched it until there was room for a large body of men, who, drawing their swords took possession of the city.[21]

Macao is to feature largely in this story because it was the threshold of an antagonistic China, until the beginning of the 'open century'. From this time foreigners began to be called 'foreign devils' from the resemblance of the typical bearded Portuguese of the day to the Chinese concept of a demon. Their truculent behaviour had serious repercussions on the Christian remnants in Ming-dynasty China. The fires of persecution were fanned and the attempt to exterminate the Church was speeded up.

Now Francis Drake came on the scene and sailed the China Seas after rounding Cape Horn. The first British commercial transaction with China, ten tons of cloves shipped from the Moluccas, was in 1579, nine years before the destruction of the Spanish Armada in 1588. When Queen Elizabeth sent an expedition to the emperor in 1597, disaster struck it. All except one man perished in the Atlantic from disease and Spanish privateers. Perhaps this was a good thing, for she asked, in Latin, for 'full and free libertie of egress and regress and in trade of merchandize' but promised,

of ourselves (we) doe most willingly grant unto all and every of your subjects . . . full and entire libertie unto any of the parts of our dominions to resort there, abide and to traffique and thence to return.[22]

On the last day of 1600 Queen Elizabeth presented a charter to the British East India Company and so opened another chapter of China's sorrows. By 1611 the East India Company had 'factories', as the trading posts came to be called, at Pattani on the peninsula between Malaya and Siam, and at Ayuthia, north of present-day Bangkok, trading with Chiang Mai in the northern hills. Trading was competitive, to say the least, and in prolonged hostilities between the Dutch and the English the East India Company was driven away from the Indonesian archipelago and lost her best commander, John Jourdain, in a battle actually in the harbour at Pattani *c* 1620. By 1636, forty years after the first abortive expedition, British merchants were again on the China coast.

Early missions   *1534–1632*

Late as the Protestant nations were in following the Catholic explorers, they were also late in attempting any missionary activity. Spain and Portugal would not have

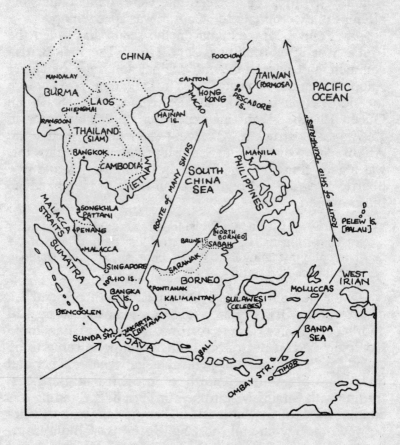

SOUTH-EAST ASIA

allowed them any footing in what they considered their own reserves. But Reformation theologians were too preoccupied with European controversies and making their own position secure. Some taught that the Lord's command to go and preach the gospel to all nations was binding upon the apostles only. Modern Christians, they said, had no obligation to engage in evangelism abroad. For three hundred years after Luther, comparative indifference to the unevangelised world persisted, although in 1534 Erasmus had written of the Christian obligation to the pagan world, adding, 'Would that God had counted me worthy to die in so holy a work!'[23] With the beginnings of the German Pietist movement, the first Protestant initiatives foreshadowed the great phenomenon of a missionary awakening. All through its history the Roman Church has been notable for its missionary spirit, in contrast with the Orthodox communion, but only the Jesuit expansion in the sixteenth century can compare with the evangelical missionary eruption, when once it began. In these books we are concerned with the flood of missionaries in tens, scores, hundreds, and even thousands with which Hudson Taylor had so much to do. It is to understand this phenomenon that we are examining the background history.

The Protestant missionary venture began sluggishly. In 1556 a Huguenot admiral obtained two missionaries from Calvin and sent them to Brazil, where they were killed. They were followed by some Swedish and Dutch missionaries. But these were sporadic moves. The Pilgrim Fathers landed in New England in 1620 and carried the gospel with them, but primarily as colonisers. A German missionary went to Abyssinia in 1632. Britain was slow to do anything. John Donne is said to have preached the first recorded missionary sermon, in 1622, and Sir Walter Raleigh contributed the large sum (at that time) of a hundred pounds 'for the propagation of the Christian religion' in Virginia, presumably among non-Christians, by which would be implied the Red Indians. John Eliot (1604–90) became known as the Apostle to the Indians. He learned the

Mohican language, reduced it to writing and by 1663 had translated the whole Bible. Cromwell's parliament in 1648 felt 'bound to assist in the work' and a 'Corporation for the Propagation of the Gospel in New England' was formed.[24]

Successive blows to papal prestige in Europe led to the founding in 1534 of the Society of Jesus, the Jesuits, by Ignatius Loyola, Francis Xavier and others, the year that papal power in Britain was ended by the Act of Supremacy. Xavier was a Basque, an ardent soul, and was chosen to inaugurate the Jesuit mission to the East. A visionary with all East Asia as his field, he showed amazing courage and energy. Heading for Japan after a spell in India he touched at Canton when the Portuguese were being expelled and knew its gates were closed to him. But Japan was at first barred to him also. Columba Cary-Elwes describes how, landing dressed as a poor priest, Xavier was treated with contempt, but returning in silks, as a sage, he was at least received civilly. After two years he had some 'converts' — by 1575 said to number fifty thousand, of which he never knew.[25]

The Japanese had a respect for China, from whom their civilisation and writing were derived, so Francis Xavier concluded that China was the key to Japan. 'For him to think was to act,' the Abbé Huc declared, so back to Canton Xavier sailed—or rather to the forlorn island of Shangchuan, south-west of Macao. He was determined to land, anywhere, and if thrown into prison 'to preach Jesus Christ to the prisoners and thus deposit a germ of the true faith in the bosom of that infidel nation'.[26] No foreign merchant would risk incurring Chinese wrath by taking Xavier up river to Canton, and the Chinese boatman who agreed to do so failed to appear. While he waited Xavier fell ill with fever and finding the motion of the junk distressing asked to be put ashore, to die in a flimsy shack in December 1552.

This courageous attempt was the first serious effort by a Christian missionary to re-enter China. Deeply discouraged by the resistance he met with in India, Xavier had

'left in disgust', but he loved the Lord devotedly and
suffered many privations to secure the salvation of the
people he went to. His dying words on Shangchuan island
were reported to have been the last phrase of the Te Deum,
'not confounded for ever'.[27] Three years later another
Valiant-for-Truth, Gaspar de la Croix, did succeed in
landing in China, but was quickly deported.

After the Spanish progressively occupied the Philippines
during 1565, soldier and priest under Legaspi together
'Christianising' with sword and crucifix, the Jesuits stationed there made several attempts to penetrate China but
each time met with failure. They were resisted by both
Portuguese and Chinese. None were allowed to stay.
Ironically, the rivalries between Spain and Portugal and
between the various Roman sects and orders for centuries
bedevilled their own efforts to Christianise China. Franciscans and Dominicans, also from the Philippines, having
succeeded in getting as far as Canton, marched through
the streets with a crucifix, denouncing idolatry and destroying any idols they could. It was indiscreet. Jesuits and
merchants alike saw their patient efforts to gain acceptance
ruined. The same happened in Japan where ferocious
persecution took place.

In 1580, the king of Spain became king of Portugal also
and Spanish priests flocked to Macao, the Portuguese *pied-
à-terre*, and Canton. Such blindness to China's aversion to
foreigners deserved the rebuff it received. The viceroy
imprisoned some and forced the rest to leave. They were
not abashed. A proposition was put to Philip II by the
governor and archbishop of Manila, that China should be
converted by conquest as the Philippines, named after him,
had been. Ten thousand Spaniards with ten thousand
Filipinos and Japanese should be enough! The scheme was
not taken up. Sub-Christian all this feverish activity may
have been, but its relevance to this story will become
apparent.

Crack in the wall — the Jesuits succeed   *1580 –1600*

At last the picture changed. New methods were adopted. A distinguished Jesuit visitor named Valignano, on the way to Japan in 1579, was halted at Macao and began to study Chinese. He saw that success depended upon fluency in Asian languages, adapting to the culture and devoting the whole of his life to the task. With another Jesuit he studied Mandarin, only to find it was of little use in the Cantonese-speaking south, the one accessible point on the coast of China. Discouraged, so the story runs, Valignani looked out of the window with deep emotion to the mountains of the mainland and 'called out with a loud voice and the most intimate affection of his heart, addressing himself to China, "Oh, Rock, Rock, when wilt thou open, Rock?" '[28]

The answer was at Valignani's elbow. He had sent for a young man born in the year Xavier died, who after being a law student had become a novice under Valignani and turned to mathematics, cosmology and astronomy. Arriving at Macao the twenty-seven year-old Matthew (Matteo) Ricci (1552–1610) also started learning Chinese. Ricci was 'a man of the world and a consummate courtier', a Jesuit of the Jesuits. A Chinese historian later described him as having 'a curly beard, blue eyes and a voice like a great bell'.[29] His General, Loyola, had believed in promoting 'the greater glory of God' by approaching the upper classes, as a stable basis for influencing the poor, and Ricci set out to do this in China. The end would justify the means. He made no secret to his beliefs but, dressed as a Buddhist monk, he veiled his intentions and spoke of having been attracted by the renown of the Celestial Empire. With companions he secured residence at Zhaoqing (Chaoch'ing), the then capital of Guangdong province, from 1583–89, and when they were driven out they moved to Zhaozhou (Chaochou) near Swatow.

For six years he used scientific knowledge to win respect. Clocks were a special attraction. His mathematics won him friends among scholars and officials. All the time he hoped that these would lead on to philosophical enquiries from which he could move to Christian doctrine. Then he discovered that Buddhist monks were not greatly respected, and changed to the dress of Confucian scholars, the gentry of China. He was inside the closed land — in fact two of his companions were taken by a friendly official on a three-hundred-mile visit to his home, at Hangzhou — but his position was still precarious. At this rate what would he achieve? He decided to make for Peking and try to get legal recognition. Attempting to make Nanking on the Yangzi river his first stepping stone he was driven out, so he lay low and succeeded on the next attempt.

The sixteenth century was ending and the Ming dynasty had less than fifty years to run. There was considerable unrest among the literati. In this situation Ricci now won some converts among the intellectuals. In a sense this was a high point in the history of Christian missions to China, for one of Ricci's converts was a Shanghai notable, Xu Guangqi (Hsü Kwang-ch'i), known as Paul Hsü. His daughter became a devout Christian and gave herself as a young widow to spreading the message. She taught professional story-tellers the gospel narrative so that as they travelled the country thousands would hear it. To leap ahead in time, the ancestral village of the Hsü family, Xu Jia Wei (Hsü Chia Wei), outside Shanghai, became the headquarters of the Jesuits in China, 'Siccawei'.[30] A descendant of Paul Hsü married a Chinese Methodist minister named Song (Soong), and of their daughters one became the wife of Sun Yat-sen (1866–1925), father of the Revolution of 1911–12 and acclaimed by the present Communist regime, one the wife of Chiang Kai-shek, and a third the wife of H. H. Kung, China's Second World War Minister of Finance. All were at least nominally Christian.

To return to Matthew Ricci and the seventeenth century. In 1600 he set off for Peking with gifts for the emperor. On the way he was robbed, and imprisoned at Tianjin (Tientsin), but the emperor knew and sent for him. By then he had become very proficient in the Chinese classics, so when he arrived in Peking on January 4, 1601, he made the right impression and was allowed to remain. The great striking clock which he presented to the emperor turned out to be a good ally. When enemies tried to oust him the powerful palace eunuchs were afraid they could not keep it going and saw to it that Ricci was not expelled. A house and stipend were assigned to him and his companions and before long they had converts among high officials, including two members of the Hanlin Academy, and even an imperial prince and his family. A colleague, Friar Claudio Aquaviva, asked if there were many conversions to report, wrote in 1608,

> We are dressed and shod in Chinese fashion, and we neither speak nor eat nor drink nor live in our house except in the Chinese manner . . . the time in which we live in China is not one of harvest.[31]

But by then there were two thousand adherents in four provinces, three hundred of them in Peking. Enquiries about the Nestorians produced no trace or memory other than a little bell, very old and bearing a cross and Greek lettering. Incidentally, Ricci's presence in Peking was reported by merchants in Central Asia to Benedict of Goes, one more factor in proving at last that Cathay and China were one and the same.

Ricci died in 1610, apparently very successful. On his death-bed he said,

> I leave you the gate open to great victories, which nevertheless are only to be attained with great pains and combats.[32]

He was one of the greatest Roman Catholic missionaries to China, honouring her culture as others failed to do. But the policy he followed, of adapting the Christian faith to Chinese religious practices was the cut-worm at the root of the Church he planted. He interpreted ambiguities in the Confucian classics in a light favourable to Christianity but without stating Christian doctrines, for the present. And he allowed the veneration of ancestors and idolatry as mere ceremonial observances, so long as the Christians directed their devotions to a cross hidden in the flowers or candles in the pagan temple. This was 'the seed of self-destruction'. It led to dire results; debacle, persecution and the withdrawal of Jesuits from China by, of all people, the Pope himself.

Ricci's death at first made little difference, for the Jesuits and no others were well established. So after his Chinese funeral, involving sacrifices and paper replicas of all he would need in the after-life, the work went on. The emperor gave a temple outside Peking for use as a Catholic cemetery and it remained as such for three hundred and forty years, until the Communist takeover, but soon the opposition showed their claws and intermittent persecutions began with an imperial decree expelling all missionaries. Those outside Peking were affected but the priest-scientists in the capital were too useful.

In 1606 an expert astronomer, Sabbatino de Ursis, had been sent from Europe at Ricci's request. He exposed a serious error in Muslim astronomers' forecasts of an eclipse, and reputedly became a victim of the 1616 persecution at their instigation, dying at Macao. Some missionaries were deported in cages, suffering hideously, but others were hidden by heroic Chinese until the pressure eased. On and off for two hundred years the Chinese Christians were to risk their own and their families' lives by secreting fugitive missionaries in cities, villages and mountain hideouts, protecting and feeding them while they taught and directed Chinese catechists at work in the provinces.

Again in 1622, a time of many local rebellions, persecution broke out on charges of sedition. Then the chief enemy died and peace returned. Members of the Court were baptised, including the Empress Dowager and Heir Presumptive. How much of the biblical gospel they knew, it is hard to say. A Chinese Catholic even became President of the Board of Rites, the body which initiated the persecutions, and a member of the Council of State. Cary-Elwes called the period between the death of Ricci and the fall of the Ming dynasty 'one of the most fruitful and most heroic in the history of the Chinese Church'.[33] But much depends on what is called success. There was more success and more heroism to come. In 1615 Pope Paul V granted Chinese priests the right to say Mass in Chinese (though as a matter of 'face' they chose to use Latin), and from 1622 to the end of the dynasty peace reigned for the Church, at least as far as the Chinese were concerned.

Among the priests it was another matter. The Jesuits did their best to keep other orders out of the country. It was partly a matter of European rivalries, but more because the Dominicans and Franciscans rejected Ricci's strategy and their methods were different. When a Dominican missionary was tied hand and foot and expelled by the Jesuits, tensions between the orders increased. In 1625 it was the Dutch who drove the Jesuits out of Formosa (Taiwan). China was a long way from Rome. Of twenty-eight Dominicans who left Spain in 1631 for East Asia, six died on the way, yet it was described as a 'prosperous' voyage. Of three hundred and seventy-six Jesuits who sailed for China between 1581 and 1712, one third died from disease or shipwreck on the way.[34]

Meanwhile Europe was in turmoil. The Thirty Years War was disrupting life. Charles I was king of England and using the Star Chamber against his enemies. Dissension was building up to civil war between the Cavaliers and Roundheads. Few in Western countries had time to concern themselves with far-off Cathay.

Half-century of hope 1625–1700

During the last twenty years of the Mings there was civil war in North China, until by an act of treachery the Manchus were invited to help. Instead they occupied Peking themselves, seized power and set up the Qing (Ch'ing) dynasty, in 1644. The Mings retreated to the south, taking Jesuit priests with them, but their cause was hopeless. The emperor's mother, wife, son and daughter were received into the Church by priests, but the displaced emperor hanged himself from a plum tree and others committed suicide or were killed.

Among the Ming loyalists who chose retreat into exile in preference to going underground in Manchu-dominated China was an ex-pirate, known to the world as Koxinga. With a desperate body of men he crossed the straits to the island of Formosa (meaning 'beautiful'), home at that time of perhaps one hundred and fifty thousand aboriginal tribesfolk but only a coastal scattering of Chinese peasants. Portuguese and Spanish adventurers had used Formosa but gave way to the Dutch when they were expelled by the Chinese from the Pescadore Islands in 1622. When Koxinga suddenly arrived in 1661 he ousted the Dutch and from that time Taiwan has been part of China.

The Manchus were a virile Tartar race, uncouth by Chinese standards, daring horsemen accustomed to a rough existence; but they were wise. In many ways they adapted quickly to the Chinese culture and set up a Qing court in Peking as glorious as anything that had preceded it. This was to be the last imperial dynasty to rule in China. Its ten rulers spanned two and a half centuries, into the twentieth century. Contacts with the West increased very cautiously, but the policy of strictly controlled isolation continued.

In the outer world exploration and rivalry had continued unabated. Early in the seventeenth century the East India Company obtained trading rights from the Mogul empire in India and traded with the Malayan archipelago under protection from the British government. Predictably in

1635 a Company ship pressed farther east and came to Macao. She met opposition from the Portuguese and withdrew, but the next year six ships under licence from Charles I (in breach of the monopoly given to the East India Company) sailed up the Canton River, bombarded one of the river forts and captured some junks. The British had arrived! This foolhardy debut met with the rebuff it deserved. They signed an admission of guilt, undertook not to repeat their offence, and sailed away with a cargo of ginger and sugar. Mainland China was not like the docile spice islands. After that the Company had to trade through the Portuguese at Macao, but also managed to establish trading points at Amoy and Ningbo.

At last, in 1650, the East India Company secured trading rights with China and before the end of the century to Britain's shame the pale spectre of opium appeared at Canton. Addiction spread as Indian opium was sold to Chinese merchants. Soon the vice spread inland. Not that the British were the only culprits. From the point of view of trade, opium had the great advantage 'of making hungry where it most satisfied'.[35] The demand from consumers went up and up regardless of cost. China's attitude hardened. After what the Portuguese and British had done, 'foreign devils' were not to be trusted, so they were restricted to a small area outside the city walls of Canton. There they began to build warehouses, a ghetto known as 'the Factory' that was to see much history. A few missionary scientists might be admitted at the emperor's pleasure, but China's doors remained fast shut to the outer world.

When the last Ming emperor was being threatened with defeat, he had called to Peking from Xi'an (Sian), the ancient capital city in Shaanxi, a Jesuit scientist, Johann Adam Schall von Bell (1591–1666), and set him to provide cannon to defend the crumbling dynasty. The Jesuits were civil servants in those early centuries, advisers on matters of which the Chinese knew little. Schall's abilities were many and when he reformed the faulty calendar and like Ricci's successor correctly predicted eclipses, he was promoted not only to be Court Astronomer but chaplain to the imperial palace. When the Manchus came to power he was retained as astronomer by the first Qing emperor, Shun Zhi (Chih) (1644–62).[36]

During attacks by Muslim astronomers on the Christians after the emperor's death, Schall was imprisoned and condemned to die. Of the thirty-eight Catholic priests in China at that time, thirty were in prison. Schall was an old man of seventy-eight and had served five emperors. He was reprieved in 1665 and died the next year. The first true martyr, however, was an itinerant preacher named Fernandez Capellas whose crucifix was probably regarded as a magic emblem.[37] When put in chains and asked where he lived, according to the Abbé Huc in his book *Christianity in China, Tartary and Thibet*, he answered,

I have no other house than the wide world,
no other bed than the ground,
no other food than what Providence provides from day to
    day,
and no occupation other than that of labouring
and suffering for the glory of Jesus Christ,
and the eternal happiness of those who believe in Him.

Such men were the soul-brothers of Hudson Taylor.

The Empress Dowager intervened in the Muslim persecution and Schall was succeeded as Court Astronomer by his assistant and companion in prison, Verbiest (1617–88). Verbiest was to become more influential than all his predecessors. When the new emperor Kang Xi (Hsi) attained his majority, he at first permitted Verbiest to practise Christianity but not to preach it, and restored the missionaries' churches to them while forbidding Chinese to become Christians. As a young man he enjoyed being taught by Verbiest, however, and became increasingly friendly and tolerant. The prohibitions were disregarded and many Chinese were baptised. As Astronomer Royal, Verbiest constructed some large bronze astronomical instruments — still to be seen at the Peking observatory. 'No foreigner ever enjoyed so great favour from the rulers of China,' was one tribute to him, and wherever they were, other Catholic missionaries benefited from that favour.

At Rome the Sacred Congregation for the Propagation of the Faith had been founded in 1622 to supervise missions and in 1659 this papal 'Propaganda', as it became known, sent these instructions to its vicars-apostolic (the titular bishops before the usual hierarchy was set up):

> Do not regard it as your task, and do not bring any pressure to bear on the peoples, to change their manners, customs, and uses, unless they are evidently contrary to religion and sound morals. What could be more absurd than to transport France, Spain, Italy, or some other European country to China? Do not introduce all that to them, but only the faith, which does not despise or destroy the manners and customs of any people, always supposing that they are not evil, but rather wishes to see them preserved unharmed. It is the nature of men to love and treasure above everything else their own country and that which belongs to it . . . do your utmost to adapt yourselves to them.[38]

Even when evil customs had to be changed, it was to be done gradually, through the people themselves seeing why. When a French priest, François Pallu, was appointed vicar-apostolic of South China and Cochin China in 1658 and set out from France in 1662, he was accordingly 'instructed to follow local customs not evidently contrary to religion and good morals', and 'to give the Faith and not European customs'. Adversity encouraged such practices but imperial favour undermined discretion.

After Verbiest's death the emperor's kindness continued and he gave the Jesuits a residence near his palace and a site and funds to build a church, the Bei Tang (Pei T'ang) or North Church. Unwisely they built it in quasi-gothic style.

In 1692 after some persecution in Zhejiang (Chekiang) province Kang Xi issued a decree granting freedom of worship and protection of Church property. He had by

then been emperor for thirty years and had thirty-one more
to reign. The edict of toleration cited the good service
rendered by missionaries and denied any danger of insurrection. Although it made no mention of proselytising, it
read, 'Let no one henceforth offer them any opposition'[39]
so local mandarins could not but allow them a free hand.
Missionaries and their converts were soon to be found in
all provinces of China except Gansu.

Fatal 'rites controversy'   1700–1725

Fifteen more years of prosperity and growth of the
Church lay ahead. By 1701 there were 117 Catholic
missionaries in the country; but the seeds of self-destruction were there and the precarious prosperity depended
solely on the emperor himself. As Latourette pointed out,
'His death or a change in his sentiments might at any
moment bring swift disaster.'[40] Christian teaching could
already be seen by many of Kang Xi's subjects to run
counter to their most cherished institutions. Meanwhile he
contributed towards the rebuilding of 'the finest Christian
temple in all China' and sent representatives to worship in
it.

The 'rites controversy' was reaching its climax. It had
been simmering for a century. Ricci's policy of cunning
compromise, like Robert de Nobili's experiments in South
India in the first half of the seventeenth century, incensed
his superiors and members of other orders. There was no
agreement on what European Church practices could be
dispensed with, and there was the problem of what term to
use for 'God'. Like the Jews, the Muslims and the Nestorians before them, the Catholics could find no uniform
opinion on what Chinese term to employ. The 'Term
Question', as it became known, was already centuries old
and would be the focus for sharp disagreement among
Protestants until well after Hudson Taylor's day. Ricci
borrowed the Taoist, Confucian and Buddhist term *Tian
Zhu* (*T'ien Chu*), Lord of Heaven — and Catholics in China

have used it ever since. Even the Jesuits were divided about rites in veneration of Confucius and ancestors being merely civil and not religious.

During the seventeenth century acrimonious debate on this 'rites controversy' increased, became an issue between orders and nationalities, and spread to Europe. The archbishop of Manila denounced the Jesuit practices to the Pope. The Dominicans put seventeen questions to the Propaganda (as the papal secretariat for foreign missions) among which were these two: if Christians concealed a cross while pretending to worship idols, might they attend compulsory sacrifices? And secondly, should applicants for baptism be told that the Christian faith forbade idolatry and sacrifice? The Propaganda supported the Dominicans in rejecting each but the Jesuits protested that their position had been misrepresented. The Pope then prevaricated, approving of Chinese Christians observing the practices described by the Jesuits as ceremonies 'of a civil and political nature'. Unfortunately the fact was that civil, political and religious practices in China were inseparable. A Dominican minority, at a forty-day missionary conference in Canton of Jesuits, Franciscans and Dominicans (Dec. 1667–Jan. 1668), at which Ricci's policy was upheld, then protested to the Pope. He replied that both papal decrees held good – depending on the circumstances to which they were applied. All this had taken the best part of the century.

In 1697 the Pope asked the Inquisition to look thoroughly into the whole matter. Europe reverberated with 'the controversy and even the Protestants joined in. Remote as they all were from the situation, and from any hope of real understanding, they saw important principles at stake. The Propaganda, favouring secular priests who were bound by no vows to a religious order, was faced by the Jesuits with claims to papal authority for doing as they thought best. Now the Jesuits made a fatal move, they appealed to the emperor. Were the Confucian Rites civil or religious? Why, civil of course! Kang Xi replied. Honours were paid to Confucius as a legislator, to ancestors in love and commemoration, and sacrifices to *Tian* (*T'ien*) (Heaven) were to the Supreme Lord, Creator and Preserver of all. Many Chinese scholars agreed.

In 1704 the Inquisition announced its decision, which the Pope confirmed. '*Tian Zhu*' (*T'ien Chu*) was approved, but not '*Tian*' or '*Shangdi*', the Supreme Ruler. Sacrifices to Confucius and ancestors were forbidden, and also the keeping and veneration of ancestral tablets as being the seat of departed spirits. This reduced the whole issue to a simple matter of supremacy, Pope or Emperor.

A papal legate was sent to China, a young Frenchman, Mgr Charles Maillard de Tournon, not yet forty. He immediately antagonised everyone, especially Kang Xi. The Portuguese regarded him as an intruder because the Pope had failed to obtain their approval of his mission. In 1706 the emperor ordered him out of the country, banished other priests with him, imprisoned another for twenty years, punished Chinese connected with the offending priests, and decreed that only Catholics of the Ricci party could stay. Not surprisingly the legate was incensed. In a choice between Emperor and Pope a Christian's course was plain! He issued his own decree, threatened excommunication for all who failed to conform, and set the whole Church in China at sixes and sevens of perplexity.

Kang Xi was an enlightened man, patronising the arts and encouraging progress. Under his patronage a considerable export trade in porcelains and cloisonné was built up, to the delight of the appreciative West. Kang Xi wanted peace and unity among his Christians. So he sent two missionaries as his own envoys to Rome. To complicate matters the Portuguese in Macao kept the legate under house arrest. Tournon therefore excommunicated the Portuguese bishop. He himself was made a cardinal by the Pope, but his biretta did not arrive until shortly before he died in June 1710. Then a papal bull confirmed the dead legate's edict and a new legate acceptable to the Portuguese arrived, the memorable Mezzabarba.

The farce had still a scene or two to run. It was now 1720. Kang Xi received Mezzabarba with contempt and was furious when he read the bull. Sick of Christian controversies he declared that Christianity had better be banned from China. Mezzabarba was equal to this. He made concessions based on loopholes in the bull. Food, incense and lights might be presented before ancestral tablets, for example. Did Ricci turn in his grave? But Kang Xi died in 1723. To pursue this subject to its conclusion is to run ahead of the period, but will make the picture clearer. The next Pope but one swept away Mezzabarba's concessions, in 1742, and prescribed an oath to be taken by all missionaries in China, on pain of punishment. Romanists far from Rome were literally to do as Rome did. The 'rites controversy' was over at last.

Ricci was an intellectual and moved among Chinese intellectuals. It is conceivable that to them the ceremonial, civic and political aspects of these rites could have been distinct from the religious and superstitious, but not to the average Chinese with his deep animistic beliefs. Their sacrifices were offered to spirits and their prostrations were fundamentally dictated by fear. The Ricci strategy had held the stage from the sixteenth to the eighteenth century, but it had failed. As for the Jesuits, worse prospects lay ahead of them.

Latourette observed that the strong feelings and vigorous action by Catholics of both persuasions were essentially due to their genuine concern for the eternal welfare of souls and the advance of the Kingdom of God. For this cause they were constantly taking great risks on arduous journeys, aware of the danger of overwhelming persecution coming upon them without warning. Nor was this a future possibility. It began with the accession of the Yong Zheng (Yung Cheng) emperor in 1723. In fact, from the time of the legate's fatal mistake until 1739 the Church was staring in the face the possibility of extinction.

For the next century the Church in China was hounded from place to place, sometimes almost beyond endurance.

But Church it was, even if of uncertain purity. Persecution sifted good from bad, true from false, but for so many of the three hundred thousand adherents in 1726 to remain faithful and to suffer without recanting indicated true life in a large proportion of them. Much pure doctrine was taught, whatever else was added. Prèmare's (c 1666–c 1734) 'sublime piece of writing', a pamphlet on God, was in circulation for many decades, valued and used by Protestant missionaries.[41] The fruit from such work cannot be assessed but the numbers willing to die horribly give some indication.

During the half-century of hope that was so cruelly dashed to the ground, reminders of harsh reality were plentiful. As soon as Kang Xi's displeasure was known, an anti-foreign memorial in Guangdong province denounced both merchants at Canton and missionaries in rural areas. It cited the subjugation of the Philippines and Java as proof of the evil intentions of both. All Christians were ordered to renounce their faith and all missionaries to leave unless required for scientific purposes and holding an imperial permit. The viceroy petitioned the throne for the extermination of Christianity in the empire and in 1724 an Edict of Expulsion and Confiscation was promulgated. Church buildings were wrecked or turned into granaries, schools and assembly halls. Church members were scattered and missionaries exiled or confined to Canton. From then on all Christian activity had to be in secret. Two years later it was estimated that only one missionary remained to care for three hundred churches.

CHAPTER TWO

THE IRREPRESSIBLE BARBARIANS
17th–18th centuries

First Protestant missionary awakening   *17th century*

Before returning to the fate of the Catholic Church under the Yong Zheng emperor who followed Kang Xi, it is appropriate to notice some new trends in Europe. In 1647 George Fox, first of the Quakers, the Society of Friends, began preaching all over England. By 1660 there were probably forty thousand Friends and the missionaries they sent out had already travelled over most of Europe and to the West Indies and the American continent. George Fox was reported to have said in 1661, 'Oh, that some Friends might be raised up to publish the Truth in China.' And he recorded in his journal that three Friends were 'moved to go toward China and Prester John's country'.[1] ('Prester John' was the name given in the twelfth to fourteenth centuries to a fabulous priest-king who ruled a vast Asian empire. He has been identified with Genghis Khan and with a Nestorian Christian ruler. By the fifteenth century, however, it was applied chiefly to the emperor of Ethiopia.) When the Act of Uniformity was passed by Parliament in 1663, the Friends were severely persecuted and forced to retrench, until the early nineteenth century when they again became an outgoing missionary force. 1672 saw the Declaration of Indulgence to nonconformists, withdrawn the following year but renewed more than a decade later. It was an intolerant age. The established Church was decadent, and the odds were heavily against dissenters and churchmen to whom Christ meant everything. Exclusion from the universities threw the Friends into commerce and in time gave rise to the influential companies of the Barclays, Buxtons, Cadburys, Frys, Gurneys, Rowntrees and others.

Gradually a new phenomenon appeared, the Protestant missionary society. In 1664 an Austrian, Baron von der Welz, proposed a Society of the Love of Jesus and appealed to the German nobility to send the gospel to the heathen. He was rebuffed by a leading theologian who protested against casting such pearls as 'the holy things of God' before 'dogs and swine'.[2] Such an attitude was characteristic of the age. However, Louis XIV was persecuting the Huguenots and scattering them as missionaries. The Acts of the Apostles were being repeated. The Society for Promoting Christian Knowledge (SPCK) was founded in 1698 and three years later, in 1701, a Society for the Propagation of the Gospel in Foreign Parts (SPG) was established under royal charter to provide what are now called chaplains in British colonies.[3] John Wesley was one, in Georgia. With sublime insight, too tragically forgotten by missions in general until long afterward, the SPCK joyfully received the news of the ordination of an Indian catechist with these words,

> If we wish to establish the Gospel in India, we ought in time to give the Natives a Church of their own independent of our support . . . and secure a regular succession of truly apostolic pastors, even if all communication with their parent Church should be annihilated.

Allowing that the reference was to bishops, hardly could a wiser comment have inaugurated the missionary era of the Protestant Church. That Church was awakening at last. In 1705 two of Francke's Pietists were sent by the Royal Danish Mission to India, and Isaac Watts gave wings to his ardent spirit by writing the first missionary hymns, in 1707. Altogether it was a small beginning, but what is significant about it is that this awakening was in a Europe and particularly a Britain so degenerate that the prominent statesmen were notorious for their debauchery, the poor for behaving like brute beasts and the clergy for their hypocrisy and worldliness. Walpole's drunkenness and foul talk were not regarded as a discredit to him. Rioting mobs set houses on fire, broke open the gaols and looted freely. 'Brutal, ferocious games' were played on Sundays when people were free from work. This (and not only in the nineteenth century) was when the gin shops of London invited.customers to get 'drunk for a penny or dead drunk for two pence'. Describing the clergy and allowing that there were many exceptions, Bishop J. C. Ryle wrote,

> The vast majority of them were sunk in worldliness and neither knew nor cared anything about their profession . . . They hunted, they shot, they farmed; they swore, they drank, they gambled . . . Their sermons were so unspeakably bad . . . they were generally preached to empty benches.

Even if he exaggerated, Britain was heading fast towards revolution and bloodshed like that on the Continent. This was the Britain which by the Act of Union united England, Scotland and Wales as 'Great Britain'.

It was more than a time of decadence. Despair gripped the Church and the conduct of the clergy was partly due to it. The Deists were sneering and launching formidable attacks. 'It is come . . . to be taken for granted that Christianity is . . . discovered to be fictitious . . . an agreed point among all people of discernment.'[4] The Church as a whole was so preoccupied with self-defence that it neglected the gospel for the world. And Bishop Butler refused to become archbishop because he thought it too late to save a collapsing Church. Voltaire predicted that Christianity would be overthrown throughout the civilised world in the next generation.

Into this midden of vice, this slough of despond, there suddenly came not a ray but a shaft of light. The First Evangelical Revival burst upon the scene and within a few years changed English society, purified the literature and social conduct, and gave a new moral tone to the poorer classes. A devastating earthquake at Lisbon in 1755 and an epidemic of cholera in Britain, never before experienced on such a scale, struck panic in the nation. Death stalked incomprehensibly into home after home. A mood for repentance developed, and a mere handful of men, at first, in the face of fierce opposition began to preach the biblical gospel. Most were clergymen. The opposition of the Church and jeers of the intellectuals were their first problem, but the evangelists took the offensive and went after sinners with no difficulty in finding them. They preached fearlessly, drumming home the message that touched the people on the raw and brought down a hail of stones and refuse on the preachers' heads, but struck home so that ringleaders fell victims of truth and joined the evangelists on haywain or 'pub' steps (the new colloquialism of the early eighteenth century) or whatever served as a pulpit. They preached everywhere, in churches if possible but if not, then in the market places, on the commons or in the fields, from their own hearts to the hearts of the listeners. They were the Wesleys and their Methodists, George Whitefield and Lady Huntingdon's Connexion, and others who remained in the established Church without compromising their evangelistic message.

In 1733 Count Zinzendorf and the Moravians of Herrnhut sent their first missionaries to Greenland and the West Indies, and later to the Tibetan borderlands and elsewhere. If concerted action to make Christ known counts most, and not titles and organisation, theirs was the first modern mission.

The Church in hiding   18th century

Europe was seething with wars. Britain and France were fighting Spain from 1718–29, ten long years, a limited warfare between professionals, while other people pursued their ordinary lives, as long as hostilities were at a distance. News of events in China reached Britain accompanied by travel journals and letters. Exchanges between the savants saw the arrival in Europe of collections of botanical specimens and scientific papers, Chinese writings, books, philosophies and art. Kang Xi's porcelain factories worked overtime for the export trade in the second half of the seventeenth century and his cloisonné works of art (a skill derived at the time of Kublai Khan from the Middle East) exceeded the Ming masterpieces in fineness of workmanship. Sedan chairs, first brought to France in the sixteenth century, became *à la mode* for the bewigged and powdered beaux and belles. Rococo art came under Chinese influence. Chinese pavilions, lacquer, incense, China tea and Chinese painting styles came into vogue; and wall-paper first became fashionable in Europe, aping the Chinese custom. To carry this topic further, in the England of the 1780s George Prince of Wales (1762–1830) made Brighton the most popular watering place of those coaching days—where swallowing and bathing in salt water was the panacea for the ill effects of society life. So 'Prinny' had to build an oriental royal pavilion with domed stables which to Sidney Smith looked 'as if St Paul's had pupped'. Voltaire (1694–1778) and his contemporaries revelled in the craze for Chinese culture, giving rise to the term 'chinoiserie'. Western intellectuals who applied the epithet 'enlightened' to themselves, preferred 'natural religion' to 'revealed religion'. They saw in Confucian philosophies confirmation of their own and took to writing of 'Heaven' instead of 'God'.

The obsession passed, and as the tensions between China and the West built up, attitudes changed. News arrived of the Yong Zheng emperor's 1724 Edict of Expulsion being implemented again, of a bishop and eight priests in hiding in Nanking, of furtive movements from place to place, of a large community of Christians in the hills of Hunan province, of new persecutions in Fujian—and yet of the emperor helping in the repair of Catholic churches in Peking after an earthquake. Peking was the only place with any liberty. The Church in China was declining fast. By disregarding matters of 'face' Russia made a treaty with China whereby a caravan of two hundred merchants was allowed to visit Peking every two years. They had the status of tribute-bearers. And a small permanent trade mission was allowed to stay quietly in the capital, with Orthodox chaplains doing no proselytising. They were content not to, until near the end of the dynasty.

As for Canton, the opium scourge was enslaving more and more people, so in 1729 an imperial edict put a ban on opium imports, with heavy penalties. No ban could prevent or curb the traffic in opium. Overt trading became covert smuggling to supply the insatiable addicts. Penalties only gave greater power to corrupt officials to line their own pockets.

The Yong Zheng reign came to an end after thirteen years and in 1736 the Qian Long (Ch'ien Lung) emperor ascended the Dragon Throne. Sixty years later he was still there. The dynasty reached the summit of its glory, if not the peak of China's glory at any time, and became more and more prosperous. Kashgar and Yarkand were subdued again. Burma and Nepal were tributary. The imperial factories poured out their *objets d'art*, now suffering from mass production, in response to the demand from the West. And the Church came under greater disfavour.

A steady oppression was maintained with periods of intensification. Many Chinese Catholics refused to recant and died as martyrs, as (in A. H. Smith's phrase) no mere 'baptised pagans' would have done. Another most heroic chapter in the annals of Christendom was being written, the more tragic because there was a quality of fantasy about it. The emperor employed Jesuits to build him a European house with a fountain and Western paintings. Missionaries were encouraged by the rumour that the viceroy of Hunan and Hubei provinces was a Christian, no doubt secretly. Baptisms were reported from Henan (Honan), Manchuria and Mongolia. Two foreign priests were forced out of Sichuan province but a Chinese priest, Andrew Li, was allowed to minister to the Christians, keeping a remarkable journal (translated by Launay). Because of the toleration in Peking, enforcement of the 1724 edict of expulsion varied from place to place.

In Fujian it was a different story. The missionary vicar-apostolic was executed in Fuzhou (Foochow), three priests were strangled and many Christians killed. In Nanking two Jesuits were imprisoned and then strangled. On and on it went, decade after decade. François Pottier, the founder in 1756 of the West China enterprise of Pallu's Paris Society (Société des Missions Étrangères de Paris, 1663) and living in Sichuan, was the only European priest in the vast western and south-western provinces of Sichuan, Guizhou (Kweichow) and Yunnan. Escorted by Chinese Christians with extreme precautions he travelled his immense parish for ten years. Arrested and on his way to Macao and banishment, he escaped and returned to the western mountains. Reinforcements were sent to join him, risking everything. One priest, Gleyo, was arrested and imprisoned for eight years until, ironically, a Peking Jesuit visiting Sichuan for the emperor interceded for him. Officials searched until they found Gleyo's training school for Chinese priests, hidden in the mountains. After release he went to the Yunnan border and opened another there. Pottier was appointed bishop and vicar-apostolic but did not know it until two years later. While all this was going on, more priests were being trained in Bangkok and Naples. Neither expulsion, persecution nor death spelt defeat to those noble souls. Their policy was not even to prepare for the day of grace to return. It was to enter the Dragon's lair, now.

Not only in China was the Roman Church under pressure. The main European Catholic countries were on the wane and continuing wars were bleeding the rest of the Western world. Hardly had peace come between Britain, France and Spain in 1729 than France was at war with Russia. In 1739 Britain was back to fighting Spain; Prussia attacked Austria; Sweden defied Russia; France declared against Holland and Britain; Charles the Pretender seized his opportunity and there was war in Scotland and the north of England, the '45, until Culloden in 1746. Then it was war in India. Then the Seven Years War; war between Russia and Prussia; in Canada, the Battle of Quebec in 1759; the American War of Independence, 1775–77; more war with Spain; then the French Revolution, the Reign of Terror, blood flowing in rivers; and the beginning of the Napoleonic wars. And that list is not half the tally. Europe was anaemic and divided, close to starvation. The last decade of the century was particularly feverish. It was the age of revolution. The spirit of it entered widely into society.

Enough has been outlined to form a backdrop to the story that concerns us, the story first of growing developments at Canton and in Britain.

Ghetto for barbarians   *1000–1750*

In *A Cycle of Cathay*, W. A. P. Martin in 1896 summed up the history of East-West relations, which now concern us closely.

> China had always prided herself on having distant nations knock at her doors; and she encouraged them to come in by allowing their tribute missions to carry on trade duty-free. But a change of policy came with the discovery of a new route to the East by the Cape of Good Hope. When she saw Europeans arrive with stronger ships and better artillery than her own, her fears began to be excited. When she observed them pocketing the islands of the eastern seas, and contending for fragments of the empire of her kinsman, the Great Mogul, she deemed it prudent to close her ports, leaving the gates ajar at one point only, namely Canton, the emporium of the South.[5]

As so much of consequence to missions in China took place around Canton, it is appropriate here to sketch the geographical situation. Canton (Guangzhou) was an ancient walled city with records from before the time of Christ and a history of overseas trading from AD 700. The

Arabs came to Canton in the ninth century, the Portuguese in 1517 and the Dutch a century later, followed by the British.

The city stands on the Pearl River, which with the West, North and East Rivers flows through an expansive, fertile, densely populated delta-plain to the estuary. The navigable North River formed an imperial highway with only a twenty-four-mile portage over a pass to join another river flowing north through the Poyang Lake to the Yangzi. The West River provided a seven-hundred-mile waterway linked by canal to the headwaters of another northward stream which led through Changsha, capital of Hunan province, to the Dongding (Tungting) Lake and the Yangzi at Hankow. The metropolis of Hankow was key to the whole of central China and the western provinces.

Canton was, therefore, the natural entry and distribution point for foreign trade. Ships could go up to Canton, but there was an anchorage twelve miles below, at Huangbo, the 'Yellow Anchorage'. Thirty miles or so downstream from the city, the united Pearl and East Rivers flow into a wide estuary or bay, the natural site for fortifications which came to be known as 'the Bogue'. And forty more miles southward the estuary opens into the South China Sea, with the Macao peninsula like a gatepost on the west and Hong Kong Island among others to the east.

Seaborne trade was nationalised in about AD 1000 and apart from some relaxation under the enlightened Kang Xi emperor, was strictly confined to Canton, especially after Kang Xi's death in 1723. His successors were difficult to deal with, but by 1757 regular commerce had begun under incredibly difficult circumstances. The technicalities of trade relations feature so largely in the international developments, with their repercussions on Christian missions, that a few must be outlined here.

The 'Viceroy of the Two Guangs', the provinces of Guangxi and Guangdong (Kwangsi and Kwangtung) in which Canton and its life-giving rivers lay, and the governor of the city itself, asserted their authority over the merchants

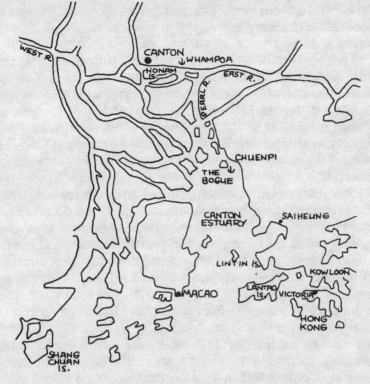

CANTON ESTUARY (diagrammatic)

through a department and superintendent of trade, the *Hai Guan Bu*, known as the Hu Bu. The foreigners of course mangled the Chinese terms and the institution became known as the 'Hoppo'. The Hoppo used and abused a guild of Chinese merchants as its agents, the 'Cohong' or business house. The foreign ghetto, 'the Factory', a few hundred yards in width on the waterfront outside the walled city, was called the *Fan Fang*, the barbarians' quarter. These nicknames convey the mutual scorn prevailing.

Almost all trading and control of the merchants' conditions was administered by the Cohong for the Hoppo, and profits remaining after each had taken its slice belonged to the central government. The mandarins' pockets, in consequence, were richly lined, and trade was important to all concerned. A game of cat and mouse went on interminably. The barbarian, for so he was invariably called, was treated with disdain and discouraged in a thousand and one ways, short of scaring him away. Hard bargains were driven, for he needed the market. He wanted the exotic foodstuffs of China in the early years, and the tea and silks, the porcelains and furniture later. And the Hoppo and Cohong wanted the profits from handling up-country and overseas products.

Literature about Canton is filled with expressions like 'the ingrained rapacity of the officials'. Life would proceed smoothly in its peculiar course for a while and then the screws would be tightened, the fear of torture and death would be held over the Cohong and their foreign counterparts, and when the end was gained all would revert to normal. This hostility was in part the legacy of the turbulence of the early Portuguese and British visitors but had been experienced for centuries. Foreign devils were not to be trusted an inch and seemed to understand firmness, so normality was a system of obduracy, restrictions and insults which foreign merchants accepted year after year as inevitable and just worth enduring. Most of them were adventurous young men. They stayed at it until they had had enough, and returned home sleek and prosperous to conduct the home end of the business and become landed gentry and members of Parliament, especially after tea and opium became the chief commodities.

They were permitted to come to Canton from September to March only, the trading season. They could bring no women, so any families, and there were few, were separated for long periods. The womenfolk had to stay in Macao, where the merchants lived through the summer. No weapons could be carried and it was forbidden to speak or even to learn Chinese. Any Chinese citizen found teaching a barbarian was beheaded or strangled, so a part-Chinese, part-Portuguese and part-English trade language developed, known as 'pidgin'. For full measure, they were debarred from riding in sedan chairs, the gentleman's mode of conveyance.

The protocol was stereotyped. Any communication with the Chinese authority had to be in the form of a petition, through the Cohong, and messages from the viceroy or Hoppo to the merchants came through the Cohong in scornfully flowery language. This protocol and terminology were used throughout the empire as a necessary means towards controlling hundreds of millions of subjects, many of them very remote, but for the barbarians it was larded with insult.

A certain James Flint, distinguished servant of the East India Company, thought to extend trading facilities with China and secured a passage in a Chinese junk to Tianjin (Tientsin) in the far north, the gateway to Peking. He persuaded a local official to present his petition to the emperor, Qian Long (Ch'ien Lung). The official was beheaded and in spite of protests from five European powers, Flint was incarcerated in a filthy prison for two and a half years.

The merchants were known as 'factors', which is why their quarters were called 'the Factory', actually becoming a row of thirteen 'factories' side by side, with the flag of each country flying on a mast in front of it. They faced on to an open space of about a hundred yards by fifty where the merchants exercised under close observation by an unsympathetic crowd of sightseers, barbers, fortune-tellers, and vendors of dogs and cats, quack medicines and trinkets, who took up much of the space. It was a public park for the townsfolk of Canton.

The 'factory' buildings were two-storeyed, with merchandise and offices below and sumptuous living quarters above. The merchants bolstered their morale by self-indulgence. Behind lay more warehouses and servants' quarters. If the barbarians tired of their ghetto life and wanted an excursion they could obtain permission to cross the river under escort for a walk, at the risk of ramming by playful or malicious shipping. Three times a month parties of no more than ten could visit the pleasure gardens on Henan Island where there was a temple or 'Dios-house' (from which comes the familiar term 'joss-sticks', for incense). Even on these expeditions they were in danger from stoning.

Opium quicksand   1750 – 90

To some extent the scene is ready for the drama that built up to the opium wars. Its action began in the wings. In India the French had taken Madras, in 1746, and when the Seven Years War broke out, hostilities engulfed the East India Company and British shipping on the high seas. On June 18, 1756, the Nawab of Bengal reputedly captured one hundred and forty-six British and confined them in an airless room about twenty feet square. Only twenty-three were alive the next morning. The details are disputed but the reply was decisive. Calcutta was retaken in January and almost a year to the day after the Black Hole atrocity, the British force of three thousand under Robert Clive confronted the Nawab at Plassey in Western Bengal and defeated his much larger force of fifty thousand. British supremacy in India had begun. The end of the Mogul empire, offshoot of Genghis Khan's conquests, was in sight. Bengal was seized and the exploitation of what Clive called 'this rich and flourishing kingdom' began.[6] The Portuguese had been exporting opium from the Mahratta States, through Goa, and Bengal had its own varieties. The best opium, commanding the highest prices, came from Patna. When Clive found himself saddled with a huge area to administer and finance, and that revenue was available from opium, he claimed the monopoly of the trade for the Company, the Company that was already established at Canton. At once the action broke upon the Eastern stage in a hubbub of activity.

When the Company in India began sending opium to its

agents at Canton the imperial ban on opium was being enforced. The agents saw the rest of their trade imperilled, or at least a reduction of such privileges as they had, if they contravened regulations. Not only so, the offending ship would be burned and both foreign and Chinese merchants and their families be executed. There was a simple way out. The Company sold its produce to Parsee and independent British merchants who either shipped the opium themselves or sold it to other ship owners.

These independent ships were known as 'country-ships' and played an increasingly significant role. Some of the owners were men of great ability who developed their businesses into major concerns. In our own day the same firms operate internationally. When the country-ships reached the Canton estuary they anchored at a safe distance from the shore and warded off interference from enquiring Chinese Customs' junks. By night Chinese merchant junks would come alongside, load up and be away to safe landing places along the coast. The Canton and coastal smuggling business had struck a rich vein. By 1767 the Portuguese were importing a thousand chests of opium into China each year, but the British were soon to eclipse them.

The ships also brought merchandise from the Malayan archipelago, spices, tin, birds' nests from Bornean caves and, as George Woodcock records,[7] sea-otter skins bought from Canadian Indians to trim the mandarins' robes — and loaded up with whatever might be sold abroad. Meanwhile the East India Company pursued its legal trading at the factory, and only carried licensed cargoes of opium for medicinal use. Chinese practitioners had known and used its properties for a thousand years. Now British hypocrisy had begun — on the face of things importing only legitimate amounts, but through the country-ships smuggling far more.

Apart from opium, the rapid development of British seaborne trade took the Chinese by surprise. Surrounded on three sides as she was by deserts and mountains, China's overland trade could never be more than a trickle, at best it looked like 'tribute'; but here she was with her 'safe' seaboard receiving increasingly importunate advances by barbarian shipping. This was patently more than tribute. Old concepts were shaken by the new trends and the dynastic government did not know how to cope. It resorted to bombast, blood and thunder.

Warren Hastings became the Company's first Governor-General of India in 1773. Although he knew the devastating effects of opium on addicts and their families and called it 'a pernicious article of luxury'[8] not necessary to life, he forced the pace of poppy cultivation in Bengal, even at the cost of destroying crops when they stood in the way of opium planting at the right time. With the exploitation of indigo the condition of the Bengali peasants deteriorated rapidly. The Company had a considerable trade with the East Indies, and when the Dutch cut it off, Hastings was desperate for funds. He armed and disguised two merchant ships and sent them weighed down with opium to Canton. One ship was wrecked, but the *Nonsuch* arrived with two hundred thousand pounds of contraband opium. The Company agents were frantic. It was too good a haul to be lost, and there were plenty of Chinese ready to take it, but it would be fatal if she were to be found loaded with contraband. The agents made the captain do a quick transformation of the *Nonsuch* to look like a merchant ship again and move downstream to the anchorage at Huangbo. There they furtively unloaded her. When Warren Hastings was impeached, this *Nonsuch* adventure was one of the counts against him.

Britain's consumption of tea was rising dramatically, coming within the means of all classes, as inferior and smuggled supplies came on the market. The Boston Tea Party was in 1773 and the American War of Independence was threatening. After that it was the Napoleonic wars. Until the nineteenth century the world's supply of tea came from China. So Britain could no more afford to lose her tea trade with China than she could take over the financing of the Indian administration. Chinese techniques of tea cultivation had not yet been acquired or exploited in India, and China did not want British textiles, though the wool trade meant so much to Britain. The difficulty was to find anything China would buy.

Having soiled her hands with opium, Britain now plunged in to the elbows. Having paddled gingerly she sank to the knees. Pitt's government supported the trade. The so-called Honourable East India Company was allowed to keep her trading monopoly on condition that she matched Chinese tea purchases by Indian exports, avoiding the opprobrium of naming the main commodity. Responsibility for the opium trade was now fairly and squarely the British government's; but it was a precarious arrangement and the twenty-four year-old Prime Minister William Pitt was anxious. Steam power had been harnessed, industrial output was increasing and expanded markets were imperative. A very systematic census of the population of China set the subjects of the Dragon Throne at three hundred million — a market to be exploited by every means possible. Pitt decided to send an embassy to the emperor of China to negotiate for better facilities and greater exchanges between the two countries. Access to northern ports was important, Ningbo and Tianjin (Tientsin) in particular. Unfortunately Pitt did not know his emperor.

Macartney debacle   1793

For over a century after the first Portuguese embassy in 1520, no attempt had been made to obtain trading rights, but between 1655 and 1793 sixteen or seventeen embassies were sent. Six were Russian, four more were Portuguese, Holland sent three or four and the papacy three. And all of them performed the *ketou*. As the Chinese word *ketou* says, this form of obeisance involved knocking the forehead on the ground as an act of surrender. A full *ketou* at court consisted of nine prostrations. At the strident command of the usher 'Kneel!' the one seeking audience would sink on both knees. 'Fall prostrate!' and he would go down with forearms and forehead on the ground. 'Kneel!' and he would raise his head and body again. After the third prostration he would stand, only to repeat the whole performance twice more.⁹ It was part of the Confucian protocol. The emperor as Son of Heaven himself did it before Heaven from time to time. And it was observed throughout the empire. There were then two ways of looking at it — as a matter of good manners, or as an admission of subservience. Even the papal envoys avoided trouble by welcoming the first interpretation. Not so the British.

When William Pitt's envoy, Lord Macartney, reached China in 1793 with HMS *Lion* bearing gifts for Qian Long, worth fifteen thousand pounds, he took one of the leading agents at Canton, George Staunton, with him up the coast. Staunton had been in East Asia since he was a boy of fifteen and knew the state of affairs well, but his advice to Macartney was not to perform the *ketou*. Trade as between equals was overdue. European merchants had licked the boots of the emperor for too long already.

Things did not go smoothly after they disembarked at Dagu, at the mouth of the Beihe below Tianjin. Somehow the loads of lavish gifts had come to be labelled in Chinese 'tribute from the Kingdom of England', and when Macartney and his entourage of over ninety attendants arrived at the Summer Palace in the country a few miles north of Peking, court officials were appalled to be told that he would not *ketou*. Tribute bearers normally entered the imperial presence on their knees. Lord Macartney was denied audience unless he did. The 'tribute' meant little to Qian Long, his palaces were stuffed with the offerings of vassal states and favour seekers like Matteo Ricci with his clocks. Instead, with great courtesy — for courtesy and a banquet could be the prelude to an assassination, even in twentieth-century China — the embassy were lavishly entertained at the Rehe (Jehol), 'Hot Stream', hunting palace beyond the Great Wall. Then, dazzled by the splendours of the imperial court they were ushered out of the country, having delivered their proposals without achieving anything. Nothing but scorn was felt by their hosts. They carried a letter from the Qian Long emperor to George III.

> . . . I have already taken note of your respectful spirit of submission . . . I do not forget the lonely remoteness of your island, cut off from the world by intervening wastes of sea . . . [As for northern ports] . . . should your Majesty . . . attempt to trade at Ningpo, Tientsin or other places, as our laws are exceedingly severe . . . I shall direct my officials to force your ships to quit those ports . . . You will not then be able to complain that I have not clearly forewarned you. Let us therefore live in peace and friendship, and do not make light of my words.[10]

For good measure he warned the king against letting his subjects 'propagate the English religion', but he did not know that Lord Macartney had smuggled two foreign priests into the country and two Chinese from Ripa's school in Naples in the guise of interpreters.[11] They were desperately needed. The Church in the Yangzi valley provinces was declining at an alarming rate, almost to extinction.

The failure of Lord Macartney's mission scarcely mattered in Britain by the time the news of it arrived. Revolutionary horrors were breaking loose on the Continent, though in Britain 'Farmer George' as the king was being called, was 'the symbol of national unity and patriotism'. Pitt's revival of prosperity in Britain had restored the king's popularity, lost through his attempt to tax the American colonies. That blunder had estranged them irreparably and brought down on his head the armed intervention of all the maritime powers of Europe. Now he made a 'triumphal progress through flower-strewn villages and cheering crowds'[12] on recovering from his first serious illness. The anxieties over the French Revolution and imprisonment of the French royal family in 1792 were intensified by news in January 1793 of the execution of Louis XVI by the guillotine and the beginning of the Reign of Terror. The Chinese emperor's letter, arriving soon after Marie Antoinette's execution, went unnoticed. King and ministers were preoccupied. However, Qian Long's own days were numbered and in 1796 the Jia Qing (Chia Ch'ing) emperor succeeded him in a country not only troubled with external pressures but increasingly distraught by insurrections and the decay of ancient loyalties.

Wesley comes to Yorkshire   1720–1800

In the unfolding of this epic, period by period, we turn aside to trace more of the antecedents of Protestant missions in China. Now parallel, now interlocked with secular events, they owed a great deal to the Wesley brothers.

At Oxford from 1720–29 John Wesley had been troubled by his own sinful nature. Instead of silencing the clamours of conscience he joined with others to search for elusive holiness. Charles Wesley, five years his junior, was already one of this coterie known as the Holy Club, whose members were called Methodists because of the devotions they observed. Whitefield joined later. On October 21, 1735, the Wesleys sailed together to Georgia as SPG 'missionaries'. There they went barefoot, slept on the ground, but failed with both colonists and Indians and were soon home again, Charles leaving in May 1737 and John in December. They had no peace in their own hearts or message for others.

On the Wesleys' ship, going to America, were some Moravians, men who lived on the sunny alpine pastures of a holy life with God through an intimate experience of Jesus Christ. When John Wesley returned from Georgia, he was still longing to know the secret of their cheerful loving nature and engrossment in useful occupations. Then he met them again in London, and within a few days of each other Charles and then John were through the faith barrier, at last able to understand, and trusting in Christ for deliverance from sin. They had indeed found *him*, and confessed to being 'thrust out utterly against our will' to tell the world. Charles was turned out of his curacy in Islington for preaching the gospel, and went to the convicts at Newgate.

John Wesley began preaching in 1739 and continued until he died in 1791. Rising at four a.m. and often preaching by five, travelling never less than four thousand five hundred miles a year by horseback, he preached on average fifteen times a week, eight hundred sermons every year for fifty-three years. 'I feel and grieve, but by the grace of God, I fret at nothing,' he wrote in his journal. Not until he was eighty-four did he mention ageing, when he wrote, 'I am now an old man, decaying from head to foot,' but still he travelled and preached, quoting, "Tis time to live if I grow old.' George Whitefield similarly never spared himself but burned out twenty years earlier, at fifty-six.

Charles Wesley's gift for hymn writing appeared almost as soon as he began working with John. From 1738 hymns had poured from his soul. Many were missionary hymns. Wherever people responded to the preaching they were banded together in 'classes' to learn and become established in the faith, and where classes met to read and study and pray, there they sang and sang for joy.

John preached in the West Riding of Yorkshire in 1742 and Methodism took root. In 1760 a great revival broke out in Yorkshire and from there spread to London and onward; but an unhealthy 'spirit of enthusiasm' developed with excessive emphasis on feelings, irreverence in prayer, hypocritical discerning of spirits and the future, and criticism of other Christians as being blind or dead. John Wesley dealt with it. He had one hundred and fifty-five travelling preachers in 1776, apart from a small army of local preachers. At a conference of these men in 1763 'Twelve Rules of a Helper' were drawn up and adopted— the rules by which Hudson Taylor's forebears lived, and in time he himself. They showed a wisdom and understanding of psychology before its time, making him the man he was, the direct product of Methodism. In brief the rules were:

1 Be diligent, never unemployed or triflingly employed.
2 Be serious — remember, 'holiness unto the Lord'.
3 Be careful in all dealings with women, especially the young.
4 Take no steps toward marriage without consulting your brethren.
5 Believe evil of no one; put the best construction on everything.
6 Speak evil of no one, till you come to the person concerned.
7 'Cast the fire out of your bosom' — confess what you think of a person.
8 Be servant of all — do not 'affect the gentleman'.
9 Do not be ashamed of manual labour, only of sin.
10 Be punctual and precise.
11 Bring as many souls to repentance as you can, and build them up in holiness.
12 Obey the direction of the leaders, 'not according to your own will but as a son in the Gospel'.

Much more was of course given as guidance to Wesley's preachers and class leaders. They were advised to give from four to five a.m. and five to six p.m. every day to the Scriptures and prayer and meditation, with the help of books; and to preach, preferably 'where there are most quiet and willing hearers and most fruit', but never to the exclusion of breaking new ground at whatever cost in danger and suffering.

In 1760 one of Wesley's travelling preachers came to Barnsley in Yorkshire, 'when they were very angry, cast rotten eggs at us and gave us hearty curses. But I think the Lord will conquer them.' 'Baiting the Methodists', like baiting the bears, was a diversion for rough elements in the town. The first 'Society' of believers was formed at a near-by village and when John Wesley preached there the following year, he stayed in the home of a respectable Anglican Church family, the Shaws, who were also

'Methodists'. The term referred to a practice, not a denomination.

In 1776, the year of the declaration of American Independence, a young stone-mason lived in the cottage next to the Shaws, a stone-mason by trade but by taste a musician—player and singer and a bell-ringer at the parish church. Apart from the Shaws' influence, he was familiar with Scripture. On his wedding-day morning the thought came to him, 'As for me and my house, we will serve the Lord.' It struck him forcibly. He knew he could not do so without first getting right with God, and was soon lost in thought. Time passed, and when he emerged from his reflections, his decision taken and his lifelong transaction with the Lord completed, he was late for his wedding and had two miles to run. His friends the bell-ringers had stopped the clock.

Immediately the wedding was over, James Taylor told Betty his bride what had happened, adding that there were to be no unseemly dancing and celebrations. 'Surely I have not married one of those Methodists!' she exclaimed. Back in his cottage she refused to read or pray with him and day after day taunted him until he could endure it no longer. He swept her up in his arms, carried her upstairs and knelt by the bed holding her by his side while he poured out his heart to God. She was overcome. The next day she too 'found peace with God' and they set out together to be uncompromising Christians.

They moved into Barnsley soon afterwards and used their home as the meeting place for Methodists, as one by one brave men and women joined them. They were the target of attack. One of Wesley's preachers wrote to him that he had been unable to stay there overnight for fear of the consequences to the home that received him. When he preached a rain of mud and stones and rotten eggs fell on him. Another wrote that James Taylor's perseverance against such odds nerved him, the writer, and others to be 'willing to be struck down in the market place, dragged through the streets, pelted with refuse, and rescued at the last moment only to preach again.'

The *Barnsley Chronicle* in 1905 quoted an 1813 writer saying, 'Scarcely any people raged against the Methodists or persecuted them with that ferocity as the people of Barnsley. For some years a preacher never went there without several persons in company.' But not only religious intolerance was involved. Strangers were suspect at any time. As late as the mid-nineteenth century a *Punch* cartoon showed one villager in north-east England saying to another as a stranger passed by, 'Heave half a brick at him!' Strangers preaching the wrath of God were doubly vulnerable, but not only strangers. When James Taylor became a local preacher, permanently exposed to attack, his life was 'once and again in peril from the violence of an angry mob'.

In the course of his work he had an accident and found employment with a Mr Beckett, owner of a linen factory and a local magistrate. One day, in Church Street a man held out his hand as if to shake hands and with the other hand 'daubed Mr Taylor's face with smudge and broken glass', the *Sunday Telephone* recalled years later. Blinded for seven weeks and unable to work for seven more, James Taylor would not prosecute his assailant, so his employer did so himself. On another occasion, when James was walking down the street in a new 'salt and pepper coat' a woman in a house near by cursed him, ran out and rubbed her frying pan down his back. He turned round quietly and invited her to do it to the front as well. When he began having meetings in his home, they were frequently mobbed by people beating kettles and pans. Turfs were laid over the chimney stack to smoke them out, where they could be assaulted again. Another time, the mob made a bonfire at the door of the home and as the Taylors and their fellow-Christians escaped, 'pelted them with the foulest filth'.

John Wesley passed through Barnsley twenty times, but stayed overnight on only three occasions. A few months before the most notable of these visits, one of his travelling preachers was stoned and seriously hurt. A friendly Quaker rescued him. Three years earlier, a man had tried to murder one of the preachers as he preached. On Friday, June 30, 1786, John Wesley, who had reached his eighty-second birthday two days before, wrote in his journal:

> I turned aside to Barnsley, formerly famous for all manner of wickedness. They were then ready to tear any Methodist preacher in pieces; now not a dog wagged his tongue . . . Surely God will have a people in this place.

God did, but not yet in any great numbers. After nine years of such fortitude there were only seven in the Barnsley 'society' at James Taylor's house. By then Wesley had over five hundred travelling preachers in the United Kingdom, thirteen hundred local preachers and four thousand stewards and class leaders. At seventy he had been the best known man in England, with brow smooth, eyes brilliant, complexion ruddy and voice strong. Now he wrote, 'I am wonderful to myself. It is now twelve years since I have felt such sensation as weariness. I am never tired (such is the goodness of God) either with writing, preaching or travelling.' Standing in 'Strutt's Yard' at the Old White Bear, with James Taylor and others around him, he spoke to an attentive crowd. Whether there were some in the town who had been impressed by the lives they witnessed day after day, or whether it was simply respect for the old man with such a reputation was not recorded. Wesley himself had only five more years to live, for he died on March 2, 1791, three months short of eighty-eight.

On that day in 1786 when 'not a dog wagged his tongue', James Taylor was still only thirty-seven. After nine more years he was still being pelted, in 1795, the year he died at forty-six. He left two sons and three daughters. John, the eldest, had been through all the assaults on their home when, at seventeen, he became man of the house, and soon afterwards a class leader. Class leaders were the pastors of the local congregations. When converts were accepted into a 'society' they solemnly undertook to attend weekly meetings as well as Sunday services for worship. The class leader taught them, met them at least once a week and enquired into their spiritual progress, advised, reproved, comforted and exhorted them. Attendance at love-feasts with the Lord's Supper was by certificate. Unfaithfulness in maintaining Christian fellowship forfeited the right to be present. Local preachers were class leaders with added responsibilities, preaching nightly in their own neighbourhood and on Sundays. They were also colporteurs, distributing Scripture and Methodist literature, all in addition to their bread-winning occupations. Itinerant preachers were like John Wesley, always on the go and preaching two or three times daily.

One of John Wesley's first seven travelling preachers, who worked with him and shared his stonings, was William Shepherd, a man of independent means. In his journal Wesley refers to him a number of times between 1743–48. In the Taylor family a strong tradition was and still is passed down that John Taylor married William Shepherd's daughter (or granddaughter) Mary.[13] Each generation, beginning with one of their own sons, had a William Shepherd Taylor, including Hudson Taylor's closest brother, but confirmation of the first William Shepherd's identity from available records is difficult.

Mary was also a class leader and together they carried on James Taylor's good work. Persecution gradually diminished, but John was known for the story that one day as he was walking along the street he was given a resounding blow with the words, 'Take that for Jesus Christ's sake!'[14] and unruffled replied, 'I do take it for Jesus Christ's sake.' Disciplined Methodism was the environment into which their children were born, and in which Hudson Taylor was to grow up as John and Mary's grandson.

Second missionary awakening   *1740–1800*

During the last decade of Qian Long's sixty-year reign, 1736–96, the 'missionary awakening' in Europe, which had dozed fitfully for a century, suddenly returned to life. It was the product of the 'evangelical movement', itself the product of the great turning to God we have seen in connection with the Pietists, Quakers, Methodists and others. Strongest in the English-speaking countries it spread to Scandinavia, Holland, Germany and Switzerland. Its emphasis was on the individual experience of meeting with Christ, and responsibility for leading others into the same kind of experience, into knowing him. It also expressed itself in love and concern for needy people of all kinds, socially and physically as well as spiritually. From it arose orphanages, care for offenders against the law, opposition to slave-trading and slave-owning, justice for those suffering oppressive conditions in factories, charities, reforms and good deeds of many kinds, including a wave of action to take the gospel to all deprived of it.

So now, after three hundred years of Protestant indifference, as voice after voice awakened the conscience of Christians, society after society came into being. It was not a movement of the Churches, the denominations as represented by their leaders, but of small groups of individuals in each section of the wider Church agreeing together that something must be done, and doing it. Some were recognised by their denominational leaders, others remained independent but with the full approval and support of their Churches.

In 1743, four years after the Wesleys began their true lifework, David Brainerd went to the American Indians and died among them.[15] Then another forty years went by. The Wesleys sang their missionary hymns and looked for the day of missionary enterprise but their own time and hands were full. In 1776 John Wesley met a young clergyman, Dr Thomas Coke, wealthy, cultured, a Gentleman Commoner of Jesus College, Oxford, who had been

ousted from his parish as a despised revivalist. He became
John Wesley's right-hand man for a time, while his heart
was set on taking the gospel far afield, to India if possible.

Wesley needed someone with Coke's qualities to super-
intend the Methodist societies in the American continent
and prevailed upon Thomas Coke to go. He was known as
the 'foreign minister' of the Methodists and referred to by
some as the 'bishop', although neither he nor Wesley
wished the term to be adopted. The Methodist Episcopal
Church originated, however, from its increasing use. Coke's
ship bound for Nova Scotia was battered by a storm and
driven south. Eventually they made land in the West Indies
and to Coke's delight he found a government shipwright,
a zealous Methodist, with fifteen hundred Christian slaves
under his instruction.

Coke published a vigorous missionary appeal on the
spiritual need of the Indies, Newfoundland, Nova Scotia
and Quebec – and also proposed a mission to Asia. It was
now 1786, the year John Wesley stayed with James Taylor
in Barnsley, and in a letter he wholeheartedly endorsed
Coke's appeal. On Christmas Day, the title 'Missions
established by the Methodist Society' was first used,
antedating the Baptist Missionary Society (BMS, 1792) by
several years. (In 1818 it was changed to the 'Wesleyan
Missionary Society'.) Wesley could have spoken of it in
Barnsley, where Methodist contributions for sending the
gospel overseas rose in the following year to £1,167.

As early as 1784 the young William Carey, 'shoe-maker,
school-master and pastor', through his concern for the
'heathen' persuaded the clergy in Nottingham at least to
pray about the matter. But in 1786, that significant year,
when Carey proposed to a meeting of Baptist ministers
that they consider their responsibility to the heathen, the
chairman retorted, 'Sit down, young man. When it pleases
God to convert the Heathen he'll do it without your help
or mine.' In the same year the bishop of Lincoln appealed
in the annual sermon of the SPG for the evangelisation of
India, as Bishop Butler had earlier done for the slaves of

the West Indies. The following year, the year when Coke's appeal was winning Methodist support, the saintly Andrew Fuller exclaimed in answer to Carey's pleadings, 'If God would open the windows in heaven, then might this thing be.'

The concept was still too revolutionary and too visionary, but Carey was not to be deterred. In 1792 he presented his treatise *An Enquiry into the Obligation of Christians to use Means for the Conversion of the Heathen* and on May 31 preached a memorable sermon before his fellow-ministers in Nottingham from Isaiah 54:2–3, 'Lengthen thy cords, and strengthen thy stakes', under the two headings 'Expect great things from God. Attempt great things for God.' A group of colleagues joined with him at Kettering to form what became the Baptist Missionary Society (BMS) with the intitial sum of thirteen pounds 'taken in Fuller's snuff-box' to open its accounts. William Carey sailed for Calcutta with his wife and children in 1793, the year of the Macartney fiasco at Peking; and at the turn of the century he joined Joshua Marshman and William Ward in the Danish colony of Serampore, a few miles away, to evade the harassments of British Indian officials.

A direct outcome of Carey's going to India was the formation of the London Missionary Society (LMS) in 1795.[16] Its founders were clergy of the Church of England (led by Dr Haweis, Rector of Aldwinckle, near Kettering) and ministers of the Presbyterian and Independent Churches, and it was intended to be undenominational, embracing all evangelical sections of the wider Church. To its honour and the glory of God, it sent out as fine as army of missionary commandos as any in the history of Christendom. Robert Morrison of China, John Williams of the South Seas, David Livingstone of Africa and James Gilmour of Mongolia were among them.

The year 1786 was also significant for William Wilberforce's entry in his diary, 'resolved to live for God's glory'. Wilberforce's role in Parliament was to make history. Supported by a coterie of friends labelled the 'Clapham

Sect' but more properly the Eclectic Society (1783),[17] and including such notables as John Venn, co-founder and first chairman of the Church Missionary Society (CMS), and the Thornton brothers, Wilberforce battled until the Act abolishing the slave trade became law. Then he went on to outlaw slavery in every form. It was banned from the British empire in 1833, the year he died.

In the same period Charles Simeon, persecuted at Cambridge as a 'Methodist', was actively influencing Henry Martyn and others to go overseas with the gospel. In 1798 he read before the Eclectics a paper entitled 'How might the Gospel be carried to the heathen?' It led to the concern among evangelicals of the Church of England which resulted in 1799 in the founding of the Church Missionary Society, established with these aims: to follow God's leading and look for success only from the Spirit; to send out missionaries who should have heaven in their hearts and the world under foot; to begin on a small scale, sending preferably ordained clergy but also lay people to work on the 'Church-Principle', that of establishing churches as a product of the gospel.

Other societies came into being around the same time. The Protestant missionary era had begun. China had hardly been mentioned, for India had the Church's attention. But a certain Reverend Dr William Moseley[18] and a series of events given too little prominence in missionary histories were already playing what proved to be the key role in the beginning of the evangelisation of China. During the Qian Long persecutions in China, in 1737–38, when there were many Catholic refugees at Canton, a certain Mr Hodgson arranged for a transcript to be made of a Catholic translation into Chinese of most of the New Testament. He took it to England and presented it in 1739 to Sir Hans Sloane, Bt. As President of the Royal Society, following Sir Isaac Newton, Sir Hans bequeathed it to the nation among his fifty thousand volumes of MSS, books and other treasures. They became the nucleus of the British Museum and Library (at Montagu House, 1759–1847).

Mr Moseley, as he then was, came upon this Chinese manuscript in the Museum and, as he wrote, '. . . nothing but a sense of decency prevented the most extravagant marks of joy.' The manuscript was found to contain 'a Harmony of the four Gospels, the book of Acts, and St Paul's epistles'. Mr Moseley could not be held in. He wrote a memoir urging the establishment of a society for translating the Holy Scriptures into the languages of the most populous oriental nations, and had a hundred copies printed.[19] On March 7, 1798, six years to a day before the founding of the British and Foreign Bible Society, he sent a copy to every bishop and to other influential men. Charles Grant, a director of the East India Company and regarded as an authority on Eastern affairs dismissed the undertaking as 'a practical impossibility. No translations of the Holy Scriptures could be made into the Chinese language!'[20] And not only he, all concerned rejected the idea as impracticable, if only because the problem of distributing it was insuperable. In China who but 'the Popish bishops' could do anything? And the Roman Church in China was in hiding, as weak as it had ever been at any time since Ricci, and getting weaker. However, the archbishop of Canterbury referred the matter to the SPCK. After four years' delay they decided not to proceed with it. Meanwhile the founders of the CMS showed considerable interest but in deference to the SPCK and the archbishop, refrained for the present from any action. This by no means crippled Moseley's initiative. More was soon to be heard from him.

The European eruption   *1796–1820*

The Jia Qing (Chia Ch'ing) emperor and Manchu dynasty were distraught by their apparent impotence to curb the decay and corruption in court and country. They had passed the apogee of their glory. The power of the palace eunuchs was growing. Insurrections followed on each others' heels and took advantage of the authorities' preoccupation in one quarter to spring up in another. Connivance by the officials appointed to suppress them, and fictitious reports and memorials to the throne gave an untrue picture of the state of affairs. Edicts were ferocious in content but weak in effect. It was a collapse of the heart-structure of the dynasty which was to continue until its end a century later. Piracy, smuggling and vice were increasing as Chinese cultivation of opium kept pace with its mounting importation from India. Attempts to check the traffic seemed useless. China's tributary states were the target of European ambition, and the wider empire was being eroded fast. Burma and Malaya, Java and parts of Indo-China were visited, occupied and finally dominated. Yet the writ of Peking followed Chinese emigrants to the remotest corners of South-East Asia (as it comparably does today), and posed a serious threat to foreign mission-aries even so far from China's coasts.

In the minds of the Manchus, Christianity was insepar-ably connected with trouble-makers and enemies. Among the ruling classes it was regarded with a mixture of scorn and fear. Confucianism presented a solid front, but Buddh-ism was almost moribund. It had been waning for a thousand years. Taoism was even more feeble. Each was kept alive by superstitious observance of its customs but there was little knowledge of the philosophies of either. Muslim minorities existed in the west and in Henan (Honan), but kept very much to themselves, for the present. The nineteenth century opened with not a single Protestant missionary in China and the Catholic Church under severe persecution, about to be violently intensified.

As so often happens, the interception of a map set the cat among the pigeons. It was intercepted by the Manchu government at a time, in 1805, when all Europe was on the warpath, Napoleon's fleet was operating in East Asia, and China was alert to attack. A priest in Peking wished to guide the parent missionary body in Rome, the Propa-ganda, in the settlement of an ecclesiastical dispute over areas of supervision and accompanied his memorandum with a map, but, taking it as a plan for invasion, the Manchus reacted swiftly. Christians were tortured and exiled. Christian books and printing blocks were destroyed. From that time no more Catholics were attached to the government, though some scientists were allowed to remain in the capital. The last astronomer died there in 1838.

An Italian Franciscan who entered the country illegally in March 1805 was arrested and condemned to prison for three years, but after a beating, at the very least a hundred heavy strokes, he was delivered to Macao and threatened with death if he entered China again. He went to Tongking, North Vietnam, and five years later reached his destination, Shanxi in the far north. Another, travelling with only a Tongking Christian who had never been in China himself, reached Shanxi in 1818. Such devotion and courage reaped its reward in courageous converts. Their success was partly due to an amusing situation. In a moment of self-congratulation the mandarins in Sichuan reported that all Christians in the province had been eliminated. They therefore dared not arrest any and for a while turned a blind eye. In 1807 over eighteen hundred adult baptisms were reported from China. Mass was always held in secret, and foreign priests remained hidden, while Chinese catechists continued to work with great caution.

Abandonment of the Ricci compromises threw Catholics into conflict with ancient customs, however, and aggravated the opposition. The Jesuits had been suppressed by the Pope himself in 1773, and Napoleon overthrew the Pope if not the papacy in 1809. This was the end of the papal 'Propaganda' and support from Europe for the hard-pressed Church in China. Its future was very dark indeed, even for the tolerated priest-scientists in Peking. As Professor Latourette summed it up, an era was approaching its end and a new era was not yet in sight. The two hundred thousand or so remaining Christians were not only suffering from the general lawlessness but, because they could only meet in secret for their all-important sacraments, they were suspected of being members of a seditious political society.

Europe was in ferment and the industrial revolution was affecting events worldwide. Scientific knowledge and curiosity were leading to new inventions and inventions to new manufacturing methods. Factories were springing up everywhere to the exclusion of cottage industries, and with them the exploitation of labour, including child labour, increased. By 1800 as many factories were powered by steam as by water, and needed a hundred million pounds of raw cotton to process. By 1840 it was five hundred million pounds. Dickens started exposing the abuses in 1812. Railways, steamships, and soon telegraphs and telephones were startling the Western countries out of long-accustomed torpor.

With the spread of education and the need for raw materials, new vigour and new enterprise drove explorers and merchants to the ends of the earth. A Frenchman, Dupleix, in the mid-eighteenth century had recognised the debilitation of the Mogul empire as France's opportunity and so kindled in Asia the strong feature of the nineteenth century, imperialistic colonialism. In contrast, the spiritual awakening of the British nation supplied a new moral and spiritual energy. But for it, who can guess to what lengths accumulating wealth and power would have led greed and ruthless ambition? For the industrial revolution was a head of steam thrusting pistons of commercial motive and military capability jointly towards national expansion.

Great Britain became the United Kingdom by union with Ireland in 1800 and British victories in India and against Napoleon gave her self-confidence. Her population was overtaking her food supply and this too spurred her citizens to look overseas for personal security, employment and gain. It enhanced the need for sea power, and strengthened Britain's interest in obtaining possession of strategic positions on the main trade routes. Hence the sparring with the Dutch at the Cape of Good Hope which changed hands a number of times; and the acquisition of Penang, as early as 1786; of Malacca, also taken from the

Dutch but returned to them until ceded in 1824; and of Singapore in 1819.

Napoleon Bonaparte had been on the march since 1796. Defeating Austria, Syria and Egypt he found himself the most popular man in France and took the title of First Consul. In 1800 he was victorious in Italy and there was no holding him back. He crowned himself Emperor Napoleon I in the presence of the Pope, and scattered kingships among his relatives. Challenging Britain and Russia was going too far. The retreat from Moscow and the Peninsula War brought him to a standstill, but he escaped from the island of Elba by a carefully laid plot while his chief custodian was on a visit to the mainland, and his old army rallied to his banner. One or two successes came his way, but the Duke of Wellington, summoned from a diplomatic reception in Vienna, proved his match at Waterloo on June 18, 1815. Napoleon died on the island of St Helena, off the West Coast of Africa six years later.

The story of this troublesome genius, Napoleon, impinges time and again upon the events we are following. Britain declared war on him in 1803 and in October 1805 the Battle of Trafalgar gave her undisputed control of the seas. Nevertheless Napoleon was a terror to Europe. When the Pope excommunicated him he arrested the Pope, at a time when the Roman Church in China most needed support; but the lull in pressure from Rome gave some respite to the Chinese Church and allowed her missionaries to lie low when they most needed to do so. Before Napoleon was brought to heel and sent to Elba, America declared war on Britain. The Declaration of Independence in 1776 had only been acknowledged after six years of fighting. Now hostilities were resumed again.

The nineteenth century opened with no Protestant missionary or convert east of Calcutta, but while Roman Catholic fortunes waned, the momentum in the Protestant Church in Europe gained strength. The addition of new missionary hymns to the Church's collection is like a barometer of her spiritual welfare. So it was no accident that between 1725 and 1832 a spate of such hymns appeared. That the early emphasis of the emerging missionary societies was on India and Africa was because to all appearances China, Japan and South-East Asia were sealed against them, either by pagan or Roman Catholic rulers. Under the Spanish the Philippines were as dangerous as or more dangerous, for Protestants, than was China. The garotte was in use for heretics and rebels.

In 1801, however, the first Annual Report of the Church Missionary Society (CMS) devoted two of its twelve pages to China and referred to Dr Moseley's proposition to print and distribute Scriptures to the Chinese.[21] It expressed the wish that the CMS might undertake this work and stood by the promise of the means to fulfil it. The decision had been made, it declared, to open a fund for this purpose. Action was to be taken when enough money was in hand, either to use the British Museum translation, 'should they also obtain sufficient evidence of the fidelity and elegance of the manuscript', or failing that a new translation if they could find ways of obtaining a reliable one. In 1802 a copy of Moseley's circular about the manuscript came into the hands of a Dr Bogue, principal of the Missionary Academy at Gosport in Hampshire. It struck an answering chord in him. His college existed for the same purposes. His immediate reaction was to urge Moseley to go himself to China. But there the matter had to rest for the present.

The first report of the British and Foreign Bible Society after its formation in 1804 also called attention to the Museum manuscript and discussed printing and distributing it. The Society's feet were firmly on the ground. To print would be futile unless the personnel were available to put the Scriptures into the hands of the Chinese. 'If a missionary society should fix missionaries in China,' it said, 'a rational method would suggest itself of conducting the business of the manuscript.' The treasurer of the LMS, a Mr Hardcastle, also called the attention of the directors to the spiritual need of China and suggested action. Seeing China itself was inaccessible the strategy they adopted was to send three or four 'agents' to establish a mission at the Prince of Wales Island, now Penang, to gather information about China, study the language, translate Scripture, and to preach the gospel among Chinese immigrants to East Asian islands under European control. Chinese Christians would then go as missionaries to their own people in China. The evangelisation of the Malay nations was to be a collateral aim. Dr Bogue knew he had the right man to nominate.

CHAPTER THREE

THE MAN IN THE MIDDLE
1782–1820

Enter Robert Morrison   *1782–1806*

The story of Robert Morrison (1782–1834) is so basic to an understanding of Protestant missions in East Asia as a whole, and so repeatedly relevant to the Hudson Taylor saga, that it too must be related in some detail.[1] When Robert Morrison was born, it was into the home of an agricultural labourer from Fife, then working in Northumbria. Home was 'four earthen walls with a thatched roof, a hole for a chimney and a hole for a window'. 'A weak leg' forced his father to move into Newcastle and there he supported his wife and eight children by making boot trees and lasts while Robert grew up from a child of three until he was twenty.

A family of neighbours were their close friends, and their destinies were strangely intermingled. While Robert's playmate George went into a colliery and worked as a brakeman, Robert was apprenticed to his father's trade, fell into the wrong company and more than once became the worse for drink. An uncle then took him on as a mechanic. No kind of craftsmanship was right for him, however, and he struck out for himself on a new line, travelling the country with a company of strolling players. For someone as stolid and devoid of humour as he was, this too was a mistake, as he soon found out. He returned to his father's workshop — and discovered his grand passion, books.

By now his father was an elder in the Presbyterian Church and young Robert acquired a love of the Bible, so much so that he began to speak in biblical language. He worked for twelve to fourteen hours a day, with a Bible or some other book beside him, teaching himself Latin, Greek and Hebrew, and enjoyed himself so much that hard work became a lifelong habit. He chose to sleep at the workshop so that he could go on reading into the early hours, and developed headaches which plagued him for the rest of his life. It was before the days of skilled refraction for spectacles, which were still simple one-inch lenses used mostly by old people. Years later he recalled in a letter to his wife,

> It is the time of life that gives the charm; whether riding on a five-barred gate or in a royal carriage. The happiest abode (so far as house goes) was my father's workshop, swept clean by my own hands, of a Saturday evening, and dedicated to prayer and meditation on the Sunday. There was my bed, and there was my study.

Two missionary magazines telling of Carey and others turned his thoughts to the world without Jesus Christ, and he hoped 'that God would station him in that part of the mission field where the difficulties were greatest and to all human appearances the most insurmountable'. On the day after his twenty-first birthday, in 1803, he arrived in London to be trained as a minister at the Hoxton Academy. This involved preaching with the London Itinerant Society in the villages around London, Bethnal Green, Hackney, Islington and Highbury. His father and seven older brothers and sisters were pressing him to return home, but he knew that God had called him to go overseas and on May 27, 1804, he wrote to the LMS. They sent him to Dr Bogue's Academy at Gosport.

At about the same time his Newcastle friend George moved to a colliery where he used a Watts static steam-engine and revealed an inventive streak when he made it move a coal truck. In 1825, when Morrison was in England on his only furlough and had been received by the King and made a Fellow of the Royal Society, George Stephenson opened the Stockton and Darlington railway, a far cry from when they played together in the slums of Newcastle. Moreover, with Stephenson's Liverpool and Manchester line and the *Rocket* doing thirty miles per hour, the railway era commenced, an era which directly contributed to anti-foreign bitterness and bloodshed, and the collapse of the Manchù dynasty in China.

In 1804 Dr Bogue was impressed by the serious young Morrison with such a passion for work and had no hesitation in taking up with him the LMS's proposition that he should go to East Asia and translate the Bible into Chinese. Morrison recognised it as the call of God. He gathered information about China and knew what to expect. To a friend he wrote,

> I wish I could persuade you to accompany me. Take into account the 350-millions of souls in China who have not the means of knowing Jesus Christ as Saviour. Think seriously of your obligations to Jesus. [And a month later] the undertaking is arduous, my brother, and I seriously entreat you to count the cost. Many among the Chinese are highly refined and well-informed; they will not be beneath us but superior. The Romish missionaries will be our bitterest foes . . . foes that are far superior.

He offered himself to the LMS, requesting that he first be allowed to qualify as a doctor. In 1805 he was accepted for service in 'China', by which the directors meant Penang in Malaya, and moved back to London. It was the year of the Battle of Trafalgar which gave Great Britain control of the world's oceans for a whole century. From lodgings in Bishopsgate he walked daily to St Bartholomew's Hospital to attend lectures and practise in the crude wards and operating rooms, and also to the Greenwich Observatory to study astronomy, perhaps because of its prominence in the history of Roman missions in China. As if that was not enough, in 1806 he also began to study Mandarin with this determination: 'If the language be capable of being surmounted by human zeal and perseverance, I mean to make the experiment.' Another missionary aspirant who started with him soon gave up.

One day Dr Moseley, discoverer of the Chinese manuscript in the British Museum, was walking down Leadenhall Street when to his delight he saw a well-dressed Chinese gentleman coming towards him. (Whether in Chinese or English clothes we are not told.) 'I could not let him pass,' he said afterwards, 'my heart was full of China.' He invited him to lunch and from him learned of another educated young mandarin named Yong Sam-tek, who had just arrived from Canton to study English.

The interlocking of events is notable. The next day, Dr Moseley and the young Robert Morrison were introduced to each other. Moseley took Morrison to Clapham to visit Yong, and as a result Yong came to live with Morrison, now at Greenwich. Together, in the course of 'several months' they transcribed the whole of the British Museum manuscript and a Latin-Chinese dictionary to which the Royal Society gave them access,[2] and used them as textbooks for Morrison's study of the language.

Morrison learned far more than Chinese from this prolonged close contact with Yong. A clash of cultures was almost inevitable. Yong was a Chinese of the Chinese, straight from the dynastic strait-jacket, and Morrison had had no experience of anyone but insular Britons. The etiquette of the two nations was poles apart. The climax of misunderstanding came when Morrison threw a scrap of paper with Yong's handwriting on it into the fire. Yong's outburst of indignation and refusal for three days to work with Morrison was the explosion of pressures that had been building up. From the Confucian who must be impassive however riled he may feel, this violent display of temper was evidence of insult upon insult already endured, and of oblique hint after hint having no effect on the uncomprehending Englishman. They soon became reconciled. To Yong's amazement he learned that in England written words were not revered as in China, and Morrison learned the Confucian principle that erudition was so vital to the 'Superior Man' that calligraphy *per se* must be handled with reverence. These experiences drew the two young men together, and when Morrison was later in danger of ejection from Canton, Yong used his influence to stop his expulsion.

To embark on the study of Chinese was in itself a very considerable undertaking. Sir George Staunton, the prestigious Interpreter to the East India Company, was believed to be the only Englishman who spoke Chinese, and not being of an academic turn of mind had done nothing to pass it on to others. After the Macartney embassy he had written a book, in 1798, and this had succeeded in stirring up interest in England. Voluminous Catholic writings about China had received little attention or credence in the country. If Morrison had known of Prèmare's *Notitia Linguae Sinicae* he would have benefited immensely. His future colleague Walter H. Medhurst, when he himself was doyen of Protestant missions in East Asia, considered it 'above praise. It embraces, within a small compass, all that can be said on Chinese grammar.'[3]

Living in Greenwich and walking between the Royal Observatory on the hilltop and the Thames ferry, Morrison and Yong struck up a friendship with the secretary to the Royal Hospital for Seamen, close to the river-bank where the *Cutty Sark* now lies. His name was John Dyer. The two young men, away from their homes, often dropped in on the Dyers to enjoy a taste of home life, and the Dyers' young son acquired an interest in China. A few years later he was to become Morrison's colleague. And in time Hudson Taylor was to marry his daughter.

During these two years of study another missionary pioneer sailed for India as a chaplain in the East India Company. Henry Martyn arrived at Calcutta in 1806, the year in which a mutiny among its Indian troops decided the Company to ban new missionaries from India, so the arrival of a young Baptist named Chater led Carey to send his own son Felix with him to Burma, the first but short-lived Protestant mission to that land.

Leap into the unknown   *1807*

At that time even a mission to 'Prince of Wales Island' or 'Pinang' (*sic*) was a great new undertaking. Only adventurers had penetrated beyond India. The commercial toeholds of the Portuguese at Macao and the Dutch at Malacca (taken from the Portuguese), and Batavia, now Jakarta, were precarious though held for many years. There was a colony of Chinese at Penang, but a bare handful of British under Francis Light, the founder of the settlement, a man with a doubtful reputation for the twin social offences of having a Eurasian wife and of changing from his English broadcloth into a Malay *sarong* after the day's work. Singapore was still a barren waste with a few fishing villages, no more. But Penang at least was out of the immediate reach of bloodthirsty mandarins. Farther east lay Bangkok with no British residents, and Canton, barred to all but merchants.

In tackling China the problem before the LMS was comparable with the problem they also faced of how to start work on a cannibal island in the Pacific, all but unknown and impossible to assess without setting foot among hostile people. The map seizure at Peking and resulting severe persecution in China were recent developments. To their great credit, Morrison and the LMS decided to scorn half-measures and to make not Penang but Canton the beachhead. At least they knew all that Yong had been able to tell them, a hair-raising story at best.

The LMS had come to know their Morrison well. He was ordained on January 8, 1807, and in Mr Hardcastle's counting-house at the end of the old London Bridge was received into the Society. With great wisdom they gave him full liberty to act 'on every occasion according to the dictates of your own prudence and discretion', for how could they hope to guide or control him at a distance of half the earth's circumference and half a year's voyaging away?

The problem of how to get to China remained. The days of scurvy incapacitating whole crews barely ended with the eighteenth century. In 1789 one ship arrived at St Helena with the captain at the helm and only four men on their feet, but by 1807 scurvy was controlled by the use of citrus fruit. The problem now was social. The East India Company had the monopoly of British shipping round the Cape. Her fleet of teak-built one to two thousand-ton vessels manned by three thousand men under naval discipline and escorted by men of war, was armed with up to forty-eight guns per ship to meet attacks by the French and Spanish fleets, even after the Battle of Trafalgar. 'With their chequered paintwork they looked so much like naval vessels that on one occasion in the Straits of Malacca a strong French naval squadron mistook a group of them for ships of the line,' and beat a hasty retreat.[4] In East Asian waters they were joined by the 'country-ships', so that the arrival of a whole fleet or convoy of fifteen or sixteen Indiamen, perhaps thirty 'countrymen' and several escorting warships, in the Canton estuary was a tremendous occasion. The captains of Indiamen had an official allowance of eight hundred pounds for entertaining Chinese officials at Huangbo, the anchorage twelve miles below Canton. The Indiamen were provided with crude cubicles for passengers—very unlike the red plush furnishings of the tea clippers of the mid-nineteenth century—but discriminated stubbornly against missionaries.

There was nothing to be done but for Morrison to go to America and find a ship from there. He sailed from Gravesend on January 31, expecting never to return, and wept bitterly as he went. With him as companions were two couples bound for India. They ran into strong westerly gales almost at once and not until February 26, after a month of misery, did they finally lose sight of the Isle of Wight. With other ships being driven ashore and their own sails in rags, Robert Morrison read Psalm 107 and the story of St Paul's shipwreck to comfort his fellow-passengers. After another month of gales during which they rescued the crew of a wreck and he helped to take in the last rags of sail and sweated at the pumps, they eventually cast anchor off New York on April 20. The crossing had taken nearly three months.

Like true Americans a ship's captain offered to take Morrison to China for nothing more than the cost of his board, when another would not hear of less than a thousand dollars, and newly-made friends introduced him to James Madison, the Secretary of State and future President, who gave him a letter of introduction to his acting-consul at Canton. Without it he would have been helpless. He was only in New York for three weeks but made his mark. 'His piety had the bark on,' they said. It was fresh and alive, sound oak that would not yield to outrageous fortune. The captain was a friend, but not the ship-owner who, when business matters were settled, turned and said, 'And so, Mr Morrison, you really expect that you will make an impression on the idolatry of the great Chinese Empire?' 'No, sir,' he replied, 'I expect God will.'

On September 4, 1807, seven months after leaving England, Morrison arrived at Canton — and met the full force of opposition. He was twenty-five years old. The China he found was all he had been led to expect, and more. To Western traders she had never been and perhaps never was again more exasperatingly arrogant and obstructive. But to those with the eyes to see, the ears to hear and the aesthetic sense to perceive, never more fascinating and entrancing.

The first sight of her massive, high-poop, ocean-going junks with their huge pleated, russet-brown sails and chanting crews, prepared the traveller for the Macao 'roads', thronged with scurrying *sanbans* (literally 'three planks') of many sizes and designs, and for the sturdy gaiety of architecture, the fabulous costumes and the music of their tonal language.

A MANDARIN'S SOCIAL CALL

As he went ashore at Macao and visited the Portuguese and Chinese quarters, Morrison heard Cantonese spoken on all sides, and understood when the educated spoke with measured dignity. He was already familiar with the simplicity of sentence structure 'which has perhaps never been equalled in the language of any cultivated people',[5] and with their literature, the teaching of the sages. He called it 'one of the largest gifts ever bestowed by [God] the Father of Lights upon any race', for in spite of admissible defects, it was 'a power for righteous living, an ideal of virtue kept before the nation', if only it were to be observed. Though the uneducated Chinese were as rough as his own forebears had been, Morrison soon found them impressively hardy, inured to poverty, to endless hours of hard work and to pain. As Yong had led him to expect, the educated were not only intellectual and scholarly but wise with the wisdom of many centuries, acquired from the Confucian classics.

At Macao Morrison met Sir George Staunton, Bt, 'most friendly', and a Mr Chalmers to whom he had a letter of introduction. What they had to tell him filled him with dismay. The East India Company itself forbade anyone to stay except for the purposes of trade, so their own hands were tied;[6] 'the jealousy of the Romish bishops and priests' made residence at Macao especially difficult; and the Chinese ban on teaching their language to foreigners under pain of death was being rigidly enforced at Canton. In his diary he wrote, 'I am full of anxiety; a great deal too much so,' but undeterred he went on, up the river to Canton, appalled by the charge of forty dollars for the hire of a boat and a tax on the journey. There on September 7 he presented Secretary Madison's letter to the American merchant consul. The winter trading season had begun. The Chief of the American 'factory' made him welcome and he moved in, not daring to let it be known to others that he was an Englishman and a missionary.

On the north side of the Pearl River the Factory now occupied about fifteen acres in the western suburbs of the city of Canton.[7] Much of the space was open, but with servants, about a thousand people lived in 'the thirteen factories', as the townsfolk called it. During Morrison's time there, only British, American and Dutch factors were in residence. With the Napoleonic wars the French had moved out and their 'factory' lay vacant. They did not return, in fact, until 1830, fifteen years after Waterloo ended Bonaparte's rampage. In 1802 British forces had occupied Macao to prevent a French take-over, and in 1808, after Morrison's arrival, they did so again — until the Chinese authorities threatened to banish all traders and close the Factory.

The conditions imposed on the foreigners were as they had been for decades — no women, no weapons, no Chinese personal servants or language teachers, no sedan chairs, the barbarians must walk, no direct dealings with the mandarins but only through the Chinese merchants, the Cohong. They were only there on sufferance. Foreign ships were referred to in official documents as 'devil ships' and this expression, with 'barbarians' and 'foreign devils', was used with zest and emphasis. It was all endured, as ever, for the sake of profit. Later on when chaplains to the foreign community were permitted, they were 'story-telling devils'. They would have been expelled at once if their primary object, the gospel to the Chinese, were known. China had the whip-hand and on the whole the factors did as they were told.

In the year Robert Morrison arrived at Canton, a Chinese was killed in a drunken brawl, and when the Company refused to hand over the British sailor responsible to be tortured and executed as had once before happened, trading was suspended for two months and an indemnity of fifty thousand pounds had to be paid before it could be resumed. Virtually imprisoned but perfectly free and secure within the Factory area, all lived in style. The banqueting room of the East India Company was 'a gilded cage' equipped for a hundred guests, each with a servant behind his chair. The banquets were displays of affluence, vying with the latest one put on by the Chinese

merchants or the other 'factories'. With cut-glass chand-
eliers, a portrait of King George III on the wall, elaborate
ceremonial and fine wines, they lived far better than they
would in England.

Morrison found the standard too lavish and too costly.
'It would be impossible for me to dwell amidst the princely
grandeur of the English who reside here.'8 So he withdrew
to a warehouse, at ground level, and 'went Chinese', to the
dismay and scorn of most of the other foreigners. He
dressed in a Chinese gown and thick Chinese shoes, let his
fingernails grow long as Chinese scholars did, to show that
they were above manual labour of any kind, and his hair
too, in a plaited tail or queue. Yet he was still known as an
American, to the Americans' great resentment. And he
ate Chinese food with chopsticks, and little else until his
health suffered. Before long, however, he realised that
while he was among fellow-Westerners this was mere
eccentricity. It alienated them and brought him no closer
to any Chinese. So he reverted to English dress and
customs.

He took more care of his books than of himself. Very
stealthily he bought hundreds of Chinese books on every
kind of subject: language, religion, philosophy, medicine,
law and history. Unscrupulous go-betweens and merchants
fleeced him for each volume, but before long he had over
twelve hundred and was still not satisfied. He rented the
French 'factory' for his own use and succeeded in hiring as
teachers two heroic Chinese Catholics who came regularly
to him, knowing it was a capital offence. To teach the
language to foreigners was 'revealing the secrets of the
Empire to enemies'. For Morrison to speak in Chinese in
the street or to read a poster or proclamation on the wall
would be to betray his teachers. They were putting their
lives in his hands. One was a Cantonese scholar with a
degree in the arts, and the other a Jesuit northerner from
Shanxi province who had lived long in Peking and spoke
Mandarin. That they lived constantly in fear of detection
and torture (and one at least carried poison in preference

to the horrors of a Chinese prison), says much for the genuineness of their commitment as Christians.

The northerner demanded a high wage. Li, the scholar, did not. He had spent twelve years at a Jesuit college in Portugal and later married and went into business. In Chinnery's famous portrait of Robert Morrison at work, the older man is a certain Chen Lao-ye, and the younger is Li Shi-gong, son of the original scholar Li. Soon they learned that to work for Morrison was an honour, for his ability was profound and his 'grave and solemn demeanour' were Confucian to perfection. The sage had said, 'The Superior Man if not dignified in bearing will not command respect.'

'Law of pains for the pioneer'[9]   1808–12

With the end of the winter trading and the departure of the great fleets of ships and their teeming rowdy crews, quietness fell on the Factory and all residents prepared to move to Macao for the summer. Meanwhile the Governor-General of India, Lord Minto, afraid that the French would seize Macao, despatched a powerful squadron of ships and troops to forestall them. The Chinese reacted strongly, stopped all supplies and service to the Canton Factory and compelled the British occupants to take refuge in their ships.

Morrison left on June 1, 1808, committing his now valuable library to the care of his friend Yong Sam-tek. Now he was in greater personal danger, as he had told his friend in England he would be. On the way to Macao he barely escaped attack by pirates, but worse still, from his point of view, the Macao priests forbade any Chinese to help him, and his teachers and attendants had to go. He hid what books he had brought with him, for fear of a visit from the authorities, both Chinese and Portuguese, and worked in secret. Years later he wrote to his children, probably about this period,

When I first came to China I prayed three times a day; I implored God's protection only for a few hours, from morning to noon – from noon to evening, [and at night when he was alone].[10]

At one point the Portuguese viceroy showed plainly that he was willing for him to stay and continue his work, but suddenly his attitude changed. The priests had shown who made the decisions. But by now he had in his own right won the respect of Sir George Staunton and 'Mr Roberts', the Chief of the English Factory. They intervened in his favour and prevented his ejection. Staunton saw his own reputation as the sole English speaker of Chinese being eclipsed but showed no resentment.

Incessant difficulties and discouragements failed to keep Morrison from working on and by the end of June he had finished transcribing a dictionary of eleven hundred pages. Life in Macao was difficult but what contributed largely to his distress was the fact that although he constantly wrote to England, ship after ship brought mail for others but few letters for him. It was to be the experience of missionary after missionary who followed him in later years. He wrote saying he knew how busy everybody was but it was by no means of no importance to write frequently to their representatives overseas. Eight months later he could refer to 'your very welcome letter . . . but the second that I have received, after having written at least two hundred'. He mentioned that some wrote asking for long letters about everything but saying they themselves were too busy to write much, or the ship was just going – as though they thought missionaries had nothing to do but their own affairs were important. Hudson Taylor wrote in the same strain when he too was desperate for the encouragement of friends.

The months passed, and Robert Morrison found a friend in Macao. Mary was the daughter of a Dr Morton. Mutual sympathy brought them together, for he was an affectionate person beneath his stern exterior, and she was ailing. 'My poor afflicted Mary' was his description of her. They were married and on the same day the East India Company offered him a post as Chinese Secretary and Translator. This would mean security, a legal position in the community and therefore a right to reside there, a salary to save the LMS and the Churches of England such great expense, and improved opportunities to progress with the language. He accepted.[11]

The LMS had given him the right to use his discretion, but now misunderstood his motives — until the vast volume of work he achieved, over and above the chores of commercial and official documents spoke for itself. He learned what he would never otherwise have learned, and laid the foundations of his major achievements. It also spared him some of the superciliousness of Company employees who knew he was a missionary. His salary covered the costs of his first year in China, and when Sir George Staunton left, Morrison was promoted and his salary doubled. Apart from this he would have been forced to leave China sooner or later, but the difficulties inherent in combining two occupations nearly drove him to resign and start again at Penang, Malacca or Batavia.

That was not all. Poor Mary's first child died on the day of its birth and the sorrowing young father could not get permission to bury it, anywhere, in either Portuguese Catholic or Chinese soil. After protracted and painful negotiations he obtained permission to bury the mite on the very top of a hill at the extremity of the foreign settlement. It was 1810 and Morrison was twenty-eight.

Far from despairing or being swamped, however, his mind was sweeping widely across East Asia and the rest of the world. In his letters to England he kept asking for information about the progress of missions in other lands and urged advance in new places. He pressed the LMS to become international, to send Americans to Canton if more British were not forthcoming, and French-speaking Protestants from Jersey to Cochin-China. News of the CMS commencing work in India and of Adoniram Judson's arrival in Burma, when the Company would not have him in India, encouraged Morrison. Judson was the first American Protestant missionary outside the Western hemisphere. Two LMS missionaries also started work in Rangoon, but one died and the other withdrew, leaving Judson and his wife alone.

After reading Henry Martyn's sermon 'Asia must be our care', Morrison raised $285 in donations in Macao towards the Bible Society's work in Calcutta. And he pressed for the creation of an institution to train European and Asian missionaries. An 'Anglo-Chinese College' was the mental picture he had. He was great enough to see beyond denominational differences to the essentials on which all were agreed. So he wrote, 'We want organised co-operation – we want a Committee of missionaries' to avoid overlapping of effort. Later, speaking for his first colleague and himself, 'We are of no party. We recognise but two divisions of our fellow-creatures – the righteous and the wicked – those who fear God and those who do not.'[12] But this was not all. They must make maximum use of 'that powerful engine, the Press', by which he meant the printing press, not the newspapers. He discussed the pros and cons of classical language and colloquial in translation work, and for his own purposes adopted a middle course, using the style of *The Three Kingdoms*, a classic in low *wen-li*, the literary language of which style the Chinese 'speak in raptures'.

Co-ordination of effort was already seriously needed, for Carey and the Serampore scholars, doing such marvels in India, still saw themselves as the primary translators for the Asian scene. Morrison was a late-comer. Carey, Marshman and Ward corresponded with him, but their sense of rivalry grieved him. Marshman had found a Macao-born Armenian Christian and began to study Chinese with him in 1806; and a Roman Catholic priest and a Chinese from Peking gave him some help. He was preparing a crude translation without the assistance of

Chinese scholars. It took him until 1811 to complete his New Testament and until 1823 to finish the entire Bible.

It was printed, using movable type, (an innovation in itself, for Chinese printing was done with carved blocks), but scarcely ever read. As Marshman's son wrote with 'regret' of his father's Bible in Chinese, 'It is now valuable chiefly as a memorial of his missionary zeal and his literary perseverance.'[13] When Morrison completed the manuscript of his book on Chinese grammar, the Company sent it to the Bengal government to be printed, and after holding it without action for three years, they submitted it to Marshman for comment. Even this Robert Morrison accepted stoically.

In 1810 Morrison had wooden blocks carved by Chinese in the greatest secrecy, ensuring a similarity to other Chinese printing. He hoped to evade detection, and printed a thousand copies of the Acts. Three copies he sent home to Britain. Others were burned by the Catholics as heretical, because the translator was a Protestant. That he had based his work on the Catholic manuscript in the British Museum was immaterial.[14] The next year he finished Luke's Gospel and the following year his Chinese catechism, essentially the Shorter Catechism with added prayers.

All this time the mandarins were aware that something was going on and were hoping to catch the culprit redhanded. Like learning the language, the printing and distribution of Christian books in Chinese was specifically made a capital offence for both European and Chinese offenders. In fact all convicted followers of the barbarians' religion were to be banished to north Manchuria. Morrison and his heroic workers took note and pressed on, merely disguising their work by pasting a false label on the covers.

Morrison had an English-speaking congregation of ten for whom he led Sunday services, and as a mark of appreciation leading Company officials offered him a salaried appointment as chaplain, to help him finance his work. He declined. Year after year he slogged on, always in danger. Twice an alarm was raised and his printing blocks were destroyed lest they be found, but he had them recarved. Even so his hardships were no greater than those of the Catholics on the mainland.

Imperial edicts in 1811 and 1812 plunged the Catholic Church in China into new distress. Napoleon's blow to the papacy and the Propaganda meant little hope of help from outside, so the long-suffering Christians prepared for the worst. This time the Church in Sichuan took the full force of repression. Only thirty-one foreign priests remained in all China in 1810, but there were eighty Chinese priests and remarkably, training schools in Sichuan, Yunnan and outside Peking. As in 1754 the clergy school in the Sichuan mountains was hunted out and destroyed. The next year, the spreading of Christianity was declared a capital crime. Three more years went by and when the clergy school was found in existence again the vicar-apostolic was beheaded in Chengdu, the provincial capital.

Persecution continued, but the end of the Napoleonic wars in 1815 heralded the recovery of the Church in Europe. Recruitment thrived and missionaries entered China in close disguise and lived secretly far in the interior for many years. Now and then they were discovered. Between 1816 and 1821 there were at least twenty-one executions. An aged Lazarist priest with a price on his head was caught at his hideout in Henan, imprisoned and finally strangled at Wuchang.[15] It is only fair to emphasise, as Latourette was characteristically careful to do, that Jia Qing's first attempts to suppress Christianity had been limited to turning missionaries out of the country and exiling Christians who refused to recant. When this policy failed, more drastic measures were considered necessary. In the Chinese view laws were being deliberately violated and inveterate criminals had to be punished. If the Manchus felt so strongly about it, the wonder is that even stronger action was not taken and Christianity effectively exterminated.

Hope of a colleague   *1813–14*

The year 1813 was a notable one for missions in Britain and for Morrison in Canton. Thomas Coke had given twenty-seven years as bishop of the Methodists in the Americas without losing his longings for India and Ceylon. At sixty-seven he pleaded with the Methodist Conference to allow him at last to go there, leading a team of missionaries. This time they agreed. In May the next year out on the Indian ocean he was found dead in his cabin, 'a smile on his face'. The news of his death sparked an enthusiasm for mission to the non-Christian world which his survival might never have done. It gave an impulse to the awakening sense of responsibility in the Church and between 1815 and 1818 over fifty Wesleyans were appointed to various foreign countries. The fact that even then there was no 'Wesleyan Missionary Society' (1818) throws into disarray the conventional dating of the succession of missions. The Methodists had for decades demonstrated that the sending body was and should be the Church, and that details of how that sending is organised are incidental. Independent and supra-denominational missions arose when the denominational Churches were slow to stir, but the 'second evangelical awakening' aroused men and women of many backgrounds to express their new faith in practical terms.

The new zeal for taking the gospel to the ends of the earth penetrated through the ranks of the Methodist churches. In the West Riding a village blacksmith named Samuel Hicks became the apostle of Yorkshire people. Travelling and preaching incessantly, emptying his pockets for the poor, he taught Methodist Yorkshiremen how to give towards overseas missions. In the ten years between 1815 and 1825 the Methodist Church gained fifty thousand members—over and above losses. The Taylor family in Barnsley were kindled by this Olympic flame and passed it on.

John Taylor, nineteen when he married Mary Shepherd,

branched out from his father's place in the linen trade to become what the *Leeds Intelligencer* called 'a linen reed and stay maker of great consequence to the staple trade of the town' of Barnsley; but his first priority in life was the cause of Christ, and his children grew up to know and serve him. James, his second son, was twelve when Thomas Coke died, and twenty-two, apprenticed to a chemist and engaged to Amelia Hudson, a daughter of the Methodist minister in Barnsley, when the missionary interest fanned by Samuel Hicks and by Robert Morrison's achievements was at its height. James Hudson Taylor was to be their first-born.

Shortly before Coke's death, another hero of the Asian scene entered the LMS as the imperial edicts revived the persecution in China.[16]

William Milne was a shepherd boy in Aberdeenshire when something the minister said at a meeting in the basket-maker's home brought him face to face with Christ. He began to pray alone as he looked after his sheep in the sheepcote and with his friends when they talked about their own good fortune 'to know the Lord' when so many in the world did not. Together they went to work as missionaries where they lived, and people who were converted through their efforts were spoken of as 'turning missionary'. In August 1812, after being ordained, Milne married a sparklingly animated girl and they sailed together on September 4 into the Atlantic as LMS missionaries to China. He was twenty-seven. Britain was at war with France, Spain and once again with America. Three times their ship was prepared for action when sails were sighted, but they reached China without mishap.

Far away in Macao, Morrison was feeling his isolation and lack of kindred spirits. He had been without a colleague for six long years. On July 4, 1813, the Lord's Day, Robert and Mary had sat down alone to a simple communion service when they were interrupted. The arrival of William and Rachel Milne was announced. It is difficult to believe that Robert's sober dignity was unruffled at that moment.

When the travellers had been brought ashore and arrangements made for their baggage to be unloaded the next day, they returned 'to the Lord's table and remembered His death' together. For all too brief an interlude it was heaven in Macao, of all places—but only for a few hours. For Robert Morrison and William Milne, as for 'my Mary' and Rachel, suddenly the joy and prospect of companionship were shattered. The Portuguese Governor was civil when Morrison requested permission for the Milnes to stay, but the next day his attitude became hostile. The full senate decreed that William Milne must leave within eighteen days. The Morrisons recognised the hand of the Portuguese priests in this and thought it unreasonable that while Britain under Wellington was fighting to preserve the integrity of Portugal, a British subject was refused admission even to Chinese territory occupied on sufferance. It was the story of the unjust steward over again. Only Rachel was allowed to stay as she was pregnant. Presumably she was considered innocuous, unlike her husband, a Protestant minister. Two days before the expiry of his permit, William left, not on a British ship but by stealth on a Chinese riverboat, for the Factory at Canton. By then he had memorised a dialogue written out by Morrison to help him with simple questions and answers, and had copied out Robert's *Chinese Grammar*. For four months he lay low, studying hard, separated from Rachel even when her child was born in October.

On the last day of the year, December 31, 1813, Morrison finished his translation of the New Testament. Most of it was already in print. He had had enough of Romish opposition and Chinese intransigence. Since the destruction of the *Acts*, the bishop had burned about a hundred copies of Luke's Gospel and more of his tracts and catechisms. He longed to find a place beyond their reach where he could work and preach unhindered. It set him thinking. It answered Milne's problem too. Armed with two thousand New Testaments, ten thousand tracts and five thousand catechisms printed for the purpose, William

Milne said another goodbye to Rachel and set off into the unknown. He was to survey the island archipelago of the Malayas and see if there was safety, out of reach of mandarins and Catholics, for them to settle. With little Chinese language or knowledge of East Asia, he was away for seven months, was nearly captured by a Chinese war junk, had been ashore at Batavia only a few hours when his ship sank in the harbour—and returned with a clear report on his findings. The direct result of bigotry had been a big forward step in the promotion of the gospel.

Back in 1810 Napoleon and the French were a threat in East Asia as well as Europe. Holland was annexed and the likelihood that they would walk into Dutch possessions in the East and dominate the all-important trade routes was considerable. Britain decided to occupy Java, an island the size of England, and deny it to the French. An exceptional young man was appointed to plan and execute the occupation of the whole thickly-populated island. Thomas Stamford Raffles was twenty-nine; but at that time few merchants or administrators were over forty. He carried out an efficient military and civil take-over. From September 1811 to March 1816 he was lieutenant-governor of Java and on his return home was knighted by the Prince Regent.

Raffles, a deeply convinced Christian, was in Batavia when William Milne arrived and 'handsomely assisted him'. He 'furnished him with the means of travelling at the expense of the government over the whole island, distributing books' which 'excited great interest among the Chinese settlers'.[17] The Dutch East India Company had sent salaried chaplains since the early seventeenth century and the New Testament in Malay had been available from 1688. Early in the nineteenth century the Netherlands Missionary Society concentrated their efforts on the Celebes (Sulawesi), but in 1811 a German watchmaker named Emde and a Dutch government servant named Coolen independently brought into being churches of converted Muslims in East Java. Not until 1849 did the first professional missionary, J. E. Jellesma, start to work near them; but the Chinese were still a virgin field when William Milne arrived.[18]

From Java Milne went to Malacca, taken from the Dutch in 1812 (and returned to them twelve years later). The Resident followed Raffles' example, and Milne returned to Macao impressed with the possibilities in both places. The two thousand Portuguese in Malacca posed no problem, they were descendants of early colonists since its occupation in 1511, and the four thousand Chinese immigrants were sheer bonus. Here was security with opportunity. The rest of the population of twenty-five thousand were Muslim Malays, descended from aboriginal people forced out of China in the days of pre-history, as were most of the inhabitants of the archipelago.

Strategy for success   1814–15

Presumably the Macao authorities granted Milne permission to come for his wife, for we are told nothing of obstruction at this point. He rejoined Rachel and the Morrisons in September 1814 and found that they were rejoicing over the baptism, necessarily secret, of Cai A-fu (Ts'ai Ya-fu or A-ko, in dialect), one of the printers and the first convert after seven long years. Morrison's entry in his journal for that happy day July 16, 1814, was

> At a spring of water issuing from the foot of a lofty hill by the seaside, away from human observation, I baptized [him] . . . May he be the firstfruits of a great harvest; one of millions who shall believe and be saved . . .

Morrison was to see only nine more Chinese converted during the next twenty years.

The three left in Macao had been through a very distressing time. The Americans had befriended Morrison when his own people failed him. When the States declared war on Britain in 1812, however, American trade at Canton was naturally affected. The British blockaded the river. The French had gone, Holland fell to Napoleon and the

Dutch had to go, now the Americans were excluded and only the British remained at the Factory. In April 1814 an American merchantman was captured and brought to Macao as a prize, and a month later another, evading capture, was chased up river. China rightly protested. Barbarian squabbles could not be tolerated within her territory. Now the East India Company were forced to leave Canton.

Ironically the brunt of Chinese indignation fell on Morrison for his part as Chinese Secretary and principal interpreter for the Company. The Company were the official arm of Britain, but Morrison was its impotent servant, pro-Chinese as well as pro-British, and doing his best for both. The men cutting the type for his massive dictionary were seized and the printer making blocks for the new edition of the New Testament, in panic, as before, destroyed most of them. Others were committed to a trusted Chinese who hid them away, only to find when they were brought out that white ants had ravaged them all.

These discouragements might have hit Morrison harder had not a member of the Company shown his sympathy by making a handsome donation of a thousand Spanish dollars, at about five and a half dollars to the pound sterling, for replacing all the losses;[19] and a legacy of the same amount from a former chief of the Company's agents at Canton came as a doubly welcome surprise. This windfall went towards the publication of another edition of the New Testament.

Mary Morrison's health was deteriorating so she was to take their two children, Rebecca and John Robert home to Britain. They could not know that it would be six painful years before they would see each other again. Robert took them out to the ship in January 1815 and returned to his desolate rooms. Together he and Milne discussed the future strategy of their work. William Milne was impressed by the freedom to work unhindered in Malacca, and Morrison selflessly advised him to settle there. He himself longed to go too, but valued being on the mainland of

China in close touch with developments. Besides, he was devoting most of his Company salary to his work. The LMS was not able to subsidise it to the same extent.

So the decision was taken. William and Rachel would go, Robert would stay. Each of them would enjoy advantages in his work the other would not have. Malacca would be a secure base, a springboard for the leap of faith and a retreat if Canton and Macao became too dangerous at any time. As soon as possible Milne was to start regular Christian worship in Chinese and, as Morrison was deeply involved in his massive dictionary, so vital to all translation work, Milne and presumably Rachel would embark on translation also. As Morrison quaintly recorded,

> the second members of the Mission shall engage in translating some parts of the Old Testament — thus uniting their labours until the whole version be completed.

The Malacca venture was only part of a far-seeing plan, drawn up in October 1815 and therefore antedating in action though perhaps not in concept, the Serampore 'College for the instruction of Asiatic, Christian and other youth, in Eastern Literature and European Science' instituted by Carey and his colleagues.

After the unforeseen delays about to be described, Morrison submitted fifteen resolutions to the directors of the LMS. They proposed the recognition of an administrative section of the LMS to co-ordinate the work of Morrison and Milne and all other members of the Mission who they hoped would join them. Because it involved all countries beyond the shores of India, they called it 'the Ultra-Ganges Mission',[20] and in the same breath it was the 'Chinese Mission' of the LMS. Its 'chief seat' was to be in Malacca, where Milne would try to obtain a site by grant or purchase, to be the property of the LMS. He was to open a school, so that Chinese children would grow up knowing and many believing the gospel, in the hope that from among them some would go to China as missionaries. He would publish a monthly magazine in Chinese, but also do what he could to present the gospel to Malays, Indians and others in their own languages, including English. Also a small periodical in English would have as its objective 'promoting union and co-operation among Missionary Societies in different parts of India . . . and the love and practice of Christian virtues generally'. He called it *The Gleaner*.

An interesting fact is demonstrated here. The government of India controlled all British subjects and territory in East Asia, so they were spoken of as being 'in India', but for years ahead the missionaries working among Chinese and for China considered the Chinese immigrants in South-East Asia and themselves as being 'in China'. At one point in 1876 the doyen of 'China' missionaries was Dr Dean of Bangkok.

Morrison's fifteenth resolution proposed keeping Japan in view, collecting all possible information, preparing for 'a voyage by some of us . . . at a future time', and assessing whether an adaptation of the Chinese translation of Scripture would be satisfactory, or an entirely new Japanese version be necessary. When the Society's formal reply was received it 'recommended strongly' that this fifteenth resolution be 'carried into effect'. But it was 1835 before an LMS missionary, W. H. Medhurst, was free to go but was prevented, and 1837 when the Americans Peter Parker and Wells Williams, actually made the attempt, only to be repulsed.

Golden handshake   *1815*

In April 1815, when William and Rachel Milne sailed away to Malacca and Morrison was on his own again, the Milnes took with them a Chinese printer, partly for his own safety, for he was known to be collaborating with the barbarians and suspected of contravening the edicts. Liang A-fa, not yet a Christian but interested in the Scripture blocks he had been carving, was to become one of the most notable Chinese Christians of all time and unknowingly the link in the chain of events which led to the devastating Taiping Rebellion against the Manchu dynasty.

Morrison returned to work on his dictionary and on an outline of the Old Testament with Psalms and hymns to tide any Chinese Christians over until the whole Bible was completed. So valuable was the dictionary going to be to commerce and government that the Company sent out a British printer with equipment to print it, and the Bengal government decided, at last, to print his *Grammar*. Like thunder-claps from a clear sky, therefore, came a sequence of shocks in quick succession. The London directors of the East India Company came into possession of a copy of the Chinese New Testament and other papers and were furious. What if China should charge the Company with responsibility for the clandestine activities of its interpreter? They voted to dismiss him and at once erased his name from their register of employees. They were clear of responsibility!

When the governing committee of the Company at Canton received notice of this they could not but pass it on to Morrison. But the deep wisdom of China had not failed to influence Mr J. T. Elphinstone, the Chief, and his colleague Sir George Staunton. They conveyed the notice of dismissal with a golden handshake of four thousand dollars, a statement of appreciation of the value of Morrison's services and of their belief that the Court of the Honourable Company were misinformed, and a request for a statement from Morrison himself. To write to London and wait for a reply would take the best part of a year, during which the almost irreplaceable interpreter would kindly continue work. Anything might happen in a year; and it did.

Morrison's response was strong and independent. His activities, he said, were the same as when he was asked by the Company to serve them. He had studiously avoided illicit action traceable to himself. 'As to "circulating" the books which I have printed, there is nothing done in this respect but with the utmost secrecy and caution, and in a way that could not easily be traced to me . . . I submit with much deference the above explanation, and am, most respectfully, gentlemen . . .' he concluded. Elphinstone and Staunton rather liked this dour divine and they recoiled from having to manage without him. Morrison's *Memoirs* reveal a long and friendly correspondence with Staunton over the ensuing years.

That was in October, 1815, four months after Waterloo. Far greater forces were at work, as the Court of the Company well knew when they decreed from a distance that this Bible-merchant in China could go his own precarious way. The need for greater outlets for British manufactures was already far more clamant than twenty-two years earlier when Lord Macartney failed to move the Qian Long emperor. The expenses of conquest and administration in India could not possibly be met from the British exchequer. The Napoleonic and American wars were too recently over. So India must pay her own way.

That meant dragooning the peasant into delivering more and more of India's 'staple product'. The word 'opium' was avoided whenever possible. The alternative was greatly increased taxation. Deleted on second thoughts from Lord Macartney's directive in 1793 were the words 'the vicious manners of the (Chinese) people call for an increasing use of that pernicious drug'.[21] The outcome of India's need for revenue must increasingly be off-loaded on to the Chinese. The British government shared this view, deciding to leave the opium monopoly in the hands of the East India Company as long as it did not jeopardise its trading concessions with China by direct handling of more than a medicinal minimum. The country-ships could do that while the Company's ships still carried manufactures to China and tea to Britain.

Brian Inglis tells us in his admirable book *The Opium War*, from which much of this information is taken, that between 1803 and 1813 the Company were producing and selling three thousand chests per annum, each a hundred and forty pounds of opium with a steady revenue of fifteen hundred dollars per chest — a two thousand per cent profit. Only men of the highest principle would give up such incentives, and from the Prime Minister to the Governor-General of India, the merchants themselves and even Parliament when it woke up to the situation, there was no moral fibre equal to cutting the skein of covetousness that enmeshed them ever more tightly. Instead they resorted to unctuous double-talk. While the peasants of Bengal suffered in grossest poverty they were discouraged from growing even vegetables for themselves, for nothing must divert them from cultivating the poppy.

Lord Hastings justified extension of the traffic by claiming that 'in compassion to mankind' it was kinder to 'regulate and palliate an evil which cannot be eradicated' from China by keeping the price as high as possible — 'as well as for the purpose of revenue'. He decided 'to crush the Mahratta rulers, seize their states and the Malwa opium trade' to keep it out of the hands of non-British traders — and to reward his government with the revenue. In his *History of Java*, in 1817, Sir Stamford Raffles denounced the demoralising trade with its 'malign influence', but the avarice of merchants and the expediency of politicians in a dilemma dictated policy. And he was writing after the Amherst embassy came back from Peking.[22]

Even while Robert Morrison was getting his golden handshake of dismissal-cum-retention in office, the British government was mounting the new embassy to Peking. The terms of reference given to Lord Amherst were substantially the same as Lord Macartney had received: greater facilities for trading were required; opium was not to be mentioned so soon after the anti-opium edict of 1815, hammered home by the execution of six Chinese dealers at Canton; but any possible relaxation of restrictions must be obtained.

The embassy reached Macao on July 12, 1816, and Sir George Staunton who had travelled as an interpreter with Lord Macartney, was appointed Chief Commissioner to accompany Lord Amherst; but in a note to Robert Morrison, Mr Elphinstone called upon him to go as interpreter, saying, 'I conclude you will be the principal person on the Mission.'[23] It appears that Staunton, the senior man, had conceded Morrison's superiority as a linguist and mediator with the Chinese.

For both Staunton and Morrison it was a relief to be aboard the Company's cruiser *Discovery*. Morrison had learned that authority had come from the emperor for Staunton's assassination and of his imperial displeasure with Morrison for his official part in the affair of the American merchantman (page 135). Perhaps time would heal some feelings in Canton, and a good reception in Peking could do much for future relations. A despatch from the emperor told Lord Amherst he would be met at the mouth of the Beihe (Peiho), the maritime gateway to the sacrosanct capital.

Arriving at Tianjin (Tientsin) at the beginning of August, Morrison was sent ashore to meet the Imperial Commissioner and discuss preliminaries. Ten days later Lord Amherst and his retinue landed and proceeded towards Peking by river-boat. At Tongzhou where they left the river, the commissioners tried to get the ambassador to practise the nine-fold *ketou*. He tactfully agreed to do whatever a Chinese of equal rank would do before a portrait of George III. The commissioner pretended to agree and they all set out in the late afternoon. After travelling all through the hot August night however, they were taken straight to the palace door unwashed and still in travelling clothes. Lord Amherst insisted on attending the audience appropriately dressed, but was told that the emperor was waiting. The impasse had been engineered. The emperor angrily instructed that the embassy be removed and they returned to Tongzhou, again by night.

Nothing had been achieved, unless some greater respect was won by the refusal to be subservient. This may have been so, for the whole retinue now progressed in a leisurely way by Chinese river-boat to the Grand Canal and along it southward for six hundred miles through Yangzhou to the

Yangzi. To Morrison this was sheer delight, a prolonged insight into the Chinese way of life, deep in the interior. They visited temples and mosques and even the College of the White Stag under the mountain of Guling, where one of the great commentators on Confucius had taught seven centuries before. They travelled up the Yangzi to the Poyang Lake and made the river journey through Jiangxi province and the inland portage to the North River which carried them through Guangdong to Canton. The party of seventy had been guests of the Chinese government for five months, at a cost of £170,000. They could have been kept closely confined at Tianjin until their ships returned for them.

As it was, the three ships made an interesting tour to Korea and Okinawa, known as the Loochoo Islands, (the Ryukyus), before sailing down the mountainous east coast of Taiwan and between Taiwan and Luzon in the Philippines to reach the Canton estuary again. Captain Basil Hall, commanding one of these ships, wrote an entertaining travelogue, *A Narrative of a Voyage to Java, China and the Great Loochoo Island, with Accounts of Sir Murray Maxwell's Attack on the Chinese Batteries and of an interview with Napoleon Bonaparte at St. Helena*. He claimed to have fraternised 'famously' with the Chinese peasantry by bartering his uniform buttons for fresh food, and walked many miles without interruption, in August after the failure of the embassy. He was 'often invited to drink tea' and formed 'a very favourable impression of the Chinese character'. When they went ashore on Corea, as he called it, it was a different matter. They were met everywhere with throat-cutting gestures — a fan or hand drawn across the throat — especially if they moved towards a house or village. Perhaps it was an indication of what the people would suffer for tolerating intruders.

They reached the Canton estuary to learn that the courtesy was over. The embassy was being treated with contempt. The ships were presented with a proclamation from the viceroy couched in most offensive terms, ordering them to stay away among the islands. This was where Sir Murray Maxwell showed his spirit. Paying no attention he sailed on November 12 up to the mouth of the river and when fired on by war junks and the fort, replied with a broadside. Apologies were quickly forthcoming. The fire from the fort had been intended as a salute!

Neither side now seemed willing to conciliate the other. The Emperor addressed a despatch to King George III and the viceroy delivered it in person to Lord Amherst.[24] It was wrapped in a roll of yellow silk and presented in a yellow tent according to Chinese protocol; so Lord Amherst insisted that the viceroy should stand in the inferior position, nearer the door, as befitted the host in Chinese etiquette. The despatch, full of factual errors, accused the embassy of insults, commanded the king to send no more, and for ever to obey it. It was Robert Morrison's job to translate these messages, giving the full import of their subtle nuances of meaning, conveyed, it might be, only by the position of a word on the page.

First goals achieved   1816–20

His journey over, and his health greatly benefited by so many weeks of country travel, Morrison returned to his solitary quarters, only to face new distresses and a threatening personal situation. The news that William Milne had baptised Liang A-fa, on November 3, 1816, cheered him immensely, but at the same time came the tragic report that Milne's own health was failing. He had pulmonary tuberculosis, and it was progressing. Then suddenly the Chinese authorities pounced.

Armed with a blacklist of Morrison's helpers and friends, including Yong Sam-tek, they broke into the printing press that was handling Morrison's dictionary and dialogues. To be captured meant execution or intolerable torture and flogging with never less than a hundred strokes on the legs and sometimes the face. Inevitably Morrison himself lived in continuing apprehension.

I hope the Almighty Arm which has been my defence hitherto will still preserve me from evil, [he wrote]. My courage and perseverance almost fail me . . . This is a very lonely situation . . . I am under continual dread . . . [My Chinese assistants] are hunted from place to place and sometimes seized.[25]

For good measure a letter arrived from Sir George Staunton in England with dire news. Morrison's friends were publishing news of his work, he wrote, and of his converts. Not only he but the Company were being endangered. As if Morrison had not repeatedly urged them to pray but tell no one! What more could he do? At least it was a comfort to hear from Elphinstone too, on his way home. He had found in his job that dealing with the mandarins 'was to me both fatiguing, disgusting generally and tiresome always, and it was satisfactory to me to see that you encountered the foremost rank and all this without a murmur'. He only regretted that he could not present the first copy of Morrison's vast Chinese dictionary to Napoleon on St Helena.

It lessened Robert Morrison's anguish a little to learn in 1817 that the University of Glasgow were honouring him with a Doctorate in Divinity, *honoris causa*;[26] but compliments and honours would neither impress the Chinese nor remove their suspicions. With a Company doctor Morrison opened a dispensary for sick Chinese, the first step towards the medical missionary work in China which was to develop so extensively; and slowly the months went by. He was at least still in Canton or Macao, still alive and still working.

After a few months at Malacca starting up his school, a magazine and Sunday worship services, William Milne went up to Penang, the seat of government of these two British settlements, to request a grant of land for the Malacca mission. This was the first visit of a missionary to the port. But he could not stay. He had too much on his hands. He was working too hard on his translation assignment, the historical books of the Old Testament and the book of Job. He was therefore delighted by the arrival in

1817 of a colleague, a young man after his own heart, Walter Henry Medhurst.

W. H. Medhurst—every missionary to the Chinese was to know this name as well as he knew those of Morrison and Milne. He was a printer by profession and soon took over the printing press and with Liang A-fa for the next few years poured out Scriptures, books and pamphlets in Chinese, English and Malay. It was all out of reach of the Manchu runners, the much feared secret state-police of mainland China. Medhurst was an evangelist at heart and it was not long before he too went to Penang, preaching the gospel and distributing Chinese books.

His ability and willingness made it possible for the Milnes to pay another visit to Canton. William wanted to go over his translation of Deuteronomy and Joshua with Morrison, and to discuss the formation of their major project, the Anglo-Chinese College in Malacca; but he also wanted to get his wife Rachel away from Malacca for a change of scene. In May the previous year an infant son, one of twins born on board ship, had died two days after birth and in April 1817 the comfort of bearing another child changed to inconsolable grief when this baby died after four days. Three other children were living but her sparkling vivacity, 'like the radiance of her eyes, unquenchable' was quenched. As a father and husband Morrison knew that kind of grief but how could he console her? He himself was heavy-hearted, for Cai A-fu, still his only convert in ten years, had died too, of that inveterate enemy of East and West, 'consumption'.

Writing home, after the Milnes sailed away again, back to the Straits, Morrison reported that more books of the Bible would be printed in 1818 'should God in mercy grant to my brother life and health . . . but appearances are against him; his lungs are weak and he is greatly emaciated'. Poor Rachel was suppressing an even greater sorrow and fear of losing her husband. Events, however, were to prove very different. In February 1819 Rachel gave birth to another son and in March she herself fell ill with dysentery and died. Again there was little Robert Morrison could do to support his stricken friend, far away across the South China Sea. They immersed themselves in their work and endured their loneliness; and William Milne called his orphaned child Robert.

The directors of the LMS had approved the plan for an Anglo-Chinese College and publicised it in Britain. It was to start with a nucleus of six educated Chinese and six European students. The first tactical objective was to develop mutual respect and understanding. With them setting the tone, others could be added in due course. The concept was far ahead of its time. In the twenty-five years of its existence at Malacca few English came to join it, but it served its primary purpose of introducing non-Christian Chinese to thoughtful Christianity and training Christians for the ministry. The LMS made a grant of five hundred pounds and Morrison trebled it with a personal gift of a thousand. His deed of gift and foundation was witnessed by the new chief of the East India Company in China, and the foundation stone laid, after Milne returned to Malacca, by the Resident in the presence of the Governor and other distinguished well-wishers. The Company made a grant of twelve hundred pounds per annum, and when its charter was revoked the British government appreciated the value of the college to the extent of continuing the grants towards its upkeep.

As for Resolution Fifteen of the Ultra-Ganges Mission, information about Japan could be collected, but the outlook for getting there was even more grim than for entering China. In both Christianity was illegal but in China there was at least an underground Catholic Church with its clergy, and a Protestant vanguard fighting for its existence. In Japan there were none of these, and would be none until past the mid-nineteenth century. Anti-Western measures were vigorous and relentless. Edicts were extensively displayed denouncing Christianity. No alien had a foothold of any kind, for the permission given to the Dutch to trade at Nagasaki was wrapped in regulations more

galling than those at Canton and could not be regarded as
a foothold. Japanese citizens were not allowed to go
abroad, and fishermen accidentally driven on to alien
shores were banned from ever returning. The overriding
objection was Christianity, to be excluded at all costs. In
the seventeeth century, under appalling persecution, Christians had died, apostatised or gone into hiding. Two
hundred years later Christianity was still proscribed. One
ray of light encouraged the visionaries. In 1818 an American
ship called at the Bay of Yedo, old Tokyo, and was visited
by some Japanese. They accepted two of Morrison's
Chinese New Testaments and some Christian tracts.

It is strange how atmosphere can be conveyed by few
words. On November 25, 1819, Morrison, the externally
stolid, unemotional plodder, tenacious, unyielding, perfectly suited to circumstances which would surely have
worn down a weaker man, picked up his pen and wrote,

> Fathers and Brethren, By the mercy of God, an entire version
> of the books of the Old and New Testaments into the
> Chinese language, was this day brought to a conclusion . . .[27]

Already his exultation is apparent. He listed the books
he and Milne had translated, and re-emphasised that the
British Museum manuscript had formed the basis of his
New Testament. He had been criticised for using it and,
erroneously, for not using it, and told that others could
have made a better job of it. Then he continued,

> It is not yet 500 years since Wycliff's bones were dug up and
> burnt, chiefly because he translated the Scriptures; and it is
> not yet 300 years since Tyndale was strangled by the hands
> of the common hangman and then burnt, for the same cause.

Admitting that it would be surprising if this humble
effort by himself and Milne did not prove to be faulty, he
wrote, 'Translation is in its infancy in China. None of its
own literati study in order to translate.' Then he went on
to explain how he had tried to convey the sense and spirit of
the original, being guided through obscure passages by the

consensus of Christian scholars in the King James version, and to express it 'faithfully, perspicuously and idiomatically', with simplicity and intelligibility in mind. Then,

> Tyndale, while he was being tied to the stake said, with a fervent and loud voice, in reference to Henry VIII, 'Lord, open the King of England's eyes' ... Let us be as fervent in a similar petition in reference to the Sovereign of this empire.

Before the century ended the emperor was steeping himself hour after hour in the Bible.

Morrison's translation had numerous and great defects, 'but not greater than were inevitable'.[28] Walter Medhurst in his *China* quotes the criticisms of Liang A-fa and two other Chinese. They agree that the idiom was seriously defective though the meaning was plain. As any use of the language was a capital offence this is not surprising. After Morrison died others revised his version and for decades it served its purpose, until the united effort of scholars who built on his foundations produced new and better translations.

The same year, 1819, saw Sir Stamford Raffles' greatest achievement. It was so simple, in comparison with the complexity of governing Java or Bencoolen, his other charge, on the west coast of Sumatra, with explorations into the mountainous interior. He had given a great deal of thought to the need for a southern location on the Malay peninsula as an entrepot for East Asian trade, and noted romantically from his close interest in history that the island of Singapore had been a trading centre in the fourteenth century. Six years previously he had read what a certain Captain Alexander Hamilton had written, 'In anno 1703 I called at Johore on my way to China and he (the prince of Johore) treated me very kindly and made me a present of the island of Singapore'.[29] He commented on the suitability of the island and its waterways as a centre for trade.

Still in 1819 only fishing villages were there. Raffles negotiated a treaty with the sultan, occupied the island and laid out plans for a settlement so methodically that the city grew into what an American described sixty or so years later as 'the handiest city I ever saw . . . like a big desk . . . where everything has its place'.[30] Certainly no sooner had the flag been hoisted than the influx of Chinese and Malays began and Raffles' dream of a free port and safe trading centre not only for the British but also for the whole of South-East Asia took shape. A grant of land was obtained for the LMS and a new young colleague of Milne's moved in. Three years later the first three Chinese were baptised; in 1824, the year in which Britain bought the island outright, a chapel was built; and schools were started in 1827 by a missionary named Jacob Tomlin of whom we shall soon hear again.

The enthusiasm for foreign missions among British students since 1813 and in the Churches from 1815 brought reinforcements to East Asia and gave William Milne a team to train and deploy under Morrison's guidance. When Bishop Heber wrote the hymn 'From Greenland's icy mountains' in 1819, however, his poetic thought in limited space was for India's coral strand, Afric's sunny fountains and Ceylon's spicy breezes. China was more remote. It was many years before China was named in hymns or reinforcements for Eastern Asia came in any numbers.

In 1817 the LMS also embarked on an imaginative attempt to penetrate China from the north-west. It appeared sound in theory, but only in ignorance of the geographical and political circumstances. A mission to western Mongolia was launched through Russia with the sanction of the Tsar, and Moravian missionaries established themselves among the Buriat Mongols in Russian territory on the western border of Xinjiang (Sinkiang) until they were forced out by order of the Orthodox Church Synod in 1841. The significance of this tribe was that its people also extended well within Chinese territory. Buddhism was firmly established among them, however, and no quick conversion was likely. After 1841 Mongolia was without missionaries for thirty years, until James Gilmour, a byword for spartan zeal, went to them from Peking in 1871.

In ten years Robert Morrison had made great strides towards mastering the forbidden language and calligraphy of China, had drawn up a grammar, compiled a vocabulary of thousands of Chinese expressions, the substance of a huge dictionary, had translated the whole Bible with Milne's help, founded a college, drafted a strategy of mission to East Asia and launched colleagues upon their life-work. This he had achieved mostly while serving as Interpreter and Chinese Secretary to the East India Company (with all that that involved of deciphering and rendering into English the complexities of mandarins' communiqués, and drafting replies), and had accompanied a royal envoy to Peking as chief negotiator. Undeterred by personally winning only one convert to the faith, he looked ahead in the belief that he was only laying foundations for a great superstructure. If the development of his embryonic Ultra-Ganges Mission was an encouragement to Robert Morrison, however, more devastating experiences were soon to come his way.

CHAPTER FOUR

TROUBLE ON THE COAST
1820–31

The spectre of opium   *1820–21*

'A national tragedy' struck Great Britain. In the words of Sir Arthur Bryant,[1] 'an aged, crazed, blind King wandered, with long unkempt white beard, through the deserted rooms of Windsor Castle.' Suffering greatly from what is now thought to have been porphyria, the popular 'Farmer George' 'sank into incurable insanity and died'. His son, George IV, had been 'the idol of society' thirty years before, but now a dissolute, flamboyant playboy, domineering or sobbing, in debt and disgrace, came to the throne. The beauties of Regency Brighton, of Regent Street and Regent's Park stand to his credit, but in him Britain acquired 'a national liability' in her sovereign. Ethical values among men in high office were debased and China was to suffer from this decline.

In India what looked like success to the biased judgment of avaricious and of ambitious men was distorting the economy to an increasing extent and grinding the faces of the Bengali peasants more deeply into the dust. More opium meant more addiction among those who looked for relief from poverty and distress in poppy-dreams; and more opium meant more profit to meet the ever-growing administrative debts of the Indian government, debts incurred by conquests over new territories. However, Bengal opium was being adulterated with poppy leaves and the Chinese were aware of it. Moreover American merchants were

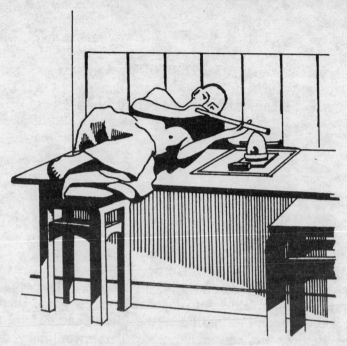

OPIUM SMOKER

challenging the East India Company's China market by shipping Turkish opium to Macao. This and Malwa opium from the Mahratta States, being carried by Parsee and Portuguese merchants, reduced the selling price of Bengal opium by half, but seizure of the Mahratta poppy-growing areas gave the Company both the Malwa and Bengali opium which Chinese consumers preferred. In 1820–21, therefore, 4,700 chests were sold to the country-merchants, whose contraband traffic with China flourished as never before.

Twenty miles up the Canton estuary from Macao and about equidistant from both shores there stands a solitary island with a tall peak, the Chinese artist's model, such as is familiar in many a scroll-painting. They called it the 'Nail', in Morrison's translation 'the Destitute Orphan'.

Lingding (Lintin) Island was well placed for smugglers and used as a distribution depot.[2] Under cover of night, fast boats with opium offloaded from the country-ships could outpace and outmanoeuvre the government war junks and the Hoppo's maritime customs boats. Deals were struck at Canton. The Chinese merchants would then collect from Lingding and the foreign merchant was rid of the stuff and free to load what he wished.

A young country-merchant in his early twenties, named James Matheson, now emerged as a very ingenious and daring businessman. He took his ships right up to Huangbo, only twelve miles from Canton, and being successful was followed by others. They set up a depot-ship at Huangbo — and a new system had begun. It was later to be used at other ports up the China coast, for many years after the opium war. Conniving officials found this close anchorage most convenient for taking delivery. 'For medicinal purposes' was a convenient term to cover both the licensed consignments handled by the East India Company in duly marked chests and an incalculable amount of Company contraband beyond that, channelled through the country-ships.

The death of Jia Qing (Chia Ch'ing) and accession of the Dao Guang (Tao Kuang) emperor was the sort of occasion, with changes of officials, when a government crackdown could be expected. Matheson and his main rival, Thomas Dent, and the other country-merchants had clear warning of this, but were confident they could cope with developments. The opium they handled was in East India Company chests to prevent imitation, prepared and packaged with Chinese consumers' preferences in mind, and the demand was insistent. The viceroy of Canton frequently issued edicts couched in the customary wording with a final 'Respect this!', but in 1821 a threatening edict was promulgated, ending 'Tremble at this!' Still the country-ship merchants paid no attention. Three British and one American ship were therefore impounded, including two of young Matheson's. He retaliated by re-establishing his depot at Lingding and exploring the coast of China for possible landing points. Contraband trade through the approved port in this way burgeoned into defiance of the laws of China by well-armed vessels with little compunction about fighting off interference by Chinese government ships.

The Hoppo ordered an end to the use of Lingding Island by the country-ships, but nothing happened. Compulsion was in any case difficult, but connivance by the officials who actually sailed down the estuary to enforce the law was easily arranged. They only had to report that anchored ships were on the move or simply invisible. It was all part of the system. The merchants had no conscience about it. Only the inconvenience of variations in practice made them change tactics. The price to the viceroy of enforcing his edicts by suspending all trade was loss of the proceeds, a measure he wished to avoid. It was better to endure a little anarchy and pocket the profits.

These were not the only make-believes. Acquiring Portuguese nationality gave one merchant new freedom in Macao. James Matheson became the Swedish consul. Thomas Dent matched him by becoming the consul for Sardinia. The advantage they gained by this ploy was not over the Chinese but the East India Company. Now they could visit Canton and conduct their illicit trade without having to get permission from the Company agents.

The agents were in the invidious position of having to enforce government regulations, for their own self-protection, although they were not British government officials. Moreover, retaliation by the Hoppo was likely to fall first on their own heads. In India the Company was both trading corporation and ruling power, but within a few years the agents at Canton were to be formally rebuked for trying to maintain discipline on the China coast. By 1824 the illicit traffic had doubled to 8,500 chests of opium with a revenue to the Company in India of over thirteen million Spanish dollars, or nearly two and a half million pounds at 1814 exchange rates. Associated violence was also twice as great.

Morrison in mourning   1820-22

Robert Morrison felt it in his bones that William Milne's remaining time with them was short. The high flush on Milne's thin cheek-bones, the hacking cough and even the cheerful optimism were a familiar picture in those days, a pointer to the approaching end. Yet he was working without remission, determined to get their Bible printed and to supply all the Scripture leaflets and explanatory pamphlets he could for the growing team to use. He was teaching in the small but demanding college at Malacca, and also helping the young missionaries in their laborious language study.

In August 1820 Mary Morrison, greatly improved in health, returned from Europe, bringing with her Rebecca, now nearly nine, and John Robert, two years younger. Morrison set them up comfortably in a house by the Macao seashore, and had a few happy weeks with them before the main fleet came in and his duty to the Company took him away to Canton. These separations were relentless. Then, the trading season over, he had another short spell with the family. Mary's confinement was due in a few weeks. Suddenly, after two days of a painful attack of cholera, Mary gave birth to a premature infant and both died. It was June 10, 1821.

> But for my dear motherless children, who are weeping around me [he wrote], I would forego my own happiness on earth and resign my Mary to go before me . . . yet oh, how great the disappointment! Oh, what a struggle!

The struggle had only begun. He wanted to bury Mary and her babe beside their firstborn on the hilltop, but the Chinese were adamant in refusing to allow it. The Catholics had a cemetery but no Protestant could be buried in it. In that semi-tropical climate he could not delay. Where could he go but to the waste ground, the 'Gehenna' outside the city walls? In his predicament and distress his colleagues, the East India Company agents, took the problem out of his hands. For a thousand pounds they bought a plot of ground and with the Chief himself present and gentlemen of the Factory as pall-bearers, saw that Mary had a proper burial. Rebecca had to be left with the Company doctor and his wife, when Morrison's work took him back to Canton, but he was able to take John Robert with him. On his return at the end of the winter there was nothing to be done but to send both children home to England. Even then they had to go separately.

Now it was only William Milne who remained to console his friend. Not long before, this 'shepherd boy' had written in an otherwise ordinary letter to Morrison in blithe ignorance of his own literary flair,

> By God's help you have set on foot what all the empires, and mandarins, and priests, and literati, and people of China can never destroy, or effectually stop; what will raze their temples, destroy their idols, change their lives and save the souls of many. Be not ungratefully discouraged, my dear friend. How many servants equally faithful have gone down to the dust without being honoured a tenth part so much? Once more, may the Everlasting Arms protect you.[3]

Even while Morrison was seeing John off in the care of a ship's surgeon, Milne was writing from Singapore that he was coughing up blood.

> Oh God [Morrison replied when he received this letter] prepare us for every event and have compassion on the feeble cause of truth in these parts of the earth . . . Oh that God may spare your life and restore your health! I am going on mourning all the day, an unprofitable servant!

But already Milne had gone, 'without a struggle or a groan', on June 2, 1822, not a year after Mary Morrison's death, and before his own letter reached his friend. He had first tried Singapore and then Penang to see if a change of climate would help him, but realised that his end was near.

He wanted to die in Malacca and the governor of Penang ordered the Company's cruiser *Nautilus* to take him. He died soon after landing, aged only thirty-seven.

Morrison poignantly recalled how the four of them had taken the Lord's Supper together just nine years before. Only he survived. 'They have left their bodies in the field of battle,' he wrote home, 'I hope I too shall die at my post', but it was hard to accept. 'I have wept much on being left alone and desolate; and I have wept over my own sinfulness . . .' The sinfulness of being sorry for himself? 'Yet, oh, how much I have to be thankful for! God save me from being ungrateful to Him.' He sent three hundred pounds to his family in Northumberland with the expressed wish that he might adopt little Robert Milne as his own son, and started to pick up the bits of the Ultra-Ganges Mission.

Key to China's awakening   *1821–24*

Walter Medhurst had moved to Batavia with his press and Malacca needed an experienced missionary. Robert Morrison planned to go there himself, but could not until after the winter trading season at Canton ended. The Company were always desperately short of men with an adequate knowledge of Chinese, but Morrison was by now a master of the subject. And not only as a linguist. His insight into the mood and motives of the Hoppo made his presence indispensable much of the time.

Two months after Mary's death he was involved in a typical international confrontation. An Italian sailor dropped or threw a jar overboard and it killed a woman in a *sanban* moored alongside. The Chinese demanded the surrender of the sailor for execution and, after long negotiations through Morrison without getting their own way, put a stop to all trade. The country-merchants would not accept this, so the wretch was handed over and publicly strangled. Robert Morrison had to watch the execution.

In another deadlock the British themselves struck their

flag and withdrew from Canton, knowing that the last thing the Chinese wanted was to lose their trading profits. The strain on Morrison of taking the brunt of accusations and negotiations was considerable, but on this occasion the lives of several British naval ratings were at stake. Then, on November 1, 1822, a few months after Milne's death, a fire broke out in the Chinese city of Canton and swept away thousands of shops and homes in an area about a mile and a half wide, with terrible loss of life. The Factory went with the rest. Saving all they could of their possessions, Morrison and the merchants retreated first to the water's edge and then to Chinese boats hired at exorbitant rates. All night they sat it out and when daylight returned on Sunday morning looked dejectedly at the smoking ruins. The area and probably the population affected were greater than in the 1666 Fire of London, and losses were seriously compounded by armed looting and robbery during and after the event.

Morrison found temporary refuge in a Chinese warehouse, and went on with his work. Only twelve days after the fire he wrote a review of *The First Fifteen Years of the China Mission*. His central aim he stated concisely: 'to preach the Gospel to the heathen and convert [them] from Satan to God.' He regarded his secular employment as a necessity comparable to a roof over his head. He noted that the Serampore College and the Episcopal Mission College in Calcutta were instituted after the Anglo-Chinese College began, and surmised that it had generated the others by example.[4] Regular Sunday worship was being conducted 'in China', by which he meant the Chinese in Malacca and the foreign community confined in Macao and Canton. The fact that his congregation was never larger than ten was of no significance. 'Despise not the day of small things.' Of course Christian literature received special mention, and he remarked that Java, Singapore and Penang also had 'Chinese missionaries', referring to British missionaries to the Chinese in these places.

The first missionaries to go to Java during the 'British

interlude' under Sir Stamford Raffles were four English Baptists led by William Robinson, a Dutchman and two Germans in the LMS, Kam and Supper and, in 1814, Bruckner, who concentrated on the Javanese.⁵ When Supper wrote, 'I have often found Chinese parents reading the New Testament to their families, and requesting instruction', the LMS had a new missionary named Slater in Malacca, so he responded to this appeal, calling at Singapore, the Rhio Islands just south of Singapore, Bangka Island and at Pontianak and Sambas on the west coast of Borneo. On this journey he distributed fifteen thousand books in Chinese and Malay, and met a Chinese at Pontianak who offered to provide a house for any missionary who would come to live there. Slater could not stay long, and when the young Walter Medhurst followed in 1822 with his printing press he had a clear field—a euphemism for being alone with a limitless job. He stayed for twenty-one years before moving on, working cease-lessly, turning out a flowing stream of Christian literature and waiting for mainland China to open up. As soon as it did, he packed up his press and was away.

After William Milne died, Morrison completed his 4,500-page dictionary and after the Canton fire, when Company activities were at a low ebb, he arranged to be absent for a few months. In January 1823 he sailed, with two skilled Chinese assistants, to Malacca and was there until July, with a visit to Penang and three to Singapore. Singapore was growing fast under the guidance of Sir Stamford Raffles, always a man full of ideas, planning a model port, curbing the opium curse, gambling and vice. He was also enthusiastic about the Anglo-Chinese College. He asked Morrison to establish another at Singapore. Of course Morrison was pleased and contributed generously towards the cost of it; but in Malacca he also found the kind of personal encouragement he needed. He set the work of the Mission on its feet again and saw the printing of his Bible well on its way to completion.

There was a naturalness about Robert Morrison that saw

value in the peripheral things of life. The premises and grounds of the college needed to be spruced up, so out of his own pocket he provided funds for making a garden and carrying out repairs, and in Singapore he addressed a meeting on the value of forwarding scientific enquiries. His generosity led, however, to his doubting whether he could now afford a visit home to Britain. He wanted to see his children and promote the missionary cause, but had spent half or more than half of his capital. In a long letter to the LMS he enlarged on the kind of people needed as missionaries, and as a new departure and an indication of the stability and security of life he was enjoying under British rule in the Straits, he included unmarried women. All, of whatever sex or occupation, should 'subordinate all their personal and domestic concerns to the cause of our Lord Jesus Christ', he wrote. That was paramount. Of all men Morrison was entitled to set such a standard. To this historic appeal he was to receive a notable response.

The same autumn he was cheered to learn that Liang A-fa's wife had become a Christian. In 1819 when A-fa returned home from Malacca to build a house for his father and to get married, he had written a tract of thirty-seven pages to explain his Christian beliefs to his clan. It was seized by the police. Before the magistrate he pleaded that it exhorted to virtue, but under a law against fraternising with rebels and enemies he was imprisoned, fined and beaten on the soles of his feet until the blood ran down his legs. His bride price and his savings for the house, and even his clothes were taken. Liang A-fa said, 'I did not dare to turn my back on the Lord Jesus,' and Robert Morrison commented, 'It is not impossible but that this land must be watered with the blood of many martyrs before the Gospel prevails generally.' The marriage took place. But only when A-fa came home again to see his firstborn did his wife come to believe, making them the first Protestant Christian family in China. Fearlessly disregarding his sufferings and danger, A-fa continued as an evangelist and colporteur whenever he returned home, so

ARBITRARY JUDGMENT

Morrison ordained him for this ministry, the first Chinese Protestant Christian to be so set apart for the work of God.[6]

Another great cheer to Morrison was that the Company undertook to print the huge dictionary.[7] Its six quarto volumes dealt with forty thousand Chinese characters and cost the Company twelve thousand pounds to print. Not only did it give the meanings both from Chinese to English and English to Chinese, but it was in effect an encyclopedia of information about China and Chinese life. When this mammoth task was complete, Morrison obtained permission to ship his library of over ten thousand Chinese books

SUMMARY PUNISHMENT

in a Company merchantman, and at the beginning of
December 1823 went aboard to return to England.

The Bible was in his own judgment his most important
work. Of it he said, 'By the Chinese Bible, when dead I
shall yet speak.' And George Woodcock tells us, in *The
British in the Far East*, that Sun Yat-sen, father of the
Republic of China and now of the Communist People's
Republic as well, regarded Robert Morrison's translation
of the Bible into Chinese as the starting point for 'the
awakening of China'.[8]

Honours and friends   *1824–26*

Recalling his eventful journey out to China, Morrison must have been relieved to find that the journey home took only fourteen weeks and at that, weeks in comfort as a respected senior official of the Company. Immense changes had taken place in attitudes towards him. As if he did not deserve a rest, he used the journey to write a memoir of Mary, his wife, and a short history of China for schools. He 'disembarked in a smuggler' and landed in Devonshire, completing the journey to London by road—presumably by coach and four. When the ship arrived with his library he was alarmed to find that Her Majesty's Customs demanded heavy duty to be paid on it. Already he had spent more than two thousand pounds of his own money in collecting the books as a gift to the nation, to promote international goodwill. Only after months of delay and interviews with the Chancellor, Sir Robert Peel and others was his library released. He was presented to King George IV, elected a Fellow of the Royal Society, and dined with the Court of Directors of the Honourable East India Company, who had dismissed him before they realised his worth. At Sir George Staunton's invitation he enjoyed a holiday at his seat in Hampshire.

He advocated a School of Oriental Languages and granted it the use of his Chinese books, lectured on China up and down the country, pleaded for understanding and justice and urged the establishment of Chairs of Chinese at the universities of Oxford and Cambridge. He did not live to see his ideas taken up, but in due course missionary colleagues of his became the first professors, Samuel Kidd at London University (1837–43) and James Legge at Oxford (1876–97). But that was not all.

At the annual meeting of the London Missionary Society he presented a copy of his Chinese Bible to the directors, and one of his great dictionary. The speaker who seconded a resolution of acceptance said that nearly twenty years before he had seen a young man poring over some Chinese manuscripts in the British Museum and thought to himself, 'What a waste of time, that language is unattainable!' but now the table was loaded with that young man's efforts and the Christian world was deeply indebted to him.

At another public meeting, as he presented a copy of the Bible to Lord Teignmouth, Governor-General of India (1793–98) and now President of the British and Foreign Bible Society, the whole audience broke into a shout of 'Hallelujah!' The presentation of Morrison's Bible was of great interest because Marshman had presented his translation the previous year. It was as if together they were striking blow upon blow for the honour of Christ and his Word. The Bible Society provided ten thousand pounds for publishing the Bible. Even that was not all.[9]

> The Secretaries of the four Missionary Societies (LMS, CMS, BMS, WMS) have requested me [Morrison wrote] to work on establishing a society to cultivate all the living languages of mankind.[10]

Since 1818 Morrison had been thinking that a joint effort of this nature was desirable,

> a society, which should be a centre of union for all philologists throughout the world . . . this Universal Philological Society should be undeviatingly kept to the diffusion of Christian truth [while not denying aid to anyone].

His prophetic dream was eventually fulfilled in the Wycliffe Bible Translators, the Summer Institute of Linguistics and the United Bible Societies. For the present a Language Institution was established in which he lectured for three months, to Samuel Dyer and Jacob Tomlin among others, young men who were to become his colleagues in Asia.

After he remarried and made a home for Rebecca and John Robert, Morrison urged the formation of a society to send women abroad as missionaries and taught a class of them at his home in the quiet village of Hackney, among the fields and woodlands outside London. One of those young women was Mary Ann Aldersey, a nineteen-year-old who not long afterwards went to Batavia. She became the first unmarried Protestant lady missionary to enter mainland China, a 'domineering and remarkable' person of whom we are to hear more as a thorn in the flesh of Hudson Taylor. Another in Morrison's Hackney class was Maria Tarn, daughter of a secretary of the Bible Society and also a director of the LMS, and the mother-to-be of Maria Dyer, who married Hudson Taylor.

Morrison compiled and published a paper called *Chinese Miscellany*, contributed articles to the *Evangelical Magazine* and by the time he sailed again in May 1826 had made a deep impression on the country. From then on, East Asia had a secure place in British Christian thinking. The LMS invited him to join their board of directors and he accepted in order to emphasise the principle that members of the Church in pagan lands have the right to be heard as equals in Christian councils, in no way inferior in status as 'agents' to those in the 'sending' countries. The CMS also consulted him about how best to use the fund opened prophetically in 1801 for the distribution of the Scriptures in China.

Of special interest to Robert Morrison was the renewal of his friendship with John Dyer, previously Secretary of the Royal Hospital for Seamen at Greenwich, who in 1820 had become Chief Clerk to the Admiralty. His son Samuel,[11] one of five boys and five girls, was at Trinity Hall, Cambridge, reading for the Bar when, as he later wrote, 'I understood I could not graduate without declaring myself a member of the Established Church; but I could not conscientiously do this.' His father was a deacon of Paddington Chapel when Paddington was still a residential suburb and Samuel was a fully committed member.

> Paddington lives in my warmest affections [he wrote from Penang in 1827]. It was there I kneeled on the separating line between Christ and the world. I kneeled and prayed for strength to side with Christ; I rose, and was inwardly assisted to turn my back upon the world. And from that day to this, Jesus Christ has been precious to my soul.

He told his father that he wanted to be a missionary and was referred to Robert Morrison who with Yong Sam-tek had known him at Greenwich as a child. That was the beginning of 'a happy and intimate friendship'. Samuel attended the Language Institution and on Morrison's advice went to Dr Bogue's academy at Gosport. He was ordained on his twenty-third birthday, and with his bride, Maria Tarn, arrived at 'Pinang on Prince of Wales Island in the China Seas' in August 1827.

Before Robert Morrison sailed for Canton in May 1826, he bought a thousand pounds-worth of books to help him in his work and reminded his friends that if they did not start writing to him and his wife while they were still on the way, it could be two years before they would have a reply. It was not easy to go. He had to draw upon his great courage to do so, saying in a note to his wife, 'In the day of battle I cannot be the coward that would stay at home.'

The return journey, this time with wife and children, was as expeditious as his solitary journey home, from the point of view of time but not of weather. In violent storms off South America the ship's men mutinied, until Robert Morrison went into the forecastle and persuaded them to obey orders and work the ship again. Forty years later Hudson Taylor was to do the same. The decision to take the children with them had a significant bearing on future developments in China, as it transpired, for John Robert inherited his father's linguistic gift and while still a youth was chosen by the Company to interpret for them and for British envoys in affairs of state.

Accolade and enemies   1824–27

While Morrison was away a great deal happened in East Asia. Malacca was finally ceded by the Dutch to Britain in 1826 and the three ports Penang, Malacca and Singapore were constituted the Straits Settlements, still under the government of India. This added security to Malacca as headquarters of the Ultra-Ganges Mission. A very different story concerned Burma. Lord Amherst of the Peking embassy debacle had become Governor-General of India. In 1824 he invaded Burma and for two years was saddled with the expense of the first Burma war. Yet all he gained was the western Arakan-Tenasserim area. Nevertheless he was honoured by elevation to an earldom and with Victorian hero-worship in its element London named parks, roads and ships after him.

Adoniram Judson and his wife Anne had been in Burma since 1813, preaching and translating for six years before they won their first convert. They were in Ava, the regal capital, when Amherst's invasion began and Judson although an American was suspected of complicity. Imprisoned in the vilest circumstances, with his feet in the stocks, and suffering from dysentery, he was dependent on the faithful Anne for food and drink and care in his illness. She continued their work and, coming in touch with Siamese prisoners in the Rangoon gaol, studied their language and produced a Gospel and catechism in Siamese. After the end of the war and Judson's release, they had only two more years together before Anne fell ill and died on the voyage home to the States.

China still regarded Burma as a tributary state, so the British aggression did nothing to improve relations at Canton. In 1825 another imperial edict attacked the activities of the country-ships. Infuriated by their adventures up the coast, Peking surprisingly praised the East India Company for its professedly law-abiding behaviour and denounced the country-ship merchants, including Americans, for being 'led away by worthless Chinese'.[12] This admission of complicity augured ill for the Chinese merchants involved, about fifty of them. They were the middlemen between the Company's agents and the smugglers in their multi-oared 'scrambling dragons' which drew the opium from the Lingding depot ships and made for shore.

Predictably the edict also denounced Christianity, allegedly the religion of these criminal barbarians. Fresh persecution of Catholics in the interior broke out. Many were exiled and some executed. But the Société des Missions Étrangères de Paris was recovering from its setbacks and in 1817 formed an association in Paris to pray for the extension of Christianity in East Asia. Its prayers were largely repetitions of the Lord's Prayer, Hail Marys and invocations of St Francis Xavier, but sincere concern for the glory of God was the motive.[13] Between 1820 and the outbreak of the opium war twelve of its missionaries infiltrated into Sichuan province, deep in the heart of China. The Catholics were showing their age-old heroism while the Protestant Church was slow to start. They had the 'underground' route, from home to home of secret Christians, without which no Protestant could have penetrated even a few miles.

The Morrisons landed at Macao on September 19, 1826, to find their home by the seaside in disrepair and the books Robert had not taken with him destroyed by the insatiable white ants. Settling in had largely to be left to Mrs Morrison and the children while Robert went on to attend to the fleet's business at Canton. What he found there was no less depressing. He was back at 'the same table in the same room'. 'Canton presents a melancholy blank' was the way he described the absence of so many friends and acquaintances who had died or gone away. After another year or two none would be left who were there when he began. But instead 'a great influx of new commercial agents, especially for opium' crowded the Factory.

With his major objectives, the Bible translation and the dictionary, achieved, he was free 'to teach Christianity in the simple Chinese phrase' and set himself to write a commentary on Scripture, and other books; but his interests were wide. He joined in opening 'the British Museum in China' and a coffee shop for sailors. The sailors of the nineteenth century, until well into the second half, were unrestrained on shore; they had been cooped up, cursed and maltreated with whip and fist on the high seas. Wild, drunken and debauched, they were constantly on Morrison's mind. He had felt concerned for them since his Greenwich hospital days with the Dyers. Now he appealed for help to care for them. He also began services for Chinese in the Factory precincts—supervision by the Hoppo and the Cohong was obviously not as stringent as twenty years before—and for foreign merchants who were not afraid of being called dissenters. A large-hearted American merchant, the ship-owner D. W. C. Olyphant, threw open his 'factory' for this purpose.

Whether from motives of jealousy or sectarian competition, a virulent attack on Morrison's scholarship and integrity developed in Europe around this time.[14] This was harder to endure than the mockery of merchants at the 'factory' tables who smirked and covered their faces with their hands when he said anything they considered pious. He was accused of plagiarism in his dictionary and imperfection in his translations. He replied denying the charge of deceit and welcoming any improvement in translation his detractors could produce.

The bitterest enemy over-reached himself by trying to buy with promises of praise the support of an up-and-coming Sinologue and diplomat, the future British Plenipotentiary, Governor and Commander-in-Chief of Hong Kong, Sir John Francis Davis, Bt. A paragraph in reply from him was enough. It agreed with Sir George Staunton in considering Morrison 'the first Chinese scholar in Europe'. It declared that he wrote Chinese as rapidly and expertly as the Chinese themselves and carried on a voluminous correspondence in the language; but more significantly, the Chinese themselves had long since given him the title of 'Ma Lao-shi', Doctor of Letters. 'This title is decisive and . . . he may regard all European squabbles regarding his Chinese knowledge as mere *Batrachomyomachia*' (battles of frogs and mice).

In Macao, however, Robert Morrison was up against the Portuguese bishop and his governor. Morrison had brought a printing press to China with him and was operating it in his own home. The Macao senate denounced his publications as heretical and demanded that the Chief of the East India Company at Macao take action to prevent him using his press. To their disgrace the Chief and his Select Committee relayed the Portuguese demands to Morrison and ordered him to stop. He returned their letter with strong comments pinned to it; he had not attacked the Roman Church; Macao was part of China, not a territory of Portugal (until 1887); the Company had its own press, proof that presses were not banned. 'I therefore protest against the whole proceeding, as an act of usurped authority, tyranny and oppression, on the part of both Portuguese and English, at the bidding of a Popish priest.'[15] He was right. The Portuguese claims to jurisdiction were at that time illegal.

Morrison was serving as assistant editor of the *Canton Register*, the first English language newspaper in China, and wrote a strong editorial on freedom of speech and the press. Open preaching was forbidden, he pointed out, and it was the inalienable privilege of writer and reader to communicate through print. Both Buddhism and Confucianism were propagated and preserved in written form, and Christian truth must be allowed the same freedom. But if the choice lay between dismissal from Macao, Canton and the Company, and obedience under protest, he could only knuckle under for the present.

It was at the time of the repeal of the Test Act and of Catholic emancipation in Britain. Morrison was in favour of both measures, but the toleration being shown to Catholics in the United Kingdom was not extended by Catholics to Protestants in Asia. Experiences and attitudes like this effectively segregated Catholics and Protestants from each other far into the twentieth century and beyond the 'open century' of opportunity for the gospel in China. Morrison used his press at Canton and printed twenty thousand leaflets showing 'the difference between Popery and Protestantism' — 'to show the Chinese that the traditions and usages of the Roman Church were not biblical Christianity'. W. H. Medhurst wrote, 'The very instinct of

Christianity is propagation', and both parties had this in common; but they also had far more in common. Medhurst went on, writing about Catholic books in Chinese,

> Many of these are written in a lucid and elegant style, and discuss the points at issue between Christians and Confucius in a masterly and conclusive way. Their doctrinal and devotional works are clear, on the Trinity and the Incarnation; while the perfections of the deity, the corruption of human nature, and redemption by Christ, are fully stated; and although some unscriptural notions are now and then introduced, yet, all things considered, it is quite possible for humble and patient learners to discover by such teaching their sinful condition, and trace out the way of salvation through a Redeemer.[16]

The trouble was that the Catholic missionaries from first to last had been more concerned 'about the quantity than the quality of their success'. Medhurst was writing only ten years after Morrison's contretemps with the Macao hierarchy.

K. S. Latourette summed up the customary teachings of the Catholics in China as being along five lines: the character of God and the incarnation, life, death and resurrection of Jesus; the ten commandments; the immortality of man's soul and the value to him of the sacraments, especially penance and the eucharist; the Church and the meaning of its symbolism; and the destruction of idols and an end of practices condemned as superstitious. There was much stress on the baptism of infants, especially dying and abandoned ones, of which there were many because of so much famine, fighting and the exposure of unwanted, usually female, children. After the formation of the Society of the Holy Infancy in 1843, and its arrival on the China scene, baptism of those *in articulo mortis* was increasingly practised. The baptism of such children, they believed, was necessary and effective for eternal salvation. To Protestants this was futile misuse of the Christian rite, but to the Chinese it was at the least magic and, at the worst, part of a fiendish perversion involving the removal of infants' eyes and organs to make charms and medicine. In addition the Catholics had all the paraphernalia of rosaries, medals and images—images or idols, they were the same to the Chinese—as well as veneration of the crucifix, adoration of the sacred heart of Jesus in emblem and picture, mariolatry and much else.

It was impossible for Protestant Christians to associate themselves with the good without involvement in the confusion of unbiblical accretions. The Catholic scholars had taken pains to learn both Chinese language and literature, often excelling the scholarship of Chinese in some aspects. For they specialised in references in the classics to God and emphasised similarities of belief. They learned to express themselves in impeccable literary forms and became experts in Chinese etiquette, to avoid giving offence, trying to fulfil and not destroy the best in the Chinese heritage; but they resorted to deceits and compromises, politics and coercion, as the history of the rites controversy and of the later vicissitudes of the gospel in China demonstrates.

The lesson Walter Medhurst derived from this was not to rely on human means 'but to trust in the living God'.

> Instead of beginning from the top of society, we propose commencing from the bottom; and aim to influence first the extremities, and then the heart of the empire. With the love of Christ our motive and the salvation of souls our end ... our work will be sure ...[17]

Before the century ended his vision had become reality. From Java he was able to go to the mainland, from the coast into the interior, and after he left China to die, missions were established in Peking, and Chinese officials at Court, including the Guang Xu (Kwang Hsü) emperor himself, were reading the Bible and being taught from it.

For all the failings of Catholics and Protestants, the words of William Milne, staunch Presbyterian himself, are clearly seen to be true, writing of the Catholics:

> Their steadfastness and triumph in the midst of persecutions,

even to blood and death, in all imaginable forms, show that the questionable Christianity which they taught, is to be ascribed to the effect of education, not design; and afford good reason to believe that they have long since joined the army of martyrs, and are now wearing the crown of those who spared not their lives unto the death, but overcame by the blood of the Lamb, and the word of their testimony. It is not to be doubted that many sinners were, through their labours, turned from sin to holiness; and that they will finally have due praise from God, as fellow-workers in his kingdom.[18]

Ultra-Ganges 1827–30

In 1827 Morrison seemed to have premonitions of an early end to his full life, and felt concerned that he was still the only missionary at Canton and Macao. On January 20 he wrote,

> Our friends in England seem to have given up the Chinese mission—in China . . . of late no measures seem even to have been thought of, how the mission *in China* . . . is to be continued, in the event of my removal by any cause. I do feel a little desolate, but I hope the Lord will not forsake me, he is all-sufficient.

This was less optimistic than his observation on December 29 had been,

> I do not feel myself now of much importance here to the cause. It will go on without me.[19]

If he undervalued himself, his associates thought otherwise. The gentlemen of the Factory sent Chinnery's portrait of Morrison home to Britain to be engraved by Turner at a cost of three hundred guineas, as a mark of appreciation and respect.

If the British would not condone the presence of missionaries apart from employment by the Company, Morrison believed the Americans would. He consulted his merchant friend D. W. C. Olyphant and on November 11

wrote two letters of challenge, one to Scotland and the
other an open letter to the Church in America appealing
for 'a preacher of the Gospel in English'. A few days later
he wrote specifically to a society of which he was a
'corresponding member'. Apart from nationality the
American Board of Commissioners for Foreign Missions
(the American Board) was the same as the LMS at that
time. It was evangelical and supra-denominational, admitting of differences between members in secondary matters
of church government and interpretation of Scripture,
while solidly united on essentials. Morrison urged them 'to
consider the claims of China'. Unknown to him, the
American Board had just received 'considerable sums' of
money for a new enterprise and his letter confirmed them
in their decision to send missionaries to China.

D. W. C. Olyphant, merchant and shipowner, supported
Morrison's appeal by undertaking to provide a missionary
with a free passage to China and personal support for a
year. So the American Board appointed their man, and to
Morrison's great joy the American Seamen's Friend
Society sent a second specifically to work among the
disorderly sailors about whom Morrison cared so deeply.
They arrived early in 1830. It was one of the red-letter days
of Morrison's life. Elijah Coleman Bridgman and his wife
were to stay, and after a year David Abeel was to go on to
Singapore.

At Morrison's elbow was more than one Chinese cast in
the mould of the apostles. Liang A-fa impressed Elijah
Bridgman when he met him: 'He bears distinctly the image
of his divine Lord and Master.'[20] A-fa was living 'fifty or a
hundred miles west of Canton' and busy preaching and
teaching from house to house, when he was not helping
Morrison with printing the tracts which he then took and
distributed, all at great risk.[21] He was robbed, imprisoned
and beaten but 'unchecked'. With one of his own converts,
Qiu A-gong, he travelled two hundred and fifty miles in
the entourage of one of the public examiners, a most daring
thing for the mandarin to allow and the Christians to do.

At every examination centre they had free access to the
thousands of students and distributed over seven thousand
tracts, whereby hangs a tale so fantastic that the dynasty
came close to toppling on account of it. But more of that
later.

There were no barriers between the Chinese and foreign
Christians for 'among those who love the Saviour, difference of country makes no difference', Bridgman's biographer, his widow, wrote of those days. During Morrison's
absence in Britain, Liang A-fa wrote a commentary on
Hebrews and submitted it to him on his return. It was good,
and so were tracts which he wrote. Morrison had ordained
him as an evangelist, but he was far more. As Chinese
responded to the gospel he was pastor and teacher as well.

With adventurous faith the American Board also set
aside funds for a mission to Japan about thirty years before
missionaries were able to land there. In the same year,
1828, Walter Medhurst in Java still without any congregation, let alone Christians, was studying Japanese books to
see if the Chinese Bible could be edited to be suitable for
Japan. Not satisfied with that, he asked the Dutch to let
him sail on one of their ships to Nagasaki. Understandably
they refused. He had been working for five years travelling
extensively among the islands of what is now Indonesia,
and publishing among the wealth of other things Milne's
Chinese magazine, discontinued when he died. He
employed a dozen Chinese to copy Chinese-Japanese
dictionaries and Confucian classics with Japanese interli-
near translations. Nothing those early missionaries did
seems to have been done by halves. They worked as if their
days were numbered—as indeed they were for all too
many. And as if China's inaccessible millions were not
enough, the pioneers' faith and prayers were battering at
Japan's hermetically sealed gates as well.

D. W. C. Olyphant is one of the outstanding characters
in the saga, 'the father of the American mission to China'.
He was an honest, godly merchant in a godless, unscrupulous world of smugglers and profiteers posing as honest

men. They dubbed his rooms in the 'factory', 'Zion's Corner'. Samuel Wells Williams, who came to Canton three years later, wrote in the *Chinese Recorder* which he later edited,

> He supported and encouraged them (American missions) when their expenses were startling and the prospect of success faint. He and his partners furnished the Mission a house rent free in Canton for about thirteen years. The church with which he was connected in New York, at his suggestion, in 1832 sent out a complete printing office . . . and when the *Chinese Repository* (which the *Recorder* succeeded) was commenced, he offered to bear the loss of its publication if it proved to be a failure, rather than that the funds of the American Board should suffer. He built an office for it in Canton, where it remained for twenty-four years. The ships of the firm gave fifty-one free passages to missionaries and their families going to and from China . . .[22]

Wells Williams could have mentioned much besides. Olyphant's deep love for Christ and for the Chinese was the root from which his actions sprang. And Wells Williams himself crossed the Pacific in an Olyphant ship named the *Morrison*. With such a benefactor and supporter, Robert Morrison was able to face his difficulties and continuing dangers more cheerfully.

Elijah and Eliza Bridgman were the first American missionaries to China, as the Judsons were to East Asia. He was twenty-eight when they arrived at Macao on February 22, 1830, to be welcomed by Mrs Morrison. Eliza had to stay there while Elijah went on his way up-river to Canton after only three days. There were few Western wives and children in Macao and the addition of another was hailed with delight.

The excitement of the twenty-two-hour journey and his first sight of the Factory is apparent in Bridgman's journal.

> With the exception of two or three narrow streets [the 'thirteen factories', rebuilt] make one solid block . . . of brick or granite . . . with the flags of the different countries [flying] — a striking and pleasing contrast with the . . . ensign

and architecture of the Celestial Empire. [It took a little time to shed the feeling that everything at home was better.] The whole number of foreigners resident here is about seventy-five, and the . . . annual visitors who speak English, four thousand. Also many Lascars and fifty or sixty Parsees.[23]

Morrison was kindness itself and Bridgman settled down to language study until the compulsory spring migration of the Factory residents to Macao and reunion with their wives. They were there when the first steamship in China waters arrived. Then back to Canton when the agents went up to prepare for the merchant fleets. One of Olyphant's partners, Charles W. King, was agent in Canton when Olyphant was away, and Bridgman and Abeel, the seamen's missionary, were his guests. With Morrison the four were a team with one mind and purpose.

> Met this evening at Dr M's [Bridgman's journal for October 25 reads], with Messrs Abeel and King, by prayer and conversation to learn what we ought to do for our Redeemer, that his glory may be promoted and souls saved. In everything we think, do and say, may the spirit of the Lord direct.

And on Christmas Eve, so often in the past lonely and bleak for Morrison, who had nothing in common with the Bacchanalian revels of the Great Hall,

> We were assembled in an upper room — four only — and celebrated there the death of Christ. As we knelt and prayed, and partook of the body broken and the blood poured out, the scenes of Calvary rose before us and we thought and spoke of the tender mercies of our God and our Lord Jesus Christ . . . It affected our hearts and made us weep.[24]

Instead of settling in Singapore, after his year at Canton and Macao, David Abeel went to Bangkok, where many foreign sailors were to be found; but his health failed and he was forced to return home. He travelled via Britain and the Continent, with his heart full to overflowing with the Orient. Both there and at home in the States he stirred up an interest in East Asian missions, especially among women. A new phenomenon, of activity by women in support of missions, was the outcome on both sides of the Atlantic, with the formation of women's societies. He moved his own Dutch Reformed Church of America to concern for China, and led their mission to Amoy after the treaty ports were opened. Then his health broke again and he returned home to die. David Abeel holds a place of honour among the pioneers who helped to open China to the gospel.

Here matters more closely related to Hudson Taylor enter the scene as the Dyers play a larger part. Young Samuel Dyer showed sound common sense and the right spirit when he and his 'darling Maria' arrived at Penang in August 1827. He knew that there were three members of the Ultra-Ganges team in Singapore and three in Malacca, but that none had been in Penang for the past two years. Walter Medhurst had distributed tracts throughout George Town, Penang, and started schools for Chinese children, handing over to two colleagues before he withdrew and went to Batavia, but they had gone and the gains of their first efforts were melting away.

The Dyers left their ship and found somewhere to live while Samuel wrote to consult Morrison and his other LMS colleagues about the rightness of staying. Penang was the seat of the Straits government, set up in the previous year, and there was a small foreign colony with its strait-laced protocol. Samuel Dyer knew what that meant, and burnt his bridges at once. He rented a Chinese house in the Chinese part of the town and began going from house to house, distributing tracts mostly by Milne and Liang A-fa, while he learned the language. The personal contact with Chinese of all kinds was his best teacher. Three years before, he had written to Robert Morrison about a plan for him to teach at the Anglo-Chinese College.

> I think I have more talent in (scholastic pursuits), yet feel the need of much additional application before I could undertake the Professorship of Greek and Roman literature . . . I

confess I should not like to be *entirely* engaged in teaching classics . . . because I wish to be personally instrumental in leading sinners to Jesus . . .[25]

His genius might have been smothered, had his superiors tied him to that 'professorship'. Even before leaving Britain he had given thought to the huge problems of printing in Chinese character. The old Chinese system of writing with ink and brush a whole page of large characters, pasting them in reverse on wooden slabs and delicately carving away the surrounding wood to leave the characters standing 'proud', was what Morrison, Milne and Medhurst had been using. The labour was extravagant, the result was vulnerable to fire and white ants, and the lettering had to be large. Samuel Dyer before sailing from Britain consulted a type-founder and was told the cost would be two guineas a character. Comparison with present-day equivalents would be startling. A full fount of type for printing the Bible and Christian books would need tens of thousands of characters. He was not deterred. He would look for an economical method.

He embarked on an analysis of fourteen books, including the Morrison Bible, to determine which characters were necessary for Christian publications, excluding all others in Morrison's dictionary of more than forty thousand characters.[26] Later on he devised a method of casting fine type in slabs, so that one operation supplied many individual characters when they were cut apart. To the Mission directors he appealed for an engraver and worker in steel to be sent out, and to Morrison he wrote, 'We are cutting steel punches for Chinese metal types at Penang.'[27]

He was not the first or the most successful in making individual movable Chinese type and arranging it for the compositors, but it was a great achievement and established his reputation, according to his memorialist, Evan Davies, as 'one of the most efficient missionaries ever sent out from this or any other country to the heathen world'.[28] Incidentally, in 1850, a Chinese printer named Tang in the Canton area made sets of four characters in one movable metal bar and built up a fount of two hundred thousand units. But an insurrection led to the destruction of his premises and some wounded government soldiers, taken aboard an American ship for surgery were found to be peppered with Tang's types, used as shot.[29]

Charles (Karl) Gutzlaff   1803–35

If Morrison, Milne and Medhurst were tranquil planets in the Eastern sky, Charles Gutzlaff was a comet, more spectacular and of comparable importance.[30] His passage during twenty-three years in East Asia was marked by a brilliance that attracted attention, and by a transient trail of glory such as escaped his less conspicuous contemporaries. For Gutzlaff was unique. His passion for the evangelisation of China drove him to measures more imaginative and daring than others attempted. While they laid foundations and prepared for China to open up to foreigners, he could not wait. He set himself to break in by whatever means he could, and to rouse Christians in Europe to do the same. His success took not the form he envisaged but one patterned on it, the missionary societies he inspired.

As briefly indicated in the prologue, Gutzlaff's influence on Hudson Taylor, through the Chinese Evangelization Society, was profound. Gutzlaff's courage, originality, adventurousness, adaptability to Chinese customs, his principles and methods, left a deep impression on the young man who was to follow him. When Hudson Taylor reached China, his own actions and attitudes suggest that he was emulating Gutzlaff, albeit subconsciously. This review of missionary endeavour in the nineteenth century must therefore take due notice of a man unjustly remembered for one guileless error of judgment instead of all his positive contributions to the spread of the kingdom of God.

Even as a boy Karl Friedrich August Gützlaff (1803–51)

was remarkable, but he became a man of immense ability, enterprise and achievement. His family were Prussian colonists in Pomerania on the Baltic coast, east of Berlin and now in Poland. When still a boy he experienced a spiritual conversion which affected him like Saul and the sons of the prophets. His father's lodgers could hear him practising his preaching in the dark at dead of night. Never flamboyant, he was always intense, highly charged with zeal to extend the cause of Christ.

He was an apprentice saddler of seventeen when King Frederick William of Prussia paid a visit to Stettin, in 1820. Young Gützlaff went to see him and threw a poem into his open carriage, an accepted practice in those days, when citizens had a petition to present. He asked to be sent to college. Gützlaff had spoken with a friend of his own age about wanting to go to China, and now, when the king asked him if a missionary college would satisfy him, he accepted, and went at the king's expense. It was Jänicke's Moravian Missionary Institute of Berlin.[31] The principal was impressed by this boy who would never pray except on his knees, so real was his sense of God.

There was no German mission at that time, but the Netherlands Missionary Society was willing to take him and in 1823 Karl Gützlaff said goodbye to his father, probably for ever, a 'most painful parting', and left for Rotterdam. Even to get back to his home town of Pyritz would have been a major undertaking, so although he might not sail for Asia for some years, this was the moment of anguish. He discovered he had an uncanny knack with languages, quickly mastered Dutch and even wrote a small book in it.[32] Then he went on to Paris and England. He studied medicine and in after years was known as 'Dr Charles Gutzlaff'. Finally, in July 1826 he was ordained and sailed for Batavia in the Dutch East Indies. From this time onward he became more British than Pomeranian.

Walter Medhurst had been in Java four years, and ten years in Asia when Gützlaff arrived. He was the ideal friend and adviser. Gützlaff quickly became proficient in

Chinese and also learned Malay. He saw the printing press at work and no doubt to Medhurst's joy set himself to supply the only rationale for publication, namely distribution of the tracts and Scriptures being turned out in profusion both there and at Malacca. While Samuel and Maria Dyer were settling in at Penang, he took to moving about among the highly mobile Chinese traders as well as settlers along the coasts of Java, Borneo and the islands. In response to an invitation from the ruler of the Rhio Islands between Java and Singapore, Gützlaff went there with the LMS missionary Jacob Tomlin of Singapore. Together they became familiar with Chinese customs and dialects, and an itinerant way of life, living like Chinese on their junks.

Intending originally to stay in the Indies, Gützlaff was captivated by the charms of the Chinese as a people, and the millions on the Chinese mainland claimed him. He and Tomlin planned a visit to Bangkok, another entrepot of Chinese merchants, and Medhurst arranged to travel with them. Walter Medhurst had had Siam in his thoughts ever since some Siamese and Indo-Chinese had visited them in Malacca soon after he joined William Milne. But Medhurst failed to arrive and on August 4, 1828, their junk went without him.

When he reached Singapore two days later, such were travelling conditions, Medhurst was disappointed but not defeated. He found another junk heading for Songkhla (Songora to the European sailors), then at the very tip of Siamese territory on the Malayan peninsula, and went aboard. They were attacked by pirates but escaped and put in at Pattani, an impoverished Malayan port since the British and Dutch 'factories' closed, and repeatedly attacked by the Siamese from Songkhla just up the coast. Then on to Songkhla itself, 'exceedingly romantic', 'pagodas gild the tops of the hills'. He could not get to Bangkok so he sailed again, this time to Pontianak in Borneo where Dutch and Chinese towns sprawled side by side, created by the lure of gold and other precious metals. This was where Slater had been asked to send a missionary to stay. The twenty-five thousand Chinese were friendly when Medhurst spoke fluently in their own Hokkien (Fujian) dialect, and an old man asked how he could find salvation for his soul. So Medhurst stayed to teach him—until suddenly the old man died 'by a stroke of apoplexy'—or poison.

Tomlin returned from Bangkok to Singapore and in 1829 on an evangelistic visit to Bali with Medhurst caught 'jungle fever' (either a virulent malaria, typhoid or tick typhus) and had to be invalided home, yet another casualty that could ill be spared. Gützlaff stayed in Siam, as Thailand was called by westerners until 1939, long enough to be thrilled by the access it gave him to the crews of great ocean-going junks from Tianjin, the gatehouse of Peking. The East India Company had concluded a friendly treaty with Siam in 1826, and Bangkok was once again what Ayuthia had been in the seventeenth century, a welcoming magnet for European traders. Gützlaff was made welcome by the Chinese immigrants and also picked up enough Thai to preach in temples, cottages and even in the palace. His medical work was an open-sesame. Crowds flocked to his lodgings and he was pressed to become court physician.

But he became insufferably bored with the hours he had to spend simply sitting and talking without achieving his aims. He had brought twenty-three boxes of books and Scripture in Chinese, and found that Siam was the ideal place for getting them into the hands of Chinese, especially sailors returning to their homeland. They wanted the books and welcomed him on board their junks, especially for his doctoring. Inevitably the vision of reaching the capital of the Celestial Empire as a member of a Chinese crew came to him. He wrote to his mission directors. By the time their reply reached him much had happened.

His contacts with the LMS missionaries led to his going to Malacca, and temporarily taking charge of the work there. A well-to-do English girl was working with the LMS in Malacca, a Miss Newell. She had arrived only two years before and had already started five schools, employing Chinese teachers. Was she, perhaps, one of Morrison's

Chinese class in Hackney? Before long she and Gützlaff were married. He was twenty-six.

From somewhere about that time Gützlaff seems to have become largely Anglicised. (Students of the period will observe that his subsequent history justifies the change in common usage of his name from Karl Gützlaff to Charles Gutzlaff. Robert Morrison frequently referred to him as 'Mr Gutzlaff' and in his 1832 list of members of the 'Chinese Mission' as 'Charles Gutzlaff'. His own *Journal of Three Voyages* published in 1834 in English was 'by CHARLES GUTZLAFF'. This, then, is the most appropriate name to use.)[33]

Together he and his wife returned in February 1830 to Bangkok. However, the Netherlands Mission directors were unwilling for him to stray so far from Dutch spheres of influence and from their remote seat of authority. And they considered his proposition of visiting China impracticable. So Gutzlaff resigned and from then on was independent. In fact, the Netherlands Missionary Society had only two representatives 'in the China field', never nearer China than Java and the Celebes.

Mrs Gutzlaff was the first lady missionary in Siam, but not the first English woman. Mary Leslie, the wife of a mercenary ship's captain in the employ of the king, had chosen in 1687 to stay in Siam when her husband was killed in a massacre of the English. The Gutzlaffs settled down to work and succeeded in translating Matthew's Gospel, preparing some tracts in rough and ready Thai, and portions of Scripture in Lao and Cambodian, while the Chinese in Bangkok claimed his first attention. Scarcely a year after their arrival, however, she and her baby died. The price of pioneering would continue to be in lives sacrificed, for decades to come.

Now he faced life alone once more and his own health was making him anxious. He could not go back to Batavia, or to Malacca where he had met his wife.

All my thoughts are bestowed on China [he wrote to a

friend]. My love for China is inexpressible. I am burning for their salvation. I intercede for hundreds of millions which do not know the gospel, before the throne of grace ... The Lord will be able to prepare the way into that country.[34]

He was convinced of that. China would open her fast-shut doors and he would have a part to play in it. There was nothing to prevent him. The Siamese ambassador to Peking offered to take Gutzlaff as his physician, but someone unwilling to lose his services from Bangkok intervened and the ambassador went without him. Although ill himself Gutzlaff accepted the invitation of a friend, Lin Zhong, to go to China with him, and 'become a naturalised subject of the Celestial Empire by adoption into the clan or family of Kwo, from the Tung-an district in Fukien'.[35]

He signed on as a crew member of a 250-ton junk bound for Tianjin, 'went Chinese' in name, clothing, diet and habits, and headed east and north, up the forbidden coast, laden with Christian books. Of the fifty men on board he was at times the only one not under the influence of opium, the captain included. For a while he himself was too ill even to read, and longed to die, but recovering, he served as cook, as mate and as surgeon. He warned the crew of the wrath of God upon their vices and was 'execrated' by them — until lightning split the mast. On June 18, 1831, they arrived at Tianjin. Then came the moment of truth. Would he be arrested, imprisoned interminably, tortured, even executed?

News of his coming had preceded him, that he was a missionary and that his wife had died in Siam. Some called him a spy, making maps, but James Flint's fate escaped him. To win favour he worked hard as a doctor and to his relief was greeted as a curiosity, a 'son of the western ocean' subjected to the civilising influences of the celestials, and now returning the kindness by sharing his medical skills with them. A prominent Fujian merchant claimed him as a fellow-citizen, and another tried to strike a bargain with the ship's captain to release him to come as an attraction in his shop. A high-ranking mandarin even promised him a passport to Peking, but how far he went is uncertain. If he penetrated 'up to the very walls of Peking', as Morrison put it, the only reference in his own *Journal of Three Voyages* is, 'It had been my intention to proceed from Teen-tsin up to Peking . . .'[36] After a month at Tianjin he sailed again, to Liaoning on the Manchurian coast, and stood at the end of the Great Wall where it goes down literally into the sea at Qinhuangdao. Another month passed 'in Chinese Tartary', and again he braved the winter storms to reach Macao twelve days before Christmas.

A man with such a passion for the evangelisation of China was a man after Robert Morrison's own heart. When this mature young adventurer with the gospel turned up, having on his own initiative already seen the great places of the north, and speaking colloquial Chinese more fluently than Ma Lao-shi himself, a strong friendship grew up between them.[37]

The news that Gutzlaff had found at various ports on the coast as far north as the Great Wall a knowledge of Christian publications from Malacca, confirmed the rightness of Morrison's and Milne's strategy. Walter Medhurst had formed a respect for young Charles too, and described him as having been 'stirred up by God to attempt the hazardous, while most missionaries were in settled and sedentary work'.[38] By 'most missionaries' he was referring to the little handful of less than a dozen east of Calcutta, living at considerable risk from tropical diseases and changes of political climate.

Gutzlaff made his base at Macao and from there made other journeys up the China coast, seven in all. But Siam was not forgotten. Already he had baptised one Chinese in Bangkok and during his absence David Abeel took his place. Congregational missionaries arrived in 1831 and a Baptist missionary, John Taylor Jones, came over from Burma in 1833, also to concentrate on the Chinese, and in ten years to complete a translation of the New Testament into Siamese. Moreover, the Bridgmans pleaded the cause of Siam and the American Board sent other missionaries to the Thai people in 1840 and the years ahead. A physician, Daniel Beach Bradley soon made a great reputation and attended the royal family, and Jessie Caswell became tutor to Prince Mongkut.

In answer to an appeal by Charles Gutzlaff, the American Baptist Mission espoused the cause of the Chinese in Siam, hoping this would be a stepping-stone into China proper, and in 1835 William Dean arrived as their pioneer. Within five years the first Chinese Protestant Church in Siam was organised. He subsequently spent twenty years in Hong Kong, but well over forty years later he was in Bangkok again and at seventy was looking forward to another ten years in active service. Though he was working in Siam, the *Chinese Recorder* referred to Dean as 'the senior missionary in China', with the care of five congregations.

In 1831 Robert Morrison was forty-nine and disappointingly had begun to feel not the strength of his prime but his age. To Abeel he wrote, 'My hard-working days are nearly over'; and thinking of Abeel's free hand to do as he wished in tolerant Siam,

> Would that our fetters were broken here. We seem to require a faithful band of confessors and martyrs, foreign and native, to open the closed gates of this proud land.[39]

Even the vicar-apostolic in Macao would have agreed with him. None of them could know how much Christian blood had yet to flow after those gates creaked open.

China's predicament   1830–32

If the Dao Guang emperor had any doubts of the evils of opium, they were banished dramatically when his three sons died, helpless addicts. The loss of two he might have borne, but to lose his heir was intolerable. He issued 'Regulations to guard against foreigners', ordering his viceroy at Canton to tighten up on controls. Something must be done at once to curb the opium traffic. More corrupt Chinese dealers were tortured; the Prefect of Canton forced his way into the East India Company's assembly room, tore down the covering of King George's portrait, seated himself with his back to it and lectured the agents. The Factory gates and the new quay were wrecked and even trees in the gardens cut down.

Aggressiveness of this nature was inept. The reaction of the Company agents was no less inept. Convinced that to reduce their dealings in opium would play into the hands of the smugglers, as well as depriving the Company of profits, they reacted strongly. Perhaps they were so blinded by their own familiarity with the opium traffic that they could see no wrong in it, but only Chinese obstinacy, provoking 'justifiable counter-measures' such as smuggling.[40] They claimed to be at a loss to account for the attitude of the Chinese, but could have been playing a double game, deliberately attempting to mislead the British government. Afraid that the long-standing system of connivance by the Chinese officials was breaking down, and feeling that the Factory was becoming too perilous for them, they proposed the seizure of an island as a base, to the delight of the country-merchants. This was precisely what they wanted. To have the British government carry it out was far better than to do it themselves without the backing of adequate forces.

Many of the country-merchants were men whose origins did not bear scrutiny. Piracy, gun-running, unscrupulous and disreputable conduct in the past led them naturally into the opium traffic. Dent, Jardine and Matheson were reputedly honourable gentlemen. Allowed to occupy vacant 'factories', they were part of the social milieu of Canton and Macao. Thomas and Launcelot Dent and their partners ran themselves into bankruptcy with their profligate life in the grand style. James Matheson was the son of a baronet and William Jardine was a surgeon. A powerful Parsee country-trader who was himself honoured with a knighthood, Sir Jamsetjee Jejeebhoy, helped to set them up in business. As merchants they drove hard bargains, but their captains had a reputation for violence at sea. If a war junk came too close to their ships a boarding party would be sent to throw all the junk's weapons into the sea and send it packing, but sometimes the opium ship would simply ram the junk and fire at its crew. The violence was not even limited to fighting off Chinese war junks. It extended to forcing other merchant ships to abandon a profitable trading sphere or landing place. The energy and initiative of Jardine and Matheson gave them the lead. They began replacing their merchantmen with fast teak-built ships patterned on American privateers. These flush-decked greyhounds of the sea streaked away from their rivals.

Because of the contraband nature of the traffic, detailed figures are not obtainable, but Indian government and East India Company reports give adequate generalisations.[41] We saw that in 1826 the Company was handling 8,500 chests of opium. Each chest consisted of forty balls of three pounds net weight of opium, nearly double what it had been handling five years previously. Four years later the amount being auctioned to the country-merchants in India was fourteen thousand chests at a value of twelve and a half million pounds.[42] Still the administration in India was not reaping enough revenue to cover its inflated needs, so all pretence of limiting the supply of opium to the amount dictated by compassion for the cravings of China's addicts was abandoned. If high profit margins did not give a big enough return, an increased turnover was needed. A mighty sales drive began, just as China was determined on a drastic reduction of the traffic. And if Canton and its estuary 'drops' were not able to take enough, other places must be found on the coast. The vicious spiral was becoming a tornado.

With conditions at Canton increasingly exasperating and India pressing hard for more trading, the merchants themselves, including the Company's agents, were being driven to desperation. They reacted in two ways. They

INDIAN OPIUM WAREHOUSE

petitioned Westminster to insist on China according diplomatic recognition and fair trading rights; and instead of accepting the humiliations for the sake of such facilities as the Chinese allowed, some merchants became defiant. One of them brought his wife to Canton, in flagrant disregard of the Hoppo's sanctions.

Chinese objections to the Westerners' behaviour were apparent as far away as Jakarta, where Medhurst was being opposed on valid grounds, fairly set out in a pamphlet cogent to every Chinese. He represented a Christian nation, it claimed, devoid of four out of the five Virtues. The opium traffic showed lack of Benevolence; territorial imperialism showed lack of Rectitude; the way Western men and women walked arm in arm where others could see them showed lack of Propriety; and their rejection of the ancient classics in favour of their own substitutes showed lack of Wisdom. Only Truthfulness was in their favour. Over and above their major deficiencies were such things as their disrespect for the written and printed page, and the fact that the coffins they supplied for their dead were only an inch or so thick. It was all too deplorable. They were not to be listened to.

Meanwhile in Canton the governor of Canton threatened forcible expulsion of the merchant's provocative lady if she did not go at once, and the agents retaliated by planting two eighteen-pounders and a hundred well-armed men at the Factory gates. The viceroy and governor capitulated and three more women came to the Factory. The Chinese still forbade the merchants to use sedan chairs, the preserve of superior men. Mere merchants should walk. So the Factory committee banned sedan chairs in the factory grounds, to force the 'superior' Chinese to walk too. It was all too petty. Serious and petty provocations were multiplying.

Perhaps the worst erosion of confidence lay in the viceroy's raid during the summer of 1831. When the agents withdrew to Macao after the fleets had sailed, the Factory quarter was tacitly in the protection of the Chinese authorities, sacrosanct. The library, valuables, records, all were safe. Even when the gates and precincts were vandalised, the residences and warehouses were unharmed. That they should now be broken into and searched was the knell of that knife-edge co-operation which had somehow survived for seventy painful years. It was a pity. As Jardine testified to Parliament, the residents had been able to sleep with their windows open, sure of immunity from intrusion. In the new climate no one could be sure of anything.

When the British government's response to the agents'

plea arrived, it was disappointing. Lord Palmerston was preoccupied with problems in Europe and the Middle East, and Parliament with the Reform Bill, so the agents received a sound rebuke. They were there for commerce, not to annex islands.

> Conquest . . . would be as dangerous as defeat . . . [he told them pontifically]. No glory can be gained by a victory over the Chinese . . . Our grand object is to keep the peace and by . . . adaptation to [them] to extend our [commercial] influence . . . It is not a demonstration of force which is required, but proofs of the advantage which China reaps from her peaceful [dealings] with our nation.[43]

If only the rebuke had expressed conviction and stable policy! But Palmerston knew well that peaceful trading largely meant opium. While his remarks could have been the policy of an honourable nation, they were hollow. For good measure the Court of the Honourable East India Company added a slap of its own. What did the agents mean by interfering in international politics? 'You are not the representatives of the British nation but of the Honourable East India Company.'[44] In this they were wrong, except technically. There were no other representatives and the agents were in the difficult position of representing Britain without authority. Their only hold over the powerful country-merchants was their prestige as agents of the all-powerful Company and their ability to apply the potential threat of disowning them to the Chinese authorities and closing all trading facilities to them.

One of the factors which had stimulated the opium trade was the growing demand in the West for tea. As a result of the inability of western merchants to find a commodity sufficiently attractive to the Chinese, tea exports diminished. At that point, before the great exploitation of opium began, China demanded silver in payment for her tea. In consequence she was able to lay up a sizeable hoard of Spanish-American dollars. Now, when her people would take however much opium was delivered to her shores, the tables were turned. Her exports of tea, silk and exotica were not enough. She began to buy opium for silver. Cargoes of silver bullion began to leave China.[45] Like King Canute, Dao Guang could order the opium tide to stop, but it advanced remorselessly against him while the under-tow sucked the nation's economy away from under his throne. What could he do? The pressure of the West was relentless, ruthless. To the emperor and his advisers it was infuriating and alarming. Retaliation was imperative.

Two factors were common to both nations: insularity, and the arrogance bred by its resultant ignorance. The self-sufficiency of China and the self-righteousness of Britain made accommodation between the two peoples difficult. It was a self-sufficiency soon to be proved false and a self-righteousness that was in fact self-delusion, merely the product of industrial expansion. Sooner or later a clash was inevitable. With hindsight we stand like spectators on a vantage point, watching the two great forces on their collision course, and are helpless to alter events.

PART 2

THE CLASH OF CULTURES
1830–50

CHAPTER FIVE

DRAGON AND LION
1830–40

Build-up to war   *1830–32*

As the British lion is not a rampaging carnivore, but a figure of strength and invincibility, quiet and peaceful until roused and then more ready with a roar than with tooth and claw, so the Chinese dragon is not always the menacing creature of European folklore. It is the emblem of the sun, of glory, warmth and power, of emperor, magnificence and benignity. 'Farmer George' and the British lion had more in common with the Chinese dragon and dragon throne than either monarch ever discovered. When their individual subjects got together and explored their differences, they enjoyed a good laugh and became good friends. The Chinese love of life and fun, of hospitality and novelty, ensured a welcome to peaceful strangers. But emperor, mandarin and subject would stand no nonsense. Intrusion in any form was sure to be resisted and loyalty to the throne was as strong as love of peace. The tragedy was that incidents multiplied to create such deep-seated suspicion that reasonable relations became impossible, apart from one side or the other yielding ground. Being forced to yield would never change dragon or lion.

'The Manchu rulers—that proud race of decayed imperialists'[1] as George Woodcock puts it, were like old men too tired and set in their ways to see the need for change in a changing world. Whoever might knock at their door was sure to be repelled. They did not want to know about the modern world or troublesome foreigners. All alike were insubordinate vassals. Let the fools who wished to have dealings with outer barbarians get on with their odious job. Not long ago they would have been condemned as traitors, as was still the case in Japan. Now the distasteful necessity was admitted, but barbarian must be played off against barbarian, the peaceful ones prevailed upon to put pressure on the assertive. 'The barbarian nature cannot be fathomed' was the frequent refrain in Chinese communiqués.[2] 'Fickle and unscrupulous' summed up the Westerner. He had nothing to offer China except merchandise of doubtful worth.

George IV, the 'national liability', died in 1830 and his brother William IV, 'the sailor king', took his place. Again Great Britain had no moral lead from the throne. Under this 'bursting, bubbling old gentleman, with quarter-deck gestures, round rolling eyes and a head like a pineapple', in Lytton Strachey's words,[3] the country fell to rioting and the political power moved under the Reform Bills towards the industrialists and middle class. These were the go-getters, the men whose success was built on exploitation, Indian adventures and contraband trade with China. But the Wilberforces and Ashleys had to continue the fight to force their bills for the abolition of slavery and child labour and for poor relief through Parliament. Eventually, the Reform Bill of 1832 opened the door to the measure for the abolition of slavery in 1833.

The opportunists were men who saw the situation in China solely from the viewpoint of profit and revenue. Self-confident, energetic, indifferent to cultural differences, they made no attempt to understand or respect the highly cultured, but vastly different Chinese. That most unfortunate of hybrid languages, pidgin English, struck the young British merchant in Canton as ridiculously funny and Chinese etiquette as ludicrous. So men of profound refinement were scorned and scoffed at. Anything Chinese was comical or wicked. The more remote from them the critics were, the more extreme their attitudes. The good-hearted merchants and the missionaries who cultivated the company of the Cohong merchants found them reliable and genuinely courteous. The opium smugglers who had dealings only with the corrupt ones, formed adverse opinions and made no attempt to understand true Chinese.

So ignorance and prejudice prevailed in the seats of government and at the point of contact in Canton. 'You cannot clap with one hand,' the Chinese proverb says. The breakdown in relations between the two countries, and other Western nations with them, could be blamed on both sides. Some would say that opium and the determination to sell it at all costs to China for the sake of the Indian revenue, was the prime cause of the hostilities that developed. Others conclude that the demands for trading outlets, the direct corollary of the production boom in the west, was the cause. The war could just as well be called the Tea War, because Britain demanded its tea and could find no exchange commodity except opium to satisfy Chinese customers. The revenue from tea imported into Britain met nearly two-thirds of the cost of maintaining the entire British civil establishment.

But while there is truth in both contentions, war could and perhaps would have been avoided if mutual respect had existed, if the clash of cultures had not become inevitable, short of a miracle. Britain's annoyance with Chinese obscurantism and obstruction was backed by her international lead in the commercial field and, despite the great distances involved, with all the logistics of war in her favour. That she used them to force her demands has never been forgiven. That opium was the poison on her swordpoint still adds bitterness to the hatred. Like lemmings in their onrush fearing no barrier, not even the sea, events in nineteenth-century China led on towards war.

The Amherst *experiment*[4]   *1832*

So successful was the opium production drive in India, doubled again since 1825, and so difficult the situation at Canton, that a glut developed at the Lingding Island smuggling base and even legitimate commerce was impaired. By 1836 opium production was tripled. Their consciences silenced, the British politicians became obsessed with the commercial potential of four hundred million Chinese. However, with Lord Palmerston's refusal of strong action to bring the Chinese to their senses, only local expedients remained possible. Knowing full well that Canton was the only authorised port for foreign trade the agents of the Company decided on a market survey 'to ascertain how far the northern ports of the Empire may gradually be opened to British commerce'.[5]

They could only do it secretly, so they chartered a Dent and Company country-ship, the *Lord Amherst*, and dispatched her under false papers with a cargo of British broadcloth, calico and cotton but no opium. In command was Captain Hugh Hamilton Lindsay, with Dr Charles Gutzlaff as ship's surgeon and interpreter. Lindsay's report to the Honourable East India Company makes fascinating reading. Impressed by all he saw he could not disguise his admiration of Gutzlaff in action. The young Harry Parkes, years later to be H.E. Sir Henry S. Parkes, British Minister Plenipotentiary in China, saw Gutzlaff as 'a short, square figure' in a broad-brimmed straw hat, with 'a great face' and 'a sinister eye';[6] but it was Gutzlaff's fluency in colloquial Chinese and his behaviour among the people that intrigued Lindsay, himself familiar with the language.

On February 26, 1832, they sailed from the Canton estuary and made first for Amoy. 'Our sudden appearance on the coast transfused general terror,' Gutzlaff recorded.[7] A mandarin junk anchored near the *Lord Amherst* and displayed a board across its bows with the characters, 'The barbarian ship is ordered to set sail and depart. It is forbidden to anchor or loiter.' 'Mr Gutzlaff was not the person to be brow-beat by angry words,' Lindsay reported. A mandarin whom Gutzlaff confronted said, 'I know you to be a native of this district traitorously serving barbarians in disguise.'[8] Somehow he penetrated beyond the official façade to the men behind and in place after place succeeded in landing and mixing with the people. Everywhere Gutzlaff's medical treatment and fluent speech were hailed with delight.

> On many occasions when Mr Gutzlaff has been surrounded by hundreds of eager listeners, he has been interrupted by loud expressions of the pleasure with which they listened to his pithy and indeed eloquent language. From having lived so long among the lower classes of the Fukien people, Mr Gutzlaff has obtained a knowledge of their peculiarities, both of thought and language, which no study of books can convey . . . coupled with a thorough acquaintance with the Chinese classics, which the Chinese are ever delighted to hear quoted . . .[9]

So much for the rank and file, but the mandarins were on thin ice. The least show of friendliness put them in danger of being degraded if reported by a superior. Some even performed the *ketou*, imploring the visitors to go away. In each place the ship visited, some official was eventually punished for the fact of its arrival. It should have been intercepted and turned back. At most places, however, trade was welcomed, outside the port. Even so, friendly mandarins had to keep up an outward show of antagonism. 'Daily insults are most galling,' Lindsay confessed.

It was usually possible for Gutzlaff to distribute tracts and copies of Morrison's Bible which Morrison himself had supplied. William Milne's tracts were always popular; a *Tract against Lying*; a *Tract against Gambling*; a *Tract in Praise of Honesty*, each began on a note approved, in theory, by the reader and led on to the gospel. Lindsay and Gutzlaff were often shown great kindness and invited to feasts, but before long the superior mandarins would drive them out.

> It is an unjust and insidious remark thrown upon the Chinese, [Gutzlaff wrote], that they hate strangers and are averse to having any dealings with them. Even in Canton province . . . we found the people exceedingly friendly and hospitable.[10]

At Fuzhou they called on the viceroy, a change of tactics, but only reached the prefect. Some Chinese told them, 'Our mandarins are rogues, the people are your friends,' and 'arrange the matters with our Sovereign and we will receive you next year with open arms.'[11] Attempts to establish regular trade were unsuccessful, however. People who approached them were bambooed and put in cangues, the portable pillories inflicted on petty offenders. Yet three days after an admiral and other officers were demoted for allowing the ship to enter port and the city was placarded with proclamations prohibiting any dealings with the barbarians, an officer accompanied by a civil mandarin introduced some local merchants and arranged a $6,200 transaction, bringing themselves three per cent in rake-off. The officer then came alongside in his war junk to effect payment.

Farther on, up the coast, their welcome at Ningbo was even friendly. Crowds came to their lodging place, welcoming trade and expressing goodwill, aware that foreigners had traded with them a century before. 'But why no opium?' They could not understand. Opium was the commodity most certain of a market. The use and abuse of it was a personal matter, and the law was enforced by the men who profited most from the traffic, so clearly the law was more a hazard than an obligation. When a naval officer warned them against the 'literary mandarins', the civil officials, it turned out that he was convinced that Gutzlaff was a Fujian Chinese.

They submitted a written address to Ningbo's chief mandarin requesting permission to trade, and asked him to forward it to the emperor. Whether this message reached

MANDARINS IN CONVERSATION

Peking they never knew but on returning to Canton they learned that from every place they visited a report was submitted, in terms of course most favourable to the local mandarins. Chinese documents show that these reports were intentionally misleading. In fact before they left Ningbo the emperor knew of their presence on the coast.[12] The mandarins were caught between the throne and the wishes of the people. 'We are afraid of you foreigners; you are too clever for us,' some said; and others, 'Keep at a distance, among the islands, then we will trade. If you come into port we are bound to obey edicts.'[13] But Lindsay understood his instructions to mean more overt access to ports than that.

The *Lord Amherst* left Ningbo on June 13 and came to the great estuary of the Yangzi river. An island, unnamed on their chart, Lindsay called Gutzlaff Island. They anchored at Wusong and by smaller boat went up the Huangpu tributary to the walled city of Shanghai. Here they tried a change of tactics. Finding the highest official's courtyard closed to them they forced their way in with a shoulder to the door and demanded to be received as equals. Surprisingly the stratagem worked and once admitted by the guard, Gutzlaff's Chinese etiquette with the correct bows, pauses and advances, at the right moment, resulted in their being seated in the great man's presence drinking tea as honoured guests. Because of their knowledge of protocol they were accused of being mandarins in disguise.

Every day Lindsay and Gutzlaff went ashore at Wusong for a walk, escorted by a mandarin and guard; and on July 1 they and the ship's officers crossed the great Yangzi to Chongming (Tsungming) Island, an alluvial flat growing in size from year to year and supporting half a million people. Marco Polo had described other islands but made no mention of Chongming. It was to become the scene of one of Hudson Taylor's early adventures.

Then the prefect feared for his neck and urged the visitors to leave. He posted a proclamation forbidding trade and ordering the expulsion of the ship. In Lindsay's account,[14] the document read 'I, the *taoutae*, imitate the great Emperor, who harbours a compassionate mind towards foreigners. I therefore clearly inform and command you immediately to get under weigh . . . Take care not to bring sorrow on yourselves!' The townsfolk were highly amused to see Gutzlaff copying the proclamation with expert calligraphy, to the officials' obvious embarrassment.

They did not want to bring sorrow on anyone and had been well received, so they did as they were told. War junks escorted them down the Yangzi and when a safe six miles lay between them, fired their guns, ceremoniously 'expelling the barbarians'.

Hawks Pott, historian of Shanghai, recorded that the expedition was rebuffed all along the coast, failed to attain admittance to Amoy, Fuzhou and Ningbo, presented a petition to the *daotai* at Shanghai and was told to return to Canton, the only permitted place for trade.[15] He was right, the expedition failed to find open ports for commerce. This was the official stance. But he was wrong in terms of potential, the prospect for trade, should the imperial attitude ever change. Fundamentally the people of China were welcoming.

Shanghai impressed them and Lindsay's main recommendation to the Company was to regard Shanghai as the best entrepot for commerce.

> I was so much struck with the vast quantity of junks entering the river (the Huangpu) that I caused them to be counted . . . Upwards of 400 varying from 100 to 400 tons passed from Woosung to Shanghai.[16]

The East India Company failed to appreciate the interim possibilities for 'island trading', but Lindsay's report became an important basis for future expansionist policy in China. He had been unable to secure any trading agreement, even at a local level, but in Fuzhou, Ningbo and Shanghai, hundreds of miles from Canton, they had seen many shops with stocks of European woollen goods and in a village three miles inland from Wusong, a shop sign advertising the Company's broadcloth 'when in stock'. Urgent enquiries for opium led several of the *Lord Amherst*'s crew into becoming opium careersmen, however. Perhaps even more influential was Gutzlaff's assessment that 'all of China's thousand war-junks cannot withstand one small frigate'. A firm demand by one government to the other would ensure access to the ports. High-handed refusal could be met by a frigate's protection of merchant ships. No one yet thought in terms of armed aggression, least of all Gutzlaff.

The *Lord Amherst* sailed on, up to Weihaiwei on the Shandong peninsula where the reception was unfriendly, and across the Yellow Sea to Korea. There they too were received with the throat-cutting gestures described by Captain Basil Hall and after delivering 'presents to the King of Corea' and lists of commodities which included Bibles and tracts, had to turn south again. Before they left, Gutzlaff wrote out the Lord's Prayer in Chinese for a Korean official. That was the last straw — it challenged the king's supremacy.

They had the greatest difficulty in landing through breakers on the beach at the 'Great Loochoo Islands', but found Chinese-speaking people to talk to and leave Scriptures with. The Ryukyus, of which Okinawa is the biggest, were still a dependency of China and did their greatest trade with Fuzhou. They were not ceded to Japan until 1895 after the Sino-Japanese War. Then on to Taiwan to revictual at a friendly village without mandarins and so back to Canton in September. Most of the six months had been spent ashore and Hamilton Lindsay was enthusiastic in his appreciation.

> We found the people anxious, beyond our hopes, for intercourse with us; and I declare that we met with more kindness and civility from the Chinese during our voyage than travellers could expect or experience from any civilised nation in the world.[17]

a sentiment echoed by innumerable travellers in China through subsequent years. Six years later Walter Medhurst wrote his classic, *China: Its State and Prospects*, and his memory of Charles Gutzlaff's account of the journey was that they had been 'invariably hailed with joy by the people, and flattered or feared by the mandarins'.

The 'Sylph'[18]   1832–33

When William Jardine and James Matheson heard what had happened to the *Lord Amherst*, they saw their chance to profit from the demand for opium. They had no political or ethical scruples about withholding 'the commodity most in demand', (of course leaving the naughty word 'opium' unsaid), so they immediately mounted an expedition of their own. The first man to enlist if they possibly could was naturally Gutzlaff. No one knew the coast or the dialects or the individual ports and even the mandarins better than he. And they knew his eagerness to distribute Christian literature far and wide; but would he co-operate? How far would his religious principles allow him to go?

Charles Gutzlaff was a medical missionary. Opium in its various forms was used world-wide as a medicine. No restrictions on its sale or use were imposed in Britain where the boon and benefits of laudanum were recognised by everyone. The fact that opium had for centuries been imported by China for medicinal purposes was the current smoke-screen for the expanding trade or traffic. There was little public outcry against the trade, the pros and cons were still a matter of opinion comparable to the tobacco debate of the 1980s. The veteran and godly Robert Morrison remained a senior servant of the Honourable East India Company, which controlled opium production in India and was the compelling force in producing it in such quantities. He had no scruples against travelling on Company ships, or for that matter Jardine's or Dent's merchantmen. Like tobacco with its high annual mortality and morbidity rate, opium had not yet been publicly ostracised as unethical.

With commendable frankness, adulterated with guile, Jardine put his cards on Gutzlaff's table.

> We have no hesitation in stating to you openly that our principal reliance is on opium, [he said]. Though it is our earnest wish that you should not in any way injure the grand object you have in view by appearing interested in what by many is considered an immoral traffic, yet such traffic is so absolutely necessary to give any vessel a reasonable chance of defraying her expenses that we trust you will have no objection to interpret on every occasion when your services may be requested.

But that was not all. The more success the voyage enjoyed, the greater would be the sum the Company would be able to devote to furthering Dr Gutzlaff's missionary efforts.

The zealous apostle was torn by indecision. With another opportunity to carry more loads of Scripture by the thousand to the northern ports, how could he sit in stifling Macao with only sedentary work to do? He would not have known of Jardine's dismissal note to one of their ships' captains who had no objection to an opium cargo but refused to load it on the Sabbath: 'We fear that very godly people are not suited to the drug trade.'[19]

Gutzlaff was a prayerful man and, according to E. J. Eitel, the early German missionary, writing in the *Chinese Recorder* in 1876, never approved of the opium traffic. So he took his time before replying. Then, his mind made up, he threw himself loyally into his job.[20] He sailed in the armed *Sylph* in October, only a month after his return in the *Lord Amherst* and was not back again until April 29, 1833.

Brian Inglis writes of Gutzlaff using his imposing presence to good effect, dressed in his best and loosing a spate of fluent dialect Chinese to dismiss interfering mandarin junks and to do a brisk trade. He was the key to opening up new markets, 'oblivious to the implications', as John

King Fairbank grants him in *Trade and Diplomacy on the China Coast*. His own words bear this out. He was cheered by the success of the voyage because 'we hope that this may tend ultimately to the introduction of the gospel for which many doors are open. Millions of Bibles and tracts will be needed.'[21]

Opium and Scripture were to enter China together. Before Gutzlaff is judged on this issue, however, the perspective of history must be considered. Those were the early days. Wilberforce's Emancipation Bill was not passed by Parliament until May 14, after this voyage, and Parliament did not outlaw Britain's opium trade with China until as late as 1913. Gutzlaff was the child of his times, and he was not alone. The Church as a whole was blind to the issue for decades to come, while the anti-opium crusades gained little ground.

Certainly Charles Gutzlaff had the right competitive spirit to please Jardine. When the *Sylph*'s captain arranged with corrupt Chinese officials to intercept junks which traded with the rival Dent & Company's ships and to leave Jardine's Chinese contacts alone, the interpreter obediently translated the message.

Medhurst was always a strong opponent of the opium trade, but in his *China* (1838) he gives unstinting praise to Gutzlaff's missionary achievements, without a hint of censure. Following the *Sylph*'s journey Gutzlaff made others up the coast distributing Scripture, and Medhurst was to follow him after his book was finished.

> It had long been supposed, [he wrote] that China was hermetically sealed against the propagators of divine truth; that it would be death to set foot on her shores; and madness to attempt to diffuse the Gospel in those regions. But here was a man, who had gone and returned unhurt; had maintained an extensive intercourse with the people; had resided, for months together, in their cities and provinces; had met the far-famed and much-dreaded Mandarins; and instead of being arrested, imprisoned, and sent back in a cage to Canton, had been, in every instance, treated with civility,

and, sometimes, with respect . . . had won the confidence of multitudes . . . who were willing to harbour and protect him for the sake of his attainments.[22]

Medhurst was generous in praise as in punctuation, but his conclusion was that Gutzlaff's achievements were no indication of what others could do. For Gutzlaff was exceptional in temperament, a versatile genius with a perfect knowledge of Chinese and 'a similar cast of features'. All of which was true in spite of what had to be admitted, that Gutzlaff had a lively imagination and gave too high a colouring to his accounts. Others then exaggerated his reports. All this Medhurst wrote knowing that Gutzlaff would read the book. He could have added what John Dyer, now Chief Clerk to the Admiralty, cited from a letter by Robert Morrison, 'that altho' he considered him to be a very zealous and good man, yet his mind was so constructed that no other person could work with him . . .'[23]

The *Sylph* attempted trade along the Korean coast and was also rebuffed with the usual throat-cutting gestures and obstruction by glum, stubborn men. Clearly China was the market to be developed, and the country above all for Christian missionaries to concentrate upon. The problem was not to win acceptance by the millions of Chinese but to get past the arrogant Manchus and their henchmen the mandarins.

The dogs of war   1833–34

The old order was changing. A parliamentary enquiry in this year 1833 was to lead to unthought-of complications. The terms of reference of the Commons Committee prejudiced the result, the old evil of cant clouded the evidence, and ethical values were short-sightedly discarded in favour of financial expediency. But that is to see the wood from afar, whereas the Committee were caught up in the trees. They spoke of trade in general, as far as possible shutting their eyes to the part played by opium.

The East India Company sanctimoniously claimed to have no responsibility for the opium trade. All they did was to sell the Bengal opium to independent merchants and to tax the Malwa opium at source from the Mahratta States. What happened to it after that was someone else's concern not theirs, they claimed. If the burden of costs fell chiefly upon Chinese consumers, it was their own choice. The advantage to the British government was that revenue covering vast administrative costs in India was coming from foreigners, not British sources.

The trading figures of the Company at Canton, on legitimate merchandise, were falling while the independent country-merchants were flourishing. In other words, the policy of hypocrisy backed by a monopoly in favour of the Company was no longer proving successful. To the lawmakers it was time the monopoly ended and the independent merchants were allowed a free hand. As the health and survival of Chinese addicts were dependent on the supply of opium, the only humane and therefore moral attitude to that trade was to continue it. So ran the argument.

Parliament agreed and the Company's monopoly at Canton was terminated, with effect from the last day of 1833. Theoretically this move looked satisfactory; but its practical effects had not been thought through. The Company would no longer represent British traders to the Chinese authorities. Unless an appointment were made, there would be no representative at all. The British Factory would be open to the country-traders, large and small, cutthroat rivals, law-abiding and unscrupulous alike, and there would be nothing to control their conduct. It was the end of two centuries of exasperating but tolerated stability, and the beginning of an unknown future full of doleful possibilities.

With the end of the year the Factory closed. The grand life of the East India Company in Canton ceased, the Agents Committee ceased to function, the agents themselves started packing up, and on January 31, 1834, the last

Company ship left Canton. The first major development was consternation in the Chinese government. What threats did this withdrawal portend? They took a posture of aggressive defence.

It is unlikely that they read Charles Gutzlaff's monthly periodical in Chinese, begun at this time, or the anonymous article in Bridgman's *Chinese Repository* of December 1833, over the pen-name 'A British Merchant', thought to be William Jardine himself. It was inflammatory. The mind of the mandarin, he asserted, was to regard conciliation as weakness. The co-operative attitude of the Company, submitting to such indignities for so long under the factory ghetto system, had nourished the scorn and hardened the Hoppo's attitude. It was time to stand no more nonsense, in fact to avenge the excess of insults and grievances. Great Britain should appoint a commissioner equal in rank to the viceroy and seen to be backed by force of arms, to demand trading rights as equal nations, with the use of an island as a trading base, safe from intrusion.

He overlooked, as all but the few persistently did, that viceroys, Hoppo and Cohong merchants had frequently tried conciliatory approaches, only to be forced back to conventional antagonism. This was as much from fears of strictures by Peking for weakness as from failure to obtain the right response from the foreigners. From the Chinese point of view, it needed bilateral conciliation to provide a demonstration to the throne that the method would work. The trouble was that these efforts never synchronised. Wise and diplomatic officials would find themselves up against demanding merchants, and co-operative Company agents found friendly mandarins replaced by truculent ones.

Now, with the rise of the unfettered independent merchants, unparalleled pressure was beginning. One of the most obstreperous, ruthless members of the Jardine–Matheson organisation was a ship's captain and agent, James Innes. It is another indication of the strange religious climate of the nineteenth century, so hard for us to understand, unless it was calculated deception, that on his coastal opium runs James Innes used to distribute Morrison's tracts. This 'coast trade' became established soon after the two surveys in which Gutzlaff played such a leading role. He had not foreseen that the merchants would arm and use their ships not only against pirates, who abounded, but against the legitimate defences of the sovereign state of China. Sporadic hostilities began.

The Chinese government's alarm was fully justified. Canton continued to be used. In fact by 1839 there were two hundred merchants of fifty-seven companies where the East India Company and a few others they admitted to the Factory had mustered only seventy or so residents, but it was the rejection of Canton, the authorised port, in favour of the forbidden trading up the coast, which challenged the imperial government. They had no way of preventing it. If the barbarians insisted on defying the imperial edicts, the people and many coastal mandarins certainly wanted to trade. Now only months remained until the emperor would cry, ' "Havoc!" and let slip the dogs of war'.

Missions in the cross-currents   *1832–34*

In 1832 Robert Morrison was fifty and beginning to tire. For a man who was affectionate by nature, the yearly absence from home during the 'factory' season never ceased to be painful. Rebecca and John Robert were adolescent and by his second wife he had four younger children. When John Robert could not be with him he took even his seven-year-old to Canton for company, so fond of his family was he.

It was now twenty-five years since Morrison arrived in China and he wrote a review of what had been achieved. His far-reaching mind had larger and more distant goals than immediate personal evangelism, but it was a disappointment to him that in that quarter-century of hard and dangerous work only ten Chinese had been baptised at Canton and Macao, mostly by Liang A-fa, (apart from many others at the Strait Settlements). He summarised his translations and compilations, the Bible and dictionary and other books, and made much of the Anglo-Chinese College at Malacca and the Mission presses there and in Jakarta. They 'have sent forth millions of pages containing the truths of the everlasting Gospel', he wrote; and that was far from a trite cliché.[24] To him it was everything. Life and death were the odds to make that possible and the price of losing Mary and William Milne and his Rachel was worthwhile.

> Here is a world of guilty rebels and the world's God has put into the hearts of men, pardoned and saved by mercy, a proclamation of mercy and pardon to all who will accept it; and has given a solemn injunction to go and proclaim it to the ends of the earth — to every creature — to each rebel; and these pardoned rebels think it, in themselves, a charity to do so; and this proclamation had been in their possession eighteen centuries, and yet one-half of mankind has even now scarcely heard distinctly of it; so indolently and carelessly have successive generations done their duty.[25]

Morrison would never patronise the heathen. He was their debtor. He could not understand the indifference of the Church at home. Of his own Mission, the LMS, there were still only five men in East Asia: Medhurst, Kidd, Tomlin, Samuel Dyer and himself. Kidd and Tomlin were soon to be invalided home. Of the five only Medhurst would be left in ten years' time. Gutzlaff, Bridgman and Abeel were the only other missionaries in China or the Straits.

But Morrison saw all other missionaries as part of the family. National and denominational differences were incidental. The American Elijah C. Bridgman and he had found each other's company congenial and enjoyed working together. Bridgman was quick with the language and a scholarly writer in English. They were concerned about the uncaring ignorance about China not only of the young merchants who came and went but also of higher ranking agents and officers.

Morrison's son, John Robert, showed such promise as he grew up that his father had great hopes of him developing into a Sinologue and translator, to revise the Morrison and Milne Bible and carry on the good work. John Robert was as enterprising as his father. He started travelling with merchants when he was fifteen, and at sixteen became an official interpreter for the Company. By the time he was nineteen, in 1832, he was the Honourable John R. Morrison, a highly respected official. He shared his father's appreciation of the Chinese, their history and culture.

Father and son, Bridgman and a few others decided to launch a journal 'to impart information concerning China, by arousing an interest in the spiritual and social welfare of her millions'. They would all contribute articles and Elijah Bridgman would be the editor. D. W. C. Olyphant was not to be left out. It was now that he underwrote all publication costs and losses if the Chinese Repository should fail to win enough subscribers, and built an office and printing shop which served the purpose for the next twenty-four years. But success was immediate and Bridgman was still editor twenty years later. He too was impressed by the precarious weakness of their very small band of missionaries to China.

> We have great need of faith, and a great need of the intercessions of our friends, [he had written in his private journal a year before]. Three or four foreign Protestant missionaries in China—Mr Gutzlaff, on the coast bound in spirit to Peking, six or eight at the Straits, in Siam and Bankok (sic) with ourselves—constitute but a feeble band, ridiculous in the world's eyes, going to convert China.[26]

So Bridgman shaped the Chinese Repository to attract as many readers as he could, and that meant an open correspondence column in addition to what became 'a storehouse of information about China'. Men of all kinds took it and views of all kinds were aired and answered. 'A British Merchant' (cited on page 212) was an example. Translations of Chinese edicts and news provided a service otherwise unavailable. Political information and comment were welcomed. As a result merchants became interested in Chinese law, literature, customs, culture, and happenings. Instead of regarding the mandarins as dressed-up clowns, they began to distinguish their costumes and regalia. From being contemptuous ignoramuses, gradually, very slowly, the merchants came to respect and honour the Chinese. And, looking ahead, during the remaining decades of the century similar articles written in Chinese by Morrison and later missionaries informed the Chinese about the Western world and equally won their respect. Morrison's insight in anticipating a linguistic and Bible-translating society found expression again,

> A Society of Translators, or original Christian writers, is a *desideratum* for evangelising the Chinese language nations.[27]

Together Morrison and Bridgman addressed a joint letter and appeal to the Churches of the world. Outlining what had already been done, they continued,

> Some tracts written by Protestant missionaries, have reached, and been read by, the Emperor himself. Still, this is but the day of small things . . . Preachers, and teachers, and writers, and printers, in much larger numbers, are wanted, to spread the knowledge of God and our Saviour Jesus Christ among the Chinese-language nations. Oh Lord, send forth labourers . . . till China shall be completely turned from . . . false hopes—'from Satan to God'.[28]

They listed the members of 'the Chinese Mission' including the names of Liang A-fa, Qiu A-gong and Li A-xin and called

> the attention of the Churches, throughout the whole of Christendom, to the evangelisation of, at least, *four hundred millions* of fellow-creatures and fellow-sinners in eastern Asia . . .

In October 1833 a young printer came out under the American Board to join Bridgman. Samuel Wells Williams also fitted in well and in 1851 succeeded Bridgman as

editor of the *Repository*. He became one of the greatest
missionary scholars in China, the author of *The Middle
Kingdom*, for more than a generation the standard book on
China, superseding Medhurst, and in later years was called
upon to serve his country as a diplomat, while 'still a
missionary in faith and purpose'. The conditions under
which he began to study the language shed a lurid light on
the situation Morrison had endured so long. Wells Williams
entered the Factory at Canton as a trader in Olyphant's
firm and for months his Chinese teacher, risking torture
and strangling, kept a foreign lady's shoe on the table
between them, so that if any unfriendly Chinese came in
he could pose as a maker of footwear for the barbarians.[29]
Such necessities were wearing Morrison down, but in the
resilience of youth Wells Williams could say, 'The work
never looked otherwise than hopeful to me.' And this was
in spite of the fact that the Portuguese forced the closure
of the Americans' press at Macao.

For decades the East India Company's harassment of
missionaries and restrictions on their activities had aroused
protest. At last its prejudices had been shorn of influence.
A new charter ensured freedom of entry and action in
India and more societies began work there. In China the
Company's sanctions had been overshadowed by the
emperor's edicts. In fact association with merchants continued to form the only safe entrée to Canton. So now the
winding-up of the Company's affairs at Canton at the end
of 1833 hurt Morrison most deeply and at the worst possible
time. Everything seemed to be folding up and he could
find no way out of his personal difficulties. His wife's health
was failing and she would have to go home with the
younger children. His own health too gave cause for alarm.
Abdominal pain and a loss of appetite could have a serious
meaning, but he could not contemplate that. It was enough
that he felt unequal to reading or writing, his main
occupation, but he was beset with anxiety about the future.
His employment with the Honourable East India Company
was to end and in spite of twenty-four years' service they

declined to grant him a pension. For the second time he was to be cut off. He had lavished his personal income on equipment for his work for the Company and the Mission, and on the colleges at Malacca and Singapore. The LMS provided barely enough for his own needs, but he had his family to provide for and educate.

He wrote to his wife in Macao, 'Macao and Canton are a long way apart—what will England and China be?' The family sailed on December 10 and he did not live to hear of their arrival, for the journey there and the letter back took longer than eight months, all he had left—eight months as full and eventful as any in his life.

He sold his empty home in Macao and made shift for himself. Again he was 'desolate', and depressed that the LMS still seemed to have no plans for continuing his work in China. They understandably preferred the Straits. Alone he sang 'one of those penitential hymns which suit me,

> "O for a heart to praise my God,
>   A heart from sin set free;
> A heart that's sprinkled with the blood
>   So richly shed for me!" '

The Chinese viceroy was apprehensive and suspicious, and Morrison was always the link between him and the British merchants. 'What sinister motive lay behind' the winding-up of the Factory? Morrison saw serious trouble ahead and started studying Chinese law to prepare for eventualities when the always flimsy protection of the Company would be removed. He was ill. 'My head and my strength fail me' was how he put it. The gloom would not have been so deep if he had felt strong; and he would have found it easier to cast his cares upon God who had always brought him through.

He need not have worried. On the day his wife sailed Lord Napier was commissioned by William IV as Chief Superintendent of British Trade with China, a responsibility to be shared, unwisely, fatefully, with another Superintendent with experience of China. The idea was that prestige and competence should go hand in hand. In England Sir George Staunton congratulated Lord Napier on having Robert Morrison to assist him. And when Charles Marjoribanks, MP ex-chief of the Canton Factory mentioned Morrison's name in Parliament, the House broke into cheers.[30]

Death of the great   1834

The monopoly at Canton ended, but in June 1834 the charter for the East India Company to govern India was extended after prolonged debate in Parliament. The main spokesman contended in vain that the Company was unfit to govern. It was exploiting the people of India. With opium sometimes selling in Calcutta at a price ten times the production costs, the Chinese trade was scandalous. 'A mischievous and demoralising traffic which now did injury to both' nations would only lead people into trouble.[31] But where else could revenue come from? Westminster could not extricate itself, and renewed the charter. The administration in India was to go on depending on what could only cause increasing harm.

Lord Palmerston, still at the Foreign Office, chose his man to supervise commerce in the China seas and blundered crudely not only in choosing a naval officer with no personal knowledge of the Chinese but in briefing him with contradictory instructions. Of all difficult appointments this one at Canton needed the greatest sensitivity and skill. Lord Napier was told to avoid antagonising the Chinese authorities in any way but to make coastal surveys if he could, to persuade the Chinese to accept free trade, and to try to obtain direct access to the Court at Peking. All this was to be done without jeopardising existing trade and without giving offence to the Chinese by using menaces by word or show of force. Nevertheless he was to go with a naval escort. He was to be the senior representative of the Crown enforcing British law in Chinese waters, but was not to interfere with the independent merchants' 'surveys' on the China coast. The experienced second Superintendent was to advise him but he was Chief.

Napier arrived at Macao on July 16, 1834, in a frigate, and Robert Morrison found that he himself had been appointed Chinese Secretary and Interpreter to Lord Napier's mission with a salary of thirteen hundred pounds per annum, a magnificent reward.[32] As a nice gesture the British government were also to contribute a hundred pounds annually to the Anglo-Chinese College. They continued it even after Morrison's death. He was to wear the uniform of a vice-consul 'with the King's button'.

Characteristically, Robert Morrison was melted. He wrote to his wife, in England he hoped, 'Pray for me that I may be faithful to my blessed Saviour in the new place I have to occupy . . . rather an anomalous one for a missionary.' Lord and Lady Napier were friendly people and took an immediate liking to Morrison and Elijah Bridgman. Lady Napier liked to talk 'religion' and to hear Morrison preach, but Lord Napier wanted to fulfil his instructions and sailed up the estuary after only four or five days, without waiting for a welcome from the Chinese.

When word reached the viceroy that a British official had arrived at Macao in a warship the fat was in the fire, but when he came upriver and appeared at Canton announcing himself as of equal rank and expecting to be received ceremoniously, the viceroy was angry beyond words. Only merchants were permitted at the Factory, and then on sufferance. Anyone else, official or not, should await permission from Peking.

It was for Morrison to translate the formal letter announcing Lord Napier's arrival as Chief Superintendent of British Trade with China, and he did his best to word it in the usual style, the only form in which it would even be read, as a petition, '. . . it is at once his duty and earnest desire to conform in all things to the Imperial pleasure.'

After they left the frigate at The Bogue, the rest of their journey up-river was made in an open cutter in a rain storm. Both Napier and Morrison were ill as a result, and

Morrison had to force himself to work. For months, in any case, he had been unable to stand, sit, eat or sleep in comfort. He made a supreme effort though he felt exhausted. The anxiety associated with his position as intermediary exacerbated the strain.

Napier was forcing his way in at China's front door without knocking, and it was not surprising that he was rebuffed. A Superintendent of Trade must communicate through the Cohong, the Chinese merchant brokers. But as emissary of the king of England Napier would deal only with the viceroy. It was stalemate less a knight's move. The viceroy's message to Lord Napier read,

> The great ministers of the Celestial Empire are not permitted to have private intercourse by letter with outside barbarians. If the said barbarian headman throws in private letters, I, the Viceroy, will not at all receive or look at them. With regard to the barbarian Factory of the Company without the walls of the city, it is a place of temporary residence for barbarians coming to Canton to trade. They are permitted to eat, sleep, buy and sell in the Factories . . .[33]

So nothing had changed after two hundred years.

Robert Morrison developed a high fever and died in his son John Robert's arms on August 1, 1834. India's great pioneer William Carey had died on June 9. They did an autopsy and were astonished. Morrison had been unfit for work for a long, long time. His body was taken back to Macao and buried 'with all possible honour' beside his Mary, in the cemetery his Company had bought for her. He was fifty-two and had worked, mostly alone, for twenty-seven years. To A. H. Smith, familiar in 1909 with missionary careers lasting forty, fifty or more years, it was 'only twenty-seven years'. But with only a toe-hold on the shores of China Morrison had 'captured a commanding position in the very heart of the land to be possessed' and laid foundations for all future work by his Chinese Bible, dictionary, grammar, and other learned writings. Never again was there to be one solitary Protestant missionary in

China without aids to language study or a Bible to use, but when he died, after so much work, so many prayers and appeals for fellow-workers only the Americans Elijah Bridgman and Samuel Wells Williams were with him, and their wives in Macao. His son, John Robert, was one in heart and mind, but not a member of the Mission.

The loss of Robert Morrison was a severe blow to Lord Napier. 'By sheer ability he made himself indispensable!' Napier had to fall back on the advice of merchants who were not Sinologues. He by-passed the ex-Company advisors and took the advice of William Jardine and his aggressive clique.

Napier proceeded to treat the viceroy's letter as studied insult. It was certainly insulting but the Company had always carried on business in that kind of language. For nearly thirty years Morrison had given the undiluted literal translation of such documents and the British agents had read them as if reading the original Chinese and made their own considered interpretation with his advice. It was not for the translators to suggest policy. Their request or report was accepted or rejected and that was that. Now without expert advice Napier bridled. He stood on his dignity and refused to act through the Cohong.

So on August 17 all trade was suspended. A week later when a Chinese deputation was expected at the Factory to confer with him he insisted on the British way of doing things and changed the seating arrangements 'in defiance of Chinese protocol'.[34] Very correctly, by their custom, the Chinese allowed time for exigencies and arrived late. Napier rebuked them for being unpunctual. Three days later he went too far. A proclamation in his name addressed to the people of China was posted on the walls of Canton streets where the viceroy's own proclamations were customarily displayed. Predictably the viceroy denounced this 'lawless foreign slave' and blockaded the Factory.

On September 7 two frigates exchanged fire with the Bogue forts, passed them and proceeded up-stream to Huangbo. Gilbert and Sullivan could well have found inspiration from the next inept stages of the tragi-comedy. In mocking parody of the viceroy's own 'warnings' Napier wrote him a threatening letter, 'Therefore tremble, Governor Lu, intensely tremble!'[35] The viceroy was Governor-General of the Two Guangs, Guangdong and Guangxi provinces with an aggregate of twenty-nine million inhabitants. He simply blockaded the river above and below the frigates and there was nothing the dejected, humiliated envoy could do. Then Napier himself fell ill, conceded defeat and accepted the viceroy's magnanimous offer of a boat to take him down to Macao, where he died. It was claimed that 'he was driven to death by Chinese official barbarities', but the blame was certainly bilateral and the humiliation hardly of that severity.

In Britain meanwhile, a change of government had taken place. Lord Palmerston was replaced as Foreign Secretary by the Duke of Wellington in Sir Robert Peel's four-month administration. The Duke reiterated too late the pacific instructions of his predecessor, namely to avoid giving offence and to conform to Chinese requirements.

> It is not by force and violence, [the Iron Duke, victor of Waterloo declared] that His Majesty intends to establish a commercial intercouse between his subjects and China; but by the other conciliatory measures so strongly inculcated in all the instructions which you have received.[36]

But Napier was dead and the merchants on the China coast were demanding tough action. They wanted a British blockade of Chinese ports until free trade was granted, and compensation from the Chinese government for trading losses from the viceroy's, in their view, high-handed action.

Back in office again, Palmerston was unmoved. For a few more years he played the dove, but he was a man of expediency, not principle. He appointed a Captain Charles Elliot, RN as Chief Superintendent of Trade with the same instructions, emphasising that he had no authority over the merchants. A more impotent stance could hardly have been devised for a representative of the Crown and Captain Elliot's skill in adopting it went unappreciated by his distant masters.

Missions after Morrison   1833–35

Such events could not but have their effects on Christians in China. Liang A-fa was as intrepid a missionary and as tireless as any of his foreign colleagues. Armed with tracts and Scriptures printed by the LMS and American Board missionaries and paid for by the Bible Societies, he and fellow-Christians continually travelled through the hinterland of Canton, secretly selling and preaching wherever they could. He was known to the authorities and publicly denounced as a traitor in a decree of 1833 which again prohibited the printing or sale of Christian books, those 'vile and trashy publications of the outside barbarians',[37] but he managed to evade arrest. The government was suppressing Christianity wherever it was found, and drastic action was taken at intervals through the next decade. Roman Catholic martyrs deep inside China again paid the price of faithfulness. In the Straits, however, 'the thirst for Chinese books increased daily, so that they could not be printed fast enough' at Malacca and Jakarta.

In 1834 A-fa was at the American Board press at Canton one day when officials arrived and arrested him. His son, a boy of seventeen, was actually living with the Bridgmans, learning Hebrew with a view to Bible translation, but he was not taken. It transpired that A-fa's first 'convert', Zhu (Chu) A-san, was a fraud, looking only for what he could make out of attachment to the Christians. He sold A-fa, his wife and relatives to the authorities. Elijah Bridgman somehow managed to rescue A-fa and put him on a ship to Malacca. The Factory was to some extent sacrosanct against such intrusions, and a strong protest could have been effective, even though the East India Company no longer ruled supreme. American merchants were increasingly influential and the courteous attitude of Olyphant and his partner Charles W. King towards all Chinese was respected.

Sitting helpless on board ship, leaving his wife and children to unknown horrors, Liang A-fa wrote a most poignant letter to his missionary friends pleading with them to pray for his family. They escaped extreme punishment, but his Chinese travelling companion received a hundred lashes to the body, a hundred more to the face, and survived to continue his work, his spirit unbroken. The little group of Christians scattered and lay low until conditions improved.[38]

The long arm of imperial influence reached well beyond the borders of China proper, and even in South-East Asia safety varied from place to place. In 1825 a decree in Indo-China had denounced Christianity as destructive of approved customs, and forbade the entry of Christian missionaries, but with increasing pressure from France the Catholic Church was expanding and in 1833 there were many adherents. Then came a vehement reaction. All Christians, whether officials or people, were ordered to recant, to trample on the Cross and destroy church buildings. Foreign missionaries went into hiding, but executions began, and in the next seven years hundreds of Christians including the vicar-apostolic, were martyred. Both edicts closely resembled the Chinese imperial decrees.

In the Dutch East Indies (Indonesia) Christian churches were coming into being among the animistic and semi-Muslim peoples of the eastern archipelago. In the Sumatran highlands virile warring Bataks resisted even Dutch rule and in 1834 killed and ate the two missionaries of the American Board, Samuel Munson and Henry Lyman, who approached them.[39] But in Malacca all was peaceful. After Miss Newell married Charles Gutzlaff, a Miss Wallace came and supervised ten schools, eight Chinese, one Tamil and one Malay. A Tamil was baptised around the time of A-fa's arrival, and three more in the following year, 1835. Progress was slow and painful, brick upon brick. An excellent missionary, a linguist and preacher but not an administrator, was in charge. So the directors of LMS asked Samuel Dyer to go down from Penang 'to promote the efficiency of this station' with its Chinese congregations totalling two hundred and fifty Christians and its nearly thirty trained men 'now ready to go forth, as preachers of the Gospel, to their own countrymen'.

Liang A-fa had proved himself as both evangelist and pastor, and was busy preaching in Cantonese and Hokkien (the Fujian dialect of Amoy). When the Dyers arrived, bringing their printing equipment, a close friendship grew up between the two men. Samuel encouraged A-fa to write, and soon reported '[he] has written nine very good tracts'. He himself was busy with the Anglo-Chinese College, training seventy fee-paying students, but also wrote some highly-regarded documents on the technicalities of printing in Chinese, on the result of his tests of the accuracy of Robert Morrison's Bible, and on the unsuitability of that Bible for the Chinese emigrants he met in Malaya. 'He loved Dr Morrison intensely and gloried in his version, and looked upon it "*as a pledge of the conversion of China to God*" ' [But Dr Morrison's translation] ' "is *faithful* to the *letter*, — faithful in the extreme . . ." ' [so literal as to be unintelligible in places].[40] Here was a man with a great future before him if he survived where so many succumbed.

The climate was hot and humid and for refreshment they used to visit a waterfall. After one of these outings a friend described how Samuel Dyer reacted to the beauty and the peace. His heart was 'always in tune to praise God'. He 'poured forth his soul in prayer . . . in such a strain as deeply to impress us with the idea — GOD is here, and this is in truth a man of God.'[41] He was also a most tender husband and father. Maria's first baby died. 'We were scarcely aware', he wrote home, 'how we loved the little darling till she left us.' But three more children followed, to play a large part in this story until well beyond the mid-century. Samuel, named after his father, was the eldest, born on January 8, 1833, Burella arrived on the last day of

May, 1835, and Maria Jane on January 16, 1837. Then their mother's health declined and two years later they all had to go back to England, her only hope of recovery.

When Robert Morrison died, John Robert was promoted to take his place, finding time to work with Bridgman and Gutzlaff, and with Medhurst in Java, on revising Robert Morrison's Bible. They completed it in 1835. Charles Gutzlaff meanwhile had written his *Journal of Three Voyages along the coast of China* and sent appeals to the Church in Europe and America to rise to the occasion and exploit the opportunities he had demonstrated. Like Samuel Dyer, anticipating the need for movable metal type, although he was not a printer, he sent manuscript Chinese characters to Germany in 1833 to be engraved. A fount of four thousand engraved into copper plates in reverse for casting into type duly reached Serampore, only to be discarded as too uneven and imperfect for use. Medhurst, in congratulating Samuel Dyer on his growing fount wrote of the German types, 'They are as far inferior to yours, as a clown is to a courtier. Yours have been surpassed by none that I have seen as yet.'[42] German craftsmen could hardly compete with Chinese educated in the calligraphy.

Intense enthusiasm was aroused among political, commercial and religious people by the news of Gutzlaff's coastal journeys. The LMS made him grants towards his work and the Christian world took a close interest in him. Eugene Stock, General Secretary of the Church Missionary Society, in his *History* of the Mission was highly complimentary. Gutzlaff was an accomplished scholar, a qualified doctor, a man of extraordinary enterprise and resource, he wrote,

> Ascending the rivers, landing here and there at the risk of his life, pursued by pirates, harassed by the police, stoned by the mob, haled before magistrates, but giving medicine to crowds of sick folk, and distributing literally hundreds of thousands of tracts and portions of Scripture. His method was much criticised but his adventures excited unbounded

interest in England and America, and certainly gave the Christian public a new idea as to the possibilities of missionary work in China.[43]

Gutzlaff himself wrote in the *Missionary Register*,

> Are the bowels of mercy of a compassionate Saviour shut against these millions? *Before Him, China is not shut!* He, the Almighty Conqueror of Death and Hell, will open the gates of heaven for these millions, he *has* opened them.[44]

The imperial edict declaring, 'The Christian religion is the ruin of morals and of the human heart; therefore it is prohibited' was no prohibition to Gutzlaff but an invitation.

> Neither the Apostles nor the Reformers [he declared] waited until Governments were favourable to the Gospel, but went on boldly in the strength of the Lord.
> We want here no gentlemen missionaries [i.e. who desire to live as single 'gentlemen' and not risk their precious lives (*E. Stock*)] but men who are at all times ready to lay down their lives for the Saviour, and can wander about forgotten and despised without human assistance, but only the help of God.[45]

To the CMS Robert Morrison had appealed in person to send missionaries to China. At the time they were unable to respond except by making a grant of three hundred pounds towards Gutzlaff's work, but three years later they sent a former officer of the Indian navy, E. B. Squire, to make a survey. He worked in Singapore and Malacca, but his wife's health failed and he had to return home. As for Gutzlaff, he was still living on the 'fortune' he inherited from his wife, E. J. Eitel[46] stated in the *Chinese Recorder*, and all the time he was at sea or in Macao he was hard at work on his own translation of the Bible and many tracts, printed at his own expense.

The CMS wrote to Robert Morrison for his advice but before the letter reached China he had died. It came to Gutzlaff and with characteristic prescience he replied suggesting Shanghai and Hangzhou as the best places to start in. Immediately after the opium war the first CMS representative in China went to Shanghai. And the first city outside the 'treaty ports' ever to be occupied by Protestant missionaries, at first tentatively and then on a permanent footing, was Hangzhou by members of the CMS.

On the Continent the same kind of interest was aroused. A representative of the Basel Mission arrived at Macao to confer with Gutzlaff and wrote home urging that two men be sent to penetrate into the interior without waiting for concessions by the emperor. Gutzlaff was visionary but not wildly so. In 1836 a Lazarist priest named Perboyre travelled through Fujian and reported seven or eight churches open for all, even the mandarins, to see. The riddle of Manchu rule was never easily solved. There were pockets of territory where discreet foreigners might lie low and be safe. Perboyre went on up the Yangzi and was executed four years later. Gutzlaff was not suggesting that it was safe on the mainland, only that it was possible to get in to live and work there, and that some brave men were doing so already. Recognition of this fact secured one of his notable advances. To anticipate by a decade, during which much admittedly transpired, some German missionaries succeeded in following Gutzlaff's advice and establishing a bridgehead in Guangdong. Eitel called him 'the originator of all the German missions in south China', three or four in number.[47]

In 1835 Charles Gutzlaff was coming to the end of his private means and accepted appointment by Captain Elliot as an assistant interpreter and Chinese Secretary to the Commission for Trade. It meant being junior in rank to young John Robert Morrison, but allowed him enough liberty to continue his missionary work and gave him added influence. As a memorial to Robert Morrison he and John Robert and others formed a society for the promotion of Morrison's objectives, the Morrison Education Society. It supported the Anglo-Chinese College and Christian schools, and sent a student to the States, the first Chinese to graduate from a Western college, and another to Edinburgh, the first Western-trained doctor. Following the death of Charles Gutzlaff's wife he had married another English woman, and she ran a school in Hong Kong supported by this society.

On January 20, 1835, Elijah Bridgman and John Robert Morrison issued a joint appeal 'In behalf and by the direction of the Christian Union in China'. This consultative body united the twelve Protestant missionaries east of Burma. Medhurst was alone in Jakarta, there were three in Canton since Edwin Stevens arrived as chaplain to foreign sailors at Huangbo, two in Malacca, two in Singapore, and one each in Penang, the Rhio Islands, Bangkok and Macao, 'All who were to be found . . . as far east as Hakodati (*sic*)', a town in northern Japan, then almost unheard of; Japan, a country never far from the minds of the China missionaries.

> But what are these, [a dozen missionaries], among the millions of Chinese to whom the Gospel is to be preached? . . . Where are the converts, the churches and the Christian families among the Chinese? . . . Where are the thousands of Christian pastors and teachers who are needed for so great a multitude? . . . Though the prospect before us is dark, *very dark*, yet we see no reason to be discouraged; on the contrary, we find much to call forth new faith, new zeal, new efforts, new labourers, and above all more frequent and fervent prayers . . .[48]

Medhurst in the Huron[49]   1835

If it was unsafe at present for Liang A-fa and other Chinese Christians to show themselves in China, perhaps it was time for foreign missionaries to make more use of such liberty as they enjoyed. Medhurst came over to Canton concerned for the beleaguered group of Christians there, and made some discreet enquiries after their welfare. He met a stony silence. If anything it made them even more secretive. But he did meet D. W. C. Olyphant, that zealously missionary-hearted merchant, and found him a good friend. Medhurst had been asked by the directors of LMS to make a survey like Gutzlaff's, up the China coast distributing Scripture and if possible to include Japan. Four years of aggressive opium-running had passed and to sail in an opium ship 'appeared very objectionable'. The Anti-slavery Bills had awakened consciences. He chose to make no voyage rather than use a smuggler.

> The opium merchants themselves, [Medhurst wrote] though exceedingly friendly, and ready to lend every possible aid . . . yet conceive it quite out of character for missionaries to [use opium ships for spreading the gospel]. But the most serious objection is that the Chinese bring it as the main argument against Christianity, that its professors send opium . . . Now the time is not far distant, when the opium trade . . . like the traffic in slaves, will be denounced by every friend to religion and morality . . . The individual who has ever kept aloof from such associations, can go to the full extent, which conscience urges, in condemning the trade.

But what other ships were there? Medhurst wished there were a mission ship, as in the South Pacific, with a doctor on board. When persecuted out of one place they could then sail off to another, interminably. The LMS had been at work in the South Pacific since 1796 and their most notable pioneer, John Williams, later to be martyred, was at the time in England raising funds for a new inter-island ship. Olyphant had another idea. His brig the *Huron* was at anchor waiting for a cargo that was delayed. He would fit it out for a voyage of a few months up the coast and cover the cost of a consignment of Scriptures and tracts for them to distribute. Edwin Stevens, the seamen's chaplain, was game for an adventure during the slack summer season, so off they went. The undergraduate Charles Darwin was sailing at this time in HMS *Beagle* for South America.

The captain had never been along the coast before; the *Huron* was a trans-Pacific merchantman, and they could find few charts of any use to them. Medhurst had learned

Mandarin from a Shandong man so they headed for Weihaiwei. The mandarins were hostile at first but relented and for two days they toured the villages and distributed a thousand books of a hundred pages each, all most warmly welcomed. At Ninghai, further along the coast, an old general told them that imperial orders were to receive foreigners courteously but to send them on their way without allowing them to propagate their opinions. People remembered receiving tracts from earlier travellers and one mandarin knew the name of Charles Gutzlaff and other members of the *Lord Amherst* expedition. Attempts were made to restrict them to the beaches but they pushed through the crowds to meet as many people in the towns as possible.

From Shandong they sailed south again and arrived off Wusong on October 6 in a fog. When it cleared the naval authorities fired blanks in their cannon to scare them away, but they rowed up the Huangpu in a long boat to Shanghai and were delighted by a smiling reception and cries of '*Kih-lae*' — visitors have come! Local officials served them with tea and cakes, but the Chief Magistrate was unfriendly. He commanded them to stand in his presence. They declined. To submit would be to suffer indignity after indignity. 'You are the Chief Magistrate and I am the chief Englishman in Shanghai,' Medhurst explained courteously. 'I sit as Lindsay and Gutzlaff did.'

Somehow he carried it off, but out in the courtyard a basket of their books was burned in their presence. Back at Wusong they found placards threatening anyone who traded with them. Twenty-five war junks fired blanks at them, but an officer was received aboard ship and his soldiers accepted tracts. Such a mixed reception was again open to the interpretation that the official Peking stance did not reflect the people's attitude.

At the mouth of the great Hangzhou Bay they were met by six war junks, but the commanders were very civil and when they went ashore on the islands of the Chusan group people came asking and even fighting each other for tracts and Scripture. In one village they discovered that every shopkeeper had a tract preserved from Gutzlaff's visits.[50] Officials spoke highly of Lindsay too and expressed the opinion that it would be better if free trade were allowed.

Then the *Huron* sailed down the Fujian coast and Medhurst went ashore. He had learned the Fujian dialect from a Chinese in Java. When he started to speak, to his amazement he, like Gutzlaff, was welcomed as a local citizen. Not only was he speaking the language of the province and county and district, but of the actual place. People were dancing with delight and coming close for a good look at them. Even the women came up and asked for tracts.

When they arrived back at Canton they had disposed of eighteen thousand volumes including six thousand of Scriptures. It transpired that Charles Gutzlaff had visited the same part of the coast and travelled thirty miles inland, to Changpu city itself. But they also found that Peking knew about their landings and a dispatch to Canton expressed the emperor's high displeasure. The governor was to prevent any repetition of this sort of adventure by 'violent and crafty barbarians'.

An imperial edict announced the discovery of barbarian books distributed along the coast and attributed to Canton. So a search of the 'factories' was mounted and for a while there was panic with all the secret printers' and teachers' lives in jeopardy. All incriminating material was successfully hidden, however, — it had to be whenever not actually in use — and only books printed in Malacca were discovered.[51] This exonerated the officials from failure to find the source, and when their boat was wrecked between Canton and Macao they dropped the whole matter. In fact, Liang A-fa managed to make a brief, surreptitious visit to his home to see his wife and children again. Once more, the people of China had been proved to be open both to foreigners and to the gospel. The mandarins, on the contrary, answerable to the throne, were justifiably afraid.

As for finding openings for settled missionary work, 'the whole coast had to be left for the opium pedlar and the smuggler', as Wells Williams put it.

Peter Parker in the Morrison[52]   1834–37

Not long after Robert Morrison died, an American surgeon arrived at Canton and went on to Singapore to learn Chinese in peace. Peter Parker is better known than many who deserve as great a reputation. It has been said that he 'opened China at the point of the scalpel'. East India Company doctors had done some medical work at Canton, and Morrison's dispensary at Macao was not the only one in existence. Both Morrison and Gutzlaff did medical work among the Chinese as a side-line. And a Company doctor taught the principles of vaccination to Chinese practitioners. But when Peter Parker opened his ophthalmic hospital at Canton he quickly disarmed suspicion and was given free accommodation by one of the leading members of the Cohong. It was he who allayed the strong prejudice against missionaries. Like Samuel Wells Williams he too in the course of time was called upon to serve as his nation's ambassador to China.

Seeing how valuable his medical work was proving, a number of influential men clubbed together in 1838 to form the Medical Missionary Society of China to support Parker's hospital and a new one in Macao.[53] William Jardine, the surgeon, was one of its vice-presidents. And when another soon-to-be-famous surgeon, William Lockhart of the LMS arrived, he took over the Macao hospital. Springing directly from Parker's appeals to Britain and America, an associated society came into being in Scotland, the Edinburgh Medical Missionary Society.

At a time when James Innes was provoking the authorities by his audacity, and incidentally the week that Queen Victoria came to the throne, Secretary Gutzlaff sailed in a naval ship, HMS *Raleigh*, on a visit to Fuzhou and the Loochoo Islands. It was two years since the voyage of the

Huron, and Olyphant had a new venture in hand. Wells Williams wrote forty years later that few people could realise what a discouraging prospect 'the Ultra-Gangetic nations presented'. 'Excepting the islands of Singapore and Pinang (*sic*), the Indian Archipelago was mostly under the control or awe of the Dutch and Spanish colonial authorities.' The Spanish prohibited Protestant missionaries from living in their territories, the Philippine Islands, and continued to ban them until two years from the end of the century, 1898, when they themselves were driven out. 'The Dutch were almost as strict and repellent', insisting on a probationary year in Jakarta (Batavia) before allowing any missionary farther afield in Java or Borneo, and nowhere else. Bangkok was the only truly open city. Elsewhere only 'a kind of underground work' was possible, 'in hope of a brighter day'. Clearly some exploration was needed to find more scope, and here it was that Olyphant rose to the occasion yet again by providing two ships.

A two-volume book describes the two-pronged venture, entitled *The Claims of Japan and Malaysia upon Christendom, exhibited in Notes of Voyages made in 1837 from Canton in the Ship* Morrison *and Brig* Himmaleh, *under the direction of the Owners*.[54] Dr Peter Parker also wrote an account of the voyage of the *Morrison*, and Samuel Wells Williams contributed an article to the *Chinese Repository* in 1837. Parker's title is another museum piece, *Journal of an Expedition from Sincapore* (sic) *to Japan with a Visit to Loo-choo, description of these islands and their inhabitants, in an attempt with the aid of natives educated in England, to create an opening for missionary labours in Japan*.[55]

Olyphant and his partners purchased and fitted out the brig *Himmaleh* at a cost of twenty thousand dollars to cruise through the China seas looking for trade and missionary prospects. He expected Gutzlaff to join her, but Captain Elliot refused to release him for the voyage. The harassed Chief Superintendent of Trade could not be blamed. Attempts to persuade Gutzlaff to resign from office failed. Zealous as a missionary, he was also a loyal man of principle, highly respected and trusted. So Chaplain Edwin Stevens and George Tradescant Lay, newly-arrived agent of the British & Foreign Bible Society, went instead. Like the sultanates of Brunei and Celebes there were still some territories retaining a shadow of independence. In fact in 1840 the adventurer James Brooke (1803–68) found himself made Raja of Sarawak by the sultan of Brunei for quelling a rebellion which threatened the sultan's rule.

The policy for the voyage of the *Himmaleh*, apart from trading, was deliberately to invite local rulers to admit missionaries to live and preach and do medical work. However, Stevens died within a month of their leaving Macao, and the two missionaries who took his place at Singapore could speak neither Chinese nor Malay. One of them was also to die that year. The captain of the *Himmaleh* was unsympathetic and would go only to Dutch and Spanish ports. So the voyage was a failure.

The voyage of the *Morrison* was no more successful in achieving its objective, but was more eventful. In Macao at the time there were seven shipwrecked Japanese sailors.[56] Three were survivors of a junk with a crew of fourteen who had been driven far into the Pacific by a gale in 1830 and after more than a year went aground off Queen Charlotte's Island, five hundred miles north of Vancouver. Eleven of the crew died of scurvy and the survivors were rescued from Red Indians by men of the Hudson Bay Fur Company and taken to England. Eventually, seven years after leaving home, they reached Macao, the last port before Japan. Four others were wrecked on Samar Island in the Philippines and were deported from Manila.

Charles W. King hoped that the charitable act of bringing these seven men home would create a favourable impression in Japan. He knew Japan was sealed against intruders of any kind and that any approach was dangerous, so he planned on handing over the seven to the emperor himself at the capital, hoping that 'if some Cyrus now sat on the throne of Japan, all would be well'. Perhaps to prove the purely peaceful nature˙of the visit, he decided to go himself, together with his wife and her maid. The *Morrison*'s anti-piracy armament was put ashore, and instead of going to Nagasaki, where the Dutch alone were allowed to touch briefly, he went first to Napa harbour. With him he had Dr Peter Parker and Samuel Wells Williams.

Gutzlaff was not to be left out of such a venture. As soon as his work at Fuzhou and the Loochoo Islands (Okinawa) was done he transferred from HMS *Raleigh* to a sloop and joined the *Morrison* at Napa. The Japanese attempted to prevent them from landing and failed, but succeeded in restricting them to the beach. It was an eerie experience. All the time they were surrounded by hundreds of people who for reasons unknown never raised their voices above a whisper. The *Morrison* then went on to the Gulf of Yedo, Tokyo Bay, and had a very different reception. They were fired on by the Japanese and took a direct hit among many shots falling all around. Only retreat remained open to them. In the Bay of Kagoshima they failed again. Giving up hope of a better reception they tried to land the seven Japanese exiles, but they too were refused admission. They were guilty of bringing the alien ship to Japan.

At the end of August 1837 the expedition returned to Macao, fifty-six days after setting out. Not one of the exiles ever set foot on his native land again. Two stayed with Gutzlaff until his death in 1851, two worked in Wells Williams's printing office in Macao, all four helped to teach Japanese and translate Scripture, and five met daily in Wells Williams's house to pray. They were the first-fruits of prayer for a Japanese Protestant Church. Their story and the report of the *Morrison* venture stirred up the Church in Britain and the States to pray for Japan.

'China Opened' — *but not yet*   *1837–38*

While the members of the expedition began writing up their experiences, Gutzlaff's eyes were still on China and his valued if controversial book *China Opened* appeared in print. The historian H. B. Morse commended it. But China was far from open; it turned out to be a prophetic rather than a visionary essay, however, for within three years there were five ports on the mainland officially open to residents, and a 'general post' was taking place, bringing most of the missionary team at last from the Straits and Jakarta to China proper. At the time no one had an inkling of what those three years were to reveal. If Gutzlaff's title was premature, this period saw the fruit of the pioneers' appeals. A flow of new missionaries into East Asia began and increased year by year. The Stronach brothers had already reached the Straits. Two American Baptists arrived at Macao, J. Lewis Shuck, who became a translator of the Delegates' Bible, the successor to Morrison and Milne's pioneer work, and Issachar J. Roberts, the eccentric, who was to spur the Chinese Evangelization Society into sending Hudson Taylor to China without waiting to qualify as a doctor. A surgeon, William Boone, arrived, who later became the first bishop of the American Protestant Episcopal Church in China; and a United States senator, Walter Lowrie, resigned from the senate to become the first great secretary of the new American Presbyterian Board of Foreign Missions, and to give two of his sons to service in China. Another was Mary Ann Aldersley, who at this time went to Java to study Chinese and start work independently but under Walter Medhurst's guidance. Because mainland China was not open these reinforcements went where freedom and early success assured a welcome.

At Malacca twenty more Chinese believers and another Siamese were baptised in April 1838, and ten more Chinese in May. Every new Christian was a potential missionary to his own people, another stone in the building that would one day be the Church of Jesus Christ in China. Samuel Dyer was seeing progress in the Malacca Church, but also in his strategic hobby. The cutting of his steel punches began. Each a work of art, he could see them in two completed founts, years ahead, printing in their thousands the kind of book every Chinese would delight to own.

This was not the only great potential. It was also a time of great progress in modern technology. The first steamships were crossing the Atlantic (1833–37), the first telegraph message in Britain was sent from Euston to Camden Town (1837), and the London to Birmingham railway was opened (1838). Significant in themselves, these advances were before long to affect East Asia and the missionary scene. Steamships, independent of wind, calms and currents, came to dominate the coastal trade of China and make the hazardous journey from Europe tolerable or even enjoyable. International telegraphy followed late in the century. The absurd situation whereby the Queen's representatives waited almost a year for instructions in response to a vital report from China, a year in which alarming changes often took place, was only slowly resolved. In 1838 China was still on the other side of the moon. Yet to Gutzlaff's faith China was in one sense open already. After all, he himself could go ashore and mingle with the friendly people. His claim was not entirely overstated.

Vicious spiral   *1838–39*

Captain Charles Elliot, now Chief Superintendent of Trade, was one of the unfortunates of history, in two senses. He had the misfortune to be in the hot seat of a situation without precedent, and to be a gentleman, a courteous man, considerate of others, forced to deal with unscrupulous merchants and intransigent mandarins at a time of mutual antipathy. The traders were more and more irresponsible and aggressive, and the Chinese more than ever determined to resist them. Competition between the coastal traders was becoming more bitter too. Undercutting, scheming with corrupt mandarins and even armed clashes were increasing. Jardine's new country-ships, such as the Calcutta-built *Red Rover*, patterned on privateers, were such a success that a fleet of these fast 'opium clippers', forerunners of the famous tea-clippers from

English shipyards, was on the drawing board. Teak-built 8 in Asian yards they lasted a century. And a score of them replaced the two or three smugglers of earlier years. Jardine and Matheson were soon making a profit of a 9 thousand dollars on every chest of opium delivered by their armed greyhounds of the sea.[57]

Although or because James Matheson published a trea-
tise in 1836 on *British Trade and China*, the people and government of Britain were ignorant of the facts. Even his 11 tables of trade statistics omitted to mention opium except by euphemisms. Britain had the merchandise. China needed, he wrote, but China's mandarins were so imbecile, 12 avaricious and obstinate that while they permitted trade through one port they refused to open others. They should be forced to agree.[58] In the *Chinese Repository* someone 13 submitted three long-term objectives to be kept in view and worked for perseveringly; foreign ministers plenipotentiary should reside in Peking itself; all ports of the 14 empire should be open to foreign ships, as in the reign of Kang Xi; and consuls should be stationed at several 15 principal ports to watch over foreign interests.[59]

The missionaries themselves were not silent. In the *Repository* 'a Resident in China', indicted the opium 16 smugglers for throwing discredit on the character of foreigners and suspicion on all dealings with the Chinese. 17 George Tradescant Lay was outspoken from the start. After three years he found so little scope for the Bible Society beyond what others were doing, that he followed 18 Gutzlaff's example, hoping to be of more use in government employment. He did not mince matters. Opium 'as merchandise blasts and withers every kind of dealing that is mixed up with it,' he declared.[60]

Walter Medhurst calculated that on a surmised average dose of one tenth of an ounce of opium each day, there were three million addicts in China.

> In proportion as the wretched victim comes under the power
> of the infatuating drug, so is his ability to resist temptation

less strong; and debilitated in body as well as in mind he is unable to earn his usual pittance . . . Shut out from his own dwellings, either by angry relatives or ruthless creditors, they die in the streets, unpitied and despised . . .

Gutzlaff wrote on the vast protection racket which grew up, involving a 'murderous and unscrupulous' horde of informers.[61] The officials were as bad. On the pretext of searching for opium, a whole gamut of evils stemmed from the drug traffic — arrest, extortion, robbery, confiscation, blackmail.

The viceroy of Canton was clamping down on all opium-dealing in the estuary but some merchants attempted to defy him. Fights took place, ships were burned and legitimate trade was threatened. Still they forced their way past the Bogue ports and right up to Huangbo 'almost under the walls of the Governor's palace at Canton'. Chinese collaborators were imprisoned and executed but others took their place. The patience of the authorities is highlighted by their restraint in the face of such insults, but there was a limit. When the obstreperous James Innes in 1838 unloaded opium at the factory wharf, such blatant provocation could no longer be tolerated.

The Cohong merchants pleaded with Elliot to stop the dumping of opium, for they were caught between the upper and nether millstones and being crushed without mercy. Elliot had appealed to Palmerston the previous year for authority to control the merchants. When he took over after Lord Napier died, with instructions to adhere to the dead man's briefing, what he read was Palmerston's strait-jacket directive: 'You must never lose sight of the fact that you have no authority to interfere with or to prevent them',[62] the country-merchants and their escapades. He had explained the situation only to receive a snub in reply.

Now the viceroy took strong action. He tortured the Chinese dockers and suspended all trade until he had James Innes's name, and ordered him and his ship out of Canton waters. A Chinese opium dealer was led on to the

Factory recreation ground in front of the American premises, as it happened, and preparations were made to execute him before a gawping crowd. This would show the merchants how determined China was to stop the traffic. To the surprise of the Chinese, the American consul lowered the flag on his flagstaff and ordered the execution party away. British sailors joined in, seized the executioner's weapons and laid about them, breaking up the show. The mob of spectators then attacked the 'factories' with stones.

Captain Elliot came up from Macao and calling the merchants together threatened strong action. The British government had declared that he should not resist the Chinese if they used force. He ordered the merchants to remove every smuggling vessel from the Canton river or he would tell the viceroy what his instructions were. They complied. On January 1, 1839, the viceroy removed his ban on legitimate trading, but it was too late. The emperor had had enough. On New Year's Eve he appointed a commissioner superior in authority to the viceroy, to end once and for all the importing, growing and smoking of opium in China. Between 1830 and 1835 imports of opium had risen abruptly from ten thousand to twenty-five thousand chests per annum; and during the next five years while China did all in her power to arrest the tide, it rose to thirty thousand.

The very pace of increase drove the emperor to all lengths to stop the traffic, but if it was difficult to stem the flood at source in India, it was impossible to dam the torrent reaching China. He could only discover this by trying; and the only reason why he failed was that the British were determined that he should. The governor of Canton took the trouble to inform all trading companies individually of the impending arrival of the commissioner with the express intention of exterminating the trade, so that they might remove their ships. His warning was disregarded. On January 2, 1839, Elliot appealed yet again to the British government for powers equal to the position he found himself in. But no reply could arrive until months later.

Commissioner Lin 1839

Appalled by the rate of deterioration of the morals of his increasingly addicted people, of the coastal security of the nation and of the economy being drained of its bullion to pay for opium, the Dao Guang emperor invited memorials on the problem from his subjects. The loss of ten million taels (the Chinese silver ounce) in 1836 had grown to sixty million taels in 1837 and even copper currency had depreciated in value by over fifty per cent. Copper coins were being used as ballast in ships unable to find merchandise.

The proposals which won the imperial favour after nearly a score of personal interviews with the dragon throne, came from the viceroy of the provinces of Hunan and Hubei, and he was appointed to implement them. Commissioner Lin Ze-xu (Tse-hsü) was the emperor's main hope for the future. He was a large, bearded, vigorous man of fifty-four with a strong personality and forbidding appearance but gentle manner. His policy was to dispense sweet reasonableness to the co-operative and stern retribution to the recalcitrant. It had succeeded to a large extent in these two provinces.

He hit the nail on the head in 'a noble letter' to Queen Victoria which never reached her.[63] It is easy to imagine the very young Queen's advisors sparing her from what they in their prejudice saw as a troublesome piece of nonsense. He was sure, he wrote, that this poisonous opium was not produced with her approval but by certain devilish persons in places under her rule; and he went on (in Arthur Waley's translation),

> So long as you do not take it yourselves but continue to make it and expect the people of China to buy it, you [are] careful of your own lives but careless of other people, indifferent in your greed for gain to the harm you do to

others. Such conduct is repugnant to human feeling and at variance with the Way of Heaven.[64]

Lin asked his own four hundred million compatriots to co-operate with him and to help each other to break their addiction. Students were organised in groups of five to discipline and help one another, and corrupt government employees were promised what they deserved. For the foreigners at Canton a practical demonstration was judged to be more eloquent than words and on February 26, 1839, the newly arrived LMS surgeon William Lockhart saw a Chinese opium-dealer strangled in front of the Factory. This time an armed guard was present as a precaution. Commissioner Lin arrived on March 10 and declared that the 'receiving ships' or opium depots at Lingding Island and Huangbo were an illegal presence, as everyone knew, and must be withdrawn. No one moved. On March 18 he appealed through the Cohong to the good faith of the merchants and asked them to hand over all opium in their possession and to sign an undertaking never to trade in the drug again. The alternative was the end of all trade of any kind. China was self-sufficient.

The minds of the merchants worked in the way they always did. They failed to see that a new phenomenon had arisen, that the 'reign of sham' was over, that this time the emperor and his commissioner meant business. Jardine was on his way to Britain with as calculated a scheme as had yet been resorted to in forcing the issue. Launcelot Dent, his high-living rival, saw only a manoeuvre to wring more personal profit out of the opium racket and advised playing for time.

Lin was irate at being told to wait a week for their decision. He closed the Custom house and issued an ultimatum. All opium must be surrendered at once or Chinese brokers would be executed. But Sunday, March 24, might be observed as usual. He would not interfere with the foreigners' religion. He did not know that Morrison had been driven to desperation and anger over the hypocrisy of a few who went through the motions of attending his services and that the rest could not care less. Sincere Christians in the Factory were fewer than ten.

Captain Elliot came up from Macao in a hurry and hoisted his ensign on the Factory flagstaff. Lin acted at once, blockading the Factory by land and water. Now it became clear that Lin meant business. The Queen's representatives and powerful merchants were virtually imprisoned. But the commissioner did not know the temper of the British lion when cornered. While Lin threatened death to foreigners involved in opium trading and the end of all trade, Elliot still had no authority over the merchants, only the status of trading representative of the Crown. In this capacity, however, he was the senior British official, expected to take the lead. He could not order the merchants to comply with Lin's demands, but nor could he encourage them to resist, and be held responsible for bloodshed. Lord Palmerston had plainly laid it down that anyone who incurred losses through violating Chinese law would look in vain to the British government for compensation, and to the end he was to stand by his word. But Captain Elliot saw British lives and property threatened by 'unprovoked aggression', and the dignity of the British Crown challenged.

He was in a cleft stick and had to make a decision. His patience with the Chinese had already given out and a dispatch from him to London was on its way calling for the means to teach them a lesson. So when on March 27 he promised compensation to the merchants and secured the surrender of 20,283 chests of opium, seven thousand of them Jardine and Matheson's, it was not in support of the emperor's anti-opium drive. As for the merchants, a grossly undeserved bonus had come their way. There was no sale for this opium in China under Commissioner Lin's restrictions and no other market for it anywhere. They jumped at Elliot's promise.

The measure of Commissioner Lin's very short-term triumph, of the guilty merchants' scoop and of poor Elliot's

major gaffe was over 1,260 tons-net of Indian opium valued
then at two million pounds. This was on average five
months' supply for three million Chinese addicts. It took
Lin and his men six weeks to destroy it. Some they burned
and some they adulterated with lime and salt and dumped
in the estuary—after sacrificial apologies to the sea-spirits
for polluting their water.

Lin was elated. He invited Elijah Bridgman and Charles
King, of Olyphants, to watch the destruction with him at
Chuanbi, near the mouth of The Bogue—Chuanbi, 'the
Nostril', so named from a perforated rock visible to
shipping, where more history was soon to be made. He was
'bland and vivacious', they recorded; and he reported to
the emperor that they were attentive and respectful to him.
When the emperor received the report he was pleased and
promoted Lin to be Viceroy of Zhili (Chihli), the highest
viceregal honour—as soon, that is, as the opium traffic and
traffickers were finally banished from China's shores. Lin
lifted the blockade on the Factory, announced that legitimate trading was re-opened, and thought all was set fair.
He had misjudged the British temper.

Kowloon affray and Chuanbi skirmish   1839

It could scarcely have happened otherwise. The lion's tail
had been tweaked. Elliot lost no time when the blockade
was lifted. He asserted his personal authority and ordered
all British ships and personnel out of Canton waters to the
protection of a single frigate, all he had, in the Hong Kong
Island anchorage. At that time there were a few small
fishing and pirate villages on the largely barren island and
opposite on the Kowloon shore. Elliot was not going to be
caught again with British hostages forcing his hand or
angry sailors precipitating trouble at Canton. By May 24
no British remained at Canton. The withdrawal was not
without difficulty, however. The Commissioner probably
suspected Elliot's motives. He harried the ships from
anchorage to anchorage and issued proclamations prohibit-

ing the supply of food or water. Loyal Chinese were to resist all landings to provision the ships. On June 5 Captain Elliot placed an embargo on all British trade with China.

At this point one of the quirks of international relations occurred. Although American merchants had surrendered one thousand five hundred chests of opium, they saw Olyphant and Company, who never touched it, benefiting by taking over the abandoned British trade, so they gave an undertaking not to handle opium again. Then they discovered that by ferrying Chinese merchandise to British ships at Hong Kong and carrying British merchandise back, both parties profited. Elliot's prophecy to Lord Palmerston had come true, the Americans had taken over Britain's legitimate trade because of British violations of Chinese law. Britain must protect her interests by controlling her unruly subjects.

Elliot then went further. When he handed over the opium to Commissioner Lin he also pledged on his own authority that British merchants would stop trafficking in opium. It was no more than a pious hope. His problem then was to enforce the pledge. Still no authorisation had come from England, but he issued an order banning ships with opium from the Hong Kong anchorage, in Chinese territorial waters, and denying them any protection by British naval vessels. The merchants laughed. Their opium clippers needed no protection. They could outpace and outmanoeuvre any war junk, and bypass the anchorage. The *Chinese Repository* reported that British smugglers were landing opium under arms on the Chinese coast. It was being held in temples, tombs and private homes, and the smugglers were buying the co-operation of informers for more than the mandarin paid them.

With news of events in Canton reaching Singapore, opium from India was being offloaded there. James Matheson was alert as ever. He shipped twenty chests back from Hong Kong to Singapore and put them up for sale. As he anticipated, the market slumped. Working with secrecy through local brokers he then bought his own and seven hundred more chests at a knock-down price, and shipped them to China. Prices on the black market there had risen to new heights, so what Matheson bought for $250 a chest he sold to Chinese smugglers for $1,500 and even $2,500. There was no getting even with these men.

Both nations were well on the slippery slope from which there was no climbing back, but so far neither could see it. To understand the seriousness of the situation, however, events in Britain must be noted first. William Jardine reached the United Kingdom in September and plunged into his mission. He had had it all worked out before he left Canton and was surf-riding to success. The merchants contributed twenty thousand dollars for him to 'secure the services of some leading newspaper', legal advice and writers.[65] Soon petitions were flowing in to Westminster from ports and industrial centres connected with the China trade. They demanded compensation for losses sustained, and compulsion to put trade on a secure footing.

A skilful writer named Warren with legal training defended the merchants as nineteenth-century Elizabethans extending the honour of the nation in the face of attack by foreigners. Justifiably he claimed that they carried on their opium trade on behalf of the government. All the responsibility rested on the government for its policy in exporting opium to provide revenue for India. Could 'our most eminent British merchants' be called smugglers? 'men whose names would command respect and confidence' anywhere in the world 'where commercial enterprise, honour and good faith are known? . . . in the name of the dear glory and honour of old England . . . why are not thousands of bayonets bristling at this moment on the shores of China?'[66] Warren was in the vanguard of Victorian jingoists.

Jardine's business activities on the China coast were one thing. In private life he was the image of an impeccable English gentleman, friendly, charitable, the model of rectitude. He called on Lord Palmerston, still at the Foreign Office, with a glowing introduction from Elliot. It spoke of the esteem in which he was held, 'honourably acquired by a long career of private charity and public spirit.'[67] True enough, he could afford it. He quickly ingratiated himself with Palmerston and was consulted at length about the East Asian situation.

Captain Elliot's dispatches were the work of an indignant man. They denounced the opium trade, pleaded for action to curb the merchants, and reiterated the necessity of authority if he was to carry out the government's commission. The traffic

> in its general effect ... is intensely mischievous to every branch of trade, and rapidly staining the British character with deep disgrace ... No man entertains a deeper detestation of the disgrace and sin of this forced traffic on the coast of China, [he wrote in November]. I see little to choose between it and piracy.[68]

He warned Palmerston that desperados would seize control.

> With this long line of unprotected coast abounding in safe anchorages, and covered with defenceless cities, I foresee a state of things terrible to reflect on.[69]

But Elliot did not foresee that British ships and soldiers would perpetrate those terrible things when he requested a force to impress the Chinese, to restore balance, to impose order on the merchants, and to support his attempts to persuade the emperor to open other ports to foreign trade. He wanted 'to teach the Chinese a lesson', but in a gentlemanly way.

Lord Palmerston had to choose between disowning his representative and the British merchants, or using force. The merchants of Calcutta appealed to the Privy Council for protection of the trade on which all the commerce of India depended and indeed of United Kingdom trade with Asia. What would happen to shareholders' dividends and taxpayers' wealth? Lose the opium revenue and what could be done to support the economy and administration? Palmerston knew it all by heart, but as Florence Nightingale was later to say of him, 'He was a humbug and he knew it.'[70] With his Chief Superintendent at Canton hobbled by his own restraints, he already had an expeditionary force in mind, and needed little persuasion by William Jardine. The confiscated opium was 'merchandise', not contraband, and the merchants were 'suffering parties'.[71] Commissioner Lin's action was unprovoked aggression, this was the argument, and China must pay full compensation. British lives and property were in danger! Elliot's pledge could be disregarded. China must apologise or pay for the insults to Britain's representative and flag, and in a solemn treaty guarantee security for her subjects. A threat to Peking by blockading the Beihe, the Tianjin river, and the occupation of one of the Chusan islands, Jardine's choice, with permanent possession in view, would be enough to make China see reason. The emperor would have to open Amoy, Fuzhou, Ningbo and Shanghai to trade, as well as Canton. Two men of war, two frigates and two shallow-draft river-steamers, with seven thousand soldiers in troop ships would be ample.

The strong merchants' lobby in London was not un-opposed. Wilberforce's success with the Anti-Slavery Bill encouraged an anti-opium campaign to mobilise public opinion against the trade. A 'small but vociferous group of pamphleteers' were taking no nonsense from Jardine and his hirelings — or from Lord Palmerston. With merciless accuracy they wrote,

> If Mr Warren's clients, though eminent British merchants, will stoop for profit to do what they are afraid to be detected in, they can be eminent only for their wealth.[72]

The Secretary of the Trinitarian Bible Society published the *Iniquities of the Opium Trade with China*. It was murder and all who shelter the murderer or 'stand by unconcerned when murder is committed' are accomplices in crime. An Assam tea plantation superintendent deplored the demor-alising effect of opium on his labourers. To obtain the drug 'he will steal, sell his property, his children, the mother of his children; and finally even commit murder'.[73]

At the Hong Kong anchorage the British crews were itching for revenge against Commissioner Lin. It only took the Queen's Birthday and celebrations on board to precipitate fresh trouble. On July 7, 1839, a ship's captain, no doubt the worse for liquor, fired on a Chinese junk, and drunken sailors from two ships landed on the Kowloon shore and stoned a temple. A fracas developed and soon a Chinese lay dead.

Up to this point Commissioner Lin had used no actual violence, only extreme pressure. This incident changed his tune. He demanded the surrender of the guilty sailor for execution by strangling according to Chinese law, and ordered that if landing parties came ashore for water the wells must be poisoned. A force of war junks gathered to impose the new blockade, but Elliot attacked and routed them. Now it was Elliot's turn to be execrated. If the British wished to resume trade, they must first hand over Elliot's head. He was the source of all this trouble and ringleader in provocation.

Elliot sent his only frigate to India for help and was left with nothing but the armaments of the merchant ships. On August 25 the British who had taken refuge in Macao were expelled by the Portuguese. Only the ships remained to them. Then in September help arrived in the form of one naval vessel, followed at the end of October by another. In all of these negotiations John Robert Morrison and Charles Gutzlaff were Elliot's interpreters. Later they were joined by George Tradescant Lay and through the events of the next three years played a major role as negotiators.

The escalation of hostilities could still have been prevented but on neither side was anyone in the mood for conciliation. The British warships sailed up the Canton estuary and on November 3 off Chuanbi met twenty-nine war junks. Lin was determined to take the Kowloon murderer; but he was a landsman. There was carnage. The greatly superior fire-power of the two British ships scattered and destroyed the junks. Without question this meant war. British observers deprecated the bloodshed, but Commissioner Lin reported to Peking that he had won three victories. Arthur Waley's study of Chinese history books revealed that someone doubled the number to 'six smashing blows'.[74] On November 26 British trade with China was prohibited, 'for ever'.

CHAPTER SIX

UNEQUAL WAR
1840–47

Commerce, cant and the 'ketou'   *1840*

The indecisive scuffles at Kowloon and Chuanbi were the prelude to war. The first campaign was more Gilbertian tragi-comedy. Only in the second campaign did Lion and Dragon really come to grips. But the whole of 1840 and first half of 1841 saw action.

Palmerston's expeditionary force sailed in September and was therefore at its destination when news of the battle at Chuanbi reached England in March 1840. It precipitated a debate in Parliament and the country, during which many home truths were exposed and the public became aware of Britain's involvement. The battle helped the government to justify Palmerston's decision to despatch the expeditionary force, but criticism came from all sides. Sir George Staunton, veteran of the East India Company and of Canton since he was a boy, supported the merchants. Their argument was just, he maintained. Even the country-merchants were the government's servants and should be compensated for their losses. Jardine's commissioned pamphlets followed one upon another. A Quaker named William Storrs Fry answered him in others, asking what Britain would do if French wines were forced by armed smugglers ón to the British Isles, with depot ships, bribed officials and French warships to sink our customs vessels. Unfortunately Fry's humanitarian argument cut little ice. It needed cold commercial facts to defeat the opium trade.

Only when the nation became convinced that contraband traffic killed sound trade and deflected Chinese consumers from British manufactures would opinion turn against it.

The government were on very weak ground and helplessly vulnerable when the contradictory instructions given to Lord Napier and Captain Elliot were exposed. The argument in Parliament which carried most weight was frankly that while morality, religion and the happiness of mankind were all very fine in their way, Britain could not afford to bestow them at the cost of £1,200,000 per annum from inland revenue. So Macaulay, for the government, inflated the insults to the Crown and the imprisonment of British subjects in the Canton blockade into their *casus belli*. The Black Hole of Calcutta was avenged by the battle of Plassey, they pleaded. Subsequent speakers urged that the insults of Canton must be avenged and commerce put on a secure, progressive footing, so that China could be given the benefits of Christianity![1]

Again and again in the nineteenth century this hypocrisy recurred, the use of such arguments as a political device with no relation to sincere religious motive. That is not to say that sincere Christians did not also approve of high-handed measures to make China willing for open relations with the West. Elijah Bridgman, the pro-Chinese American missionary, wrote in his private journal as hostilities began,

> We are on the eve of a new era and a great revolution has commenced ... And now, we trust, the God of nations is about to open a highway for those who will preach the Word.[2]

No cant there, but sincere conviction, welcoming the opening of China without judging the justice or injustice of the war.

John Quincy Adams, Secretary of State, and sixth President of the United States, addressing the Massachusetts Historical Society after the opium war, insisted that opium was no more the cause of it than tea was the cause of the War of Independence after the Boston 'teaparty'.

> The cause of the war is the *kow-tow!* . . . The insulting and degrading forms of relations between lord and vassal.[3]

In his opinion China had to be brought to her knees; in an expanding world such obscurantism had no place; isolationism, especially with insults, was intolerable.

The debate continues today. Professor Latourette included the wide gap between Chinese and Western concepts of law and justice as a main contributory factor. In the tangled skein of history it is impossible to put a finger on one thread and say, 'That caused the war.' China said 'opium' and says it still. Lord Palmerston himself summed up the Parliamentary debate in 1840 by saying, 'This is an exportation-of-bullion question, an agricultural interest question.'[4] With this reference to silver, Sun Yat-sen agreed. Again the evasion of any direct reference to opium was noticeable. Even Chinese protocol, however degrading, was acceptable so long as trade could flourish, the trade Britain wanted to encourage. If that was obstructed, then insults were intolerable.

The war had started, but the ulcerative issue of Anglo-Chinese relations would go on festering until ministers plenipotentiary were admitted as residents in Peking twenty years later. Even then they would be called 'barbarian chieftains'. Beyond that, the tensions would provoke violence until after Hudson Taylor became the unwilling centre of a major diplomatic storm and the murder of a British consul was the final turn of the key which unlocked China for Christian missionaries to travel, live and work where they pleased.

Elliot and Qi Shan   *1840–41*

Palmerston's expeditionary force under General Sir Hugh Gough[5] reached Macao in June 1840. It was immensely impressive, the greatest display of strength ever to appear in Chinese territorial waters. In actual fact it was impressive for that reason rather than by its composition, except in one respect. It included four side-wheel steam warships of shallow draft for service in estuaries and rivers. HMS *Nemesis* was an ironclad of six hundred and thirty tons and drew only six feet of water. Manned by ninety men and armed with two 32-pounders, she was impregnable to attack by Chinese junks and fire-rafts. She was also highly manoeuvrable and under an energetic commander. In all, twenty-seven troop-ships arrived carrying four thousand men, escorted by sixteen ships of war; or according to one account, a total of ten thousand men. Commissioner Lin reported their arrival to Peking, describing the paddle-steamers as 'cartwheel ships' and adding that they were 'fast, with axles put in motion by fire'.[6] Charles Gutzlaff was appointed interpreter to the commander, Sir Hugh Gough, and was attached to his staff from then until the war was over.

Lord Palmerston's directive came to Captain Elliot, RN, still only the Chief Superintendent of British Trade but still being treated as senior authority in the East, though by June 9, 1841, he could sign himself 'Charles Elliot, Her Majesty's Plenipotentiary'. Justice was to be seen to be done, the injured parties were to be compensated, ports were to be opened for unrestricted trading, and an island base for British ships was to be provided, but this demand could be withdrawn if ports were opened to trade.

Ports mattered most to Palmerston for European competition was developing so fast that, as he wrote, 'We must unremittingly endeavour to find in other parts of the world new vents for the produce of our industry.'[7] To the merchants an island was most important. Their estimate of the Chinese character was summed up in one word, 'perfidious'. With a safe island base in Chinese waters they could go on running merchandise ashore, while if other ports were anything like Canton, only more trouble lay ahead.

Another important point was to be handled very carefully. No demands were to be made or pressure applied, but the Chinese negotiators were to be advised that it would be to China's advantage to legalise the opium trade and draw revenue from it.

To the emperor Palmerston addressed a manifesto in which he protested against what he called unprovoked outrages against British merchants at Canton. China was perfectly within her rights to make laws and enforce them, but Her Majesty could not tolerate unjust and violent treatment of her subjects. Innocent merchants had been imprisoned in the Factory along with the guilty, and the blockade meant starvation if their stocks of 'merchandise' were not surrendered, again without mention of opium. So Britain demanded 'satisfaction'. Captain Elliot would spell out what that satisfaction entailed.

The facts were very different. The Canton Factory siege was called an 'atrocity', but in accounts written at the time, in books and letters to *The Times*, it was, as Brian Inglis says, 'all a great lark'.[8] With no Chinese to impress, the merchants enjoyed doing their own chores and played host to each other on turkeys, capon and mutton provided by their 'oppressor', Commissioner Lin.

So Captain Elliot and Sir Hugh Gough started with a show of strength. Two thousand men were landed at Canton and established themselves on the walls of the city. Let the million inhabitants and their rulers tremble! But what next? The men had to be kept supplied, and began to fall ill. Elliot was the last man to countenance the indiscriminate sacking of a city, or the capture of the commissioner, so he withdrew his forces. To the Chinese this was retreat. Masters of display, they were unimpressed by the show of force. After all, they knew it was trade the British wanted most.

At the end of June the expedition turned north, blockaded Amoy, Ningbo and the mouth of the Yangzi, occupying the island of Chusan at the mouth of Hangzhou Bay. The intention was to teach the ruling classes a lesson but to show goodwill to the common people and avoid disturbing their lives. The Chusan mandarins, however, were courtesy itself and only the people were hostile. Why bring trouble to Chusan? the mandarins asked 'with pained surprise'. The wrongs complained of were in distant Canton. 'We know that opposition to a force as strong as yours will be madness', they protested, 'but it is our duty to resist you.'[9] When the British persisted, the Chinese opened fire with antiquated cannons from the shore and some junks, and were silenced by the British guns. The chief magistrate, head of police and warden of the jail then committed ritual suicide. And the British began to loot. China was entirely new and fantastic to them. Silks, painted fans, 'fairy shoes' and porcelains were too enticing. In fact the Bengali word for plunder came into the English language as a result of this expedition – 'loot'.

The 'indestructible Gutzlaff' as Brian Inglis calls him, was left at Chusan as chief magistrate, with a garrison of troops ready for action when called upon. But here again malaria, dysentery and heat stroke played havoc with the men. Dr William Lockhart opened a hospital for them but could do little to help. One-sixth of the total force died and hundreds more were incapacitated.

With a heavy squadron of ships Captain Elliot proceeded to the mouth of the Beihe in the far north, arriving on August 15. This was serious for Commissioner Lin. Far from controlling the barbarians he had turned them loose on the empire. He and the governor of Canton were disgraced and sent into exile, Lin to remotest Xinjiang (Sinkiang).

Qi Shan, the elderly, aristocratic governor-general of Zhili (Chihli) whom Lin was to have replaced, now came to Dagu at the mouth of the Beihe below Tianjin. On August 30 he greeted Elliot with honeyed words, and had little difficulty in persuading him to return to Canton for talks. After all, the pother was all about Canton and events there, and Elliot was anxious to avoid pressing things too far. To topple the emperor by going on to Peking, for example, could lead to unpredictable developments. So once more the British 'retreated', this time a thousand miles, driven from the gates of the capital city by judicious words. It is recorded that Qi Shan enjoyed the joke with Dao Guang. These bold and defiant barbarians were vulnerable to praise even if deaf to reason.

They met again at Canton and Elliot succeeded in getting Qi Shan's agreement to some moderate demands. He was too gentlemanly for Palmerston and the merchants, but he might have been even more lenient if the crew of a British ship and an unfortunate woman named Mrs Noble had not been taken prisoner when they ran aground in Hangzhou Bay. Manacled in chains and exhibited like animals, each of them crouching in a three-foot cage for all the long journey to the south, they suffered shamefully until handed over by the authorities at Canton. An independent Anglican missionary, Rev Vincent J. Stanton, was also imprisoned for four months, in chains which were 'to be seen at many missionary exhibitions' when he returned home. Indignation and demands that the Chinese should pay for such barbarity hardened Elliot's attitude. He insisted on the lease of Hong Kong, as Chusan was so unhealthy, on six million dollars in compensation, which amply covered the confiscated chests of opium, and on direct dealings between himself as the Superintendent of Trade and the viceroy of Canton, instead of by the insulting procedure of petitions through the Cohong merchants.

Qi Shan was adamant that even the lease of an island was out of the question, so to his surprise Captain Elliot attacked and destroyed the Chinese batteries at Chuanbi and later the Bogue forts also. With Canton obviously the next objective Qi Shan capitulated and on January 20, 1841, signed the Convention of Chuanbi. Hong Kong Island was occupied on January 26, 1841, and a harbour master and magistrate appointed. All comers were promised freedom of social and religious customs and on June 7 duty-free trading facilities.

Not surprisingly the almost barren island began to blossom. By December twelve thousand Chinese had arrived, the promise of free trade attracting successful merchants. The two American Baptists, J. Lewis Shuck and Issachar J. Roberts led the way as the first missionaries there. Four years later there were six hundred European residents and twenty-three thousand Chinese. Palmerston's taunt about 'a barren island with hardly a house on it' must have given him some uncomfortable moments. Merchants returned to the Factory at Canton and trade was resumed. They found that the Cohong merchants had carefully preserved all their property from harm. But all concerned were in cloud-cuckoo-land.

When Palmerston heard on what terms Elliot had concluded his treaty he was furious. Instead of news of a resounding victory and massive indemnity in truly imperial style, this insipid treaty was all he could report. 'You have disobeyed and neglected our instructions,' he wrote.[10] What use was a barren rock and only leasehold? Six million dollars might cover the twenty-thousand chests of surrendered opium, but what of the lost trade and immense cost of the expedition? Was the taxpayer to make up the deficit? Elliot's belief that moderate terms and greater goodwill would soon compensate for losses by extending healthy trade was pooh-poohed by the merchants' lobby. Only immediate maximum compensation would satisfy them. So, with scathing comments from twenty-one year-old Queen Victoria, Captain Elliot was to be replaced and the Convention would not be ratified.

For Qi Shan it was no better. The terms he had accepted were repudiated by the emperor and this 'noble and gracious' man as the Abbé Huc described him, imperturbably suave and tactful under provocation, was disgraced and led away from Canton by chains by his imperial master's command. His attempt to soften the blow for China was rewarded by denunciation for double-dealing intimacy with barbarians. For him it was banishment to the coldest north-east of Manchuria. The degradation of Lin and Qi Shan was symbolic of the deep wound suffered by China as a whole. With their failure the nation suffered decades of demoralisation. Qi Shan died, and too late the emperor deplored his loss, remitting all the censures levelled against him.

Yet again the Factory became untenable and hostilities reopened in February in a desultory way while the Chinese built up their forces to exterminate the barbarians. The Factory itself was invaded and partly burnt down. Fire-rafts were assembled to attack the British ships, and the price of fifty thousand dollars each was placed on the heads of Elliot and the commodore of the fleet. Elliot then threatened to sack Canton and wrung another six million dollars' indemnity from the viceroy. In March he could muster only two thousand four hundred disease-free men to enforce his demands. Of nine hundred and thirty Cameronian Highlanders only a hundred and ten were still on their feet. Any thought of pressure upon Peking was out of the question.

Pottinger and Qi Ying   1841–42

Lord Palmerston by now had forgotten that so recently he had cooed piously like a dove. He was all hawk. Only another, more powerful expeditionary force could undo Captain Elliot's mistakes and exact Britain's demands in full.[11] Though his Prime Minister, Lord Melbourne, demurred, Palmerston won the ear of the queen and in the summer of 1841 Sir Henry Pottinger, a major-general in the Honourable East India Company, arrived at Hong Kong as plenipotentiary to succeed Charles Elliot with the authority he had for so long been so blindly denied. Sir Henry had a reputation for social success with Indian princes and ruthlessness when necessary. Captain Elliot continued to serve in high office in other parts of the world, but lived in the wrong times for a gentleman of his cast. A public figure who could describe the Chinese as 'the most moderate and reasonable people on the face of the earth'[12] had insight too far in advance of most contemporaries.

When Pottinger arrived he cold-shouldered Elliot and

went to the home of James Matheson at Hong Kong. This insult and other indications of his close association with William Jardine in England showed the course events were soon to take. 'Dr William Jardine, MP' as he now was, could run his finger over Palmerston's maps and talk about China with firsthand knowledge. The advice he gave was closely followed. Blockade the coast, occupy three or four islands, send a force up to the threshold of Peking and demand trading rights at five ports.

Sir Henry Pottinger lost no time. With John Robert Morrison and Charles Gutzlaff as his negotiators, and Tradescant Lay also on his staff, simply because they were the best linguists available, his expedition proceeded up the coast from port to port. His intention was to demolish defences and give land forces a taste of defeat, but to preserve strict discipline. No looting would be tolerated this time. Gulangsu Island alongside Quemoy and dominating Amoy harbour was occupied, and held until 1846 as a hostage until reparations had all been paid. Amoy was attacked and taken on August 26. To the troops' surprise, out came Chinese looters on the grand scale. 'If they can loot, why can't we?' the soldiers asked. Chusan was retaken on October 1 and Ningbo, where British prisoners had been so maltreated, was occupied by the expeditionary force throughout the winter. They fought off Chinese counter-attacks, but British stragglers and prisoners were carted off for execution. In March 1842 the troops at Ningbo repulsed a surprise attack with heavy Chinese losses, and this time the British sacked the city in retaliation. It was the time of the first Afghan war, shortly before the massacre and Britain was in no mood for moderation, quite the reverse.

Savagery and slaughter continued as they pressed on up the coast and took Shanghai on June 19. The paddle-steamers towed the sailing ships up the Wusong river, running the gauntlet of bombardment from both war junks and shore batteries. The incredible daring of these barbarians did as much to demoralise the Manchu resistance as the devastating fire of their guns. Advance parties scaled the walls of the old city of Shanghai and flung open the gates. Before the main force arrived both British and Chinese indulged in an orgy of plundering.

From there they went on up the Yangzi river, bombarding and taking Zhenjiang (Chinkiang) on July 21 and blockading the Grand Canal. Charles Gutzlaff went ashore and did his best to stop the wholesale suicides and self-elimination of the Manchus, while the peasant rabble fell to and plundered as if justice were on their side giving them the opportunity of a lifetime.

The emperor now ordered ships to be built in Sichuan and divers to be sent from Yichang to bore holes in the British hulls and to wreck their rudders. He was out of touch with reality and was as alarmed by the increase in banditry, riots and anti-dynastic sects as by the barbarian threats. When the British took the imperial grain from the swarming grain junks and distributed it to the common people, the government became afraid of popular support for the invaders. The antagonism of the Cantonese was lacking farther north.

Nanking, the ancient southern capital of the previous Ming dynasty, was the next objective. On August 9, Sir Henry Pottinger's fleet appeared. He was on the point of attacking when the arrival of an imperial envoy was dramatically announced. The Dao Guang emperor could see that his dynasty itself was in danger. By controlling the Yangzi the invaders had cut the empire in two. He sent as his plenipotentiary an envoy at least as remarkable as Qi Shan. Qi Ying was a diplomat of the same type, aware that Pottinger could dictate his terms and exact whatever he liked from a helpless China. But he also put himself in Pottinger's shoes and recognised his difficulties. An expedition was not an occupying force.

'Diplomatic honeymoon' and unequal treaties   *1842–44*

Qi Ying made a bad start. He stayed in the background and sent inferior officials deceptively dressed in the robes of superior ranks to open negotiations. They were to draw out the British negotiators and learn their intentions without making valid commitments. Charles Gutzlaff was actually doing the negotiating when he suspected chicanery, they were so non-committal. He could get nothing. When the truth was exposed Pottinger was furious and the British merchants' accusations of Chinese perfidy seemed confirmed. In fact, however, though every commercial subtlety might be employed to strike as favourable a bargain as possible, the Chinese did establish a reputation of honesty in fulfilment of what they finally agreed; but this perfidy at Nanking and British perfidy at a later stage sowed the seeds of deep discord which it took decades to dispel.

Qi Ying was unperturbed. He made his personal appearance with an ease that was disarming. His immediate aim was to win the favour of the British and get them out of the Yangzi. He saw that affability held out the greatest hope of tolerable terms and embarked on a remarkable farce which came to be known as the 'Diplomatic Honeymoon'. Somehow he sustained it for four years. Only then, disgusted by its failure, did he bitterly change his tune.

Banquets set the stage for discussion and Pottinger rose to the occasion. In view of the issues at stake and known attitudes of both sides, the familiarities and levity displayed by both men amazed every subordinate. To see His Excellency Sir Henry Pottinger, Bart, Her Majesty's Plenipotentiary, standing with his mouth wide open while His Excellency the Imperial Plenipotentiary Qi Ying deposited sweetmeats in it, was inexplicable except to the principal performers. Pottinger knew what he was doing. A diplomatic honeymoon suited his purposes. He had no need to negotiate and merely coated his dictated terms in appropriate pleasantries. The pill needed plenty of sugar, but he wanted Anglo-Chinese relations to recover and be warm, once open trading was re-established.

The emperor and Qi Ying began on the wrong assumption. With such power the British must surely intend the conquest of China. They could not believe that the repeated insistence on sound trading facilities was the sum and end of their demands, so stiff terms appeared lenient. It was a relief to concede so much less than they had feared. On August 29, 1842, the Treaty of Nanking was signed. The five ports of Canton, Amoy, Fuzhou, Ningbo and Shanghai were to be opened to foreign trade, fair tariff rates were to be imposed, and the Cohong was to be abolished. Consuls were to reside in each, with equality of rank and access to the senior mandarin in each place. British citizens 'with their families and establishments' were to be guaranteed freedom from 'molestation or restraints' in the ports and 'close environs'.[13] Hong Kong was to be ceded to Great Britain. And within three years an indemnity of twenty-one million dollars was to be paid. Pottinger had secured all that Palmerston stipulated under the merchants' prompting. Hong Kong was a bonus which Pottinger justified by saying,

> Every hour I have passed in this superb country has convinced me of the necessity and desirability of our possessing such a settlement as an emporium for our trade, and a place from which Her Majesty's subjects may be alike protected and controlled.[14]

This time Lord Palmerston was elated. This was the resounding victory he wanted. He patted himself and William Jardine on the back with specious talk about 'an epoch in the progress of the civilisation of the human race' and truer sentiments of 'not unimportant advantages to the commercial interests of England';[15] and Pottinger was decorated with the GCB (Knight Grand Cross of the Bath). Opium could be conveniently forgotten.

Pottinger had not failed to put it to Qi Ying that it would be to China's advantage to legalise opium trading. Apart

from customs revenue, the occasion of clashes with foreign
'merchants' would be removed. Not to legalise it would be
to recreate the circumstances which precipitated war.
Where then would the blame lie? To the honour of China
these blandishments and threats had no effect. The debase-
ment of her people mattered more. 'The misery and
demoralisation are almost beyond belief,' Marjoribanks,
ex-Chief of the East India Company at Canton, had said.[16]

Duty on opium would never check the amount imported,
however. It would only hasten the degradation of the
addict and of officials who handled it. Responsibility rested
squarely on the British who produced and carried the drug.
If they could coerce China they could control their own
merchants. Clearly they did not wish to. For the next
fourteen years this was the bone of contention which kept
the two countries on the brink of war. The merchants were
not satisfied, the Chinese were indignant at continued
smuggling, and the foreign consuls were on a tight-rope
between the two. The second opium war was not only
foreseeable but foreseen. Lord Palmerston was Prime
Minister and aged seventy-five when it erupted.

The mood in Britain was very different. The headmaster
of Rugby, Dr Thomas Arnold, expressed the conviction of
the Christian public when he wrote in 1840,

> Surely you will agree with me in deprecating this war with
> China, which really seems to be so wicked as to be a national
> sin of the greatest possible magnitude, and it distresses me
> very deeply. Cannot anything be done by petition or other-
> wise to awaken men's minds to the dreadful guilt we are
> incurring?[17]

Two hundred British merchants signed a document
addressed to Sir Robert Peel, Prime Minister in 1842,
pointing out that an impoverished China unable to trade
helpfully with Britain would be a promising market ruined.
How could she buy British manufactures if her own exports
of tea and silk were already exceeded by opium imports?

The Times commented on the news of the Treaty of

Nanking with the suggestion that this was the time for Britain to extricate herself from involvement with opium. She owed China some compensation 'for pillaging her towns and slaughtering her citizens in a quarrel which would never have arisen if we had not been guilty of an international crime'.[18]

Palmerston's son-in-law, the future Lord Shaftesbury — at that time Lord Ashley, giving himself to the care and protection of the mentally ill, of 'cotton children', child slaves in English factories and of the 'climbing boys', child chimney sweeps wild with terror — was nauseated by the news from China.

> We have triumphed in one of the most lawless, unnecessary and unfair struggles in the records of history, [he said] this cruel and debasing war.
> The whole world is intoxicated with the prospect of Chinese trade. Altars to Mammon are rising on every side and thousands of cotton children will be sacrificed to his honour.[19]

But when he read the terms of the Treaty he denounced them equally. The peace was as wicked as the war itself. So he added the anti-opium campaign to the causes he espoused. For him as for Wilberforce before him, to champion any moral cause was to fight for God. On March 23 he wrote,

> Prayer to begin, prayer to accompany and prayer to close any undertaking for His service is the secret of all prospering in our ways. [And on March 28] Oh what a question is this opium affair; bad as I thought it, I find it a thousand times worse, more black, more cruel, more Satanic than all the deeds of private sin in the records of prison history.

On April 4, 1843, he introduced the resolution in Parliament:

> That it is the opinion of this House that the continuance of the trade in opium and the monopoly of its growth in ... India are destructive of all relations of amity between England and China ... and utterly inconsistent with the

honour and duties of a Christian kingdom; and that steps be taken as soon as possible . . . to abolish the evil.[20]

The war and treaty settled nothing, Gladstone said,

A war more unjust in its origins, a war more calculated to cover this country with permanent disgrace, I do not know and have not read of.[21]

Britain's crime was plain, for all to see, but her international reputation suffered more from her falsehoods than from her actual deeds. Balzac's epithet 'Albion perfide' clung to her well into the twentieth century. 'The English flaunt their perfidiousness in the face of the whole world.' Seventy more years were to pass before the infamous traffic was ended.

All on the band-wagon   1842–43

Unfortunately Qi Ying's taste for histrionics and deception extended to his version of the treaty and his report to the Court in Peking. The emperor's directive had not been closely followed, so some provisions were never fulfilled. The version submitted to him differed from that approved by the negotiators, in that recognition of equality was omitted. It should have been demonstrated by elevation of Britain's name above the level of the text in keeping with Chinese custom. On June 26, 1843, however, the treaty was ratified and the cession of Hong Kong proclaimed. As on all great occasions Charles Gutzlaff was interpreter when Qi Ying was brought with ceremony from Huangbo to Hong Kong in HMS Vixen. A supplementary Treaty of The Bogue was then negotiated and signed in October, to deal with deficiencies in the first.[22] This time Britain agreed to discourage opium trading. Apart from lip-service she never fulfilled her promise. On the contrary, pressure from Hong Kong continued until relations became so unstable that only a spark was needed to explode the situation into war again.

Pottinger himself attempted to enforce legitimate trading at the treaty ports only, but it was quickly shown that the authority of the Crown did not extend to foreign soil or the high seas. Jardine and Matheson now had five fast opium clippers on the India run and half a dozen more on the China coast. Dent and Company matched them closely. Before long the old devices of depot ships and islands were re-adopted beyond the reach of Chinese and British authorities, but not before another gambit was tried with equal success.

As soon as other nations saw what Britain had achieved, they concluded treaties of their own. Elijah Bridgman and Dr Peter Parker, whose Chinese was imperfect, were the best interpreters America could find, but a satisfactory treaty was negotiated in 1843 and signed at Macao in July 1844. It was more explicit on matters of 'extraterritoriality' (the privilege of jurisdiction in the territory of another state) than Pottinger's treaty had been.[23] America had not been belligerent or as commercially active as the British but was morally entangled as much as any in opium trading.

When Pottinger's strictures were enforced, Jardine, Matheson and Company bought three American ships and carried their opium under the Stars and Stripes, and others followed suit. No one could win against these men. The clamour they raised was so loud when a naval officer enforced Pottinger's orders that he complained to the government that suppression of the traffic was impossible. Naval protection was withdrawn from ships going to other than the five treaty ports but that did not trouble them.

Without stirring from Canton waters the French, through M. Lagrené, negotiated a similar treaty in 1844 and, adopting a role as champion of the Church, included a clause granting toleration of Roman Catholic Christianity in China. During the war, persecution of Christians had been intensified and this was a very live issue. The Chinese agreed, with the proviso that as travel was prohibited beyond the five treaty ports, so propagation of Christianity was banned. According to the missionary historian Servière, however, an oral promise was made to Lagrené by Qi Ying that if missionaries were prudent, officials would close their eyes to their presence farther inland. But in the ports organised churches would be allowed. This was a far cry from the secret meetings of Robert Morrison, Liang A-fa and their friends. In fairness, by an imperial rescript issued on December 28, 1844, the Chinese extended the same privileges to all Christians and every nation requesting them.

Ever since Commissioner Lin was flouted and lost face so severely the morale of the nation had been weakened. Their helplessness in the face of Western arms further undermined the prestige of the emperor and the will of his better mandarins to restrain the illicit opium traffic. Others connived so that the forbidden cargo was welcomed and the illegal in theory was tolerated in practice.[24]

Why was there no stronger reaction from China? For what could a handful of ships and men do against hundreds of millions of Chinese? The answer is not difficult to find. The Manchus and Chinese loyal to them were hostile to foreigners but most of the nation were friendly, tolerant and apathetic about affairs of state. They were inured to suffering and content to accept whatever came their way. But the Court and government machine was highly centralised, based on decrees and plagued by corrupt court eunuchs and intrigue. It could not cope with events outside its experience. An entirely new situation had arisen and everyone concerned must wait and see how it developed. What they saw was the merchants' dreams come true. As a by-product there was also a dramatic revolution in the prospects for missions.

As soon as the Treaty of Nanking was concluded, the foreign community in East Asia leaped into action. That is hardly an overstatement. Among merchants, missionaries and administrators there was a 'general post', a winding up or handing over of existing commitments to others and a move into the mainland ports. Charles Gutzlaff returned to Chusan Island as governor for nine months, John Robert

Morrison to Hong Kong as Chinese Secretary-in-Chief, and George Tradescant Lay as consul to pivotal Canton, then to Fuzhou and then Amoy to establish consular procedures.

A member of Sir Henry Pottinger's personal staff, Captain George Balfour, later one of Hudson Taylor's benefactors, went as consul to Shanghai. Merchants and missionaries arrived in the ports hard on their heels, and consuls like Balfour, now and later, who knew little or no Chinese, depended on the missionaries as interpreters and go-betweens with the Chinese. They would have been almost helpless without them. Mistakes were made by inexperienced administrators. Robert Thom, first consul at Ningbo, was provided by the Chinese with a farmhouse among rice fields and malarial swamps as his consulate. He died and his successor, a remarkable young man named Rutherford Alcock, who is to feature largely in this story about Hudson Taylor, was shocked and driven to strong-arm tactics by what he found. He, like Thomas Francis Wade, a lieutenant in the forces wintering in Ningbo in 1841, set himself to learn the language and culture of China. Both became ambassadors to Peking and Wade's romanisation of the Chinese language was the system most widely used outside China.

Tradescant Lay, a naturalist and still primarily a missionary, was given the most difficult task—for Canton was the seat of bitterness. Pottinger wanted to restore good relations with China and Lay's brief was to heal old wounds; but the British merchants would not co-operate. They protested against Lord Palmerston's allocation of indemnity. A court had ruled that the value of each surrendered chest of opium was two hundred dollars and for every chest an additional three dollars would be just compensation for the debts of bankrupted Chinese merchants. By that reckoning a total of $4,120,000 would have been ample, but Palmerston had promised six million and kept his word.

The merchants behaved insufferably towards the

Chinese. The tables had turned and they treated cultured men as servants, an unpleasant attitude which spread to other ports and never quite died out. Another riot occurred and again part of the Factory was burned down. On July 8, 1846, after Lay had gone, mobs completely sacked the Factory area and closed that chapter of history. The British and French then took possession of an eighty-acre sand-bank in the river called Shamian Island, built retaining walls, raised the level and established a secure foreign settlement under their own control.

Before the revolution of 1911–12 Chinese cities were densely inhabited and closely built up. For this reason both Chinese and foreigners preferred that the new treaty settlements should be outside the city walls. When Captain Balfour went to Shanghai in 1842 he was shown the mud flats on the banks of the Huangpu River. The people of Shanghai did not have the xenophobia of the Cantonese, but if a mixture of fear, contempt and tongue-in-cheek led them to encourage the barbarians to accept marshland and tidal wastes for occupation they can be forgiven for lack of clairvoyance. Like Sir Stamford Raffles, Balfour knew what he was doing and initially claimed twenty-three acres of low-lying swampy ground bounded by stagnant ditches.

During 1843 twenty-three foreign residents and some families moved in, and eleven merchant houses were erected. These forerunners, with the two LMS missionaries, W. H. Medhurst and Dr William Lockhart, and the consul, constituted the beginning of the greatest port in China, opened to foreign trade on November 17. Forty-four merchant ships made Shanghai their main port, on average less than four a month, and trading began. Balfour drew up his rules, marked out the roads-to-be and with Medhurst as his interpreter sorted out his relationship with his Chinese opposite number, the *daotai* or prefect of the old city.

The new era had begun. Chinese law and authority ended at the borders of the Settlement and within it all, including Chinese, were under British rule. This extraterritoriality was to develop with the growth of the settlements until many thousands of Chinese as well as foreigners were governed by aliens in their own land.[25] It was a period of uncertainty and confusion, of foreign dominance by prestige, with Western life and technology on show to the curious populace. They watched with disapproval as foreign women with low-cut dresses perambulated on the river path arm in arm with their menfolk, behaviour that was pert and indecent by Chinese standards. But they worked out profitable ways of trading under regulations so fair and straightforward that commerce quickly gathered momentum.

Repercussions on the Church   1840–42

The Chinese have not forgiven Britain for what she did. In 1836, when Christianity was banned in China, pockets of toleration still existed, as 'the frail but heroic' Perboyre demonstrated. In Fujian province he claimed to have found forty thousand adherents; and when the Church in the Yangzi valley requested more priests, three were sent. In September 1840, however, when persecution was intensified after the war broke out, Perboyre himself was executed at Wuchang. And in 1842 a member of the imperial family died in prison for his faith. After the treaties and court edicts to implement them, any foreign priests discovered outside the five ports were merely sent to their consuls at the coast.

When hostilities began and Dr Peter Parker found it impossible to work at Canton, he went home to the States to promote the cause of missions, and addressed the U.S. Senate. The Protestant Episcopal surgeon, William Boone, was on Gulangsu Island with David Abeel during the war, but succeeded in making a twenty-five-mile evangelistic journey on the mainland and planted 'the Seed of the Church' at Amoy — a phrase used as the title of his recent biography.[26] Amoy was his natural stamping ground after learning the Hokkien dialect in the freedom of Batavia

(1837–41), on Gutzlaff's advice. After the Treaty of Nanking he too went to the States. He returned a bishop, in 1845, to be joined in Shanghai by six colleagues shortly afterwards.

News of the treaty also alerted the Church Missionary Society in the United Kingdom and a fund was started to send missionaries to China. Since Robert Morrison reached Canton in 1807 a total of only fifty-seven missionaries had come to East Asia, most of them in the Straits, Java and Siam. Ten had died, fifteen had withdrawn and thirty-two were still at work when the treaty was signed. Through the upheaval of war China also lost a notable recruit. Inspired by reading Gutzlaff's *Journal of Three Voyages*, David Livingstone offered himself to the LMS for service in China; but with the future unpredictable the Society asked him to consider Africa, and meeting Robert Moffat he agreed to join him there instead.

Now with treaty rights in the five ports and Hong Kong offering security under British rule, the way was at long last open for missionaries to study Chinese on Chinese soil, and even to build homes, schools, hospitals and places of worship in the British and later the international settlements. In Hong Kong where the Chinese city was growing rapidly there was unrestricted freedom. The Roman Catholic Church made a good recovery, but the phenomenon of Protestant activity became the more remarkable.

Predictably, when cynics saw how the missionary work expanded, they questioned whether missionaries should have accepted the privileges secured by force of arms, let alone have helped in the expeditions and treaty negotiations. Neither the missionaries themselves nor their supporters in the West were troubled by the problem. Until vigorous missionary condemnation of the opium traffic highlighted the issue, it was too complex for those close to it, even Medhurst, to see themselves as tainted by association. All along the war had been in the name of justice, a defence of the right to trade and to be justly treated as equals. The people of China had a right to hear the gospel;

and for thirty-five years the missionaries had waited for this moment. 'We . . . recognise the inscrutability of Divine Providence in bringing so much good apparently out of that unmixed iniquity,' was how Evan Davies put it in his *Memoir of the Rev Samuel Dyer*, stigmatising the opium traffic and opium war as 'one of the vilest that has ever polluted human hands'.[27] The gates of China were ajar. The only right course was to enter.

The general deployment which followed the signing of the treaties therefore affected the missionary body as acutely as anyone. Their migration from South-East Asia to China was mainly governed by which Chinese dialect each missionary had learnt. Leaving a skeleton staff behind, a score of them with basic knowledge of the land and people formed the spearhead. Almost all were British or American, and although widely represented across the denominational keyboard, all sprang from the Evangelical Awakening and shared the same gospel in commendable harmony. Both medical and educational work were regarded not as a lure but as part and parcel of the Christian message.

To the grief of the Bridgmans and other missionaries of the American Board, the American Baptists and Presbyterians, the great day had come and only enough of them were in the field to maintain existing work. The Boardmans were among the Karens in Burma, the Deans and Bradleys in Bangkok, where Josiah Goddard had duly arrived in 1840, and one or two more in Singapore. They were established in as good a cause, and not free to leave. Only Dr William Dean moved to Hong Kong. The missionary-minded church he proceeded to found there was to reproduce itself in a daughter church at Swatow. In Jakarta the Walter H. Medhursts and the indomitable Mary Ann Aldersey were poised to take off. Java was only their springboard and mainland China their destination.

In 1841 Henry Venn became Honorary Secretary of the CMS in London, another gem in the starry crown of an illustrious society.[28] Born two days after Charles Simeon's address to the Eclectic Society which gave rise to the CMS, Venn grew up breathing the air of missionary springtime and gave thirty-one years of inspired leadership. The year after his appointment two missionaries, George Smith and Thomas McClatchie, were sent on a survey and visited Amoy. They were amazed by the reception they received. The five chief mandarins invited them to a feast, placed them in the seats of honour and complimented them on bringing a religion 'tending to the peace and harmony of mankind'![29] In 1849, through the influence of Henry Venn, George Smith became the first bishop of Victoria, the embryo city of Hong Kong.

America also responded promptly with three new missions sending members in 1842 and another, the Southern Baptists, in the following year. The American Presbyterian Mission, one of the greatest, began not only in China but also Siam at this time.

The LMS added to its remarkable tally of missionary giants by sending James Legge to the Anglo-Chinese College at Malacca. Legge was sure that 'Hong Kong and China are certainly more promising fields for missionary labour than the settlements in the Straits' and 'longed to transport himself into the heart of the Celestial Empire'. So he wrote to John Robert Morrison who received the letter at Nanking actually during the treaty negotiations. He replied from there on September 11, 1842, 'Your scheme for removal to Nanking or rather Peking is, my dear friend, too imaginative . . . Make up your mind then, to Hong Kong.'[30]

Samuel Dyer   *1840 – 43*

We left the Dyer family in 1839 on their way home round the Cape to England because of the mother's illness. Apart from narrowly escaping shipwreck on the Goodwin Sands they had a good voyage and two years in a temperate climate restored Maria to health, while Samuel travelled widely, lecturing on East Asia.

A delightful file of his surviving letters reveals the kind of man he was, an ardent soul and a tender lover.[31] 'My dearest Love', 'My Darling girl' they began, with news of his work and little messages to his children.

Then, in 1841, while the opium war was in progress, the family returned to Malaya. With Legge at the Anglo-Chinese College, Samuel was free to join his close friend, the scholarly John Stronach, in Singapore. John's brother Alexander was at Penang. The completion of steel founts of moveable Chinese type was now Samuel's most urgent objective. He believed they could revolutionise the printing of Christian literature and the time looked increasingly right for them to be put to use. At last, to his great joy he would have less academic work and more time to preach the gospel, to go personally to men and women and tell them about Jesus whom he dearly loved.

In August 1842 they moved to Singapore and learned of the Treaty of Nanking being signed. Samuel wrote of those stirring days, '. . . every missionary to the Chinese felt he ought to be in China'; but he himself was convinced that he should stay at Singapore. 'We have full liberty to teach from house to house and we proclaim the Lord Jesus all over the town . . . But the people are so given to idolatry . . . Oh, might I but see a bonfire of idols, I would sing and leap for joy.'[32] John Stronach and he fitted in with one another 'like the pinions of a clock'. The future was bright.

About this time one of their children fell dangerously ill, and in a letter Samuel said,

> Our little sweet babe is now on the very verge of Jordan . . . sometimes I seem to say, Go, sweet babe, go — and become another gem in the Crown of Jesus. Then I say — stay, sweet babe, stay . . . Do you ask me . . . what I think of China looking at it from the gates of the grave? Oh, my heart is big to the overflow . . . nigh to bursting . . . If I thought anything could prevent my dying for China, the thought would crush me. Our only wish is to live for China, and to die in pointing the Chinese,

To his redeeming blood, and say,
Behold the way to God.

Again three days later he added, 'Our little darling seems to be recovering. "His strokes are fewer than our crimes, And lighter than our guilt." '[33] The comment of Evan Davies, his biographer, was, 'Samuel Dyer was a holy man, and that heavenly-mindedness was his habitual state.'

The East Asian missionaries called a series of conferences to be held in Hong Kong in the summer of 1843, the first of their kind on Chinese soil. After a meeting of the Ultra-Ganges Mission of the LMS to wind up Robert Morrison's administrative unit and separate the mission in the Straits from the LMS in China proper, there was to be an inter-Mission conference.[34] All agreed that their plans and activities must be co-ordinated to complement and not duplicate or compete with each other's efforts, and a joint team and strategy for Bible translation must be drawn up.

On July 18, 1843, a month after the Treaty of Nanking was ratified, Samuel Dyer and John Stronach sailed from Singapore to Hong Kong, spending four days in Macao *en route*.

> I have been obliged to discard both drawers and flannel waistcoat, [Samuel wrote to Maria]. . . . we scarcely know what prickly heat is at Singapore; my thighs were just flayed with it; the skin was off and my clothes and sheets stuck to the raw flesh . . . at Macao; it is cooler here . . .

A fever of excitement was in the air. William Milne's son, W. C. Milne, already in Ningbo, had written to say he was setting off overland disguised as a Chinese. The conference was more than due to begin and he had not arrived.

> I believe Sir Hen. Pottinger will feel obliged to report the affair to the Chinese Authorities, and it is possible that Milne may arrive in a cage at Canton. [But a few days later he continued] . . . disguise ill becomes the Christian. He has had some very narrow escapes of being detected.

No doubt to secure official countenance for the LMS conference, the Honourable John Robert Morrison as Chinese Secretary to Sir Henry Pottinger and the British administration and perhaps in tribute to his father's memory, was made chairman, though Walter Medhurst had already been a missionary for twenty-six of John's twenty-nine years of life and had recently been honoured by Glasgow University with a D.D. Samuel Dyer was elected conference secretary and consultations began.

> Our future station is to be Fuh-chow [he wrote] . . . (Hong Kong) appears to be a very unhealthy place; many are dying. A namesake of mine, Samuel Dyer, is dead . . . We seem to look each other in the face and ask whose turn may come next.

The missionaries of the American Board also met in Hong Kong and resolved to appeal for reinforcements. Although no one was free to move at present, they too had each port except Fuzhou in mind. The General Inter-Mission Conference followed in August and it was agreed to start on a translation of the Bible into literary Chinese. In each treaty port work would be done individually on different books and a committee of delegates would do the final revision. Then differences of opinion emerged which were never fully resolved. Debate became acrimonious over the Chinese terms to be used for 'God', as among the Catholics, and for 'baptism'. Only a word meaning total immersion would satisfy the Baptists and 'others, denying that this was the only possible meaning of the Greek word, felt that a more flexible rendering was needed.' It was a tragic start which soured relationships between and within missions for a century. But this was only one of many difficulties,

> . . . opposition shows itself in high quarters, and we are driven back upon the promises, that our hopes may be sustained . . . our work has this seal upon it that it is the work of God; viz. that we shall meet with difficulties in performing it.

Opposition and ill-feeling were tempered however by the illness and death of John Robert Morrison. Now the epidemic was among the delegates. In the state of medical ignorance of the causation of disease, everyone was at the mercy of every pestilence. The disease was 'raging extensively' — 'persons sicken and die in a few days. It is very awful.' The delegates dispersed and Samuel Dyer went to Canton on a visit. But he and John Stronach had already been infected and were soon desperately ill. In delirium he preached in a loud voice exhorting his imagined hearers to come to the Saviour. Dr Peter Parker was there and under his treatment Samuel improved. On October 4 he wrote to his children, 'I thought I was just going to heaven . . . but I am coming back to Singapore in a few days.' Then followed a paragraph about his thoughts when so ill and a statement about God's love and Jesus coming to save sinners so clear that any of his children would understand; and to Maria his wife, that Dr Parker had asked him if he would like his body to be buried beside Robert Morrison's in Macao.

> I said no, let me be buried here *in* China, and so let us take possession of the land by our burying places. But no . . . I shall soon embrace again the darling of my heart.

He recovered enough to start homewards but had a relapse and died at Macao on October 24, 1843.

Parker was not there to mention Dyer's wish, so they buried him in a grave beside Robert Morrison, and John Stronach had to write breaking the news to Maria. In Singapore Sir Thomas Norris, the Chief Justice, and Lady Norris, good friends of the Dyers, took Maria and the children under their care.

General post   *1843*

Hardly were the conferences over than the missionaries began to deploy their new locations. Dr Medhurst and William Lockhart, the surgeon, visited the ports and stayed at Shanghai. Until the settlement was developed they lived in a suburb and worked in the Chinese city, preaching, doctoring and going on itineration of a few miles into the surrounding countryside. Such freedom was revolutionary, unthinkable in the Canton Factory days. Medhurst as Captain Balfour's interpreter was an invaluable adviser to the army officer, new to things Chinese.

Before he died Samuel Dyer wrote to his wife about Miss Aldersey having already 'gone north', to Ningbo where before long she settled and opened a school for girls. An American Baptist physician named Macgowan also went to Ningbo in 1843 and set up a small hospital for a few months.

James Legge, Principal of the Anglo-Chinese College in Malacca, now wound that up and reopened it in Hong Kong. He had the conviction that anyone wishing to convert the Chinese must understand their mind and to do that must know their literature. He would not consider himself qualified as a missionary until he had mastered the classical books. So he proceeded to translate the chief classics into English and went far towards making Chinese thought comprehensible to the westerners. 'He opened the door to the mind of China.'[35] He was also a faithful preacher of the Word. The English services he held in his home developed into a Union Church, and out of his preaching to the Chinese grew a self-supporting church in Hong Kong.

Very different from the studious Legge was the ebullient Charles Gutzlaff. During the exasperating and then frivolous negotiations at Nanking he presented a New Testament to every representative on the Chinese team, asking them to read it. Being an important official made him no less a missionary evangelist. It is unlikely that he ever thought of how incompatible with one another his work with the invaders and his message of the gospel must appear. When John Robert Morrison died, Gutzlaff was recalled from his governorship of Chusan and appointed first Chinese Secretary to Her Majesty's plenipotentiary.

He held this post until he died, serving first under Pottinger and then Sir John Francis Davis. All his spare time he devoted to missionary work. Every evening he preached the gospel in idiomatic Chinese and on Sundays often six times. Reputedly he sometimes used Japanese, presumably in teaching the exiled sailors.

His thoughts roamed far across China. Amidst all the commotion of comings and goings he began to express his conviction, born of long experience and of observation of his fellow-foreigners' potential, 'China can be evangelised only by the Chinese.'[36] The foreign missionaries' work was to train and guide them until they developed their own momentum. These missionaries should as far as possible be like the Chinese. They should live and work with them, but always humbly aware that they could never lose their own foreign-ness or be adequate substitutes. He saw them always on the move, lighting the gospel flame in place after place, feeding it but never imposing Westernisms upon the Church that came into being. He began to pray for a thousand Chinese evangelists to start groups of Christians all over China, Christians who in turn would preach the gospel to others. The flame that fired Hudson Taylor was beginning to burn more clearly.

Father and son[37]　　　　　　　　　*18th century — 1845*

The moment is approaching when in this history of God's working to create 'The Chinese Church that will not die',[38] Charles Gutzlaff's torch was passed on to James Hudson Taylor. We left the Taylor family back in the eighteenth century, so we must pick up the threads and bring their story up to date.

John Taylor and Mary Shepherd his wife were carrying on the brave work of his father James. As local preacher and class leaders they were fully committed in all their spare moments and facing calumny and violence. A blow and 'Take that for Jesus Christ's sake!' was an accolade, for in the words of Charles Spurgeon, friend and confidant of the adult Hudson Taylor,

> It is impossible that any ill should happen to the man who is beloved of the Lord. Ill to him is no ill, but only good in a mysterious form. Losses enrich him, sickness is his medicine, reproach is his honour, and death is his gain.

John and Mary had a family of eight children, brought up strictly on Methodist principles, with the usual variety of effects. William, the third son, went his own way and became a well-to-do stockbroker. Samuel Shepherd Taylor, the youngest, became a Methodist minister. James junior, the second son, was apprenticed to a 'chemist and druggist' in Rotherham and became an apothecary or 'prescribing chemist', part pharmacist, part doctor, in those days of scanty medical knowledge and evolving professions. At the weekend he would walk the ten or fifteen miles to return home and spend Sunday with the family.

After two years, in 1823, a jovial Wesleyan minister, the Rev Benjamin Hudson, was appointed to Barnsley. He was known for his irrepressible fund of humour. When the moderator of a ministerial conference chided him for levity he apologised in words so witty as to have all his colleagues holding their sides with laughter. He too had sons and daughters of about the same age and the two families discovered a love of music in common. They sang and played together in each other's homes. John had done well as a maker of 'reeds and stays' for linen-weaving looms. On the strength of it he built a good stone house and there they enjoyed their musical evenings. John Taylor had 'a very beautiful voice and a perfect musical ear', and so had Amelia Hudson, 'the nightingale', one of the minister's daughters.

When Amelia was sixteen and the young James twenty-two they became engaged. It was about the time that Samuel Dyer offered his services to the LMS and fell in love with Maria Tarn. But after another year the Hudsons moved elsewhere in the Methodist circuit. Amelia went to

Polam Hall, a Society of Friends girls' school with a Froebel training department for teachers, a music and arts 'conservatoire' and a domestic economy department, and James faced the fact that although his father could have helped him he could not marry until his apprenticeship ended and he could himself provide for Amelia and a family.

In 1830, however, while Amelia was governess to a good family, James Taylor launched out on his own, aimed high, leased a pharmacy in the best location, 21 Cheapside, Barnsley, and with the help of a loan from his father and elder brother bought the freehold. Cheapside faced on to May Day Green, the market place from which the main streets of Barnsley radiated. He began to build up a reputation. Soon it was known that James was 'scrupulous to a farthing and to a grain' and made it a rule to pay any debt the day it fell due. 'If I let it stand,' he said, 'my creditor is defrauded of interest . . . if only a fractional sum.'

He had been a local preacher since he was nineteen and already since reading Captain Basil Hall's *Voyage of Discovery along the Coast of China*, had more than an interest in East Asia. He was concerned that the people of China should hear the gospel. There is no record that Robert Morrison came that way during his year in England, 1825, but James cannot have failed to share in the excitement and repercussions, the missionary zeal which Morrison's advent created in the Churches of England.

James and Amelia were married in April 1831 and began to pray together for a son whom God would use for the evangelisation of China. Very solemnly they read in Exodus 13.2 about the consecration of the first-born, and in the same spirit knelt side by side and dedicated their own to God, months before he was born on May 21, 1832. They named him James Hudson and lived not only to see their prayer answered, but to witness the growing success of the mission he founded. There was no precedent by which they could have imagined the part their son was to play in the opening up of China to the gospel; and they did not tell him of their prayer until he was an experienced missionary in his thirties.

The years of Hudson Taylor's childhood were eventful ones for Britain and the world. With so much travel and such ignorance of disease it was inevitable that sooner or later epidemics should spread. Asiatic cholera had struck England devastatingly for the first time in November 1831. Sixteen thousand died in London alone, but Barnsley was spared. It was to strike again several times. Those were days of political unrest too. Ireland's attempts to secure Home Rule were put down; the trades unions failed for lack of resources; electoral and administrative reforms, poor relief and factory acts came in. The pillory and whipping posts were abolished; and the Corn Laws were repealed.

Hudson Taylor lived at a time of immense progress and change. When he was two, all slaves in the British empire were freed, and the Methodist world with its stake in the Caribbean plantation islands and thousands of Christian slaves celebrated their rejoicing on Emancipation Eve, July 31, 1834. Services were held in all Methodist chapels in Britain. As midnight approached all knelt in prayer and as the hour struck and eight hundred thousand slaves became free men, James and Amelia, their family and fellow-Christians, sang the doxology.

In October John Taylor died and one of Hudson Taylor's earliest recollections was the sight and feel of his grandfather's dead body, for they made him touch it. The solemnity of life and death must be inculcated in the young. His sixth birthday was also the centenary of Charles Wesley's conversion; and the following year Hudson and all his family were caught up in the centenary celebrations of the Methodist movement. At seven he was impressionable and consciously taking part. There were by then more Wesleyan missionaries overseas than all John Wesley's enrolled ministers put together and Hudson's parents talked often about them. His father was a great reader of theology, sermons, medicine and French literature, but now he devoured all he could find on the work of missions. Livingstone was asking the LMS to send him to China as Morrison had asked them to send him to Africa. Why was it, James Taylor asked, that so many Methodist missionaries were sent to India and elsewhere? 'Why don't they send them to China?' If Roman Catholic missionaries could live and work in the interior of China at such low cost, why not Protestants? Hudson soaked up the influence of his parents' zeal. 'When I am a man I shall go to China,' various members of his mother's family heard him say.

In 1839 a young Scotsman, William C. Burns, was preparing to go as a missionary to China and speaking at farewell meetings, when he found himself the greatly beloved centre of a spiritual revival. To his joy and amazement it swept through Scotland and northern England, and then Canada when he went over there. It delayed his departure to China for eight years but resulted in others becoming missionaries as well. Barnsley was affected and revival in the Churches fanned the flames of missionary zeal already burning in the Taylor home.

A year or two after Hudson, his first brother William Shepherd was born. He died at the age of seven. After him came the first girl, born on September 20, 1835, and named after her mother, Amelia Hudson Taylor. Another boy came next, but he also died in childhood. Not until 1848 did the Public Health Act make a start towards reducing the infant mortality rate in the towns of England. It still stood at an average of one in every two babies, followed closely by morbidity among surviving children. Finally in 1840 Louisa Shepherd Taylor arrived, when Hudson was eight.

If a few pages on Hudson Taylor's home and childhood at first seemed excessive in a book of this nature, their relevance will become apparent as his personality and life story are revealed. No. 21 Cheapside had four storeys, the kitchen and medical stores in the basement, the shop and dining room, used as a consulting room, above it, the sitting room and parents' bedroom above that, and finally the children's and servants' rooms. James's assistant shared Hudson's bedroom. Outside at the back was the stable-yard with stable and warehouse.

Every day James Taylor would take his children into his bedroom and kneel beside the four-poster with arms spread over them, to pray for them by name. It made a deep impression on them. He took Hudson on some of his engagements, and rejoiced that 'his face glowed with delight' when people responded by going up to the penitent form. For James was always an evangelist. His unbounded faith in God and his Word inevitably rubbed off on Hudson. His characteristic expression, 'He cannot deny Himself, He would not be God if He could,' was the bed-rock belief by which Hudson came to live, and the cornerstone of the China Inland Mission he founded. By then the old man and his wife were convinced that God had accepted the offering of their first-born and intended to do great things through him.

James Taylor was a complex character, and suffered from being his own worst enemy. He was painfully shy even among equals, and only at ease among familiar friends. His rich and influential clients who came to him because of his reputation for sound diagnosis and treatment, as well as honesty, found him uncommunicative. He would even go upstairs rather than face some of them. But his home was wide open to his Methodist friends when they came into town, and those who entertained him in their homes when he went to preach had a standing invitation to lunch when they in turn were in Barnsley.

Friends with the same intellectual interests saw a very different side of the man. He could expand very knowledgeably on many subjects. K. S. Latourette in his Tipple Lectures spoke of his wide reading and called him a competent mathematician of scrupulous integrity, with a reputation for carrying through whatever he undertook. His tables of interest were calculated to four or five places of decimals, but he never pressed for payment of accounts or sued for bad debts. When he knew his customers could not afford the cost of treatment he often remitted part of the charge or simply said, 'It's all right James, we'll send that account to heaven and settle it there.' He was genial and kindly, especially to the poor, strangers and foreigners.

In another way James Taylor was tight-fisted. It began when he saved every penny to pay off his family loans as quickly as he could, and continued throughout life because he set out to give his widow and children a secure future. Unfortunately it made life almost intolerably difficult for his wife as she struggled to feed the household on a barely adequate allowance. James earned enough to send the children to good schools but kept them at home to be taught by their mother and himself, both well able to do it. She also helped as his secretary. He would pace up and down with his hands behind his back, as Hudson Taylor was to do in later years, dictating his sermon notes while his dutiful spouse wrote fast and meticulously, enjoying herself but counting the minutes lost from her other duties.

Fortunately Hudson's mother was a selfless person, unobtrusive, intelligent, well read herself and a good listener. Latourette says she inherited her father Benjamin Hudson's sense of humour, and certainly Hudson Taylor had a good streak of humour, and his mother needed all she possessed. Another record says she lived in 'painful subjection' to James. In fairness, however, it has to be remembered that the idea of the paterfamilias as lord and master of the home was well-established and, in the judgment of the day, ordained by Scripture.

After her own home in Barton-on-Humber where her father settled, the cramped and busy house in Barnsley must often have seemed a prison. The Barton home was an old red-bricked house covered with creepers, with broad low windows with window seats, a beautiful garden with trees, flower beds, orchard and garden wall decked with well-trained fruit trees, and a lawn leading to a park-like field beyond. She was a 'beautiful character' and the children knew only her warm and affectionate nature.

From the correspondence she preserved after Hudson

left home, it is clear that a strong bond of confidence existed between them. In many ways Hudson, and his sister Amelia too, were very like their mother. Few were more affectionate than Hudson Taylor as an adolescent and adult. Foremost in his mother's thoughts, however, was the desire not only to point but to lead other people to Christ. Like her husband she was a 'soul-winner'. Their example played a decisive part in making Hudson Taylor a missionary even while still a boy.

School was at home. Their father taught them arithmetic, French and Latin, and their mother applied her Froebel principles, and later taught them English, music and natural history. The educational methods of the contemporaries Froebel and Pestalozzi were new to Britain. By their emphasis on the child's right to personal autonomy and self-conceived play in the 'kindergarten' they introduced a new understanding of child psychology. So it was a happy arrangement in the Taylor home. The children learned to read and observe for themselves. For the rest of his life Hudson Taylor was a nature-lover and collector. The journal of his first voyage to China is full of evidence of this. Still preserved are botanical specimens collected by him on an island in the South Pacific on one of his journeys.

A twentieth-century tradition seems to have grown up that Hudson Taylor as a child was frail and even sickly, that this was the reason for his not going to school. He was slight and pale, perhaps from too much indoor life and too little exercise; and during the months when he eventually attended a school he did miss many days through colds and minor ailments; but until he was nineteen he never had a day's serious illness. A close study of the archives discloses no other information. It looks as if previous authors' interpretations rather than the facts are responsible for the legend. The description of him as 'sunny, bright and nature loving' belongs more to a healthy boy.

Both children learned how to work, and the parents found they themselves could cope with schooling at home and all preferred it that way. When a school in the town

was first talked of, Hudson was full of the new book
Nicholas Nickleby and, imagining himself under the rod,
pleaded to be spared. For two years from the autumn of
1843 he did attend as a day boy, but when Mr Laycock, the
Master, left and an unsatisfactory successor took over,
Hudson at thirteen and a half returned to be taught at
home and to help his father in the pharmacy, mixing,
pounding and wrapping medicines.

Those were the Hungry Forties after a disastrous series
of wet summers; and the Irish potato famine deprived the
poor of their staple diet. The Queen's friend and adviser,
Lord Melbourne, was out of office and young Prime
Minister Peel's concern for economic stability took precedence over the sufferings of the poor. Destitute Irish
families flocked to the factories, roads, canals and railways
of England earning their pittance as 'navvies'. It was also
the period of imperialist expansion in India, and of
exploitation of the concessions wrung from China through
the first opium war. Brunel's *Great Britain* inaugurated the
era of propeller-driven ocean-going steamships, and rapid
travel to China was in sight.

Hudson all at sea   *1844–48*

During the four years following the revival movement
and Wesleyan centenary, the attention of Britain and the
Church was focused intently on the events in China. News
may have travelled slowly but when it arrived the thought
of what might have happened in the meantime only added
force to the excitement. The East-West conflict had burst
into flames, had fizzled and died down, but had then been
fanned again and spread from port to port up the coast to
the Yangzi and Nanking.

James Taylor must have followed events closely, for
China was constantly in his thoughts and prayers. His
conversation at table, while the children sat silent and his
wife and apprentices listened dutifully, can be assumed
from after-events to have had a profound influence on

Hudson Taylor. Amelia in later years drew a diagram of how they sat, with her father's books filling the recess behind the red plush curtain from floor to ceiling. The memory of that room and of her father's voice were printed on her mind. Hudson and Amelia were becoming inseparable, entering into their parents' life, even to going out together distributing tracts in the poorer parts of Barnsley. So they grew up with a deepening interest in China.

In 1843, when Hudson was eleven, Peter Parley published his book on China, the latest in a series introducing the world to his young readers. Even today its elfish, chuckling cheerfulness is infectious. 'Once more, my young friends, old Peter Parley greets you.' Hudson and Amelia, intellectually older than their years through close association with adults, read and re-read Peter Parley's *China and the Chinese* 'until they could almost recite it'. The preface introduced:

> one of the most interesting nations on the face of the earth. If I had called it *the* most wonderful I should not have been far from the truth . . . It is the oldest government . . . the most populous nation . . . acquainted with the art of printing, the use of the mariner's compass and the art of making gun powder . . . for several hundreds of years before the Europeans discovered them. . . . If the books which formed their standard literature were all destroyed, then at least a million of persons now living . . . could restore them all from memory. They have the most extensive public works in the world . . . the Great Wall and the Grand Canal, either of which has as much work in it as all the pyramids of Egypt . . .

—good factual information with a playful lilt for over two hundred pages.

The part that John Robert Morrison and Gutzlaff were still playing in Asian events was probably well known to the Taylors for they took *The Evangelical Magazine*. The editor's daughter was married to James Legge and close to the action. An 1843 edition of Captain Basil Hall's racy travelogue about his 1816 voyage, published when the opium war brought China into the public eye, was full of absorbing details. Hamilton Lindsay's report of the *Lord Amherst's* survey was available, Gutzlaff's *Voyages* and Medhurst's *A Glance at the Interior of China* followed. Strange to say the major work, Medhurst's *China*, is not actually mentioned in the family papers until 1850. From these and other sources Hudson probably heard of Samuel Dyer's and John Robert Morrison's tragic deaths, and of others like saintly, ailing David Abeel who went home from Amoy to die.

In the summer of 1844 Hudson Taylor was taken to a 'camp meeting' in a park at Leeds to hear an evangelist named Henry Reed. Reed told the story of a 'ticket of leave man' in Australia, who kept on putting off the decision to turn to Christ, in spite of repeatedly thinking of the words 'My son, give Me thy heart' before it was too late. The twelve-year-old took note and thought about it. He had grown up in the Christian circle and entered into everything, but had never had consciously personal dealings with God. Not until he was fourteen did he act on what he knew was God speaking to him. Then, as he wrote years later, 'I gave my heart to God.' But life went on much as before.

The religious atmosphere at home was unusually intense. He was having perhaps more than was good for him of his father's company. Morning prayers at the table after breakfast involved a reading of Scripture so that the children soaked it up involuntarily. But James Taylor would then pray for twenty minutes in the rich biblical language of the Reformed tradition. Hudson can be forgiven if at his age he suffered from spiritual indigestion. Amelia seems to have absorbed it more easily and at twelve was called upon by her father to pray aloud when she went with him to meetings in the district. But in spite of giving his heart to God, Hudson was in the doldrums.

Soon after his fifteenth birthday, May 1847, he went into a local bank as a clerk. His father, who wanted to give him more experience of book-keeping and to let him see something of a wider world, spent anxious months as he watched Hudson come under the influence of the 'banker', the cashier and others. They laughed at Hudson's ideas, tied him in knots with their arguments, shocked him with their language, and gave him grand ideas of owning a horse and a fine house and being 'successful'. He longed to go hunting with them. This is the first mention we have of his ability to ride. How James travelled to his circuit meetings is nowhere stated, for horseback was the common-place way and an 1850 letter confirms that they had more than one mount in their stables.

Hudson's spiritual life shrivelled up. He stopped praying and became miserable with doubts about what he believed. The Chartists, the socialists of the day, were at their strongest; and, after years of study at the British Museum, Karl Marx published his *Manifesto* in 1848. Politics, scepticism and atheism were all of a piece. A Chartist second-hand bookseller took to sniping at Hudson's fragile faith. When he tried it at 21 Cheapside he met his match in Hudson's father, but Hudson Taylor alone was sitting prey. Both cashier and Chartist harped on the inconsistency of Christians and, from the state of some prominent Christians' balances at the bank, Hudson knew what was meant. He decided that if he was going to be a Christian he would be a thorough-going one. If not, far better throw it all overboard. In a sense the opposition was tempering his beliefs, but because of his state of confusion he came to think of himself as a non-Christian.

As winter drew on Hudson Taylor's eyesight began to give trouble. Working by candle-light he strained to see and could not. 'My eyes gave out at balancing time' was how he put it in his recollections. So he had to leave the bank — 'very fortunately for me or I might have been swamped'. He had been there only nine months, but with his father's teaching it was enough to give him a very adequate grasp of books and of business principles. The reputation he later acquired as an administrator owed a good deal to this and to the meticulous accuracy his parents instilled. Spectacles of a sort had been in use for centuries, but by twentieth-century standards were still primitive, with very small and simple lenses. A portrait of Benjamin Hudson, the grandfather, shows his humorous eyes twinkling over such a pair, and there is a portrait of Hudson Taylor as a medical student of twenty wearing lenses no more than an inch in diameter.[39]

For the present he could only return to work in the pharmacy, sick with himself for his spiritual backsliding and exasperated by his father's strictures and sometimes short temper. After a few weeks he reached sixteen, as unhappy as any adolescent wrestling with a turbulent self-awareness he could not fathom. And so he remained, wilted and rebellious, all through that year and into the next. His mother and thirteen-year-old sister tried without success to help him, so they agreed together to pray until the Lord delivered him.

In the house next door there lived a nineteen-year-old, staying with his sister who was married to a business friend. Benjamin Broomhall was intrigued by James Taylor's apparently inexhaustible fount of knowledge. He called him the 'Oracle' and was immensely impressed 'by the enormous pains he took to memorise' whatever he wanted to remember. Benjamin found him 'inspiring' and would spend hours in the Taylors' home. Naturally a friendship grew up between him and Hudson, a stabilising influence in a shaky world and a bond which bound them both to China.

CHAPTER SEVEN

AFTER NANKING
1844–49

International adjustments *1844–45*

The unequal treaties of 1842–44 gave the Western powers not only a foothold in five ports and on the island of Hong Kong. With the American and French treaties of 1844 the Chinese conceded the principle of equality for all foreigners, and the benefits of French insistence on religious liberty for Roman Catholics were also applied, as we saw, to Protestant missionaries and Christians. Edicts of persecution were rescinded, and missionaries found outside the treaty ports were merely to be handed over to their consuls. In the event, the implementation of the treaties depended largely on the attitude of local mandarins. Many were only too ready to disregard them.

In 1846, however, the French government went further and set itself up as champion of Roman missions. They insisted on Chinese observance of the privileges granted, exemption from penalties previously imposed, and liberty for Christians not only to hold but to exercise their faith. But that was not all. A further demand sowed the seeds of deep resentment, litigation and conflict. They demanded and an edict decreed the restoration to the Catholic Church of buildings confiscated since the reign of Kang Xi. Those converted into temples or private homes were exempt, but others were to be surrendered. Property had changed hands frequently in the one hundred and twenty-three years since 1723 and gross injustice and bitterness resulted. For the

Church to re-occupy such premises could only presage trouble; and it did, especially as the French interpretation of the agreement went to extremes.

Understandably Qi Ying, the chief negotiator and 'barbarian tamer' changed his tune, and 'stopped trying to get his way by cordiality'. The 'diplomatic honeymoon' fell apart. In 1858 when relations between China and the Western powers collapsed again, Qi Ying tried to save the dynasty and himself, but a copy of his 1844 report to Peking was found at Canton and cruelly used 'to laugh the aged diplomat into his grave'.[1]

Restrictions on Westerners travelling beyond the treaty ports were plain enough, but disregard for the laws of Asian nations was inherent in the attitude of British merchants. In the treaty ports of China it was even more so. The air of conquest bred such scorn that opium and gun-running continued to be blatant evasions against which the Chinese authorities and Western consuls were powerless to do more than protest. This attitude affected everyone. The vogue was to test the constraints as far as possible. For any but the armed ships an element of real risk made treaty-stretching fair sport. If you were not stoned or stabbed to death, you could expect to be delivered back to the coast under escort and receive no more than a reprimand.

Robert Fortune, a botanist collecting for the Royal Horticultural Society, began in 1843 a series of four long journeys spanning nine years. By careful disguise as a Chinese subject from beyond the Great Wall, a world of mystery to people in the south, and by close observation of customs and behaviour, he made friends and penetrated wherever he wished. The tea plantations of Assam and Darjeeling resulted from his success in collecting seeds and thousands of plants, and even in recruiting tea growers from the native places of China's fragrant teas.

In 1844 the renowned Abbé Huc and his companion Joseph Gabet visited congregations in the far north and in a truly epic journey went on westward disguised as Mongol lamas into Tibet. In the company of a Tibetan dignitary with an escort of two thousand mounted men they succeeded in reaching Lhasa; but then the discovery that they were foreigners caused consternation. They were taken as prisoners all the way to Chengdu, tried, despatched to Canton and deported. In other circumstances strangling would have been the least they would have suffered.

The Protestant missionaries were grateful for the great progress they were making and with few exceptions stayed within the limits of the ports and twenty-four-hour excursions.[2] Walter H. Medhurst was an exception, going out in 1845 'in defiance of existing political regulations . . . yet in dependence on the Divine guidance'.[3] His account of the journey through Zhejiang (Chekiang) and Kiangxi was published after a discreet interval of four years yet still anonymously, to avoid recrimination, as *A Glance at the Interior of China, obtained during a journey through the Silk and Green Tea Districts.*

The detail with which he described his disguise and procedure throughout the journey was clearly intended as a *vade mecum* for others contemplating a similar adventure. In the event he found that he had to keep hidden, often feigning sleep or sickness. He paid a generous tribute to his Chinese guides who took such risks for his sake, and to the Catholic missionaries who travelled and lived in this way year after year. Twice he almost gave himself away — by speaking Malayan in his sleep. Robert Fortune escaped detection on encountering a Shanghai Chinese acquaintance who happened to have come inland.[4]

Under successive governors Hong Kong expanded in a haphazard fashion, unlike Singapore in Sir Stamford Raffles's control. By the time Sir John Bowring, plenipotentiary in 1854, attempted some town planning, the vested interests of the merchants made it impossible and he had to swallow his exasperation. Shanghai was a very different picture.[5] Captain Balfour had allowed building at first to be haphazard but had soon laid out a pattern of roads. His successor, Rutherford Alcock, was a methodical hardliner. When he took over in 1846 the settlement had grown from twenty-three acres to one hundred and eighty and sound planning was imperative. Four years later it was four hundred and eighty acres, and the hundred or so foreign residents almost doubled. Twenty-five merchant firms were represented and before long Shanghai boasted five shops for European goods. European women were few, only seven in 1844. Hudson Taylor had been in China for five years before the first ladies' dress shop opened in 1859. In addition a constantly changing population of seamen brought their own problems of law and order.

The river front was a muddy bank when the British moved in, and the first development undertaken was to drive wooden retaining piles and build a simple towpath for the Chinese tracker-coolies towing their grain ships upstream. Gradually this embankment was improved and widened on to the tidal foreshore, with simple jetties for visiting ships. It came to be known by the Persian-Hindi word as the Bund. As steamers came and went, their clinkers and ashes were tipped on shore and slowly the mud tracks became all-weather roads.

The consuls, merchants and missionaries gradually built bungalows with cool verandahs and moved out of the Chinese houses they had occupied at first. Then business houses in 'compradore' style followed: square buildings with four large offices on the ground floor, company dining-rooms and dormitories for the young bachelors upstairs, and warehouses in the 'compounds' behind. Upstairs and down were wide verandahs, cool and airy, usually over-looking the Bund, the Huangpu river and shipping.

Senior merchants, seldom over forty-five as in the early days, were known as *taipans* and their juniors as 'griffins' after the Tartar ponies they kept for exercise and later for racing. Debarred in the larger commercial houses from marrying for five years, they lived in semi-collegiate fashion often with 'kept' Chinese women. The old Canton 'factory' days were over but the new Shanghai set-up was its first cousin, with the marked difference that here the foreigner did as he liked so long as the consul turned a blind eye.

In 1845 the P & O Steam Navigation Company began a monthly mail and passenger service from England to Singapore, and a year later extended it to Hong Kong and Shanghai.[6] The *Lady Mary*, a paddle steamer, halved the time previously taken for the voyage, and the China coast was more on the map than ever before. Even so the first 'hotel' was not opened in Shanghai until 1848, six years before Hudson Taylor arrived.

In political turmoil at home, the French were troublesome allies in Asia. At Shanghai they occupied a separate area between the British settlement and the ancient Chinese city. With the arrogance of the revived Napoleonic empire they claimed jurisdiction and refused unification as an international settlement. The first Americans to arrive were the missionaries led by Dr W. J. Boone, by then a bishop of the American Episcopal Church. Looking for less expensive Chinese premises to rent, they occupied the north bank of the Suzhou (Soochow) Creek outside the Settlement, but co-operated closely with the British. A separate American settlement therefore developed.

Rutherford Alcock   *1842–48*

The early consuls were an outstanding group of men. Among them the mortality rate was as alarmingly high as among the missionary pioneers, but they shared a dedication to their job and some survived to make a name for their nations and themselves.

Rutherford Alcock was such a man, 'a philosophic man of action'.[7] As a boy he made artificial limbs in Paris to pay for a medical education, and qualified as a Member of the Royal College of Surgeons at twenty-one. For the next four years he was a house-surgeon at Westminster Hospital, until in 1832 a surgeon under whom he had studied was appointed Surgeon to the British Forces in Portugal. G. J.

Guthrie invited Alcock to go with him and within twenty-four hours they set off.

For five years young Alcock showed such courage and ability that he returned to England with the rank of Deputy-Director of Hospitals and several Portuguese decorations. He was married at St Margaret's, Westminster, won the Jacksonian prize of the Royal College of Surgeons for studies on concussion and injuries to the thorax, and became a lecturer with a view to a professorship in military surgery at King's College Hospital. He was made Inspector of Anatomy and called to serve on Royal Commissions on the Peninsular Wars, for his gifts of administration were as great as his surgical skills. Then suddenly he fell ill with fever and paralysis of both arms. He was thirty-five.

When he recovered Rutherford Alcock was left with residual paralysis of both thumbs and some arm muscles. Teaching without practical surgery held no charm for him, so he entered the Diplomatic Service and was posted at once to China. Appointed as British consul at Fuzhou, he went to Amoy for a four-month interregnum. At once he demonstrated his characteristic energy, clear-sightedness and forthrightness. As an interpreter he took with him a fifteen-year-old boy in whom he recognised qualities of greatness. H. S. (Harry) Parkes had come to China only two years before but had learned Chinese from Charles Gutzlaff and John Robert Morrison and been present at the Treaty of Nanking negotiations.[8]

When the mandarins at Amoy tried to disparage Alcock by relegating him to unsuitable premises he had a good consulate built on a good site. At Fuzhou he found a similar state of affairs. The consulate Tradescant Lay had accepted was a mere farmhouse on a mud flat, so Alcock built a substantial Chinese house on a hill in the heart of the city, disregarding the mandarins' objections. He quickly established a reputation for firm action and was posted to Shanghai to succeed Captain Balfour. Again he took Harry Parkes with him, training him for promotion to assistant consul.

A consul was responsible to his own government for the safety and good behaviour of his compatriots, and to the Chinese government for their observance of Chinese law. In Shanghai when Rutherford Alcock went there, the mere one hundred and twenty Europeans were not all British, but the drifting population of hundreds of seamen was a ripe source of trouble and might outnumber the residents by ten to one. Debauched and riotous, they provided work for the consul as magistrate and representative of the Crown.

Even the missionaries contributed their quota of problems, welcoming every concession but rejecting any suggestion that the treaties fettered them to the ports.

In 1846 the adventurous W. C. Milne moved from Ningbo to join Medhurst and Lockhart at Shanghai, and the following year a fourth LMS missionary arrived. William Muirhead was to become one of the outstanding figures of the century in China. The countryside around Shanghai was full of game, pheasants, quail, snipe and wild fowl, close to the Settlement and even flying into the residents' gardens. Sporting parties would therefore mount excursions and be away for twenty-four hours at a time. The country folk learned to trust them and would accept a chit, a scribbled IOU in exchange for food or services, knowing that it would be honoured in the settlement or even in the city. There was always the risk, however, of being stoned by anti-foreign Chinese. The missionaries joined in the sport but also went preaching from village to village, selling books and distributing pamphlets. Trouble was not long in coming.

Qingpu and Canton outrages   1848

In March 1848 Medhurst, Lockhart and Muirhead were on one of these missionary excursions when they were attacked by a mob at the market town of Qingpu.[9] The great grain fleet which carried rice from the south by sea and by the Grand Canal to Peking and the northern cities, was seasonal in operation. During slack periods the discharged crews were left to shift for themselves and roamed the countryside together almost as brigands. One of these bands set upon the unresisting missionaries with hoes, clubs, iron bars and chains, beating them to the ground and hauling them to their junks to hold them for ransom. Rescued by militiamen of the *daotai*, the city Prefect, they returned to the Settlement bruised and bleeding. 'Undoubtedly [they] were able to reach the point of rescue only because of "the rare example of Christian forbearance and temper which marked their conduct," ' Consul Alcock reported.[10]

Rutherford Alcock acted at once,[11] calling on the *daotai* to deal with the junk-men. This was the first incident of the kind in Shanghai and the *daotai* did not know his man. When evasion of responsibility failed to get rid of the consul he tried intimidation by threats. Immediately Alcock showed his mettle. His instructions were to conciliate the Chinese. Careful Confucian etiquette and civility however were unsuccessful. The treaty was bilateral. If he kept his own rowdies in order, so must the mandarins theirs. Alcock was a just and honourable gentleman. The victims happened to be missionaries but merchant sportsmen could as easily have been molested. Weakness now would certainly lead to greater provocation later.

Fortuitously there were still fourteen hundred laden grain-junks in the river and some British frigates visiting Shanghai. It was characteristic of Rutherford Alcock to size up the situation and act decisively. He arranged for the ten-gun brig *Childers* to blockade the river and demanded action from the *daotai*. The *daotai* was made of the same stuff and ordered the rice-fleet to proceed downstream protected by fifty war junks. Had the fleet obeyed, a major clash would have developed, but the junk crews had seen foreign warships in action six years previously and refused to budge.

At the same time Alcock sent his vice-consul and Harry Parkes[12] direct to the viceroy at Nanking. The viceroy was a realist. He ordered full redress and the punishment of the offenders by execution. The LMS missionaries intervened and instead the ringleaders were exposed in cangues outside the old temple in the settlement, doing duty as a customs house, as an example to the rest, and the *daotai* was replaced.[13]

The British government's reaction to reports of this 'Tsingpu Outrage', as it is known in Parliamentary Papers, was a muted reprimand to Alcock that read more like congratulation. Their dispatch had overtones which shaped the actions of British consuls until after 1870. It could be read as, 'Repeat this at your peril, leaving us to applaud or repudiate you, according to the circumstances.' The next time it was put to the test, Alcock was Sir Rutherford, Her Majesty's Minister in Peking; Medhurst's son, Walter H. Medhurst Jr., was consul-general at Shanghai; and the victims of mob violence were Hudson Taylor, his wife and children, and several young colleagues. However, in the meantime Alcock was promoted to the senior consulate, that at Canton, a stepping-stone to the highest rank.

The Qingpu outrage was not the only one, or the most serious. On December 5 of the same year 1848, six British clerks from Hong Kong business houses went on an excursion three miles upriver from Canton and were attacked by villagers. One of them shot a Chinese dead and wounded two more, whereupon all six clerks were butchered with great cruelty and their mutilated bodies thrown into the river. Both Chinese and British authorities were aghast. The bodies were recovered by dragging, and the attackers were arrested.[14]

Then began one of the most lamentable episodes between the two nations. Sir John Francis Davis was governor of Hong Kong, superintendent of British trade and minister plenipotentiary, and Qi Ying was still imperial commissioner at Canton, no longer playing the 'diplomatic honeymoon' game. Sir John demanded justice and Qi Ying acknowledged Chinese responsibility for the affair.

Although the 'diplomatic honeymoon' was over, the

records show that Qi Ying was from beginning to end courteous and reasonable, while the British were high-handed and crude in their demands for vengeance. Enlightenment was on the Chinese side. Sir John insisted that the guilty Chinese all be executed and their villages razed to the ground. Not content with that, and interpreting Qi Ying's conciliatory but balanced communications as prevarication, he also threatened to end all trade and chastise the city of Canton. Qi Ying was prepared to execute the murderers but protested against punishing their wives and children and fellow-villagers. The populace would not tolerate that. He feared a general rising. To this Sir John replied offering to 'help' the commissioner with a gunboat and four hundred men. A compromise was reached. Only the guilty were punished, but heavy indemnities were exacted. Quiet descended once more, but not true peace. Foreign intransigence and Chinese resentment had replaced the Chinese intolerance and foreign resentment of the old Factory days.

Missions after the treaties   1844–47

With the revoking of the edicts of persecution, the Catholic Church in China rapidly recovered from the suffocating pressure of decades. The Jesuits took over the Siccawei property near Shanghai, ancestral home of Matteo Ricci's convert Paul Xu, and made it their headquarters. Before long an orphanage, an industrial school and a library were built, and later on an observatory and a cathedral church, with a bamboo pipe-organ like that which survives today in a suburb of Manila. Thirteen new churches were erected in Fujian in the first five years.

On his travels the Abbé Huc found the Church in Sichuan more flourishing than elsewhere and attributed the fact to the higher educational level of its members. The Société des Missions Étrangères de Paris, the Paris Mission, took responsibility for Tibet and made many heroic attempts to establish themselves there, but in Sichuan province itself there were large and well-cared-for communities. In 1848 as many as eight hundred and eighty-eight adult baptisms were recorded.[15] If these are accepted as merely meaning declarations of adherence to the Church the figure is still significant. But the parallel figure of eighty-four thousand baptisms of infants in danger of death is ominous in the extreme, for they were popularly believed by superstitious people to be associated with the basest motives. The Society (or Association) of the Holy Infancy (or Childhood), the Catholic sisterhood, existed to rescue destitute children and to give expression to their belief that baptism before death would ensure a welcome to heaven. Death so often followed the rite that cause and effect were assumed and guilt was pinned mercilessly on well-meaning Catholics all over China.

In 1846 the first Sisters of St Paul arrived at Hong Kong and among them was the Wuchang martyr Perboyre's own sister.[16] The following year some Sisters of Charity came to Ningbo. It was many years before unmarried Protestant women came to China in any numbers. Even though Mary Ann Aldersey had led the way in 1844, it was largely left to Hudson Taylor to defy public opinion and bring about the change in the latter half of the century.

If the Catholic recovery was good and more daring, the Protestant response to the opening of the ports was at first stronger.[17] Their occupation was immediate and purposeful. Only the essential outline can be related here.

The LMS team were the vanguard. As soon as Walter H. Medhurst reached Shanghai in 1843 as interpreter to Captain Balfour, the consul, he began to conduct Church of England services of worship in the consulates and went regularly into the Chinese city to preach the gospel. With the arrival of other nonconformists he also held services for them. When CMS missionaries came he handed over the consulate services to their care.

After his spell on Chusan Island with Charles Gutzlaff, William Lockhart, the LMS surgeon, moved to Hong Kong, the first medical missionary there, but with the occupation of Shanghai this pioneer with a zest for new frontiers made sure of being at the fore again. He moved in with Medhurst and opened a hospital in the Chinese city. Seven years later he was the first medical missionary to go on to Tianjin and Peking.

For nearly forty years the LMS had been the only British mission in China. Now the CMS and English Presbyterian Mission joined them with the coming of George Smith and Thomas McClatchie in 1844 and of William Burns in 1847. Three years later two more CMS men, W. A. Russell and C. H. Cobbold arrived and went to Ningbo.

The opening of the treaty ports was in part at least the fulfilment of the early missionaries' dream and they had already consulted together in the Hong Kong conference about co-operation and avoidance of overlap. In the event, however, the unsectarian unity of Robert Morrison, Elijah Bridgman and others was not achieved. Each mission and each denomination started its own work. Even the two Anglican Church societies, American and British, went their own ways and in time had separate bishops. The result was not as divisive as might be expected. The danger of competition and overlap so clearly foreseen and forewarned against by the men who paused to think was not disregarded by late comers. In the words of Professor Latourette, who of all men was entitled to his judgment, some 'unfriendly and wasteful competition' caused confusion in the minds of the Chinese, but 'by no means as much as might be supposed'.[18] Each mission established its own work with its own emphases and biases, and the Chinese Church developed with built-in divisions as foreign to it as the noble frock-coated missionaries who brought them. In fact there was ample room for all and close agreement on doctrinal essentials. 'Modernist' teaching did not come to China till some decades later.

Confinement within the foreign settlements encouraged a Western life-style, however, even though much of the work was in Chinese cities and countryside. Insidiously, therefore, a pattern of norms and conventions developed from which it was difficult for far-seeing missionaries with originality and initiative to deviate. Such eccentricity as adopting Chinese dress and treating Chinese as equals was heavily frowned upon and semi-ostracism became one of Hudson Taylor's tribulations when he followed this course.

Of the new arrivals in China one must now be introduced more fully—William C. Burns,[19] from whose preaching revival had spread in the churches of Britain and Canada, with a resulting concern for the non-Christian world. Burns was a Scotsman, a man of 'fine mind and cultured intellect', a tutor in Greek before he left the academic world. But the Church of Scotland and Free Church were burdened with the problem of recent schism when Burns was ready to go overseas. Like Samuel Dyer he abandoned plans for a career in law and prepared to become a missionary to India. It was then that the revival broke out during his preaching at his father's parish and kept him fully occupied from 1839 to 1847. Andrew Murray, the saintly divine, and his brother were profoundly influenced by him while still boys in Scotland, and G. L. Mackay, one of the first Protestant missionaries to Taiwan, was converted through him in Canada. Burns left it all to join the English Presbyterian Mission and start again in China.

After great audiences and great popularity Burns turned to Chinese language study and suffered from the frustrations of initial inability to make himself understood. For seven years he preached in Amoy and the surrounding countryside and slowly became fluent in the language of the common people. Only then did he have the encouragement of seeing his first Chinese convert. But he overcame his linguistic difficulties. For many years his translation of Pilgrim's Progress was in great demand.

Latourette wrote that Burns's 'transparent devotion and saintliness made a profound impression on many' and that 'in Amoy the LMS, Dutch Reformed and the English Presbyterian missionaries so collaborated that the Chinese Christians did not know that denominational differences existed'.[20] The Chinese Recorder added that Burns was also known for being satisfied with the simplest of living conditions. In 1856 he was to contribute to the spiritual growth and missionary methods of Hudson Taylor at a critical period in his early missionary career, and humbly to acknowledge benefit to himself from their friendship. Perhaps more notable than any of those tributes to William Burns, however, is Latourette's statement that at Amoy he left an independent Chinese Church when he moved away.[21] It was (in Henry Venn's words) self-governing, self-supporting and self-extending—the fruit of his personal humility. Other missionaries served it by teaching and advising, until it was able to stand and grow without them.

The Delegates' Committee who met in Shanghai in 1847 after preparatory work on their own were an impressive group of veterans and scholars, led by Medhurst and Bridgman. John Stronach, William Boone, William Muirhead, J. L. Shuck and some newer arrivals from America made up the team, including William Lowrie, a son of the U.S. Senator who had resigned in order to become Secretary of the American Presbyterian Mission. They completed the New Testament in 1850 and the whole Bible in 1853.

Miss Aldersey had opened a girls' school in Ningbo where the shipwrecked Mrs Noble had been so barbarously maltreated, and William Milne's son, W. C. Milne, returning after his overland journey to the conference at Hong Kong, was there until he joined other members of the Bible translation team in Shanghai. W. H. Medhurst moved the mission press to Shanghai and set it up, powered by buffaloes. He himself wrote and published scores of books in Chinese, Malay and English, as well as being one of the delegates translating the Bible into simple *wen-li*, the lower literary form of Chinese. William Muirhead, who joined him in 1847, specialised in itinerant preaching, and in 1848 Joseph Edkins, another pioneer preacher, arrived. All of these were to be Hudson Taylor's close friends and associates.

The Stronach brothers, John and Alexander, went to Amoy in 1844[22] and John remained there for thirty-eight years, building up a strong Chinese church. His only break was the six years he spent in Shanghai working on the Bible. Both as an apostle and a translator he had exceptional gifts. When educated Chinese attacked him in his preaching by quoting the classics to refute what he was saying and so to alienate his hearers, to the amazement of all John Stronach would give as good as they gave, in the sages' own words. He had studied and memorised until he was their master. This ability to quote large sections of the classics enabled him to express Scripture in rhythmic idiomatic *wen-li* to the delight of all.[23]

The Delegates' Committee and their scholarly Chinese informants faced not only an immensely difficult task of translation, but problems of internal dissension arising from their international and sectarian complexity. The 'term question' and basic principles of translation divided the committee and a minority worked alone to finish their version nine years later. A compromise term for 'baptism' was adopted and 'God' was expressed in alternative ways, by '*Shangdi*' or '*Shen*'. Even the disagreement worked out for the best, however.

> The literati were so exacting in matters of style that a translation of scriptures if it were not to repel them as hopelessly barbarous, must be the fruit of the labour of all the best scholarship that the missionary body could provide.[24]

This goal was achieved. Condensed *wen-li*, the literary form of the language, existed in three degrees, high, medium and low, but because *wen-li* was too classical for most Christians, a minority of translators went on to complete a simpler, less polished but still not vernacular version. An incidental by-product of this was more precise and therefore more accurate rendering of the meaning. The Bible Societies rose to the occasion and eleven editions were published in seven years. In the various dialect areas the missionaries then produced vernacular translations.

Such a 'daring and noble innovation' was liable to incur 'the contempt of Chinese scholars, if indeed they ever deigned to notice' it, but they scarcely did.

Some further reference to the American, Continental and British missions remains to be made. After the LMS, the American Board led by Elijah Bridgman, held the longest record in China. Before moving to Shanghai with the Delegates' Committee the Bridgmans rejoined Liang A-fa, now pastor of the church in Canton. To stay there after the hostilities of the opium war required great courage. In 1846 there were riots, and from time to time foreigners were stoned. With a delightful sense of the dramatic or perhaps of news-value, the Bridgmans kept and took home with them an eighty-five pound rock which was hurled into their river-boat on one of these occasions; but after 1846 it became possible at last for missionaries to live in the city.

Bangkok was still spoken of as 'China' by the old guard of missionaries, using the word as a contraction of the idea that wherever they worked among Chinese the evangelisation of China's hundreds of millions was their aim.[25] After thirteen years in Bangkok the Bridgmans' colleague Stephens Johnson moved, in 1846, to Fuzhou, the first missionary to live in the port the Dyers were to have occupied. Four years later CMS missionaries joined them, but sickness worked havoc among them and tangible results were seen only after eleven years of hard and sacrificial work. The opening of medical work by Dr W. Welton of the CMS appeared to be the key which unlocked the closed hearts of the people.

The American Baptists followed suit when Josiah Goddard moved from Bangkok to Ningbo in 1847 and started to translate the New Testament into the local dialect. A Mr and Mrs Edward C. Lord also came to Ningbo that year. More of Hudson Taylor's future friends are moving on-stage. Dr D. B. McCartee and Mr and Mrs R. Q. Way of the American Presbyterian Mission, and William Lowrie were in Ningbo already. In 1847 they were joined by Mrs

Way's brother, J. W. Quarterman, for whom Hudson Taylor was to risk his life and earn the Ways' unending gratitude, and in 1850 by the Martin brothers, one of whom was to become famous.

However many missions or missionaries followed each other to China, only Hong Kong and the five ports were open to them. For the present some duplication and jostling for position could only be avoided by sinking their differences for the common good. Unfortunately not all were ready for that.

This is not the place to name every mission to enter China, but relevance to the unfolding story earns a brief mention for a few more. Christian naval officers who visited Okinawa during the opium war formed the Loochoo (Ryukyu) Naval Mission, and supported a Dr Bettelheim as medical missionary to the island for several years.[26] And now Charles Gutzlaff began to reap the reward of his industry and faith.

The Berlin Missionary Society, founded in 1824, was too committed to Africa to contemplate adopting China also. When Gutzlaff saw that his appeals to existing missions were not resulting in immediate action, he acted in two ways himself. He founded in 1844 a 'Christian Association for Propagating the Gospel', for Chinese Christians only and under Chinese management; and he appealed in a voluminous correspondence to European Christians in general, reiterating his claim 'China is open; the time has come when we must act.'

As a direct result several German-speaking societies came into being and sent missionaries to work under his guidance. Like Gutzlaff himself, all had and used some knowledge of medicine and surgery. The Evangelical Missionary Society of Basel or Basel Mission was first on the scene in 1846. The Rhenish Missionary Society, known also as the Barmen Mission; a Berlin Missionary Society for China, and Berlin Men's Union; the Berlin Women's Missionary Society for China; and the Berlin Foundling House of Hong Kong, all took shape within two or three

years. The Pomeranian Mission Union for the Evangelisation of China followed. As the 'Pied Piper of Missions'
Gutzlaff unquestionably had a gift for inspiring others.[27]

Gutzlaff's appeals reached the United Kingdom also,
but response was slow to be seen. A group of ministers and
businessmen corresponded with one another, but not until
he was on his way home to Europe did they form their
Chinese Association. Interest in China was by no means
confined to this circle, however. The Dyers' friend, Evan
Davies, published his *Memoir of the Reverend Samuel Dyer*
in 1846, but already he had published a collection of
learned discourses, given originally to his own congregation, under the title *China and her Spiritual Claims*. As a
one-time missionary himself he was well-informed about
the country and its religions and made good use of all the
information that had come his way to stir up the Christian
conscience on behalf of the land for which Samuel Dyer
had given his life. The heart of his appeal was in the words
of Robert Morrison when asked, 'What do the Chinese
with all their ancient civilisation and wisdom require from
Europe?' His reply: 'The knowledge of Christ.'[28]

Revolution   1848–49

In Europe the spirit of revolution was once again in the
air. Karl Marx had been driven out of France in 1845 and
went to Belgium. When his revolutionary movement failed
in the Rhineland in 1848 he found sanctuary in London
and for the rest of his life worked towards the overthrow of
the system that defended his liberty. Hours, weeks and
months spent in the British Museum resulted in his
Manifesto (1848) — and years later the monumental *Das
Kapital* (1867–83). His fellow-revolutionaries of the Communist League held their stormy meeting in London, and
scattered to change the world. With the February Revolution, France was on the rampage again in 1848, and Louis
Napoleon crossed the Channel from his sanctuary in
England to become president of the Second Republic and

then emperor, and to invade Italy and capture Rome. Queen Victoria, niece of the two unprepossessing monarchs before her, was 'the one hope on which the English Crown seemed to depend', for most liberal-minded people then believed that Britain would follow the example of the United States and soon be a republic. With her Consort, Prince Albert, she set a pattern of family life and integrity in a nation which had largely lost its ethical standards. Again in Sir Arthur Bryant's words she was becoming the acknowledged representative of 'her subjects' moral convictions and aspirations'. Overseas they were increasingly imperialistic aspirations.[29]

At the time of the monster meeting of the Chartists on Kennington Common, the barometer of the British social temper, revolution was the prevailing atmosphere of Continental and national life while Hudson Taylor was serving his apprenticeship to his father, and Charles Gutzlaff's appeals were exciting the zeal of Christians on behalf of China. In China itself, while the foreign settlements in the treaty ports were taking root, an insignificant religious movement among peasants in the south was taking a sinister turn, enough to attract the attention of the Peking Court.

Back in 1834 a twenty-year-old Hakka student teacher in Guangxi province who had been disappointed by repeated failures in the classical degree examinations essential for appointment as a mandarin, was handed by Liang A-fa a copy of William Milne's *Good Words to Admonish the Age*. He was impressed and put it aside. Two or three years later he fell ill and over a period of about forty days had visions or hallucinations in which he was taken to luminous palaces and met venerable sages with flowing beards. They were lamenting the depravity of the world and commanded him to exterminate demons and reform society. A middle-aged man then appeared to instruct and help him. He called him his Elder Brother.

But Hong Xiu-quan (Hung Hsiu-ch'üan),[30] the student, recovered and saw no connection with Liang A-fa's tract until in 1843 a cousin was so impressed by it that Hong read it again. Then he 'understood' his visions. The chief sage was God the Father, the Elder Brother was Jesus, and the demons were idols. Hong Xiu-quan and his cousin proceeded to baptise themselves and to preach to their relatives. His parents and family turned from idolatry and for two years Hong travelled through Guangxi preaching and teaching. In 1846 he met the American missionary Issachar J. Roberts, who invited him to come for fuller instruction. Roberts taught him for two or three months and Hong returned home 'before we were fully satisfied of his fitness' for baptism.

When Hong Xiu-quan returned to Guangxi he found that a confused sect of Hakkas and Miao tribes-people, calling themselves 'Worshippers of Shangdi' had arisen as an outcome of his preaching. They confessed their sins before baptism, promising not to worship evil spirits and to keep the heavenly commandments. Together with praying and preaching they made animal sacrifices, fell into trances and mouthed ecstatic utterances. The authorities were alarmed as the cult grew, and imprisoned a local leader. Hong went to Canton and secured his release.

In 1849 Hong Xiu-quan was the accepted leader of the Worshippers of Shangdi and beloved by his followers. He was abstemious, self-denying and kind to all, treating the poor with respect and generosity. He was also keeping in touch with Issachar Roberts. By then Roberts had great hopes of the movement and was reporting developments in his missionary letters.

The Qing (Ch'ing) dynasty had been degenerating perceptibly as the imperial family lost the vigour of the illustrious Kang Xi and Qian Long. The indolent and oppressive Dao Guang and the mediocre Jia Qing were to be succeeded in 1850 by the weak and contemptible Xian Feng emperor. For decades discontent with the imperial government and armed insurrections increased. Secret societies perpetuating the nationalist, pro-Chinese anti-Manchu cause revived and were on the lookout for ferment of any kind. Bad harvests added to the unrest and more peasants resorted to arms. Cults like Hong's remained under suspicion and were increasingly harried. The Worshippers of Shangdi added the destruction of idols to their activities, and when the authorities tried to arrest their leaders thousands of followers flocked to protect them.

Another failed examinee, a Hunanese named Zhu Jiudao (Chu Chiu-tao),[31] with military training and a grudge against the Manchus, saw in the harassed Worshippers of Shangdi the allies he wanted. He brought in veterans of the Triad Society, sworn to the restoration of the pure Chinese Ming dynasty, and began to drill formidable fighting units. Local hostilities began in 1848 and through the next year taxed the provincial governments beyond their strength. The imperial government was forced to intervene. No one, neither 'Patriot Army', as the British in Hong Kong began to call the rebels, nor Manchus, nor foreigners had an inkling of the holocaust about to devastate China. These were the beginnings of the Taiping rebellion which was to dominate events in China for the next fifteen years.

'The Chinese Union' 1844—49

Far from the story nearing its end, with the general activity following the Treaty of Nanking the plot thickens. Against the background of centuries the tumultuous events of the mid-nineteenth century stand silhouetted. As the open century prophetically foreseen by Charles Gutzlaff and soon to be welcomed by the Chinese Church unfolds, the subject of this biography, Hudson Taylor, emerges into manhood with China filling his thoughts. Most influential under God in forming and shaping those thoughts and ambitions was Charles Gutzlaff, renowned as the missionary adventurer of the 1830s, and the indispensable interpreter-negotiator of the still acclaimed treaty. On John Robert Morrison and Charles Gutzlaff, Her Majesty's plenipotentiary Sir Henry Pottinger had leaned heavily. John Morrison was dead, but Gutzlaff remained.

If the structure of this book mattered more than its content, the story of Gutzlaff should now be curtailed. But a slim volume of his collected papers of 1849–50, partly in his own hand, deserves more attention than it has in the past received. If his achievements had ended with his death he would still have an honoured place in the history of the Church, but his significance extends far beyond that point. One distressing error of judgment and a habit of hyperbole, the flowering of an ardent spirit, have tended to be emphasised by writers, to his detriment. Therefore the balance needs to be restored by a more adequate presentation of his aims and policies; but not only for that reason. More significantly, Gutzlaff's vision and some of Gutzlaff's ideas live on to the present day by having taken root in Hudson Taylor, in whose life a projection of him can be seen. In a sense Charles Gutzlaff was a prototype of Hudson Taylor. In the remaining pages we turn away from the broad history of events in China to focus on this unusual person, Gutzlaff, and on the youth through whom he made as great a contribution to the preaching of the gospel throughout China as anyone in the whole eventful story.

As Chinese Secretary to the governor of Hong Kong, the British plenipotentiary, Charles Gutzlaff was a busy man. But even such eminence and responsibility could not deflect him from his primary calling. He lived to carry 'the knowledge of Christ' to the Chinese people. Daily from seven to eight a.m. scores of Chinese came to the government offices to hear him expound the Bible in Hokkien, the dialect of Fujian province. After a hasty breakfast in his own office he then taught in Hakka or another dialect from eight-thirty to nine-thirty before starting the day's work. After office hours he went into the Chinese town or the villages to preach, or worked at home on his own translation of the Old Testament and his voluminous personal correspondence.

His most attentive Chinese listeners he armed with bags of New Testaments and tracts, contributed towards their fares and made them an allowance of four to six Spanish dollars a month from his own pocket. These were the men he organised as The Christian Association for Propagating the Gospel, soon to be known variously as the Chinese Christian Union, the Chinese Union[32] or the Christian Union—to be distinguished from Bridgman's 'Christian Union of China'. Further to forestall confusion we may here add that after 1849 when European groups were formed to support Gutzlaff's Chinese Union, they came to be called Chinese Associations or Chinese Societies—a confusion of names but not of organisation.

Gutzlaff was a Lutheran and the Word mattered more to him than the messenger, but he had high standards and chose the colporteurs carefully. He travelled with them when he could, on the Guangdong and Fujian coasts, and worked out an ambitious plan for reaching the remotest parts of the empire with the gospel. Soon there were six hundred Chinese connected with him, of whom forty were colporteur-evangelists. The members of the Chinese Union were all Chinese and it was under Chinese management. He was their advisor and patron. By April 1847 there were sixty-four colporteurs and by August 1848 as many as eighty. The Union sent them out singly on short itineraries and in pairs for journeys lasting weeks or months. They planned the routes, budgeted the expenses and implemented the policy for gathering converts into groups for simple worship and reading of the Bible.

In 1844 in Hong Kong and farther afield two hundred and sixty-two Chinese were reported as having been baptised. Many of these were the men whom Gutzlaff taught day by day. The following year a more modest eighty-eight baptisms were recorded, but in 1846 after the declaration of tolerance towards Christianity the work apparently acquired new momentum and altogether six hundred and one baptisms were reported from all regions. A peak of six hundred and fifty-five was reached in 1847.

At a time when converts elsewhere were numbered in tens or single figures, this success was outstanding.

The colporteurs were encouraged to bring their leading converts back to the base in Hong Kong for assessment and training, especially any who volunteered to do colportage work themselves. From among them some were chosen, taught and sent out with experienced men. The Chinese Union published its own books and tracts with two grants of a hundred pounds from the British & Foreign Bible Society, and as the work became known in Europe received other donations including four hundred dollars from the king of Prussia. The total expenditure climbed to forty thousand dollars and colporteurs reported a good reception to the gospel in every province except Gansu in the far north-west.

Dr E. J. Eitel described how Gutzlaff

> spent hours every night writing to every missionary society and to every friend of Missions he knew, urging them with all his powers of eloquent persuasion and enthusiastic zeal, to send him men who would not settle down in the ports like other missionaries, but adopt the Chinese costume, live in Chinese style, and be prepared to live and die in the interior of China. And such missionaries did come . . . and went into the interior, patiently submitted to being robbed and plundered, driven from place to place, till stricken down with fever they died, or returned to Hong Kong to recruit their shattered health . . .[33]

In 1847 Gutzlaff received the first answer to his prayers for reinforcements. The Evangelical Missionary Society of Basel was sending a young Swede, Theodore Hamberg, and a companion, Rudolf Lechler, to Hong Kong in September; and two from the Rhenish (Barmen) Missionary Society were to sail with them. In due course they arrived and began to learn Chinese, gradually entering into Gutzlaff's work. The names of some of these young men deserve a more familiar place in the history of the opening of China to the gospel: Lobscheid, Genähr, Vogel, Winnes and others.

In April 1849, however, Gutzlaff's wife was visiting Singapore when she was taken ill and died. Death claimed its victims as capriciously and freely as ever. Medicine was advancing and slowly becoming a science, but little was yet known of the causes or cure of most diseases. Louis Pasteur, the discoverer of the bacteria of cholera and many other diseases was still in his twenties. Sir Patrick Manson, who first suggested that malaria was transmitted by mosquitos, was only five. Decades must still pass and many valuable lives be lost before enough was known about the avoidance and cure of the chief killers in either Asia or the West.[34]

Charles Gutzlaff had twice been bereaved. This time he had to provide for his children. The prospect of visiting Europe, for the first time since his harrowing farewell from his father more than twenty years before, filled him with enthusiasm. News of the Chinese Union had reached the United Kingdom from Germany in 1847, and more recently Gutzlaff had corresponded with Richard Ball, a businessman in Taunton. Ball published the information in pamphlets, and they inspired a new confidence among Gutzlaff's acquaintances.

During the summer of 1849, while still in Hong Kong, Gutzlaff planned a tour of Britain, Scandinavia and the Continent to arouse the Church to China's spiritual need, and not only the opportunity but the accomplished fact of her evangelisation in progress. 'China can only be evangelised by the Chinese,' he claimed, but so far only young and inexperienced Chinese Christians were available. They would need teaching and help from the West for years to come.

Assertive though he was, Gutzlaff was also truly humble and self-effacing. His practice of putting Chinese in the forefront and himself staying in the background was typical. But it had unforeseen consequences. He compiled a statement of the aims, objects, members and achievements of the Chinese Union in Chinese and English[35] and sent it to England (and, the evidence suggests, the continent of

Europe) without any mention of himself or his part in the enterprise. The only name given was that of a Chinese secretary. Richard Ball and his friends jumped to the conclusion that the documents had been drawn up by a Chinese Christian, clearly a man or men of deep spirituality and insight. Here was tangible proof that the grindingly slow progress of missionary work in China was reaping its reward. It must be supported more vigorously by Christians in the West.

What they read was none the less remarkable because it came from Gutzlaff's mind and not a Chinese gentleman's. First the motto of the Chinese Union in Chinese characters and then English:

> Behold these shall come from far; and lo, these from the north and from the west; and these from the land of Sinim. Sing O heavens; and be joyful, O earth; and break forth into singing, O mountains; for the Lord has comforted his people, and will have mercy upon his afflicted. Isaiah 49th chapter, 12th & 13th verses.

Then followed the 'Constitution of the Chinese Union', the 'Objects', 'Future Intentions', 'Means', and 'Remarks' on its administration. The 'Rules and Regulations' in columns of neat little Chinese characters led on to a list of members, province by province and city by city, signed by the Union's Chinese secretary. 'Preachers and their Assistants sent out by the Chinese Union from the first of January to the thirty-first of August 1849' came next, tabulated in Chinese on the left and English on the right with 'Time Departure', 'Preacher's Name', 'To what Place', and 'When to return'. The first entry read 'January 2, Kwok Kao, Szechwan, Kiating, Six Months', and so it proceeded day by day following the lunar and solar calendar until the 126th preacher was listed on August 31, shortly before Gutzlaff sailed for home. Some men featured more than once as they returned and went out again. The full complement of preachers was one hundred and thirty by then, and four hundred and eighty-seven baptisms had been reported with four more months to go before the year ended. This was what Morrison and Milne had dreamed of.

The list of the Chinese Union publications says a good deal for the quality of its teaching. The Bible and histories of the Bible and of the Church are listed with the *English Prayer Book*, the *Augsburg Confession*, two expositions of Christian doctrine and booklets on the birth, death and resurrection of Christ, on *God the Creator*, the *Lord of All Things, Who is Jesus?* and, *Saviour of the World*. For good measure there was a general history, a general geography, a *Short Account of England* (suitable for Hong Kong) and various admonitions from Scripture, on *Moral Principles in the Bible, God's Love to Mankind*, and so on.

The names and locations of every reported baptism were then given in full, in Chinese, and after that each place was identified by latitude and longitude (echoes of the seafarer Gutzlaff), again signed by the Chinese secretary to the Union. Next came an audited statement of accounts and, country by country, notes on the Chinese empire and dependencies, 'Corea', Japan, 'Manchooria', Mongolia, 'Soungaria' [after the Dzungar tribe of what is now called Xinjiang (Sinkiang) or Chinese Turkestan], and finally 'Thibet' and the 'Kochin Chinese Empire', 'Annam', 'Laos' and 'Kambodia'.

> The Laos are a scattered race, serving many masters [this section began]. They inhabit all the interior of the peninsula beyond the Ganges, from the northern frontiers of Siam to the boundaries of Yunnan. Those in the south own the Siamese monarch as liege lord, those in the west the Birmahs, those in the north the Chinese, and only a few tribes of the central part are independent . . .

Rough estimates of the population of each country were also given, but without naming the census China was confidently stated to be 'about 1,379,999 square miles in extent, with a population of 367,642,907 inhabitants'!

Bound with the foregoing were papers more clearly written by or copied from Charles Gutzlaff. Because they remained in some ways the legacy of one of the greatest of missionary pioneers and are the source from which Hudson Taylor and through him many modern missions derived their inspiration, they also deserve to be examined closely. The first was some advice addressed to Theodore Hamberg. The second, advice on establishing Associations in Europe for the support of the Chinese Union by prayer and co-operation. The third set out 'Requisites for the foreign preachers of the Gospel who wish to combine their efforts with the Associations now forming for the conversion of Eastern Asia'.

China's allegedly four hundred millions were only part of his concern. Gutzlaff saw the eight to ten million Koreans, fifteen to forty million Japanese, the hermetically sealed land of mystery, and perhaps twenty millions in South-East Asia in the same light.

He left Hamberg in charge and sailed away from Hong Kong. But as Hamberg entered more into the activities of the Chinese Union his phlegmatic nature saw things very differently from the sanguine Gutzlaff; and two LMS missionaries, James Legge and J. F. Cleland, shared his alarm.

CHAPTER EIGHT

CREST OF THE WAVE
1849–51

Gutzlaff's principles   *1849*

In September 1849 Charles Gutzlaff was on the way to
Europe. To be the Honourable Dr Charles F. Gutzlaff,
Chinese Secretary, etc, etc, was an open sesame in Britain
and on the European continent. Since 1827 his name had
been well known. His early books had stirred the hearts of
the Christian public, and his exploits on the China coast
for the last eighteen years were a byword among merchants,
naval officers and politicians. An aura of romance such as
is associated with Lawrence of Arabia and Orde Wingate
clung to him, but he had no desire for the limelight. He
wanted above all to set up an international organisation to
work with the Chinese evangelists of the Union.[1]

Gutzlaff arrived in England in January 1850 and was met
by warm-hearted Christian lawyers, manufacturers, stock-
brokers and ministers who wanted to hear from him about
the Chinese Union and his plan for Associations in Europe.
At last they could talk with this phenomenon with the
'great face' and 'sinister eye' of Harry Parkes's description.
It was disappointing for them to learn that he and not a
Chinese was the author of the documents they had received,
but that made little difference. They were impatient to hear
what he had to say. His views on how to carry the gospel
to every corner of China and East Asia impressed them as
much as the reports he gave of the development and success
of the Christian Union. In view of subsequent developments

and of the documents preserved, enough must now be quoted from his papers on the Chinese Union to bear their own evidence to the truth about Charles Gutzlaff himself.

With the object of 'simply preaching the Word of the Cross . . . from house to house, from city to city', Gutzlaff declared, 'the colporteurs aimed to circulate the Scriptures as the power of God unto salvation for all that believed . . . and to furnish Christian literature to their countrymen . . .'[2] They were penniless but 'still they think it their duty to press forward in faith and hope', anxious to establish a fund so as

> not to be constantly hampered by appeals. How this is to be done they do not know, but leave the whole with entire childlike confidence in their father in heaven. If he withdraws his support we must naturally sink, if he upholds, he will do it with his miraculous power as hitherto . . . Far more necessary and powerful are the Holy Spirit and Prayer to help on the good work . . .

So fellow Christians were implored to join in prayer with them, and the establishment of the fund was as clearly but tactfully left for their consideration.

The best way to achieve the indigenous aims of the Union was by Chinese evangelists under Chinese superintendents going out among their own people.

> All the men employed write their journals which they present to the Society on their return . . . Their pay on their excursions is from $4–$6 (Spanish) per month and a small allowance for travelling expenses . . . The whole is a work of faith from first to last . . . hitherto has the Lord helped us, and the futurity we leave to him . . . and when this paltry institution is on the point of being crushed, we look up to yonder eternity where Christ is sitting at the right hand of God . . .

The essence of Charles Gutzlaff's convictions about a missionary's share in the work is exposed in his 'valedictory remarks' to Theodore Hamberg, dated September 1849. He could have been writing for his spiritual heir, Hudson

Taylor, who mirrored and echoed so much of Gutzlaff's principles a decade and more later. They are a revelation of his own soul.

> Perfectly nothing can be done without the Spirit of God, and unless the prayer for His powerful assistance is constant and earnest there can be no success. There must be a relation, a communication with Heaven opened, and then only we can anticipate the glorification of Christ in the souls of men, otherwise the whole becomes mere form . . .
>
> The love of Christ in and through us must bear us up, and actuate all our thoughts and actions . . . It must be the tender love of a mother, which bears and forbears in all things . . . [or] we can make no progress in the evangelisation of this nation . . . It must be love from first to last, real, ardent, never failing love, flowing from the great fountain, Jesus Christ.[3]

With hindsight his next points are now of particular interest. He had faced criticism from Hong Kong and the colporteurs had been called in question, so he grasped the nettle firmly.

> Lying and falsehood are ingrained in the Chinese character and can only be expelled effectually by the Spirit of truth . . . It will never be by any other means.

After all, the pagan children of the 'father of lies' could be expected to be like him. This was why they needed the gospel. The Holy Spirit of God could 'make of the most crooked creature a vessel of his grace'. It would be useless simply to employ people to sell Christian books. They would never act with vigour.

> They must be engaged as if the work were their own, their responsibility towards their Lord . . . Hence the necessity of . . . committees . . . of deep and long enquiry respecting the capacity of the candidate, of earnest entreaties before the throne of grace, on behalf of the individuals proposed . . .[4]

Gutzlaff was wide awake to the danger of being hood-winked for false motives. He continued, 'We ought to avoid as much as possible every contact with unknown men, who might bring disgrace upon the Union.' All the colporteurs had memorised whole chapters of Scripture, the Ten Commandments and the Creed, and most had written 'essays about the saving faith'; but the recommendation of fellow Chinese Christians was the surest safeguard.

> If the members gave them their testimony, that they were indeed sincere believers, and if they themselves made confession and repentance of their sins, firmly believing in an all-sufficient Saviour, they were received among us, not otherwise. As no worldly prospects attached to the profession, we have had very few hypocrites, and witnessed in many instances the power of saving grace.

After advice about members of other congregations attending meetings of the Chinese Union, and on observance of the Lord's Supper, Gutzlaff went on to speak of discipline in the Union.

> Light and darkness can never go hand in hand, and to think for a moment that evil-doers can belong to a Union, whose grand object is the conversion of China, would be sinful absurdity ... Whoever is clearly proved to have sinned against the Lord and committed crime, must be expelled.

And then, with worldly-wise awareness he set down his own precautions.

> One of the most necessary things to introduce true Christianity, is to keep the idol of the world — money — which has no greater power than in China, entirely out of view. Men ... ought in no way to be encouraged to look forward to any compensation ... or hopes that they may perhaps in future be employed as teachers ... true believers must aid the glorious cause by their own substance, and the churches established in various parts of the country provide finally for themselves ...
>
> The members of the Christian Union know each other better than any foreigner. They ought therefore to be applied to, if choice of a labourer is to be made ... and if they

demur . . . it is certain that the individual proposed is unfit for his calling.

The care in selecting men to be sent out can never be too great . . . people who do not show here [in Hong Kong] a paramount interest in the Gospel, will not do so at a distance . . . those who cannot on the spot readily communicate Christian doctrines, will not do so when far away . . . Though there have been disappointments, as there have been amongst foreign missionaries, still the great body has pursued the grand aim, and proved beyond contradiction that the Lord was with us.

To test the truth of the (colporteurs), there are certain infallible signs, that do not deceive. The tone that runs through the journal, the subdued, earnest spirit of the preacher, the people that accompany him on his return, and other tokens . . . If such proofs do not exist . . . the individual should not again be sent out, or at the highest, once more, to be tried. The scrutiny of the members . . . can never be too strict. We want effectual workers, men prompted by the love of Christ.

Experience has proved that men who are actively and constantly employed, very soon wear out; most of the first preachers have either attained early decrepitude or died. The loss of men every year is astonishing . . . with disease or death in every direction . . . By establishing an affectionate relationship with the preachers, and eliciting in private conversation their views, by praying often and earnestly with them and for them, by calling upon the Saviour to keep them from all evil . . . we shall find that their progress (in) divine grace will be perceptible . . .

For years Charles Gutzlaff had been trying to get a firm footing on the coast and to penetrate inland, but with little success. The odds were still heavily against the foreigner. But even if he could gain free access, how many would be needed to reach the hundreds of millions of Chinese? The handfuls of Christians in Hong Kong and the treaty ports 'must be cherished, enlarged and multiplied to form the nucleus for future operations'.

The impossibility of foreigners doing anything on a large

> scale . . . is generally admitted, and the myriads of Chinese
> must either be left to themselves, or claim the operations of
> their own countrymen, there is no alternative.[5] [Over and
> above all that, the whole work is God's, and] the only safe
> mode of proceeding [is to be] instruments in his hands
> [prayerful and obedient to his will]. Thus apparently insur-
> mountable obstacles are removed, mountains of difficulty
> disappear, God is with us, we cease to labour, and omni-
> potence takes the sway. It is thus alone, that by such feeble
> means the evangelisation of China can be accomplished.

Finally he declared his principle of complete dependence
upon God for the supply of material needs, through normal
financial channels.

> Pecuniary means are the least of all things, in the darkest
> mind the first and foremost. If God pours out the spirit of
> prayer and supplication and does not withhold the Comforter
> from above, Christ will always be glorified, while otherwise
> the most ample supplies will be of no avail. Let us strive for
> this with a single heart, and leave the earthly substance to
> him who is rich over all that call upon him. Thus I have been
> trusting and confiding these many years, and never yet found
> that the Lord's love forsook me, or that supplies were
> wanting, when work was to be done. You may be assured
> that your experience will be the same, and that my efforts to
> procure a permanent [fund] to the Union will not prove in
> vain . . . Be strong in faith and hope, for God is with you.

If the Christians of the West would not support them,
Gutzlaff concluded, the preachers would have to be told
that their own converts must find the means. Whether from
one source or another, the work must go on.

The 'indigenous church' concept   1844–20th century

Charles Gutzlaff's 'voluminous correspondence' had been
with approving supporters in Britain and several European
countries, and the principles he had outlined for young
Hamberg were what he himself had been practising in
embryo for five years, and urging Western Christians to

adopt.[6] The term 'indigenous principles' has become a cliché in missionary parlance for much of what was his emphasis on Chinese evangelists working under Chinese supervision, on believers contributing and churches providing for their own needs, and on the evangelisation of China depending on Chinese preachers, not foreigners, all with the prayerful co-operation of the Western Church. His arrival in Europe was therefore welcomed by many who were ready to organise themselves into associations to support the Chinese Union.

The *Church Missionary Intelligencer* of November, 1849, contained an article by Henry Venn entitled *Native Churches, under European Superintendence, The Hope of Missions*, based upon the words of St Paul, 'The heir, as long as he is a child . . . is under tutors and governors', with the comment, 'What a high office, for the European missionary!' The indigenous church concept was implied in the words 'as long as he is a child', but not specifically taken up. In 1851, however, after Gutzlaff's return to Hong Kong, Venn presented a paper to the CMS Committee which was accepted and issued to missionaries, setting out the objects of a mission as 'the settlement of a Native Church under Native Pastors upon a self-supporting system', in such a way that the missionary is freed 'to resign all pastoral work into their hands, and gradually relax his superintendence over the pastors themselves, till it insensibly ceases . . . Then the missionary and all missionary agency should be transferred to the "regions beyond" '.

In Sierra Leone three African Christians, including Samuel Crowther, had been ordained by 1850, but a proposal in 1853 to apply the indigenous principle deliberately in Sierra Leone was not applied until 1860, and then under an English bishop, to establish 'a genuine branch of the Church of England'. In the event it was a paucity of both funds and men that drove the mission to encourage African autonomy, the *Intelligencer* noted in April, 1869. Eugene Stock wrote at the end of the century that the 'true *euthanasia*' of a mission would be by the emergence of a purely or predominantly native church, independent of its founding parent body, and thought that,

> the subject had never been touched when [Venn] took it up. There is no sign in the first half of this [nineteenth] century — or at all events in the first forty years — that any one, either in the Church of England or outside it, had given a thought to the matter. Henry Venn led the way with his powerful mind; and with no experience or precedent to guide him, he gradually ... worked out plans which have since been adopted, in substance, by most missionary societies sufficiently advanced to have Christian communities to think about.[7]

The difference between Gutzlaff's concept and Venn's lay in the stage at which autonomy was to be enjoyed by the Christian converts. Gutzlaff recognised the missionary's task as tuition short of tutelage, the helping but not the controlling hand — *autonomy from the very start of the relationship*, yet with close spiritual and pastoral oversight of the emerging church. Deep disappointment and unbelief led to departure from the principle by some who followed Charles Gutzlaff. Those who took control and supplied funds to the churches they established found it difficult or impossible to extricate themselves. But the principle was rediscovered, and clearly demonstrated by J. O. Fraser in the Lisu church,[8] since when it has been widely applied. Meanwhile Gutzlaff himself remained adaptable; he still believed in Christians with the financial means contributing to the support of the less well-off who were preaching the gospel.

'Chinese Associations'[9]   *1849–50*

Strong support for Gutzlaff's principles quickly led to the formation of two associations in Scotland and a 'Chinese Society' in England 'for furthering the propagation of the Gospel in China and the adjacent countries by means of native evangelists'. Much of it came from outside the main denominations, but the committees were more representative. Gutzlaff had not yet been over to Europe to visit his own family and the new German missions; apart from his reception by Richard Ball and his friends, he had another reason for delay. He met and later married a Miss Gabriel of Liverpool, his third English wife. It was she who wrote his biography.

To guide the associations and 'to avoid misconceptions' he wrote another paper. By 'misconceptions' he seems to have meant the mistaken idea that he was to be the leader or director of the associations. He decried mere organisation. The name and form of the association 'matters not'. Love and concern by prayer and co-operation were everything. It was not for a stranger from the Continent to suggest how they should run their affairs, but he would put the Continental associations in touch with the British through the London one, 'that there may be unity of design and execution'. 'Making the conversion of the Chinese empire a European cause' would 'at once disarm antagonism and place the whole on a basis worthy of so great an enterprise'. 'The most open way of proceeding here as well as in China, without concealment or reservation' would disarm criticism and accusations.

The object of the associations was to select and send the right kind of European missionary, 'Not above twenty-four years of age . . . (with) a ready talent for languages . . . They ought to be men of the first order in every respect.' 'Only foreigners of an expansive, tender heart should be admitted . . .' They were to proceed into the interior and take charge of twenty or thirty evangelists, setting them an example in 'preaching Christ crucified, constantly, from village to village, from city to city, wherever hearers may be found'. When they reached Hong Kong Charles Gutzlaff would arrange for their welcome, help them to learn Chinese and show them where to start. So far only men had been talked about, but a few women had already shown that they could do valuable work in China, and

Gutzlaff was not thinking primarily of wives for the men when he added,

> It is sufficiently evident that without the aid of pious females no permanent impression can ever be made upon families, and that Christianity therefore will have no hold amongst the nation; hence the necessity of female labourers of the same stamp as the above male agents.[10]

That he was a man of immense breadth of vision and not merely visionary is demonstrated not only by these statements but by the outcome in missions based on his principles, not least the China Inland Mission. Each found its inspiration in the man and his great sweep of ambition for the evangelisation, not only of China but of all Eastern Asia, including inaccessible Japan, Korea, the Philippines, Tibet and Chinese Turkestan, all apparently hermetically sealed against the missionary. His paper to guide in the selection of suitable 'pious females and male agents' was headed,

> Requisites for the foreign preachers of the Gospel who wish to combine their efforts with the Association now forming for the conversion of Eastern Asia.

Not only the conversion of individuals 'from darkness to light' but the Christianising of national life appears to have been his aim. His thinking was far ahead of most of his contemporaries.

The whole emphasis of the missionaries responding to his appeals was to be to arouse the co-operation of Chinese (and other) Christians in taking the gospel to their own people, to train them and multiply their number 'to the utmost of their power'. 'They are not to be surprised when converts relapse into the pagan ways they have always known,' but they should be careful not to delay baptism unduly. 'It is a matter of fact that no congregations have been obtained where baptism was either refused or delayed beyond a certain period.' For a young man to aspire to leading twenty or thirty Chinese colleagues, 'some of whom are really distinguished men', was a big undertaking in itself. It would not only be hard work but would entail 'much suffering'.

> It is necessary that he should entirely live with the natives, identify himself with them . . . penetrate further and further in the country, and give up all foreign society and connexions. The interior is the sphere of our labours, not the sea coast, the farthest land of Central Asia constitutes the area where the contest for the cause of Christ is to be fought. Although there is at present religious toleration in the Chinese empire, local opposition will always be experienced wherever the Gospel of salvation is announced. Circumstances may occur when it will be necessary to lay down one's life in the Saviour's cause, and for all such emergencies a champion of Jesus Christ ought to be prepared . . . His pay therefore will be small, his troubles many and unless he be a heavenly minded man, he will soon sink under them.

Heavenly-mindedness he knew to be the antidote to petty-mindedness. Relations with missionary colleagues needed especially to be guarded.

> The spirit which induces one to fire upon a comrade and not upon the enemy, is not of Christ; we can do much by kindness . . . but nothing by bitter malice.

He had reason for writing like this, which was soon to become public property.

As for the missionaries' financial needs, 'the Associations who send the individuals, should also provide for their necessities . . .' It was exceptional in Gutzlaff's day to think in the terms he then went on to use.

> No real workman will ever be left to starve, no great enterprise for the glory of God be allowed to stand still for want of means, for God who is rich above all that call upon him, never abandons his own. It is often an exercise of faith to believe this fully, what you do not behold with your own eyes, yet this very exercise fits one for the important duties of the station. How little is required when one can live with

contentment among the natives, what happy hours can be passed in sharing the meal with them.

So trust in God, reliance on his faithfulness, by the individual missionary and by those who sent him, was to be matched by responsible support of the 'workman' and the 'enterprise' by the organisation behind them. Good stewardship neither replaced nor was excluded by faith in God who would provide whether through 'supporters' or other means. But Gutzlaff's faith was securely bound up with self-support, as in his own case by a nest-egg and employment, and with financial backing by the associations. This was still a far cry from the position to be expressed by Hudson Taylor in his *Principles and Practice*[11] for members of the China Inland Mission.

> . . . their faith must be in God, their expectation from Him.
> The Mission might fail them, or it might cease to exist; but
> if they put their trust in Him *He* will never fail nor disappoint
> them.

Meanwhile Gutzlaff worked strenuously to arouse concern and support.

George Pearse, a London stockbroker, was invited by Richard Ball and the circle of Gutzlaff's friends to act as honorary secretary to the Chinese Society, and links with the Scottish Associations were forged.[12] Cheered by the progress, Gutzlaff crossed over to the Continent. He had a demanding schedule of meetings and interviews.

On April 10 he addressed a meeting in Brussels and in May was in Rotterdam and going on to Basel in a few days' time, then to Sweden for three weeks. His travels took him also to France, Denmark, Norway and Russia. On June 11 he arrived in his home town of Pyritz, north-east of Berlin, to be welcomed by the burgomaster and given the freedom of the town. 'Immense crowds and a spirit of devotion' as he put it, greeted him wherever he went in Europe. He formed 'a male and female Chinese Missionary Society' or Association, with a boyhood friend as the secretary, and was off again to Berlin. From there he wrote to Richard

Ball, 'I am again on my feet after a very severe attack of rheumatic fever, and hope to work until I sink.' 'Rheumatic fever' was a popular term used indiscriminately as 'flu is today.

In 1841 the Tsar had accepted the advice of the Synod of the Russian Orthodox Church and withdrawn permission for the LMS to work among Mongols on the Russian border east of Lake Baikal.[13] Hearing that Charles Gutzlaff was urging the Moravians to send missionaries to Mongolia, the son of one of the ejected missionaries wrote to him.

Thomas Stallybrass[14] had been born in Siberia, spoke Mongolian and knew the customs of the people. He had offered to go with the LMS as a missionary, and had been to Glasgow University with their help. Then Mongolia was put out of reach. While he waited he studied surgery, looked for new routes to Mongolia and served as minister of a church. When he heard of Gutzlaff's arrival and activities he wrote to Richard Ball and understood from his reply that the Chinese Association would support him. He resigned his pastoral charge, wrote asking Gutzlaff about the best route to go by, and how many of his library of a thousand books he could take with him. Gutzlaff appears to have favoured an approach through north China.

Stallybrass's congregation was anticipating his intended departure to Asia when he learned that Ball's 'promised support' had been withdrawn, or never given. The incident is significant as the first hint of Richard Ball's enthusiasm outpacing his discretion. As a result of Gutzlaff's urging, however, the Herrnhut Moravians sent three missionaries (not including Stallybrass) to north India in 1853 to penetrate through central Asia to Mongolia. They failed repeatedly and in 1857 turned instead to the Tibetans at Leh. The Moravian Mission to Tibet was the outcome, another of Gutzlaff's 'grandchildren'.

Gutzlaff meanwhile was having great success in Germany. The Berlin Missionary Association for China was formed, so named to distinguish it from the Berlin Mis-

sionary Society working in Africa since 1824. 'The celebrated Professor Krummacher . . . was in the chair . . . The
members intend to ask Her Majesty to become the Patron.
I visited both the King (and) Queen, both are exemplary
Christians . . .' King Frederick William IV was the son of
Gutzlaff's former patron. 'Several of the most noble and
influential of the whole land have come forward for the
support' of the work.

'We must make the Association *European*,' he wrote to
Ball. 'Be of good cheer! The Lord is for us . . .' He had
enthusiastic supporters 'from Ireland to Hungary'. It was
the high point of his endeavour to promote missions. To
George Pearse he wrote on July 6, 'The Continent now
looks to you for that direction which alone can give
stability to the whole,'[15] for Victorian Britain was the
acknowledged leader in world affairs.

Gutzlaff then called upon the associations to take
responsibility for the evangelisation of definite areas.[16]
China was parcelled out by provinces. 'I recommend to
your association', Gutzlaff told George Pearse, 'the provinces of Shantung, Chekiang and Fukien . . . accessible by
sea' and therefore suitable for a maritime nation. Students
of Berlin University formed their own association and
Berlin undertook to send the gospel to the provinces of
Shaanxi, Gansu, Sichuan and Tibet. The Pomeranian
Association (of Pyritz) chose Shanxi in north China. Other
'friends of the sacred cause' adopted Zhili (Chihli) in the
north-east and Manchuria. The Danzig Association 'took
charge' of Guizhou and Königsberg of Yunnan. In late
August Gutzlaff was in Herrnhut in connection with the
Moravian Mission to Mongolia and was urging Bremen to
send a missionary 'forthwith for each province', so long as
they go to preach the gospel as the power of God, through
Chinese preachers and while themselves living among the
people, 'otherwise they may remain at home'.

In September he was writing from Chepstow to Theodore
Hamberg in Hong Kong 'that he would soon be back
there', and the Berlin Missionary Association for China

appointed a young man named Robert Neumann to join him at Hong Kong. The Committee of the Chinese Institute at Kassel invited all missionary societies to send delegates to a conference on October 17 and 18 to meet Dr Gutzlaff and consider the proper division of China, either independently or in connection with the Chinese Union. This was the crest of the wave. Everything would have looked promising but for that ominous undertone in correspondence from Hong Kong which was soon to become a roar.

'The Gleaner' 1850

In March 1850 the Chinese Association in England launched a magazine, *The Gleaner in the Missionary Field*, to circulate news not only about China but worldwide, with Richard Ball as the editor. Leading articles from his pen through most of the next ten years included original and influential thinking. The first was a call to ecumenical co-operation in the cause of world evangelism. Then followed a note of 'the presence of Dr Charles Gutzlaff in England', a 'General View of Eastern Asia' from his pen, a column each on Japan, 'Corea', 'Manchooria', and 'Soungaria' and an exhortation in florid rhetoric. Quite an achievement by any Englishman but remarkable for a Pomeranian in an acquired language, it is an extreme example of prevalent attitudes.

> Whilst the human spirit soars high in the West . . . there is in the East a total debasement of the human mind. . . . Lamed in its spiritual efforts, it is debased by the most degraded idolatry, without one heaven-born thought . . . Notwithstanding, however . . . there exists no determined hostility to the introduction of truth . . .

That at least was more generous, if debatable while Japan and Korea were sealed against missionary and merchant alike. If given to hyperbole in this prophetic statement, he was only two years ahead of Commodore Perry's successful pact with Japan. Gutzlaff was no fool.

A translation of a Chinese letter to the Churches of the West on the departure of Gutzlaff from Hong Kong, gave the authentic atmosphere, 'We indite this desultory letter, to pay the various honourable brethren our respects . . .', and the writers 'knocked their heads' in a farewell *ketou*.[17]

In the early issues of the *Gleaner*, articles appeared about other parts of the world, Greenland, Labrador and Madagascar in the first, North-West America and Canada, India, Tahiti and Italy in the second, Livingstone and Africa in August. Later on, as interest in East Asia built up, the scope was narrowed first to China and her dependencies and neighbours, and finally to China alone; and with the changes the title became *The Chinese and General Missionary Gleaner* and finally *The Chinese Missionary Gleaner*. Its reception had been so good that the subscription was reduced from two pence to one penny per copy, though 'at very considerable loss'.

The *Gleaner* was not only non-sectarian, it was suprasectarian. In April readers 'wearied with controversy' were encouraged to take note of 'efforts for the promotion of Christian union'. 'Let the Christians of one neighbourhood who may be individually praying for an increase of love and unity, seek out those who are similarly disposed in the same vicinity . . . to manifest the unity that already exists.'[18] The formation of 'The Chinese Association' was then announced, to support the evangelists of the Chinese Union with whom Dr Gutzlaff was working. Dramatically the news that Theodore Hamberg and Rudolf Lechler of the Basel Missionary Society and two Rhenish missionaries, Ferdinand Genähr and Wilhelm Lobscheid were already on the mainland, in Guangdong province, between Canton and Hong Kong and many miles from both, showed that China was open as never before.

The editorial in May was an *Appeal on Behalf of China*, quoting again from Charles Gutzlaff. Saying that more missionaries were deploying to the Five Ports and Hong Kong, and clarifying the April claim it declared:

Whilst several others, who by the laws of China are permitted to be enrolled as adopted members of some Chinese family, are, in conjunction with a considerable number of native teachers, penetrating into the very heart of the so-called Middle Kingdom.

No explanation of that cryptic sentence was given, but a clue was present in news of the Germans and Swedes. To call Guangdong the 'heart of the Middle Kingdom' was more hyperbole, but to be there at all was no little achievement. 'At present the former [in the ports] are only permitted to penetrate a day's journey into the interior.' While residents in the treaty ports were limited to brief excursions, the Basel and Rhenish missionaries were making extènded visits. Reports of the Chinese Union's exploits followed.

In June the death of the Dao Guang emperor was reported, and Qi Ying's promotion from viceroy of Canton to guardian of the nineteen-year-old Xian Feng emperor. This led on to an account of Gutzlaff's visit to Brussels applauding 'this man, so remarkable for strong faith, and abounding joy, whose soul is devoted to the service of his Lord'. The report of his address in Brussels was continued in the July issue telling in detail of his early missionary days in Java, Siam and China, exciting narrative in itself.

> Nevertheless, the interior of this vast empire was scarcely touched; Japan, containing 20,000,000 of inhabitants; Mongolia, 15,000,000; Thibet, 8,000,000; Cambodia, 15,000,000; Laos, 5 or 6,000,000; all without any knowledge of the Gospel.

So zealous Christians had formed the Chinese Union and started work. Now more missionaries were needed,

> men of apostolic spirit; and pious females . . . who are willing to become Chinese, to adopt the dress and customs of the country, to show the natives the horrors of their pagan abominations, and to lead them to the feet of Christ.

Gutzlaff had just been describing how he failed to find

any educated Chinese in Java willing to be seen talking with a foreigner, so that he spent much of his time with a group of men with leprosy, cast out by their own people.

'We have determined to publish a million copies of the New Testament,' he continued, and then enlarged on the Chinese law 'for the civilisation of Barbarians'.

> On arriving in China, you have nothing to do but to enter some family, and be received as the son or daughter of the house ... Once adopted by a Chinese father, you have a *right* to all the privileges of one born in the country.

Gutzlaff himself, he reported, had been adopted by the family of Guo (Kwo) in Tianjin and used their name.

Strangely, the *Gleaner* for August was almost devoid of references to China. India, Africa, George Müller's Orphan Houses, a short letter from William Burns in Canton and another from the Loochoo Naval Mission, but silence about Charles Gutzlaff and the Chinese Union. Something was in the air.

Gutzlaff in trouble   1850

Like an ocean breaker on the shore the whole exciting world of Charles Gutzlaff's Chinese Union and its European associations collapsed as dramatically as it had built up.[19] The shock to responsible supporters in many countries, to find that the venture they were backing was largely hollow, provoked a backlash of indignation. On calmer reflection it need not have been so. Charles Gutzlaff in his enthusiasm had exaggerated, but in his humility and love for the Chinese he had been cruelly victimised. Only about thirty of the Union's evangelists were found to be genuine, the rest were confidence tricksters from Hong Kong's underworld co-operating in a great hoax. For all Gutzlaff's sound advice to Hamberg, he himself had been utterly deceived. The story is as instructive as it is pitiful.

Theodore Hamberg was astute. Before Charles Gutzlaff had left Hong Kong to return to Europe, Hamberg had

had his suspicions and mentioned them to Gutzlaff. He may have been alerted by James Legge or J. F. Cleland, of the LMS, or been their source of information. But Gutzlaff would not listen to criticism of the Chinese with whom he enjoyed such confidential fellowship. He consulted the leading colporteurs and was reassured. He knew that neither Legge nor Cleland had firsthand knowledge of the Chinese Union. They were acting on hearsay. So he wrote his defensive memorandum for his friends in Europe, 'to avoid all mistakes'.[20]

'Mr Cleland in a letter to the Foreign Secretary of the London Missionary Society accused the members of the Chinese Christian Union of the most heinous crimes'; he could produce no evidence to substantiate his charges. The Christians prayed for him to be forgiven, and that they would be kept from falling into the sins imputed to them. Dr Legge also brought accusations through the LMS, but he also had no personal acquaintance with the Christian Union. Who were his informants? The members would be the first to invite him to accompany them on their preaching trips if he would go. The accusations were being made in England while the accused were in China, unable to reply. Was Dr Legge not afraid of fighting against God? The associations in Europe would answer in their defence.

As for Gutzlaff himself, he chose not to contend with anyone, he said. Accusations against himself he would answer; yet he was not 'the pivot on which this holy work turns' but 'a mere fellow-labourer'. He would meet Dr Legge to answer accusations relating to the work as it was before he left Hong Kong, but not since. And he would do all he could 'to remove obstacles to a good and friendly Christian understanding'. The best answer would be for plenty of missionaries to join in the work and verify its integrity.

Still Gutzlaff had no qualms. To his mind the criticisms were all mistaken. Even the rapid growth of the Union was nothing but a matter for praise to God, though it should have alerted him to danger. As he had written for Ham-

berg's guidance, he always prayed and watched most
carefully for 'lying and falsehood' in the 'crooked creatures'
who might try to slip in. He knew the limitations of any
foreigner in seeing through the craftiness of the Chinese.
To them it was all a delightful game of Grandmother's
Footsteps, to see how far they could get without being
detected. Their wry sense of humour was fathomless. But
the Chinese understood each other, the Chinese Christians
were the best ones to rely upon for advice in selecting new
colporteurs; and 'certain infallible signs' of a spiritually-
minded Christian were apparent to anyone who lived close
to the Lord. Even so he was deceived.

In April and May 1850 when Gutzlaff was in Rotterdam,
Basel, Switzerland and Scandinavia, more disturbing letters
were being written in Hong Kong. They probably arrived
in June and July. Karl Vogel, one of the new missionaries,
reported that Hamberg had no confidence in the Christian
Union, but Dr Legge was the chief enemy. Wilhelm
Lobscheid was, however, faithfully continuing Gutzlaff's
work with the Christian Union.

> His narratives fully coincide with Dr Gutzlaff's account . . ,
> he practises medicine and his skill is spoken of far and near.
> Palankins with bearers are constantly sent to fetch him . . .
> He is often for months together, in places where no European
> has ever been before, and from whence he, with his compan-
> ions in the Chinese Union, are fetched and transported from
> place to place — of these men he speaks very highly.[21]

The true state of affairs was difficult to establish. A brief
enquiry into Hamberg's discoveries was held in June in the
presence of William Burns and other trusted men, but it
was inconclusive.[22] Hamberg himself reported,

> I came out with three other German brethren three years
> ago to take the advice of Dr Gutzlaff and work in union with
> him, and we all entertained the highest opinion of him and
> of the Chinese Union . . . Gradually, upon acquiring the
> language, and being constantly with these men, we saw very
> well that the Chinese were deceiving Dr Gutzlaff to get

money . . . Every representation from our side was in vain.
Dr Gutzlaff would not investigate the real state of his
disciples.[23]

In Europe Charles Gutzlaff's friends rose in his defence.
The foulest calumnies were being spread in Germany
against him, Dr Elvers of Kassel protested. On July 6
Gutzlaff wrote indignantly to Hamberg.

> I hold you responsible for every preacher you have sent
> away . . . I weep tears at your conduct and still more since
> you are so infatuated as to throw the blame upon the
> Chinese.[24]

On August 3 he wrote again, protesting that he knew
personally and intimately every Christian Chinese concerned. They had given full evidence of faith in Christ and
brought others to him. A fortnight later he wrote accusing
Hamberg of taking his cue from Legge, the academic who
criticised without ever visiting the hovels, villages and
shipping at his door, 'but the Christian public, your own
countrymen in Sweden, the Society at Basel, cannot be
deceived'; and in September, saying he was coming back
to Hong Kong, 'you mistake your position'. Calling him an
'unjust steward', Gutzlaff said he would give Hamberg's
statements 'a very narrow scrutiny'. It was not, as sometimes, that a missionary on furlough was seeing his work
undone by uncomprehending deputies. Tragically, Hamberg was right.

It was too late. Truth must out. A bundle of reports in
Chinese from members of the Chinese Union came into
George Pearse's hands. He met Harry Parkes at the
Oriental Club, on leave in Britain, and asked him to
translate them. They were descriptions of evangelistic
journeys in the interior. Both men smelled a rat. There
was something suspiciously complete and successful about
all of them. George Pearse recorded, 'They all seem to be
composed on one model, and the impression on reading
them was unfavourable as to their being *bona fide* reports
of actual missionary work.' At the same time reports were

getting back to Hong Kong of Gutzlaff's addresses to his European audiences. He was publicising the information reported by the now discredited colporteurs. Missionaries in Hong Kong raised their eyebrows even higher, and Hamberg intensified his scrutiny. He and James Legge were vindicated. They had only performed their painful duty in the interests of integrity and truth.

Dr E. J. Eitel in after years gave this account of what had happened.

> [The colporteurs] came and went with the utmost regularity, starting from Gutzlaff's office with bags full of Bibles, travelling money and directions for the route; returning at the proper time with well-written journals of travels they had never made, skeletons of sermons and lists of converts they had never baptised. Poor Gutzlaff—he believed them all to be inspired with his own holy zeal; . . . the very Bibles he bought from the printer with his hard-earned money . . . were sold by them again to Gutzlaff. He was too charitable to find serious fault with his men . . .[25]

Vindication   1850

Hudson Taylor, a great believer in Gutzlaff at the time of the debacle and unshaken by it, gave the following explanation in his own old age:[26] Hamberg made a secret mark on the literature he issued to the colporteurs, and found it repeatedly on 'new consignments' from the printer. The false members of the Union were selling it back to the printer. Both he and they were making their profit repeatedly from the same books at Gutzlaff's expense. After that it was not difficult to prove, by having them watched, that the scoundrels spent their time and travelling money in the tea shops and low dives of Hong Kong. But tares grow with the wheat and the nets bring in bad fish with the good. The scandal was exposed and Gutzlaff's grief was unbounded, but many men of sense and understanding gave him full credit for the positive facts and forgave his gullibility.

Henry Venn wrote from CMS House, 'I cannot accuse Dr Gutzlaff of an attempt or connivance at an attempt to impose on the Christian public. I think he has been deceived by designing [people].'[27] In July William Burns made a warm and generous tribute to Gutzlaff's own devotion and work.

> I . . . have been disposed to believe that he was an instrument of no ordinary kind employed by God to prepare the way for the Gospel among this people . . . But I desiderate more convincing evidence [of the conversion of some of the colporteurs]. While it is but too plain from indisputable proofs . . . that in the case of not a few the Christian profession is but a cloak of covetousness.[28]

Dr George Smith, the CMS missionary and bishop of Victoria, Hong Kong, wrote to Henry Venn and to the British & Foreign Bible Society that he had retained some ten or twelve of the best colporteurs of the Chinese Union. And a William Tarrant wrote to George Pearse that Bishop Smith agreed that 'the good done with these men gives evidence that all Dr Gutzlaff's labours have not been in vain'. Ferdinand Genähr had seven others working with him on the mainland.[29] A few weeks later William Burns wrote from Canton that two of the colporteurs were giving the CMS 'considerable satisfaction'.

From Gutzlaff's own converts a church of twenty-six members in 1850, when the total in China and the Straits Settlements was about two hundred, more than trebled its size to eighty-seven members in the five years after he died. Latourette's balanced judgment was that Gutzlaff was 'by no means a failure' but 'the organiser of an enterprise which in spite of ill-judged features, led to solid continuing missions'. Not only local and contemporary results stood to his credit, but 'solid continuing' societies of which the China Inland Mission, which Hudson Taylor founded, (now the Overseas Missionary Fellowship), 'was to have a larger and more widely distributed foreign staff than any other Christian Society whether Roman Catholic or Protestant'.[30]

In Europe the revelation shocked the new missions and associations. While Basel and Barmen missionaries severed their connection with Charles Gutzlaff, Hamberg, Lobscheid and Genähr continued working as before. The other associations and missions sympathised, holding to their conviction that Gutzlaff's principles were right, and sent missionaries to China during subsequent years.[31] The facts will show what stuff these men were made of. Rudolf Lechler lived into the twentieth century to see most of Gutzlaff's dreams come true.

In Britain the leaders of the Chinese Association were philosophical after the initial shock. China's millions of men, women and children had been brought to their notice, and they accepted responsibility as from God, not Gutzlaff. If Chinese evangelists were unreliable or not available, who else should rise to the occasion? They appealed for missionaries. The Christian public, however, were not as resilient and there was a marked drop in contributions to the cause. It took three years and the exploits of Hong Xiu-quan's 'Patriot Army' to restore confidence.

In a commendably catholic spirit Richard Ball, George Pearse and their committee encouraged the German missionaries to find reliable Chinese colleagues and to go on as before. Lobscheid's and Neumann's faith in Gutzlaff and the aims of the Union weathered the storm. Richard Ball himself remained an ardent admirer of the 'indestructible Gutzlaff' and in his book *China*, published four years later, he expatiated not only about the man but also the Chinese Union, simply writing off the renegades. In it fact and fiction are regrettably indistinguishable. Not surprisingly, Latourette does not list it in his bibliography, as we do with this caveat, for it has its place in the history. The Chinese Society, however, took up another of Gutzlaff's projects. They sponsored the manufacture of stereotyped plates for printing his translation of the Bible, and found a faithful promoter of the project in Lobscheid.[32] George

Pearse preserved and bound together the papers received from Gutzlaff, and it is from them that much of this information is taken. Some of his collection, including bound volumes of the CES *Gleaner* with his personal annotations (and the Howard Taylors') are in the Hudson Taylor archives. Whether Hudson Taylor himself had access to them at any time is not certain, though his close co-operation with George Pearse for many years spanning the formation of the China Inland Mission makes it highly probable.

Charles Gutzlaff and his wife reached Hong Kong in January 1851 to find the accusations all too tragically true. He 'withdrew' from the Chinese Union and it was disbanded. Reference in the *Gleaner* to 'sleepless nights and silent tears' drew sympathy from his friends at home, but Gutzlaff wrote a biography of the Dao Guang emperor[33] and spent all available time preaching the gospel. Young Neumann gave a picture of a Great-heart wounded but fighting on.

> His heart was truly in the work, he went out daily, in wind and rain, frequently at the peril of his life, on the mountains, and in the vallies (*sic*), visiting the fishing boats on the sea, and even the pirate ships, to carry the light of the gospel to those children of darkness.[34]

Neumann sometimes went with him and 'invariably returned deeply humbled' by Gutzlaff's love, untiring patience and self-denying humility. After a brief illness Charles Gutzlaff died on August 9, 1851.

> Even in his last hours, all his thoughts were directed to the evangelization of China ... He spoke of it with great confidence, and even in the delirium of fever, frequently in different languages he expressed his bright hopes for the future glory of his beloved Sinim.

Some modern writers have said that he died 'of a broken heart', whatever they meant by that. The evidence is that Charles Gutzlaff began again among the fragments of his dream and was building on strong foundations until his last illness in which

> he scarcely knew how to rest his thickly swollen feet through pain, and was seized with a consuming fever ... He complained to no man of severe inward struggles. 'But', he explained joyfully, 'they are overcome! ...' This was made manifest by the serenity and joy which shone forth amidst the severe pain in his looks and words. ... Thus was his house set in order, and his heart how joyous it was![35]

After the doctor told him he was dying, Gutzlaff prayed for China and when his wife said, 'God be praised who has given us the victory,' he exclaimed with a feeble movement of his arm, 'Yes, victory, victory!'[36]

'All the high officials of the English government, the governor at the head, took part in the solemn funeral' and 'a great crowd' of foreigners, Chinese and Japanese, went in procession to the cemetery. Robert Neumann carried on Gutzlaff's work with seven faithful members of the Union until his own health broke after four years and he was invalided home.

Gutzlaff's failings must be recognised, assessed and assigned to their just place in history. It is apparent that they have been over-stressed. The facts require a new attitude to the calamity in which Gutzlaff's faith in his converts was so bitterly disappointed. He has been pilloried for long enough. Only intimidation is a valid explanation of why those thirty true colporteurs did not expose the scheming majority. Gutzlaff was right to trust his genuine Christians and in view of their silence merits only qualified reproach for being blind to the rest. Those who have lived many years in China can understand his predicament. That Liang A-fa was similarly deceived and betrayed reveals the intricacy of the problem; but the significance of that incident, though it cost Gutzlaff the respect of two European societies, is trivial in comparison with the movement he set in motion. Far from the 'signal failure' they have been labelled, his achievements were only less than he had been led to believe. In justice to a great man, his qualities and successes are at last receiving the credit they deserve.

Gutzlaff was a byword for his adventurous travels long before David Livingstone earned the attention of the public. Even his exaggerations do not detract from those exploits. His strategy of action was far-sighted and is still in vogue. His travels were missionary journeys solidly devoted to propagating the gospel. Fluent as he was, he emphasised the dissemination of Scripture and other Christian literature as a continuing influence after he and his exhortations had gone. That the books he distributed were preserved and shown years later to other missionaries proves the soundness of his judgment. He not only distributed but wrote to suit the needs of his readers. In the *Chinese Recorder* (successor to the *Repository*) Wylie summed up Gutzlaff's own published books and booklets as sixty-one in Chinese, two Japanese, one Siamese, five Dutch, seven German and nine in English.[37]

Whether or not he had read Carey's five principles,[38] Gutzlaff practised them: he preached the gospel widely by every possible means; he supported the preaching by the distribution of Scripture in the languages of the people he went to; he established a church as soon as believers were called out; he studied the thought and culture of the people profoundly and sympathetically; and he trained at the earliest opportunity the beginnings of a native Christian ministry. He also insisted that the Chinese must be evangelised by Chinese; but for years ahead there were unlikely to be enough Chinese Christians and those there were would need training and help from Western fellow-Christians. So he called upon the West to send the men; and he went far beyond Morrison in calling for 'pious females' to 'become Chinese' to bring the gospel to China's women, with whom even Chinese men could have few dealings.

To these could be added other tenets of policy and practice adopted in turn by Hudson Taylor. Like Morrison, Gutzlaff kept the Church in Europe informed about East

Asia and the work of missionaries; and without soliciting funds he encouraged participation by prayer, by personal commitment and by responsible financial involvement.

The *Gleaner* declared, 'Charles Gutzlaff is no more', and honoured him in an obituary; but 'the indestructible Gutzlaff' had initiated a train of events unmatched by all the steady output of his contemporaries. On all counts the prescient Gutzlaff was an outstanding man. Eccentric because exceptional, his vision outreached what was feasible in his day, but many modern societies remain as monuments to his concepts of how best to carry the gospel to the world's unevangelised millions. Ironically, some of the fastest-growing cults are those which are using precisely his methods, while the conventional 'establishment' plod slowly in their wake. If like a mountaineer he strove to attain the unattainable in the conditons prevailing while he climbed, all honour to him. Others succeeded.

The turning point   *1849*

The mantle of Elijah fell upon his successor in dramatic circumstances. Back in 1849 when Gutzlaff was preparing to visit Europe for the first time in twenty-three years, Hudson Taylor was in the doldrums. Seventeen on May 21, 1849, he was taking more responsibility in his father's shop, but his four or more years of apprenticeship were dragging painfully.[39] His teenage restlessness and rebellion made the close quarters with his impatient father difficult for both of them, though he enjoyed the work itself and was mastering the technicalities. When eventually he went to China he made sure of having the equipment with him to do chemical analysis of Chinese drugs and to make his own photographic plates and process them. It was distasteful for him to live at home with a lay preacher father and class leader mother while he was so out of sympathy with their religious enthusiasm. The spiritual wilt that his months at the bank had begun showed no sign of ending. He simply endured it all while they prayed for him and hoped for the day when he would emerge the wiser for the experience.

One day in June Mrs Taylor was away and work was slack. Hudson was off duty and bored. Amelia and Louisa were probably tied to their lessons. He looked through his father's library for something to read. The shelves always held books of natural history and travel that interested him; but he could find nothing. It was one of those days when nothing was right. So he tipped out a tray of pamphlets and turned them over to find anything that might be worth reading. Picking on one he went over to the warehouse in the stable-yard, as he often did when he wanted to be alone. He knew exactly what the tract would be like, a story with a moral, then a pious application and appeal to the reader to believe in Jesus and be saved. None of that interested him. He would skim the story and leave the rest.

The tract has been preserved. It is about a coalman in Somerset, desperately ill with consumption and living in squalor while his wife took his place humping coal to people's cellars. The filth and stench of his home was so bad that the doctor could not bring himself to go in but spoke to him from the doorway. This would have caught Hudson's attention. He was learning to diagnose and to prescribe for patients who came to the pharmacy. Then came a paragraph of Victorian clichés about the patient's soul, but the narrative continued. Some Christians in the same village kept visiting the sick man. One day when they told him the story of the woman who touched the hem of Jesus's garment the coalman exclaimed, 'Oh that I could reach him!' Nothing else they said or read to him apparently had any effect until he heard the words, 'Who his own self bare our sins in his own body on the tree.' He raised his head from his pillow and said 'Then it's done!' Hudson Taylor was still reading. 'Yes,' they answered, 'Jesus said, "It is finished!" ' Immediately the sick man cried, 'Then my sins are gone . . .' From that time on until he died he was jubilant, praising God for saving him. So went the tract.

Hudson had seen too many similar instances of conversion to question the truth of the story; but this time there was a new element in it. He himself was involved. He could barely finish reading. Years later when he wrote his *Retrospect*, he recalled the words that revolutionised his life as being 'the finished work of Christ'. The thought is the same. The conviction certainly mastered him that Jesus had done everything necessary for him, Hudson. There was nothing he himself needed but to accept 'the finished work of Christ'. As he expressed it, nothing but 'to fall down on one's knees and accepting this Saviour and His salvation praise Him for evermore'. Then he went and told his sister Amelia, now thirteen and his closest friend, swearing her to secrecy. He wanted to be the first to tell his mother what had happened.

Attached to the tract as we have it now is a slip of paper with these words in Mrs Taylor's handwriting. 'The reading of this tract was the means of restoring dear Hudson to the favour of God.' That was how she saw it. She had known him as a child, happy in loving God and trying to please him; and at fourteen when he 'gave [his] heart to God'; and again at fifteen when he was moved by another tract and began to read the Bible and pray again, until he went into the bank.

When she had left home for a few weeks Mrs Taylor was anxious about him, and so was Amelia; and during her absence this concern for her son had increased to what she described as 'an intense yearning'. She had gone to her room in her sister's home at Barton-on-Humber and for hour after hour had prayed for him until she could pray no longer, convinced that her prayer had been answered.

Two weeks later Hudson was the first to welcome her home. There on the doorstep he told her that he had news for her. 'I know,' she answered. 'I have been rejoicing for a fortnight about it.' Had Amelia broken her promise? he asked. No, the Lord had told her.

Amelia and Hudson had identical notebooks. One day he opened hers by mistake and saw his name with the note that she would pray daily until he was converted. The date was a month before it happened. For the rest of his life he called June 1849 the time of his 'new birth'. Now friendship with Amelia became fellowship at a spiritual level, more adult and ageless. But in September Amelia went away to the boarding school run by 'Aunt Hodson' at Barton and their cousin John Hodson came to Barnsley as an apprentice to James Taylor.

John was a poor substitute. He shared Hudson's room and his cheerful schoolboy flippancy was out of harmony with Hudson's new mood. Hudson was determined to make a success of his spiritual life this time and wanted peace and quiet to make up lost time with his Bible and prayer. The need to do it in the presence of the scuffling, garrulous John was the first test of his resolve. The greatest test was to start at Christmas and go on for more than two long years in the least expected form.

The autumn came and went and Hudson Taylor soaked up Scripture until he thought in its language. He threw himself into his parents' preaching work and helped to counsel people at the penitent form in district chapels. His own experience of forgiveness and joy was so fresh that he could understand and help others with the same sense of sinfulness and alienation. But a fear of failure again depressed him. By 'backsliding' as he said he had done before, he would dishonour the Lord and lose all confidence in himself. 'After a few days or weeks of joy there followed a time' of painful deadness of soul when 'something was wrong, so wrong' that he was afraid he 'might fall away from grace and be finally lost'. He still had a great deal to learn. While he was at the bank he had vowed that if ever he became a committed Christian he would not do it by halves. He would go all the way, at any price.

On Sunday, December 2, 1849, Hudson wrote as he often did to Amelia at Barton. Thanks to her maturity and love, this and many other letters have survived to show the millrace of turbulent emotions and spiritual agitation he went through. In the next four years he was to grow rapidly to a spiritual manhood in which he continued and developed for the rest of his days. They were the most formative years of his life, and in many ways the most critical. As the decisive time when he adopted courses of action from which he never deviated, it was possibly the most important. If this is so, it is also true that his great accomplishments stemmed from his thoughts and actions between seventeen and twenty. Because it is a period of spiritual significance to his missionary career, it deserves closer attention than can be given to most phases.

For the first page and a half his letter to Amelia was a tissue of quotations from Scripture expressing his love and prayers for her, and then, with Wesleyan overtones,

> Pray for me my dear Amelia. Pray for me, I am seeking for entire sanctification. O! that the Lord would take away my heart of stone and give me a heart of flesh . . . My heart longs for this perfect holiness . . . What a happy state it must be.
>
> > Oh! for a heart to praise my God,
> > A heart from *sin* set *free* . . .
> > A heart in *every* thought renewed . . .
> > Perfect, and right, and *pure*, and *good*,
> > A *copy*, Lord, of thine . . .

He told her about evangelistic meetings, how he talked with penitents, and how John Hodson was responding.

The same evening his longing to be holy and fit for God to use came over him again. He was in his room, alone and on his knees. The following year and also in his *Retrospect* he described what happened.

> How in the gladness of my heart I poured out my soul before God, and again confessing my grateful love to Him who had done everything for me . . . I besought Him to give me some work for Him, as an outlet for love and gratitude; some self-denying service, no matter what it might be, however trying or however trivial. Well do I remember, as in unreserved consecration I put myself, my life, my friends, my all upon the altar, the deep solemnity that came over my soul with the assurance that my offering was accepted. The presence of

God became unutterably real and blessed, and . . . I remember stretching myself on the ground, and lying there silent before Him with unspeakable awe and unspeakable joy. For what service I was accepted I knew not. But a deep consciousness that I was not my own took possession of me . . .

In a letter to George Pearse of the Chinese Evangelization Society dated April 25, 1851 he said,

Never shall I forget the feeling that came over me then. Words can never describe it. I felt I was in the presence of God, entering into covenant with the Almighty. I felt as though I wished to withdraw my promise, but could not. Something seemed to say, 'Your prayer is answered, your conditions are accepted.' And from that time the conviction never left me that I was called to China.

His own memory of dates and sequences played him false as the years passed, and it is difficult to be precise about what happened, except that his consecration and his commission to China were a single transaction. Whether in her own words or quoting him is not clear, but his mother's recollections give a further detail. When he made his promise, she wrote, it was as if God answered, 'Then go for me to China.' From that moment and increasingly in the months ahead he was heart and soul committed, not in mystical terms of the holiness he had been seeking but in practical terms of preparation for going to China as soon as he was ready. He could not go to bed that night until he had told Amelia what had happened. So he added this postscript,

Bless the Lord, O my soul, and all that is within me shout His praise! Glory to God, my dear Amelia. Christ has said 'Seek and ye shall find,' and praise His name, He has revealed Himself to me in an overflowing manner. He has cleansed me from all sin, from all my idols. He has given me a new heart. Glory, glory, glory to His ever blessed Name! I cannot write for joy. I opened my letter to tell you.

It was no passing euphoria. In the thrill and power of the

experience begun that night Hudson Taylor went on. Elation there was, and if he had cracked or regressed it would have been condemned as an empty psychological experience. He had been lifted into life on a higher plane and there he stayed. Time and its difficulties sobered him. Surviving documents show that during the next three years he became a mature man, knowing his own mind and acting independently of the adult pressures upon him; but much more than that. Even in the process he exerted an influence which shaped the lives of his friends, made new and influential friends, and struck out in directions original and foreign to the world of Christians he had known.

Though they did not tell Hudson so until he had been seven years in China and returned the worse for many harsh experiences, his parents' act of consecrating him to the Lord to be a missionary was in a sense confirmed by God that night. It was the real beginning of his story. Looking at the short, slender, gentle youth, they had long ago resigned themselves to his never being strong enough to go abroad. He would settle down at home and eventually take over the business. Instead they now saw him take on a new lease of life and show a surprising purposefulness. He entered one of the most tumultuous periods of his life, but in some ways the most productive. They neither encouraged or discouraged him in it, but advised that if he intended going to China he would need to develop his body as well as his mind, and to 'wait prayerfully on God'. He set himself to learn all he could about China and to make himself physically fit.[40] In his *Retrospect* he summed up this period in the words,

> Brought up in such a circle and saved under such circumstances, it was perhaps natural that from the beginning of my Christian life I was led to feel that the promises [of God] were very real and that prayer was a sober matter-of-fact transacting business with God, whether on one's own behalf or on behalf of those for whom one sought His blessing.

Hudson Taylor was young. No doubt he turned again to Peter Parley's *China*, re-read everything in his father's shelves like Gutzlaff's *Journal of Three Voyages*, Captain Hall's *Voyages* and Evan Davies's *Spiritual Claims*, but apart from Marshman of Serampore's *Clavis Sinica*, the bigger and more expensive books were not available. After the New Year he found new ways of satisfying his great obsession, but Christmas was upon them first.[41]

Their mother's family, the musical Hudsons, were intelligent people and the fact that he began to have more to do with them contributed increasingly towards Hudson Taylor's development. Of old Benjamin Hudson's seven sons and daughters, Mrs Taylor was the eldest. The second ran the private school at Barton-on-Humber Amelia was attending, and was a little confusingly married to an absent-minded scholar, Hodson, who lived wrapped up in his research for an Oxford thesis. Hannah, the third daughter, was a portrait painter married to a professional photographer in Hull named Richard Hardey. They lived round the corner from his brother Robert Hardey, a surgeon. Thanks to Hannah and her husband there are good portraits of the Hudsons and Taylors which bring them alive in a way words cannot do, especially of Hudson Taylor at twenty and Amelia at ten. Of the three sons of old Benjamin one who was an artist died early, but the youngest, another Benjamin, was also a portraitist, living in London's Soho.

At Barton 'Aunt Hodson' not only made a home for Amelia and her own son Thomas, John's brother, but also for two of her young teachers. Marianne Vaughan and Elizabeth Sissons were a few years older than Amelia but near enough to be good friends. With Christmas coming the Taylors arranged that 'Miss Vaughan' the music teacher should escort Amelia home and stay for the whole holiday—with unforeseen consequences. Most of the family played, but with her at the piano it was an exceptional Christmas. The parents both sang and Hudson all his life found relaxation in singing at the piano or harmonium. Marianne, however, sang beautifully. Before the brief holiday was over he was head over heels in love.

If he had been free to reveal it, it might have been easier to bear, but he could only tell Amelia. With no hope of being able to support a wife, the prime consideration in those days, how could he even hint at how he felt. Even if she was prepared to go to China, would her parents ever consent? And what society would look at him, unqualified, unordained and saddled with a wife and family? Suddenly, without warning, had come as strong a test of his consecration and obedience to the Lord he had promised to serve as he could well have met, and in the age-old form.

Life returned to normal, or as near to it as could be. If he was to lead the rugged life of a pioneer, Hudson decided, he had a great deal of leeway to make up. He started taking more outdoor exercise, discarded his feather bed for a hard one and cut down on 'home comforts', whatever they might be, 'to prepare for a rougher sort of life'. He took to visiting the poor and sick, returned to his childhood practice of distributing tracts, and began teaching in the Sunday School. It was his architect friend, John Whitworth, who provided the next link in the chain. He had become the local treasurer of the Bible Society and gave Hudson Taylor a copy of Luke's Gospel and the Acts in Mandarin Chinese.

This was bliss. Hudson and John Hodson worked together, and he described the book to Amelia in a February 14 letter as 'decidedly the most beautiful book I ever saw'. He copied out the Lord's prayer in Chinese characters for her. A dictionary would cost fifteen guineas and a Chinese grammar four guineas, quite out of the question, so by using the English New Testament and a concordance, 'We have found out the meaning of many characters . . . (and) are making a dictionary'. Already they had four hundred and fifty-three characters identified for certain, with their meaning, and two hundred tentatively identified. 'In the parable of the Prodigal Son the word "kid" occurs and we could not find any likely character for it for a long time. When we knew a few more characters we found that instead of "kid" there were three characters signifying "little hill sheep".' It was an enthralling game; but he soon realised that it was too early to take the language seriously, and turned to more immediate priorities.

> I have begun to get [up] at five o'clock in the morning so I have to go to bed soon at night for I must study if I mean to go to China. I am fully decided to go and am making every preparation I can. I intend to rub up my Latin, to learn Greek and the rudiments of Hebrew, and to get as much general information as I can . . . I must have books, and some of them very expensive ones . . . Enclosed is your valentine. It is half a sovereign between some cardboard. We all send you our love . . .

So Chinese was put into the background and basic study took precedence. All his missionary life he used 'polyglot' Bibles with English, Hebrew and Greek interleaved, and recommended them to others.

John Whitworth then did him another good turn, lending him a magazine from which he learned of the Chinese Society and the publication of its new journal, *The Gleaner in the Missionary Field*.[42] He immediately subscribed and received its first issue in March 1850. The opening sentences of the editorial struck the right note for him (in the idiom of the day),

> In proportion to the enlightened acquaintance of the believer with the finished work of Christ, and the realised enjoyment of a free and full salvation, will be his desire to impart these unspeakable blessings to those around him. To such an one, the injunction of our Lord, 'Go ye into all the world and preach the gospel to every creature,' is not a dry precept, but has a willing response . . .

Hudson Taylor devoured it all as the theme developed: 'The times in which we live are most eventful. . . . The interests of the Church are but one, [Christians should enter into] the success of each other's labours.'

The column on Soungaria caught his eye. This was the remotest region, Xinjiang (Sinkiang) as we know it today, as full of desert and steppe can ever be of indigenous tribes and descendants of Chinese garrisons from centuries past. Farthest west, beyond Urumchi (Dihua) was the canton called Ili. To Hudson Taylor it typified the ultimate challenge to a soldier of Christ. Amelia had to be told. Though he expected it to cost him his life, to Ili he would probably go.

Month by month Hudson and his family looked forward to the next issue of the *Gleaner*. Silence about Gutzlaff hinted that all was not well, but recovering from the shock of the disclosures the Chinese Society rallied loyally and renewed their campaign, calling for commitment to the cause. Hudson Taylor could hold back no longer. 'It seemed to me highly probable that the work to which I was thus called might cost my life; for China was not then open . . .' he later recalled, but the die was cast and go he must. On July 29 he wrote to George Pearse of the Stock Exchange and Honorary Secretary of the Chinese Society.[43]

> Feeling deeply interested in the spread of Christianity among the Chinese [he wrote with the right amount of starch if not of commas] and, having determined, as soon as Providence shall open my way to devote myself to that extensive and almost unbounded field of Christian Enterprise I wish during the interim to promote the work as much as possible.

He asked for pamphlets, information, collecting cards, and the rules of procedure, to help him introduce the subject to his friends. A week later he was writing again to acknowledge receipt of a letter and enclosures from the Society. What he read in a personal note from Mr Pearse was apparently a frank statement of the situation in Hong Kong — revelations which could have alienated him as they alienated many others. Instead he wrote again, encouraging the man he had not yet met, in the first of many letters which George Pearse was to keep and value.

> I think though the aspect of the Institution [the Chinese Union] is at present in many respects discouraging we may hope for better days; . . . we have the promise that *all* shall know Him whom to know is life eternal . . . May the Lord raise up suitable instruments and fit me for this great work.

Not only was he seeing beyond the tactical setback to Gutzlaff's sound strategy, but was declaring his own hope of following the great man's lead.

So began Hudson Taylor's lifework.

POSTSCRIPT

This long introduction to the biography of James Hudson Taylor is no more than a vignette of the whole missionary endeavour leading up to China's 'open century'. No biography of Hudson Taylor could be complete without due credit being paid to his predecessors, but only a sketchy acknowledgement has been possible, even at such length. Robert Morrison by his painstaking scholarship forged the key to China's awakening. Walter Medhurst's immense output of Christian literature in Chinese prepared the minds of multitudes for the coming of the preachers. Dr Peter Parker 'by his scalpel' overcame prejudice and resentment, paving the way to receptiveness even in Canton. Elijah Bridgman and Samuel Wells Williams through their *Chinese Repository* and other publications taught insular Westerners and Chinese to understand and admire the good in each other's culture and character. Others equally deserving of mention made their costly contributions. All of them through their prayers and urging brought reinforcements to their constantly dwindling ranks as death and disease struck them down. Perhaps none by example, appeals or personal influence effected more for the ultimate evangelisation of China than the luminous prophet, Charles Gutzlaff. That such a claim could be justified was due to Hudson Taylor taking up his torch.

Nor can such a biography be adequate without some understanding of the land and people of China; yet it is impossible to portray them. This outline of the encounter between East and West across the centuries must serve as the backcloth to the great events unfolding in forthcoming chapters. Those events moved rapidly after 1850, with the growing rebellion of the Worshippers of Shangdi and the

Patriot Army; and for Hudson Taylor as he schooled himself to become fit to play his part, for they swept him into the strong current flowing towards China. The Chinese empire was no longer in the maelstrom of external threats but of internal forces, as the world watched, sizing up the advantages to be gained from the changes taking place. Commerce was to see its great opportunity, governments to be weighed in the balances and found wanting, and missions to find themselves on the threshold of the century of open access to China—unprepared. A decade later, as civil war ended and uneasy peace at last returned, upon Hudson Taylor was to fall Charles Gutzlaff's mantle of pioneer, founder and prophet. As centuries of resistance to the 'barbarian' presence and to Christian missions gave place to increasing tolerance, in Hudson Taylor the right man was ready at the right time—by then the scarred veteran of his first campaign.

ESSENTIAL WADE–PINYIN DIFFERENCES

Initials

Wade	p	ts'	ch'	t	k	ch	k'	p'	ch'	j	t'	hs	ts	ch
Pinyin	b	c	ch	d	g	j	k	p	q	r	t	x	z	zh

Finals

Wade	-ien	-ieh	-iung	-üan	-üeh	-uei	-ün	-o
Pinyin	-ian	-ie	-iong	-uan	-ue	-ui	-un	-uo

Monosyllables

Wade	ch'ih	tz'u	eh	erh	ho	ko	k'o	tzu	jih	shih	ssu
Pinyin	chi	ci	e	er	he	ge	ke	zi	ri	shi	si
Wade	yeh	i	yu	chih	tse	tzu				shih	
Pinyin	ye	yi	you	zhi	ze	zi				shi	

Examples

Wade	pei/peh=north	tz'u=kind	chien=build	
Pinyin	bei	ci	jian	
Wade	kiang=river	ching=capital	ch'ien=money	
Pinyin	jiang	jing	qian	
Wade	ch'ing=green	je=hot	hsi=west	tzu=son
Pinyin	qing	re	xi	zi

PROVINCES AND CITIES IN WADE, (POSTAL) AND PINYIN

PROVINCES

Wade &c	Anhwei	Fukien	Kansu	Kwangtung	Kwangsi	Kweichow	Ninghsia
Pinyin	Anhui	Fujian	Gansu	Guangdong	Guangxi	Guizhou	Ningxia
Wade &c	Hopeh	Honan	Hupeh	Hunan	Kiangsu	Kiangsi
Pinyin	Hebei	Henan	Hubei	Hunan	Jiangsu	Jiangxi
Wade &c	Jehol	Shantung	Shansi	Shensi	Szechwan	Sinkiang
Pinyin	Rehe	Shandong	Shanxi	Shaanxi	Sichuan	Xinjiang
Wade &c	Yünnan	Chekiang	(Chihli)
Pinyin	Yunnan	Zhejiang	(Zhili)

CITIES

Wade &c	Peking	Fuchow (Foochow)	Canton	Hangchow	Nanking	Ningpo
Pinyin	Beijing	Fuzhou	Guangzhou	Hangzhou	Nanjing	Ningbo
Wade &c	Tsingtao	Suchow (Soochow)	Tientsin	Woosung	Wusih	Sian
Pinyin	Qingdao	Suzhou	Tianjin	Wusong	Wuxi	Xi'an
Wade &c	Yangchow	Yentai (Chefoo)		Chaochow	Chinkiang	
Pinyin	Yangzhou	Yantai		Zhaozhou	Zhenfiang	

EAST and WEST in PARALLEL

Based on H. C. Fenn 1926

CENTURY	DYNASTY	CHINA	WEST	PARALLELS
BC 1800	SHANG 1766–1122	Bone records of rites, poems and silk weaving	Aegean culture Egyptian shepherd kings Moses David and Solomon	
1500				
1000	ZHOU (CHOU) 1122–255	Bamboo books bronze arts eclipse recorded 776 BC Laotze Confucius	Carthage	
500		Great Wall 214 BC	Gautama Buddha Greek philosophers Julius Caesar	Pax Romana & Pax Sinica East-West contacts begin
ANNO DOMINI	QIN (CHIN) 221–207 HAN 205 BC– AD 221	Paper invented	JESUS Jerusalem destroyed	Persians Jews flee to China
AD 100		Taoism the state religion		

CENTURY	DYNASTY	CHINA	WEST	PARALLELS
200	THREE KINGDOMS 220–280			
300			Constantine Goths sack Rome	Dark Ages, West and East
400	SIX DYNASTIES 265–589			
500		Compass in China China's renaissance creative painting greatest poets	Mohammed 622	Muslim militancy
600	SUI 581–618		Nestorian Alopen 635 Charlemagne	Nestorian Tablet 781
800	TANG 618–907	Porcelains Gunpowder Peking Court Gazette		
900	FIVE DYNASTIES 907–960	1,200 Christians, Muslims, Jews in Hangzhou	Dark Ages in West	
1000	SONG 960–1280	Printing movable type	Holy Roman Empire Norman conquest	
1100	JIN (CHIN) 1115–1234			
1200			Crusades Magna Carta	Paper and compass to Europe Franciscans to China
1300	YUAN 1271–1368	Mongol emperors Genghis and Kublai Khan	Renaissance	Marco Polo with Kublai Khan

[continued]

CENTURY	DYNASTY	CHINA	WEST	PARALLELS
1400	MING 1368–1644		Wyclif, Chaucer	
1500		Renaissance of Chinese arts Peking built	Age of Discovery Columbus, Magellan	Xavier died 1552
1600	QING (CH'ING) 1644–1911	Shun Zhi takes Peking 1644	Reformation Loyola founds Jesuits Armada AV Bible	Mogul Empire in India Matteo Ricci, S. J. Adam Schall von Bell East India Company to Canton 1644
1700		Qian Long Opium banned 1727	American Revolution 1776 French Revolution 1789 Industrial Revolution	Porcelains to Europe Macartney Mission 1795
1800		Jia Qing rebellions Dao Guang 1821		R. Morrison 1807 Canton Amherst Mission 1816
1850		Taiping Rebellion 1850–64	Crimean War 1854–56 Slavery ends 1863 in US Suez Canal opens 1869	Expansion of Christianity in China 1860–1950
1900	REPUBLIC 1912	Boxer Rising		

REIGN TITLES OF THE QING (CH'ING=MANCHU) DYNASTY

	Wade	Pinyin	Duration
1644	Shun Chih	Shun Zhi	18 years
1662	K'ang Hsi	Kang Xi	61 „
1723	Yung Cheng	Yong Zheng	13 „
1736	Ch'ien Lung	Qian Long	60 „
1796	Chia Ch'ing	Jia Qing	25 „
1821	Tao Kuang	Dao Guang	30 „
1851	Hsien Feng	Xian Feng	11 „
1862	T'ung Chih*	Tong Zhi	13 „
1875	Kuang Hsü*	Guang Xu	34 „
1908	Hsüan T'ung*	Xuan Tong	3 „

* Empress Dowager Ci Xi (Ts'u Hsi) mostly in power until her death in 1908

BIOGRAPHICAL CHARTS

Seventh to seventeenth century

	600	700	800	900	1000	1100	1200	1300	1400	1500	1600	1700	1800

Alopen
Marco Polo
Ricci, Matteo
Schall von Bell
Valignano
Verbiest
Xavier

Nineteenth century

	1790	1800	10	20	30	40	1850	60	70	80	90	1900

Abeel
Amherst
Bridgman
Carey
Dyer
Elliot
Gutzlaff
Hong Xiu-quan

Jardine
Legge
Liang A-fa
Lin Ze-xu
Macartney
Matheson
Medhurst
Milne
Morrison
Moseley
Napier
Olyphant
Parker
Pottinger
Qi Shan
Qi Ying
Raffles
Staunton
Wells Williams

EUROPEAN MISSIONS attributable to Charles Gutzlaff organisations sending missionaries or supporting the Chinese Union with leading members mentioned in this biography

Basel German Evangelical Society (Evangelical Missionary Society of Basel or Basel Mission)
Theodore Hamberg; Rudolf Lechler; Ph. Winnes; E. J. Eitel

Berlin Foundling House of Hong Kong

Berlin Missionary Society for China (distinguish from the Berlin Mission) (Chinese Evangelization Society of Berlin; Berlin Society)
Robert Neumann; August Hanspach

Berlin Women's Missionary Society for China

Chinese Evangelization Society (CES)
Wilhelm Lobscheid; Hudson Taylor; Arthur Taylor; Wm Parker; John Jones

Kassel Missionary Association
Karl Vogel

Moravian Mission to Tibet

Netherlands Chinese Evangelization Society
Hendrick Z. Kloekers

Paris Evangelization Society

Pomeranian Mission Union for the Evangelization of China

Rhenish Missionary Society (Barmen Mission) (1872 incorporated the Berlin Society)
Ferdinand Genähr

CURRENCY EQUIVALENTS IN NINETEENTH CENTURY CHINA

Documents dealing with East Asia in the nineteenth century refer haphazardly to values in pounds sterling, American dollars, Spanish dollars, often called Mexican dollars, of various dates and differing quality, and Chinese silver taels. It is impossible to establish relative values with any accuracy. In response to an enquiry citing a score of statements quoted in this biography, the Banking Information Service replied: 'We do not have historical data going back that far'; the Institute of Bankers' Library had no relevant information; the librarian of the Bank of England suggested: 'It will be necessary to consult a great many published sources . . . (but) in trying to equate monetary values of a previous era with present day equivalents it is not possible to be precise.' Inflation has progressed at varying rates.

H. B. Morse: *The International Relations of the Chinese Empire* Vol. I p. xxxix states: one tael (the Chinese ounce)=525–585 grains; three taels of Canton=one pound sterling; the tael of Shanghai about 10% less.

Brian Inglis: *The Opium War*, p. 6 gives: one pound=five Spanish dollars=ten rupees.

Marshall Broomhall: *Robert Morrison*, p. 87: circa 1814, one pound=five and a half Spanish dollars.

NOTES

Page Note

8   1   Wang, Mary: *The Chinese Church that will not Die:* Hodder & Stoughton

8   2   Latourette, K. S.: *A History of Christian Missions in China,* 1928, p 4

8   3   Foreign Office Records Library: *A Century of Diplomatic Blue Books*; Parliamentary Papers; British Library, State Papers.

9   4   *see* page 397

9   5   *see* Appendix 6

9   6   Howard Taylor: *Hudson Taylor: The Growth of a Soul:* p 88 caption

9   7   *see* Broomhall, Marshall: *The Jubilee Story of the China Inland Mission,* Appendix 1

9   8, 9   Latourette, K. S.: op. cit. p 382, cf. p 259

10   10   *ibid*: Tipple Lectures 1950: *These Sought a Country*

10   11   Carlyle, Thomas: op. cit. pp 3–4

12   12   C E S *Gleaner: The Gleaner in the Missionary Field,* Mar. 1850–May '51; *The Chinese and General Missionary Gleaner,* June 1851–53; *The Chinese Missionary Gleaner,* June 1853–Oct. '60; organ of the Chinese Association, renamed Chinese Society, re-formed as the Chinese Evangelization Society.

PROLOGUE

29   1   Population of China: *Statesmen's Yearbook,* 1907, citing Chinese Government census gave 426 million; 1937 Chinese sources gave 450 million; Hook, Brian: *China's Three Thousand Years,* (The Times) Part IV p 149 says 430 million by 1850; see also *Gleaner,* 1850, p 11; Bridgman, E; 1864, p 106; Broomhall, M: *Chinese Empire,* p 23; Morrison's *Memoirs,* Vol II, p 473. Hudson Taylor

later considered most of these early figures excessive.

33 2 An imperial edict, 1729, banned opium imports under pain of heavy penalties, when addiction began to spread from Canton, port for foreign trade.

Chapter 1

36 3 Historical parallels drawn from encyclopaedias, and wall charts by Henry C. Fenn, 1926–7: *see* Appendix 3.

41, 4, 5 Cary-Elwes, Columba: *China and the Cross*,
42 pp 9–12, 24; Latourette, K. S.: *A History of Christian Missions in China*, p 48 footnote, details his sources.

43 6 Broomhall, M.: *The Chinese Empire*, pp 202, 433–5.

43 7 Cary-Elwes, C.: op. cit. p 24.

44, 8, 9 Legge, J.: *The Nestorian Monument*: lecture at
45 Oxford Univ.; cf. Cole, R. A.: *Tyndale Commentary, Mark*, p 13; Latourette, K. S.: *A History of Christian Missions in China*, pp 52–54.

46– 10–13 Cary-Elwes, C.: op. cit. pp 33–5; 72; 39; 48
52

52 14 Broomhall, M.: op. cit. p 7.

52 15–16 Neill, Stephen C.: *A History of Christian Missions*, p 137, 126.

53 17 Latourette, K. S.: op. cit. p 72

54 18 ibid: pp 73–4, sources were 'unknown missionaries'

55 19 Fairbank, J. K.: *Trade and Diplomacy on the China Coast*, p 32

55 20 Stock, E.: *The History of the Church Missionary Society*, Vol I p 28. Behaim's Globe of the same date showed the Azores and Canary Is. separated by a narrow sea from a large island called Jipango (cf. Jihpenkuo, Ribenguo) and another group of islands in the south called Jawa, off a continuous coastline called Cathay in the north and India in the south. So when Columbus sighted land he thought he had reached Asia.

57 21 Martin, W. A. P.: *A Cycle of Cathay*, 1896, p 20

57 22 Broomhall, M.: op. cit. p 2
59, 23, 24 Stock, E.: op. cit. I. 18–19; 20
60
60 25 Cary-Elwes, C.: op. cit. p 79
60 26 Latourette, K. S.: op. cit. p 87; Huc, Abbé: *Christianity in China, Tartary and Thibet*
61 27 Stock, E.: op cit. p 463
62 28 Latourette, K. S.: op. cit. p 91; Broomhall, M.: op. cit. p 9 'open to my Lord'; Smith, A. H.: *The Uplift of China*, p 124; etc.
62 29 Latourette, K. S.: op. cit. pp 92–8
63 30 Latourette, K. S.: *A History of the Expansion of Christianity*, pp 264; 324; 339; Burke, J.: *My Father in China, passim.*
64– 31–33 Cary-Elwes, C.: op. cit. pp 93; 94; 103
66
66 34 Neill, S. C.: op. cit. p 208
68 35 Inglis, Brian: *The Opium War*, p 16
69 36 Chinese emperors had personal names and dynastic titles, but are usually known by a third label, the title of their reign. The first Qing (Ch'ing) emperor's reign was known as Shun Zhi (Chih) so he was the 'Shun Zhi emperor'. In Western convention the title is used as the man's name, simply 'Shun Zhi'.
69 37 Fernandez Capellas, 1647; Cary-Elwes, C. op. cit. p 110
70 38 Neill, S. C.: op. cit. p 179; note also: Robert Morrison's 'A Christian missionary is not sent . . . to introduce English customs but Christ's Gospel.' Broomhall, M.: *Robert Morrison, Master-Builder.*
71 39 Cary-Elwes, C.: op. cit. p 132; Bridgman, E. J.: *The Life and Labors of Elijah Coleman Bridgman*, p 129
71 40 Latourette, K. S.: *A History of Christian Missions in China*, p 129 ff
75 41 Latourette, K. S.: op. cit. p 189; Edinburgh Conference Reports, Vol II, p 250; Smith, A. H.: op. cit. p 133

Chapter 2

76   1   Latourette, K. S.: *A History of Christian Missions in China*, pp 209–10

77, 2, 4   Stock, E.: *The History of the Church Missionary*
78   *Society*, Vol I pp 19, 20 ff; 32–4; Neill, S. C.: *A History of Christian Missions*, p 222; Justinian von der Welz (1621–68) himself led a mission to Surinam and died in the attempt.

77   3   The first S P G was 'the Society for the Propagation of the Gospel in New England' under Oliver Cromwell, 1648; the second S P G was a reorganisation under Charles II and Robert Boyle, so the S P G of 1701, still extant, was the third, under royal charter.

83   5   Martin, W. A. P.: *A Cycle of Cathay*, p 19

88   6   Inglis, Brian: *The Opium War*, p 18 ff

89, 7, 8   Woodcock, George, *The British in the Far East*,
90   pp 12; 24

92   9   Fairbank, J. K.: *Trade and Diplomacy on the China Coast*, p 29

93   10   ibid: pp 57–8; Broomhall, M.: *Morrison*, p 1

93   11   Latourette, K. S.: op. cit. p 174

93   12   Bryant, Sir Arthur: *A Thousand Years of the British Monarchy*

100 13   *Attested*: 1. William Shepherd 'of independent means' was one of John Wesley's travelling preachers, 1743–48; 2. William Shepherd, Gov., died 1828; 3. Mary Shepherd, daughter of Gov. William (born 1776, died 5 Jan. 1850 aged 74) and Mary.
J. Wesley's *Journal*: Sept. 12, 1743; June, July, Oct, 1745; March 17, 1746; April 1746; July 5, 1747; Sept. 14, 1788 at Bath.
Family tradition: Mary was daughter of Wesley's preacher.
Conjecture: If Wesley's preacher became Gov. and father of Mary, and if 30 in 1748, then born 1713, 58 when Mary born, 110 at death, 1828; but if older in 1748, then increasingly improbable. Or, 2. If father of Wm. Shepherd, Gov. and grandfather of Mary, then if Wm. Gov. born, say, 1748, 28

when Mary born 1776, 80 at death, 1828; more
probable.
O M F A: 211a '(He) might have been his father.'
(Mrs Howard Taylor)

100 14   O M F A: A113; A211–3
101 15   Brainerd's life and death influenced William
          Carey, Henry Martyn and Thomas Chalmers of the
          South Pacific. Stock, E.: op. cit. I.27
103 16   Stock, E.: op. cit. I.57, 59–60
104 17   Members of the Clapham Sect also included Charles
          Grant, three times chairman of the East India
          Company, later a member of Parliament; Sir John
          Shore (Lord Teignmouth) of the East India
          Company; Zachary Macaulay, governor of Sierra
          Leone, father of Lord Macaulay, the historian. John
          Venn was rector of Clapham. Stock, E.: I.41–2
104– 18–20 Broomhall, M.: op cit. pp 27–9; Latourette, K. S.:
105   op. cit. p 210; *A History of the Expansion of
          Christianity*, pp 295–6; Stock, E.: op. cit. I.463–4
          and Appendix, nine pp quoting his pamphlet.

Chapter 3

112 1   Morrison's *Memoirs*, 'by his widow', 1839, 2 vols, is
          the primary source; Broomhall, M.: *Robert
          Morrison, A Master-Builder*, 1924, 238 pp, is a
          succinct biography, based on the former, cited here
          because more readily available.
115 2   Morrison's *Memoirs*, Vol I p 78; Medhurst, W. H.:
          China: Its State and Prospects, said Royal Asiatic
          Society; but as it was founded 1823, he was in
          error; but Morrison became a member.
116 3   Medhurst, W. H.: op. cit. p 250
118 4   Woodcock, G.: *The British in the Far East*, p 23;
          much interesting information on nineteenth
          century conditions is summarised in this fine,
          lavishly illustrated book, qv
121 5   Smith, A. H.: *The Uplift of China*, pp 35, 37
121 6   *Chinese Recorder*: Vol 7, pp 174–8; Broomhall,
          M.: op. cit. p 52
121 7   Woodcock, G.: op. cit. *passim*; very informative;
          Broomhall, M.: op. cit.; Medhurst, W. H.: op. cit.

123	8	Morrison's *Memoirs*: I. 153; Broomhall, M.: op. cit. pp 53–6; Medhurst, W. H.: op. cit. p 250 ff
124	9	Carmichael, A.: *Walker of Tinnevelly*
125	10	Broomhall, M.: op. cit. p 202; Latourette, K. S.: *A History of the Expansion of Christianity*, p 297
126	11	£500 per annum: Smith, A. H.: op. cit. p 139
127, 128	12, 13	Broomhall, M.: op. cit. p 108, 66; 70–3
128	14	The Hodgson-Moseley MS he had transcribed: Broomhall, M.: op. cit. p 118
129	15	Decapitation was lenient because instantaneous, but because garotting left the body intact for the after-life it was considered a still more lenient form of execution.
131	16	Broomhall, M.: op. cit. p 74 ff; Smith, A. H.: op. cit. p 140; Latourette, K. S.: op. cit. p 299 with sources; *A History of Christian Missions in China*, p 213
133	17	Broomhall, M.: op. cit. p 83; Medhurst, W. H.: op. cit. p 306
134	18	Neill, S. C.: *A History of Christian Missions*, p 291; Bentley-Taylor, D.: *Java Saga: Christian Progress in Muslim Java, passim*
135	19	Inglis, B.: *The Opium War*, says £1 = Span. $5 = Rupees 10; but see Appendix 7.
136	20	Broomhall, M.: op. cit. p 84 ff; Latourette, K. S.: *A History of the Expansion of Christianity*, p 298; MacGillivray, D.: *A Century of Protestant Missions*, pp 3, 17–18
139, 140	21, 22	Inglis, B.: op. cit. p 35; pp 46–7, 59–61, 202
141	23	Broomhall, M.: op. cit. p 92 ff
143, 144	24, 25	Chia Ch'ing (Kia King), 11 September 1816; Broomhall, M.: op. cit. pp 96–7; 99 ff
144	26	William Milne received the same honour one year later: McNeur, G. H.: *Liang A-fa*
147	27	Broomhall, M.: op. cit. pp 117–25; the letter at length.
148	28	Smith, A. H.: op. cit. p 140
148, 149	29, 30	Wurtzburg, C. E.: *Raffles of the Eastern Isles*, p 501; also Woodcock, G.: op. cit. p 74; 138

Chapter 4

151 1   Bryant, Sir Arthur: *A Thousand Years of the British Monarchy*

153 2   Morrison's *Memoirs*: Vol II, Appendix p 10–32, the 'Lintin' story in full.

156 3   Broomhall, M.: *Robert Morrison, Master-Builder*, p 125. It was William Milne who wrote that 'to acquire Chinese is a work for men with bodies of brass, lungs of steel, heads of oak, hands of spring-steel, eyes of eagles, hearts of apostles, memories of angels, and lives of Methuselah!'

158 4   Morrison's *Memoirs*, II. 182, letter dated November 12, 1822. Bishop Stephen Neill has found no evidence to support this conjecture and believes 'that minds were independently drawn in the same direction'.

159 5   Bentley-Taylor, D.: *Java Saga, passim*; Medhurst, W. H.: *China: Its State and Prospects*, p 329 ff

161 6   McNeur, G. H.: *Liang A-fa, China's first Preacher, 1789–1855*; Clarke, Agnes L.: unpublished MS, OMFA

161 7   Dictionary: Broomhall, M.: op. cit. pp 111, 158, 173; Smith, A. H.: *The Uplift of China*, p 140; MacGillivray, D.: *A Century of Protestant Missions in China*, p 2, adds '4595 pages'.

162 8   Woodcock, G.: *The British in the Far East*, p 102

164 9   Morrison urged the CMS in 1824 to send missionaries to China. In 1832 they resolved to do so when funds were available, but in 1834 no men were offering to go, so the CMS made a grant of three hundred pounds to Charles Gutzlaff: Stock, E.: *A History of the Church Missionary Society*, Vol I p 468

164 10   Morrison's *Memoirs*: II. 298–302

165 11   Davies, Evan: *Memoir of the Rev. Samuel Dyer*, 1846; Broomhall, M.: op. cit. p 298

167 12   Inglis, B.: *The Opium War*, p 76

168 13   Latourette, K. S.: *A History of Christian Missions in China*, p 203, citing Launay: *Hist. de la Soc. des Missions-Étrangères*, Vol II p 504

169 14   Broomhall, M.: op. cit. pp 174–80

170 15   Morrison's *Memoirs*, II. 479–80 (1833) 'It has been
               fully proved that Macao belongs to China, and is
               no part of the territories of the king of Portugal;
               the claim is therefore usurpation.'

171– 16–18   Medhurst, W. H.: op. cit. pp 248, 250; 250 ff; 247
173

173 19   Morrison's *Memoirs*, II. 504, 502

174 20   Bridgman, E.: *The Life and Labors of E. C.
               Bridgman*, p 43; McNeur, G. H.: op. cit.: Liang A-
               fa's own comment on meeting the two young men
               was, 'I have been a believer in the Saviour for
               several years, but have never yet done anything
               worthy for God.'

174 21   70,000 tracts and Scriptures yearly, by hand-carved
               blocks: Wells Williams.

176 22   *Chinese Recorder*: Vol VII, Nov.–Dec. 1876

177 23, 24   Bridgman, E.: op. cit. pp 39–40; 54–5

179 25   Davies, E.: op. cit. pp 38–9

179 26   *Chinese Recorder*: Vol X, 1879, p 208

179 27, 28   Davies, E.: op. cit. p 95 ff; *China and her Spiritual
               Claims*, p 13

180 29   *Chinese Recorder*: Vol VI, p 26

180 30   Gutzlaff, C.: *A Journal of Three Voyages, passim*;
               Chinese Repository: Vols II, IV, V, VII, X, XI,
               XII, XIII, XVI, *passim*; *Chinese Recorder*, 1925:
               '*The Early History and Development of the Berlin
               Missionary Work in South China*': J. Weise,
               Canton Missionary Conference, 29 March 1924;
               Latourette, K. S.: op. cit. p 216; *A History of the
               Expansion of Christianity*, pp 243, 300; Broomhall,
               M.: op. cit. pp 194–5; also Medhurst *passim*;
               MacGillivray; Smith, A. H.: op cit.' OMF A111

181 31   Latourette, K. S.: op. cit. p 300: Stock, E.: op. cit.
               I. 111: J. Jänicke of the Berlin Seminary was made
               an 'Honorary Life Governor' of the CMS in 1813.

181 32   Latourette, K. S.: loc cit.; *A History of Christian
               Missions in China*, Vol II pp 6, 7, 'a versatile
               linguist'

184 33   Morrison's *Memoirs*, two vols *passim*, eg p 472; cf.
               Medhurst, W. H., other contemporaries, and CES
               Gleaner

185	34	*Chinese Recorder*, 1925, loc. cit.: *Early History of the German Missions*
185, 186	35, 36	Gutzlaff, C.: op. cit. *passim*; adoption was 'long before leaving Siam'; p 146
186	37	Broomhall, M.: op. cit. pp 194–5
186	38	Medhurst, W. H.: op. cit. p 329 ff
187	39	Broomhall, M.: op. cit. p 194
188	40	Inglis, B.: op. cit. pp 63, 78
189	41	Morse, Hosea Ballou: *The International Relations of the Chinese Empire*: introduction, Vols I–III: 'Every statement regarding the quantities of opium consumed in China appears to differ from every other statement.'
189	42	Fairbank, J. K.: *Trade and Diplomacy on the China Coast*, pp 59, 64, *passim*; Inglis, B.: op. cit. pp 66, 74, 181 ff, *passim*
192	43, 44	Inglis, B.: op. cit. p 79
193	45	Fairbank, J. K.: op. cit. pp 74–6; Hook, B.: *China's Three Thousand Years*, p 149 ff; Woodcock, G.: op. cit. p xxiii; Eames, J. B.: *The Englishman in China* (Rutherford Alcock): £2 million of silver exported annually.

Chapter 5

197	1	Woodcock, G.: *The British in the Far East*, p 70
198	2	Fairbank, J. K.: *Trade and Diplomacy on the China Coast*, p 176
198	3	Bryant, Sir Arthur: *A Thousand Years of British Monarchy*
200	4	Many contemporary sources: Official Publications Office, FO Records Office, Br. Library State Papers: Parliamentary Papers Vol. XXV, 1833, p 599 ff; Lindsay, Capt. H. H. and Gutzlaff, C. reports; Gutzlaff, C.: *Journal of Three Voyages*; Medhurst, W. H.: *China: Its State and Prospects*, p 360 ff; also, Fairbank, J. K.: op. cit. pp 66–7; Inglis, B.: *The Opium War*, p 79 ff; MacGillivray, D.: *A Century of Protestant Missions in China*; Pott, Hawks: *A Short History of Shanghai*; Smith, A. H.: *The Uplift of China*; Stock, E.: *The History of the Church Missionary Society*; etc.

200	5, 6	Lindsay, H. H. cited by Inglis, Brian: op. cit. pp 79, 82
200– 202	7–11	Parliamentary Papers, XXV (1833) pp 599–622
204	12	Fairbank, J. K.: op. cit. p 69
204, 205	13, 14	Parliamentary Papers: loc. cit., also quoted by Fairbank, J. K.
205	15, 16	Pott, Hawks: op. cit. pp 4, 5
206	17	Parliamentary Papers: loc. cit.
207	18	Again many sources (see note 4) but not Parliamentary Papers; Gutzlaff, C.: op. cit.; Medhurst, W. H.: op. cit. p 364 ff; Fairbank, J. K.: op. cit. p 70; Inglis, B.: op. cit. pp 81–2; also Woodcock, G.: op. cit. pp 102–3; Stock, E. etc.
208	19, 20	Inglis, B.: op. cit. p 81–2 quotation
209	21	Woodcock, G.: op. cit. p 103 quoting Collis, Maurice: *Foreign Mud*
210	22	Medhurst, W. H.: op. cit. p 364
210	23	Dyer letters: John Dyer to son Samuel, 29 Nov. 1843; property of Hudson Taylor family
214	24	Medhurst, W. H.: op. cit. p 522 ff; over 8 million pages, 10,000 New Testaments, 2,000 complete Bibles, 750,000 books and tracts, mostly in Chinese
214	25	Broomhall, M.: *Robert Morrison, Master-Builder*, p 191
215	26	Bridgman, E.: *The Life and Labors of E. C. Bridgman*, pp 65, 74
216	27, 28	Morrison's *Memoirs*: Vol II p 469; Broomhall, M.: op. cit. p 201; Morrison's *Memoirs*: II. 471; II. 472
217	29	Martin, W. A. P.: *A Cycle of Cathay*, p 20
219	30	Morrison's *Memoirs*: II, 508, Marjoribanks to Morrison
219	31	James Buckingham, MP; Inglis, B.: op. cit. p 87
220	32	Morrison's *Memoirs*: II. 524
221	33	Morse, H. B.: *The International Relations of the Chinese Empire*, Vol I p 126
222– 223	34–36	Inglis B.: op. cit. pp 99–100; 103
224	37	Bridgman, E.: op. cit. p 96
225	38	Full story in McNeur, G. H.: *Liang A-fa*
225	39	Neill, S.; *A History of Christian Missions*, p 348

226 40, 41   Davies, E.: *Memoir of the Rev. S. Dyer*, p 104; 234.
Samuel Dyer cited (*Memoir*, pp 186 ff) the use in
translation of words, idioms and word order
peculiar to another language, e.g. 'a cold laugh' to
mean 'a smile'. Evan Davies commented (*Memoir*,
p 199) 'The views that Mr Dyer had entertained for
years before were confirmed by the united and
deliberate opinion of the General Missionary
Conference in Hong Kong, 1843.' W. H. Medhurst
had already attempted a revision.

227 42   *Chinese Recorder*, Vol VI p 26

228 43   Stock, E.: op. cit. I. 466; quoted by MacGillivray,
op. cit. p 22

228 44, 45   *Missionary Register*, 1835: p 85; Stock, E.: op. cit.
I. 467–8

228 46   E. J. Eitel, PhD, Sinologue; Basel Mission 1862–5
(*see* Personalia)

229 47   *Chinese Recorder*: Vol VII, 1876, p 22

230 48   Bridgman, E.: op. cit. pp 96–8

230 49   Medhurst, W. H.: op. cit. pp 359 ff

233 50   *Chinese Recorder*: I. 1, records finding Medhurst's
books, 1866.

233 51   Medhurst, W. H.: op. cit. pp 499–508

234 52   *Chinese Recorder*: VII, Nov.–Dec. 1876, article by
Wells Williams

234 53   ibid, p 199

235 54   Two volumes publ. by E. French, New York, 1839,
pp 238, 310; also *Chinese Recorder*: VIII,
Nov.–Dec., Wells Williams

235 55   *Chinese Repository*: VI, 1837; publ. by Smith,
Elder & Co. 1838

236 56   Latourette, K. S.: *A History of the Expansion of
Christianity*, pp 381–2; *Chinese Recorder*: VII.
391–6

240 57   Fairbank, J. K.: op. cit. p 64

240 58   Inglis, B.: op. cit. p 126

240 59   Bridgman, E.: op. cit. p 106–7

240, 60, 61   Inglis, B.: op. cit. pp 127–9, 179; Medhurst, W. H.:
241   op. cit.

241 62   Inglis, B.: op. cit. p 114; 195

243 63   Arthur Waley's expression; the style of address to
             a vassal; Martin, W. A. P.: *A Cycle of Cathay*,
             p 21 ff

244 64   Waley, Arthur: *The Opium War through Chinese
             Eyes*

248– 65–74   Inglis, B.: op. cit. pp 132–3; 124; 151; 147–51, a
252   fascinating account; 133; 129–30; 148; Waley,
             Arthur: op. cit. (Waley's recurrent comment, that
             statement after statement could bear little relation
             to the facts, may be applied also to references to
             Gutzlaff, some scurrilous.)

Chapter 6
254 1   Inglis, B.: *The Opium War*

254 2   Bridgman, E.: *The Life and Labors of E. C.
             Bridgman*, p 113

255 3, 4   Inglis, B.: op. cit. pp 176–7; Bridgman, E.: op. cit.
             p 74, 'the real problem is not the opium trade but a
             conflict between two powers each considering
             herself the greatest.'

255 5   This is the General Gough who in 1845 conquered
             the Sikhs, and in 1849 was disastrously defeated at
             Chillianwallah but by victory at Gujerat annexed
             the Punjab. Stock, E.: *A History of the Church
             Missionary Society*, Vol II p 196

256– 6–9   Inglis, B.: op. cit. p 151; 154; 157; 171
258

260 10   Inglis, B.: op. cit. pp 156–8; 173

261 11   Hook, Brian: *China's Three Thousand Years*,
             p 153 ff; Pottinger's force was 2,500 men, increased
             by 10,000 from India in 1842.

261 12   Inglis, B.: op. cit. p 173

265 13   Pott, Hawks: *A Short History of Shanghai*,
             pp 10–13; Bridgman, E.: op. cit. p 179

265– 14–18   Inglis, B.: op. cit. p 163; 181; 179; title page; 204–5
267

267 19   Stock, E.: *The History of the CMS*, Vol I p 469–70

268 20, 21 OMFA; Gladstone's sister was an addict; Ball, R.:
             A Handbook of China

268 22   Fairbank, J. K.: *Trade and Diplomacy on the
             China Coast*, p 270

269 23   (*see* note 25) This ungainly international legal term came into use in 1836 (Oxf. Dicty.) but more widely after the Treaty of Tientsin, 1858; Hook, Brian: *China's Three Thousand Years*, p 153 ff; British jurisdiction over her subjects in China was provided for.

270 24   Boone, M.: *The Seed of the Church in China*, p 74; (biography of Rt. Rev. W. J. Boone Sr) 'the very officials appointed to control the trade are growing rich through condoning it', E. C. Bridgman; also Eames, J. B.: *The Englishman in China*.

273 25   Pott, Hawks: op. cit. p 14 (*see* note 23)

273 26   see note 24

275 27   Davies, E.: *A Memoir of the Rev. S. Dyer*, p 247

275 28   Henry Venn 'the elder', vicar of Huddersfield, was a leading promoter of the first evangelical revival; John Venn, his son, rector of Clapham, was a member in the eighteenth century of the Eclectics, and first chairman of CMS; died 1813; Henry Venn 'the younger', but 'Sr', was Honorary Secretary and virtually director of the CMS for thirty years; Henry Venn 'Junior', second son of the second Henry Venn, was Associate Secretary of the CMS *c* 1869–72. Stock, E.: I. 368–9

276 29   Stock, E.: op. cit. I.472; II. 15

276 30   Legge, H. E.: *James Legge: Missionary and Scholar*

277 31   Property of the Hudson Taylor family

277 32   Davies, E.: *A Memoir of the Rev. S. Dyer*, pp 233–4, 245, 247; 'we are exhilarating in glad tidings from China'; Medhurst, W. H.: *China: Its State and Prospects*, 'His chief employment consisted in going about from house to house, and preaching the Gospel to every creature.'

278 33   Davies, E.: op. cit. pp 271–2

278 34   MacGillivray, D.: *A Century of Protestant Missions in China*, p 3, the Ultra-Ganges staff and dates in full.

281 35   Legge, H. E.: op. cit.; Smith, A. H.: *The Uplift of China*, p 149

282 36   Gutzlaff, C.: *Chinese Union*: OMFA 1–4

282 37 OMFA: A111, A211–222, 2–1; Latourette, K. S.:
Tipple Lectures, 1950

282 38 Wang, Mary: from book title, Hodder &
Stoughton.

294 39 OMFA: photograph of oil portrait (now lost)

Chapter 7

296 1 Fairbank, J. K.: *Trade and Diplomacy on the
China Coast*, p 112

297 2 The 'Institution for the Propagation of the Faith'
(of Lyon, not the Propaganda of Rome)
commented on: 'the innumerable hawkers of
Bibles, whose prudent zeal extends no further than
to introduce along the coasts of China, with
smuggled opium, the sacred writings which they
profane.' CMS *Register*, cited in Stock, E.: *A
History of the Church Missionary Society*, Vol I
p 378; Robert Fortune: *Journal of the Royal
Horticultural Society*, Vol 105, Part 5, p 218

297 3, 4 Fairbank, J. K.: op. cit. p 294

297 5 Shanghai: many sources, notably Fairbank, Eames,
Medhurst, Latourette, but especially Morse, H. B.:
The International Relations of the Chinese Empire;
Pott, Hawks: *A Short History of Shanghai*;
Woodcock, G.: *The British in the Far East*;
Chinese Recorder; North China Herald

299 6 A regular mail service between Suez and Bombay
had been running since 1841, 'with steamers of the
great size of 1600 tons and 500 horse power'.
Stock, E.: op. cit. I. 298

299 7 Eames, J. B.: *The Englishman in China —as
illustrated in the career of Sir Rutherford Alcock*:
passim

300 8 Fairbank, J. K.: op cit. p 162

301 9 Pott, Hawks: op. cit. p 22 ff; Morse, H. B.: op. cit.;
Eames, J. B.: op. cit.; Boone, M.: *The Seed of the
Church in China*

302 10, 11 Morse, H. B.: op. cit.; Morse, Eames, Fairbank,
Pott, Boone

302, 12, 13 Vice-consul Robertson; Boone, M.: op. cit. p 133
303

303   14   Morse, H. B.: op. cit.; Parliamentary Papers: Sir J. Davis to Lord Palmerston, 13 December 1848, *passim*

305   15, 16   cf p 171; Latourette, K. S.: *A History of Christian Missions in China*, pp 234, 239, 242, citing *Annales de la Propagation de la Foi*, Vol 26 p 431

305   17   The CMS Report for 1847 lamented: 'While the Church of England for a whole year seeks in vain for one missionary to China, the Romish agent at Hong Kong negotiates for a contract with a Steam Navigation Company to carry to China 100 priests within the year.' Stock, E.: op. cit. I. 378

306   18   Latourette, K. S.: op. cit. p 260

307   19   *Chinese Recorder*: Vol VIII p 193; Latourette, K. S.: op. cit. pp 257–8; 264–5; Latourette, K. S.: *A History of the Expansion of Christianity*, pp 310–12; Smith, A. H.: *The Uplift of China*, p 150

307,   20, 21   Latourette, K. S.: op. cit. pp 312, 327; ibid p 259
308

309   22   MacGillivray, D.: *A Century of Protestant Missions in China*, p 4

309   23   Smith, A. H.: op. cit. p 148

309   24   Latourette, K. S.: *A History of Christian Missions in China*, pp 262–4

310   25   MacGillivray, D.: op. cit. p 4: 'both these well-known missionaries had been in China some years as members of the Ultra-Ganges Mission' – note this 1907 use of 'China' to include the Straits Settlements.

311   26   Latourette, K. S.: *A History of the Expansion of Christianity*, p 382; CES *Gleaner*, August 1850, p 48 ff

312   27   Latourette, K. S.: op. cit. p 305; *A History of Christian Missions*, pp 253–5, largely using German sources; OMFA, A111; CES *Gleaner*, Dec. 1850, p 73, 'a great many societies' formed: (*see* Appendix 6)

312   28   Davies, E.: *China and her Spiritual Claims*, 1845

313   29   Bryant, Sir Arthur: *A Thousand Years of the British Monarchy*

313, 30, 31 Many sources, well summarised in Latourette, K.
315   S.: op. cit. p 283 ff
317 32   A bound volume of early papers in Chinese and
English, from Gutzlaff to the Chinese Association
in Britain provides much of the following
information: OMFA 1–4; also from *Chinese
Recorder*, Vols II, IV, V, VII, X–XIII, XVI; CES
Gleaner; Latourette, K. S.: *A History of the
Expansion of Christianity*, p 305 and footnote
bibliography.
318 33   *Chinese Recorder*, VII. 22–3
319 34   Smith, A. H.: op. cit. p 151: of 214 male
missionaries, 44 and 51 wives died, 1807–60,
averaging 7 years' service; but average is
misleading because several lived long, even 40
years, e.g. Medhurst, Bridgman, Wells Williams,
Martin.
319 35   OMFA 1–4: *The Chinese Union*

Chapter 8
323 1   Gutzlaff: *see Chinese Recorder, passim*; CES
Gleaner, passim; OMFA 1–4, summarised in
preceding chapter and here; *Chinese Recorder*,
1925, Weise, J.: *The Early History and
Development of the Berlin Missionary Work in
South China*
324– 2–4 OMFA, 1–4; Gutzlaff has been called 'gullible';
325   this paper suggests that 'deceived' would be more
just.
328 5   ibid
329 6   CES *Gleaner*, May 1850, quoting letters of August
1844, April 1847, August 1848
330 7   Stock, E., *A History of the Church Missionary
Society*, Vol II pp 411–7
330 8   Taylor, Mrs Howard: *Behind the Ranges*, CIM
330 9   OMFA, 1–4; CES *Gleaner*, April 1850, p 10
332 10   OMFA, 1–4; an emphasis supporting Robert
Morrison's and taken up by the Chinese
Associations but attacked when Hudson Taylor
applied it in 1866
334 11   OMFA, 10–411

334	12	CES *Gleaner*, June 1850, pp 29–30; July, pp 28–9; June, 1851, pp 1–8; Latourette, K. S.: *A History of the Expansion of Christianity*, pp 305–6; OMFA, A123
335	13	Latourette, K. S.: op. cit. p 300; *A History of Christian Missions in China*, p 255
335–336	14–16	OMFA, A123; cf Broomhall, M.: *The Chinese Empire*, pp 353, 413, 417; ibid; ibid
338	17	OMFA, 1–4; clearly stated in CES *Gleaner*, March 1850, p 5 as being from Gutzlaff himself in Chinese style and using his Chinese name
338	18	CES *Gleaner*, April 1850 *passim*
340	19	OMFA, 1–4, A1; *Chinese Recorder*: Vol 7 p 22 ff; Vol 8 p 31 ff
341	20	OMFA, 1–4
342	21	CES *Gleaner*, Sept. 1850, p 56; tribute by Karl Vogel
342	22	OMFA, A123: William Tarrant to C. Gutzlaff, from Hong Kong, 14 June 1850, re report made by Hamberg in the presence of Col. Philpotts, Major Hill, William C. Burns, a Swedish missionary and himself; cf W. C. Burns's letter to C. Gutzlaff, Canton, 17 July 1850
343	23, 24	ibid, Th. Hamberg, Hong Kong, 23 August 1850
344	25	*Chinese Recorder*: VII. 22 ff
344	26	OMFA, A123
345	27–29	ibid, 14, May 1850; ibid, 17 July 1850; CES *Gleaner*, June 1851
346	30	Latourette, K. S.: *A History of the Expansion of Christianity*, pp 300, 305–6
346	31	Notably Berlin and Chinese Evangelization Soc. (British). In the *Chinese Recorder*, 1925, *The Early History and Development of the Berlin Missionary Work in South China*; (Canton Conference, 29 March 1924) J. Weise says Basel and Barmen (Rhenish) missionaries severed their links, but Latourette: *Expansion*, loc. cit., says the missions 'continued'.
346	32	Latourette, K. S.: op. cit. p 306
347	33	Published 1852, posthumously

347, 34, 35 CES *Gleaner*, Jan. 1852, p 62; Feb. 1852, pp 66–9;
348   *Last Days of Dr Gutzlaff*; ibid 'The uncommon
             strength of the powerful, robust man was broken'.
348 36   Bridgman, E.: *The Life and Labors of E. C.
             Bridgman*, p 189; CES *Gleaner*, Nov 1851, p 43
349 37   MacGillivray, D.: *A Century of Protestant Missions
             in China*, p 22
349 38   Neill, S.: *A History of Christian Missions*, p 263,
             summary
350 39   OMFA, A221–2; 2112–4; Latourette, K. S.:
             Tipple Lectures
356 40   Latourette, K. S.: *A History of the Expansion of
             Christianity*, p 327
357 41   OMFA, 212–3; A2; B1; Latourette, K. S.: ibid
359 42   OMFA: 11 Book 4, publ. March 1850–Oct. 1860
             by Partridge and Oakey, J. Nisbet & Co.
360 43   OMFA, A221; B112

PERSONALIA: to 1865

ABEEL, David, American Seamen's Friend Society, chaplain; 1830–33 Canton (Guangzhou), Bangkok; 1839–45 Am. Board (ABCFM); 1842 Gulangsu Is., Amoy; initiated women's missionary socs. in UK, USA.

AITCHISON, William, Am Board; 1854 Shanghai, Pinghu.

ALCOCK, Sir John Rutherford, (1809–97); MRCS at 21; 1832–37 Peninsular Wars, Dep.-Director of Hospitals; 1835 partially paralysed; 1843 Diplomatic Service; 1846 HBM consul Fuzhou (Foochow), Amoy, Shanghai; 1861 knighted, HBM minister, Peking.

ALDERSEY, Miss Mary Ann, (c 1800–64); 1824–5 learned Chinese from R. Morrison; 1832 Malacca (Melaka); Batavia (Jakarta); 1842 Hong Kong; 1843–59 Ningbo (Ningpo).

A-LO-PEN, Syrian Nestorian named in Nestorian monument, Xi'an (Sian); AD 635 arr. China.

AMHERST, William Pitt, Lord Amherst, 1816 Peking embassy; 1823 Gov.-Gen. of India; first Burma war; 1826 earldom; d. 1857.

BALFOUR, Capt. George, officer 1840 opium war; 1843–46 first consul Shanghai; Major-Gen., CB, nominated J.H.T. (Hudson Taylor) for FRGS.

BALL, Richard, businessman, Taunton, Somerset; moving spirit in Chinese Association and Chinese Evangelization Society (CES); editor, *Chinese Missionary Gleaner*; author, *Handbook of China*, 1854.

BARCHET, Stephan Paul, German; 1865 Ningbo (Ningpo), sent by J.H.T.; later doctor of medicine.

BAUSUM, J. G., independent, Penang; m. Maria Tarn Dyer, mother of Maria Jane.

BAUSUM, Mrs, 2nd wife of J. G. Bausum; mother of Mary; later m. E. C. Lord (qv).

BAUSUM, Mary, daughter, m. Dr S. P. Barchet.

BERGER, William Thomas (c 1812–99); London starch manufacturer; J.H.T.'s friend, supporter, co-founder of China Inland Mission (CIM); first Home Sec., benefactor.

BERGNE, S. B., co-Sec. British & Foreign Bible Society.

BIRD, Charles, Gen. Sec. Chinese Evangelization Society (CES).

BLODGET, Henry, DD (1825–1903); Am. Board; 1854 Shanghai; first to preach at Tientsin (Tianjin); translator, Peking.

BOGUE, Dr, principal, Missionary Academy, Gosport, c. 1805–20; friend of Dr Wm. Moseley (qv); nominated R. Morrison, S. Dyer to LMS for China.

BONHAM, Sir George, c 1856 HBM plenipotentiary, Hong Kong, after Bowring (qv).

BOONE, William Jones, Sr, MD, DD; Am. Prot. Episcopal Church; 1837 Batavia; 1840 Macao; 1842 Gulangsu Is., Amoy, with Abeel; 1844 bishop, Shanghai; d. 1864.

BOURGEVINE, H. A., Am. soldier of fortune; after F. T. Ward, commanded Ever-Victorious Army; later joined Taipings.

BOWRING, Sir John, (1792–1872); HBM consul, Siam, Canton; 1854 plenipotentiary, last Supt. of Trade; Sinologue.

BRADLEY, Daniel Beach, MD, Am. Board (ABCFM); 1840–49 Bangkok, physician to Thai royal family.

BRIDGMAN, Elijah Coleman, DD (1801–61); Am. Board (ABCFM); 1830 Canton; 1832 first editor *Chinese Repository* with R. Morrison; 1843–44 US interpreter-negotiator; 1845–52 translator, Chinese Bible, Delegates' Committee, Shanghai.

BRIDGMAN, Mrs, 1845 Canton; 1847 Shanghai; 1864 Peking.

BROOMHALL, Benjamin, (1829–1911); m. Amelia Hudson Taylor; 1878–95 Gen. Sec. China Inland Mission (CIM); editor, *National Righteousness*, organ of anti-opium trade campaign, to 1911 (*see* Maxwell).

BRUCE, Sir Frederick, brother of Lord Elgin (qv); 1858 envoy, rebuffed by emperor; 1859 repulsed at Dagu (Taku), Tianjin.

BURDON, John Shaw, (1829–1907); CMS 1853 arr. Shanghai; pioneer evangelist; m. Burella Dyer (qv); 1862 Peking; 1874 3rd bishop, Hong Kong; Bible translator.

BURLINGAME, Anson, (1820–70); barrister, Congressman, Methodist; 1861–67 US minister, Peking, appointed by Abraham Lincoln; ambassador-at-large for China.

BURNS, William Chalmers, (1815–68); first English Presby. to China; 1847 Hong Kong; Amoy; 1855 Shanghai; 1856 Swatow; 1863 Peking; d. Niuchuang; translator of *Pilgrim's Progress*; close friend of J.H.T.

CAREY, William (1761–1834); Baptist Miss. Soc., founder; 1793 India; 1800–30 Prof. of Oriental Languages, Calcutta.

CARLYLE, Thomas (1795–1881); historian, biographer.

CASWELL, Jessie, Am. Board (ABCFM) Bangkok, tutor to Prince Mongkut.

CHALLICE, John, deacon, Bryanston Hall, Portman Square; member, first CIM council.

CHAPDELAINE, Auguste, Paris Mission (Société des Missions Étrangères de Paris); 1856 executed.

CHAPMAN, Robert, (1802–1902); High Court attorney; 1832 Strict Baptist minister; 2nd Evang. Awakening evangelist; J.H.T.'s friend.

CHATER, Baptist, with Felix Carey, first Prot. missionary to Burma.

CH'I SHAN, see Qi Shan; CH'I YING, see Qi Ying; CHIA CH'ING, see Jia Qing; CH'IEN LUNG, see Qian Long; CHU CHIU-TAO, see Zhu Jiu-Dao; CHUNG WANG, see Zhong Wang.

CI XI, (Tz'u Hsi) (1835–1908); Empress Dowager; Yehonala, the Concubine Yi; empress regent to Tong Zhi (Chih); 1860–1908 supreme power in China.

CLARENDON, Earl of, (1800–70); Foreign Sec. to Lord Aberdeen 1853, Lord Palmerston 1855, Lord Russell 1865, Gladstone 1868.

CLELAND, J. F., LMS, 1850 Hong Kong.

COBBOLD, R. H., CMS, 1848–62, Ningbo (Ningpo); translator, Ningbo romanised vernacular NT.

CONFUCIUS, c 551–479 BC; Chinese philosopher-sage.

COKE, Thomas, Oxford Univ.; Anglican clergyman; 1776–1813, Wesley's colleague; 1786 appealed for missions to New World; first bishop, Am. Methodist Episc. Church; d. 1813 on way to India.

COX, Josiah, (–1906); Wesleyan Meth. Miss. Soc.; 1852 Canton; 1862 Hankow; 1865 Jiujiang (Kiukiang).

CROMBIE, George, Aberdeen farmer; 1865 J.H.T.'s second recruit, to Ningbo.

DAO GUANG, (Tao Kuang); 6th Qing (Ch'ing) emperor, 1820–51; China torn by rebellions.

DAVIES, Evan, LMS Malaya; author, 1845, *China and her Spiritual Claims*; 1846 *Memoir of the Reverend Samuel Dyer*.

DAVIS, Sir John Francis, Bart., Chief, Hon. East India Co., Canton; friend of R. Morrison; 1844 HBM plenipotentiary, after Pottinger (qv); Supt. of Trade, Hong Kong.

DEAN, William, (1806–77); Am. Baptist; 1834 & 1864 Bangkok; 1842 Hong Kong.

DELAMARRE, Abbé, Paris Mission; 1858–60 interpreter, French treaty; falsified Chinese version.

DE LA PORTE, Dr, French Prot. medical; 1847–57 Swatow, Double Island.

DENNISTON, J. M., Presby. minister, London, Torquay; associated with W. C. Burns revivals and J.H.T. founding CIM; co-founder Foreign Evangelist Soc.

DENT, Thomas and Launcelot, high-living merchant ship-owners; chief rivals of Jardine, Matheson.

DE TOURNON, Charles Maillard, (1668–1710); papal legate to China 1705; antagonised Kang Xi (K'ang Hsi) over Confucian rites.

DEW, Capt. Roderick, RN, 1862 commander, Ningbo front, against Taipings.

DOUGLAS, Carstairs, LL D (1830–77); English Presby. Mission; 1855 Amoy; introduced J. L. Maxwell (qv) to Formosa (Taiwan); knew J.H.T. Shanghai, London.

DYER, John, Sec., Royal Hosp. for Seamen, Greenwich; 1820 Chief Clerk to Admiralty.

DYER, Samuel, (1804–43); son of John Dyer; Cambridge law student; LMS; m. Maria Tarn, daughter of LMS director; 1827 Penang; 1829–35 Malacca; 1835–43 Singapore; d. Macao.

DYER, Samuel Jr., Burella and Maria Jane, children of Samuel and Maria Tarn Dyer; Burella m. J. S. Burdon (qv); Maria m. J.H.T.

EDKINS, Joseph, (1823–1905); LMS evangelist, translator, philologist, expert in Chinese religions, author, well-known to Taiping rulers; 1848–60 Shanghai; 1860–61 Shandong, Yantai and Tianjin; 1861 Peking.

EITEL, E. J., Ph D; Basel Mission, S. China, 1862–65; 1865–78 LMS Peking; Sinologue; Dec. 1862 baptised first Peking Prot. Christian; 1878 et seq adviser to Hong Kong govt.

ELGIN, Earl of, son of Thomas Bruce, 7th earl (Elgin marbles); 1857 Indian mutiny; 1858 envoy, Treaty of Tientsin; treaty with Japan; 1860 second opium war, captured Peking, burned Summer Palace, negotiated Peking Convention.

ELLIOT, Capt. Charles, RN, 1835 third Supt. of Trade, Canton; 1836 Chief Supt.; confronted Commissioner Lin (qv); 1840–41 political chief in first phase of first opium war; HBM plenipotentiary, negotiated Convention of Chuanbi.

ELPHINSTONE, J. T., president, Select Committee, East India

Co., Canton; friend of R. Morrison; later Member of Parliament.

FAULDING, Jane E., (1843–1904); m. J.H.T. 28 Nov. 1871; 1877–78 led CIM team, Shanxi famine relief; first Western women inland.

FISHBOURNE, Capt, RN, rescued Amoy victims; strong supporter of missions and anti-opium soc.; later, evangelist.

FLINT, James, East India Co. official; petitioned Qian Long (Ch'ien Lung) emperor for trading rights; imprisoned.

FORTUNE, Robert, Royal Hort. Soc. botanist; 1843 arr. China; explorations 1843–46, 1848–51, 1853–56, 1861–62, disguised as a Tartar; supplied India with tea-plants.

FRANCKE, August Hermann, pietist, 1696 founded Orphan Houses, extensive by C 19; prof. divinity, Halle Univ. Germany; d. 1727.

FULLER, W. R., first United Meth. Free Ch. missionary to China; 1864 Ningbo; trained by J.H.T.

GAMBLE, William, Am. Presby. Mission Press; 1858 Ningbo; 1860 Shanghai; friend of J.H.T., CIM, received Lammermuir party.

GENÄHR, Ferdinand, Rhenish (Barmen) Mission; 1847 Hong Kong, Guangdong (Kwangtung) under C. Gutzlaff; m. R. Lechler's sister; one of the first Prot. missionaries to reside outside treaty ports; d. 1864.

GENGHIS KHAN, (1162–1227); Mongol conqueror of N. China, W. Russia, Central Asia, N.W. India to Adriatic; military genius.

GLADSTONE, William Ewart, (1809–98); three times prime minister, 1868–97.

GOBLE, William, Am. marine under Commodore Perry, to Japan as missionary; 1870 invented rickshaw.

GODDARD, Josiah, Am. Baptist, Bangkok; 1848 Ningbo.

GORDON, Col. Charles George, (1833–85); 1860 Tianjin, Peking campaign; 1862 Shanghai, commanding Ever-Victorious Army; 1864 Taiping Rebellion ended; honoured by emperor and Queen Victoria (CB); 1865–71 London; donor to J.H.T.; 1880 adviser to Chinese govt.; 1883–5 Major-Gen., Sudan.

GOUGH, Frederick F. DD; CMS 1849–62 Ningbo; 1862–69 London, Ningbo vernacular NT romanised edition, with J.H.T.; 1869 Ningbo; m. Mary Jones (qv).

GRANT, General Sir Hope, 1860 commander, land forces, under Lord Elgin.

GROS, Baron, 1860 French plenipotentiary, second opium war, Peking treaty.

GROVES, Anthony Norris, (1795–1853); early exponent of 'faith principle'; brother-in-law of G. Müller; missionary to Baghdad; initiator of Brethren movement.

GUINNESS, M. Geraldine, (1862–1949); daughter of H. Grattan Guinness (qv); m. F. Howard Taylor (qv); author, biography of J.H.T.

GUINNESS, H. Grattan, DD; gentleman-evangelist, 1859 Ulster revival; J.H.T.'s friend; founded East London Institute, trained 1,330 for 40 societies of 30 denominations.

GUTZLAFF, Charles (Karl Frederich August), (1803–51); 1826–28 Netherlands Miss. Soc., Batavia (Jakarta), Java; 1828 independent, Bangkok; m. Miss Newell, Malacca, first single Prot. woman missionary to E. Asia; 1831–35 voyages up China coast; 1839 interpreter to British; 1840 & '42 governor of Chusan Is.; 1842 interpretor-negotiator, Nanking Treaty; 1843–51 Chinese Sec. to British govt. Hong Kong; initiated Chinese Union, Chinese Associations and missions.

HALL, Capt. Basil, RN, 1816 voyage up China coast, Korea, Ryukyu Is.; author, *Narrative of a Voyage* . . .

HALL, Charles J., 1857 CES missionary Ningbo; 1860 Shandong; d. 1861.

HALL, William, deacon, Bryanston Hall, Portman Square; member of first CIM council.

HALL, William Nelthorpe, Methodist New Connexion; 1860 Tianjin; d. 1878.

HAMBERG, Theodore, Basel Mission; 1847 Hong Kong, under Gutzlaff (qv); with R. Lechler to Guangdong (Kwangtung) Hakkas; first Prot. missionaries to reside outside treaty ports; d. 1854.

HANSPACH, August, Chinese Evangelization Soc. of Berlin (Berlin Missionary Soc. for China); 1855 Hong Kong; 11 years extensive inland travel.

HAPPER, Andrew P., DD; Am. Presby. 1844 Macao; 1847 Canton.

HARDEY, Richard, early photographer, Hull; m. Hannah Hudson, portraitist.

HARDEY, Robert, surgeon, Hull Infirmary & medical college; J.H.T. his assistant.

HART, Sir Robert, 1835–   ; 1854 Ningbo, consular interpreter; 1857 Canton; 1863 Inspector-General, Chinese Imperial Maritime Customs.

HOBSON, Dr Benjamin, LMS; 1841 Macao; 1843 Hong Kong; 1846 Canton; 1856 Shanghai.

HOBSON, J., CMS, chaplain to Br. community, Shanghai; J.H.T.'s friend.

HODSON, Thomas & John, sons of Mary, née Hudson; J.H.T.'s cousins.

HOLMES, J. L., Am. Southern Baptist; 1860 pioneer of Shandong, Yantai (Chefoo); killed.

HONG XIU-QUAN, (Hung Hsiu-ch'üan) (1813–64); Taiping Wang, leader of Taiping rebellion; 1837 visions and fantasies; 1844 began preaching; 1846 with Hong Ren (Hung Jen) (qv) taught by I. J. Roberts (qv); 1849 led Worshippers of Shangdi; 1851 began hostilities; 1852 assumed imperial title; 1853–64 Nanking; 1853 advance to Tianjin halted; 1864 suicide.

HONG REN, cousin of Hong Xiu-quan; known as Gan Wang, Shield King; ex-evangelist.

HOPE, Vice-Admiral Sir James, 1860–62 naval commander-in-chief, China; 1861 negotiated 'year of truce' with Taipings; 'opened' Yangzi River to foreign shipping.

HOWARD, John Eliot, FRS; Fellow of Linnaean Soc.; later Lord Congleton; manufacturing chemist; early leader of Brethren, Tottenham; J.H.T.'s close friend.

HOWARD, Robert, brother of J.E.; also chemist, leader of Brethren.

HOWARD, Luke, meteorologist, father of J.E. and R.

HSI SHENG-MO, see Xi; HSÜ KUANG-CH'I see Xu; HSIEN FENG see Xian.

HUC, Abbé Evariste Régis, travelled with Gabet 1844–46, Mongolia, Tibet; 1846 in Lhasa, deported; 1857 author, *Christianity in China, Tartary and Thibet*; d. 1860.

HUDSON, Benjamin Brook, (c 1785–1865); Wesleyan Methodist minister; portraitist; grandfather of J.H.T.

HUDSON, Amelia, (1808–64); m. James Taylor; mother of J.H.T.

HUNG HSIU-CH'ÜAN, see Hong Xiu-quan; HUNG JEN see Hong Ren.

INNES, James, obstreperous ship's captain, Jardine, Matheson.

JARDINE, William, surgeon, merchant ship-owner; 1841 Member of Parliament; d. 1843.

JIA QING, (Chia Ch'ing); (1796–1820); mediocre 5th emperor of Qing (Ch'ing) dynasty.

JOHN, Griffith, (1831–1912); LMS; 1855 Shanghai; pioneer evangelist; 1861 Hankow; 1863 Wuchang; 1867 Hanyang.

JOHNSON, Stevens, Am. Board, Bangkok; 1847 Fuzhou (Foochow).

JONES, John, CES 1856–57 Ningbo; independent, 1857–63; early exponent of 'faith principle', influenced J.H.T.; d. 1863.

JONES, Mary, wife of John; 1863–66 with Hudson Taylors, London; 1866 m. F. F. Gough.

JUDSON, Adoniram, (1788–1850); Am. Board, became Baptist; 1813 pioneer with wife in Burma.

JUKES, Andrew, East India Co. officer; deacon, Anglican Church; c 1842 independent minister, Brethren congregation; 1866 built Church of St. John the Evangelist, Hull.

JUNG LU (historic spelling retained); imperial bannerman (equiv. Brigade of Guards); perhaps father of Yehonala's son, Tong Zhi (Tung Chih) emperor; long-time adviser to Ci Xi, Empress Dowager.

KANG XI, (K'ang Hsi); (1622–1722); 2nd Qing (Ch'ing) dynasty emperor, for 60 years; aged 7 dismissed his regents; one of China's strongest rulers; pro-Christian; 1692 Edict of Toleration; 1700 pro-Jesuit, anti-Rome.

KEW A-KANG (Chiu A-Kung), see Qiu A-gong.

KIDD, Samuel, (1799–1848) LMS; 1824–32 Malacca; third after Morrison and Milne, before Dyer, Tomlin; Prof. of Chinese Language and Literature, University College, London.

KING, Charles W., Am. merchant ship-owner, partner of D. W. C. Olyphant (qv).

KINGDON, Edwin F., BMS recruit trained by J.H.T.; 1864 Shandong, Yantai.

KLOEKERS, Hendrick Z., Netherlands Chinese Evangelization Soc.; 1855–58 Shanghai; 1862 BMS 1862–65 Shandong, Yantai.

KNOWLTON, Miles J., Am. Baptist; 1854 Ningbo; friend of J.H.T.

KONG, Prince, (Prince Kung); (1833–98); brother of Xian Feng (Hsien Feng) emperor; 1860 et seq, leading statesman.

KREYER, Carl T., Am. Baptist Missionary Union; 1866 Hangzhou (Hangchow); lent his home to Lammermuir party.

KUBLAI KHAN, Mongol ruler, 1216–94; conquered Song (Sung) dynasty, founded Yuan (Yüan) dynasty; ruled all China, Central Asia, Persia, E. Europe.

LAGRENÉ, M., French envoy, 1843 treaty; negotiated edicts of toleration by Qi Ying (Ch'i Ying), for Prots. as well as RCs.

LAOZI, (Laotze) 'the Old One'; alleged, possibly mythical, originator of Taoism, fifty years before Confucius.

LATOURETTE, Kenneth Scott, late Willis James and Sterling Prof. of Missions and Oriental History, Yale Univ.; author, *see* bibliography.

LAUGHTON, R. F., BMS; 1863 Shandong, Yantai.

LAY, George Tradescant, naturalist; 1836–39 agent for Bible Soc. (BFBS); 1840–42 interpreter, opium war; HBM consul, Canton, Fuzhou (Foochow), Amoy; co-founder of 'Medical Missionary Soc. in China'; d. 1845, Amoy.

LECHLER, Rudolf, (1824–1928); Basel Mission pioneer; 1847 Hong Kong, Guangdong (Kwangtung) Hakkas, under Gutzlaff, with Hamberg (qv); 52 years in China, to 1899.

LEGGE, James, DD, LL D, (1815–97); LMS; 1839–43 Anglo-Chinese College, Malacca; 1843–70 Anglo-Chinese College, Hong Kong; translator, Chinese classics; 1877–97, Prof. of Chinese, Oxford Univ.

LEWIS, W. G., Baptist minister, Westbourne Grove Ch., London; urged J.H.T. to publish *China's Spiritual Need and Claims*.

LI HONG-ZHANG, (Li Hung-chang) (1823–1901); holder of the highest academic degrees, highest honours after defeat of Taiping rebels; the Grand Old Man of China, leading statesman until death.

LIANG A-FA (1789–1855); Canton engraver-printer; 1815 to Malacca with W. Milne; 1819 Canton, colporteur; arrested, flogged; 1821 Malacca; 1828 Canton; 1834 arrested, escaped, betrayed, escaped; 1839 returned, tolerated by Lin Ze-xu (qv); first Prot. pastor; 1845 mobbed; d. 1855.

LIANG A-DE, (Liang A-teh); son of A-fa; translator to Lin Ze-xu (qv); interpreter for British, Nanking Treaty; Chinese Imperial Maritime Customs.

LIGHT, Francis, captain of merchantman; 1786 occupied Penang Is., founded Georgetown.

LIN ZE-XU, (Lin Tze-hsü) gov. gen. of Hubei-Hunan; viceroy-commissioner, Canton, to control opium traffic; 1839 strong-arm methods contributed to war, 1840–41; disgraced, exiled.

LINDSAY, Capt. Hugh Hamilton, RN, 1832 commanded ship *Lord Amherst*, on survey of China coast, Korea, with Gutzlaff (qv).

LOBSCHEID, Wilhelm, Rhenish (Barmen) Mission to China;

1852, first medical 'agent' of Chinese Evang. Soc., Hong Kong, Guangdong (Kwangtung); 1855 interpreter, *Powhattan* voyage to Japan.

LOCKHART, William, (1811–96); surgeon, FRCS; LMS; 1839 Macao; 1840 and 1843 Shanghai; 1840–41 Chusan with Gutzlaff; first British missionary Hong Kong; 1848 mobbed in 'Qingpu (Tsingpu) Outrage', Shanghai; 1861 first Prot. missionary in Peking.

LORD, Edward C., 1847 first Am. Baptist, Ningbo; 1863 independent Am. Bapt. Mission, Ningbo; 1877 still there; J.H.T.'s friend.

LOWRIE, Walter, US senator, resigned to become Sec. of Am. Presby. Mission.

LOWRIE, William, (Walter, in some sources) son of senator; 1845 Am. Presby. Mission, Ningbo; 1847 drowned by pirates.

LOWRIE, Reuben, (Robert, in some sources) took brother's place; 1854 Shanghai.

MACARTNEY, Lord, 1793 embassy to Peking, failed.

MACGOWAN, Dr D. J., Am. Baptist physician; 1843 Ningbo.

MAGELLAN, Ferdinand, (c 1480–1521); Portuguese explorer; served Spain; via Cape Horn to Leyte, Philippines; killed, but expedition completed first voyage round world.

MARJORIBANKS, Charles, ex-Chief, East India Co., Canton; 1834 Member of Parliament; friend of R. Morrison.

MARA, John, United Meth. Free Ch.; trained by J.H.T.; 1865 Ningbo.

MARSHALL, Thomas D., minister, Bryanston Hall, Portman Square.

MARSHMAN, Joshua, (1768–1837); 1799 with Carey, Serampore; 1811 completed Chinese NT; 1822–23 OT.

MARTIN, William Alexander Parsons, DD, LL D; (1827–1916); Am. Presby. Mission; educationalist; 1850–60 Ningbo; 1862 Peking; 1869 president, Tungwen Imperial College; 57 years in China; book on Christian evidences had huge circulation, China, Japan.

MARTYN, Henry, (1781–1812); 1801 Senior Wrangler, Fellow of St John's, Camb.; 1806 Calcutta; 1810 completed Hindustani (Urdu) NT; 1811 Shiraz, Persia; 1815–16 Martyn's Persian NT published.

MATHESON, Donald, merchant partner, Jardine, Matheson; 1837 Hong Kong; converted, resigned 1849 over opium traffic;

active in Presby. Missions; 1892 chairman, Soc. for the Suppression of the Opium Trade.

MATHESON, James, heir to baronetcy; merchant ship-owner, partner of Jardine (qv); Member of Parliament.

MATHIESON, James L., gentleman-evangelist in C 19 revivals; active in anti-opium campaign (see Maxwell).

MAXWELL, James L., MD; (1836–1921); English Presby. Mission; 1863 Amoy; 1865 pioneer, Taiwan; 1885 founder, Medical Missionary Association (London); 1888 co-founder with B. Broomhall (qv), 'Christian Union for the Severance of the Connection of the British Empire with the Opium Traffic'.

McCARTEE, Dr D. B., MD; Am. Presby.; 1844 Ningbo; adopted orphan became first Chinese woman doctor educated in USA.

McCLATCHIE, Thomas, CMS; 1845 Shanghai with George Smith (qv).

MEADOWS, James J., (1835–1914); J.H.T.'s first recruit to Ningbo Mission, 1862, and CIM; wife Martha d. 1863.

MEADOWS, Thomas Taylor, heroic interpreter; HBM vice-consul, Ningbo; certified J.H.T.'s marriage.

MEDHURST, Walter Henry, DD; (1796–1857); LMS printer; 1817–20 Malacca; 1820–21 Penang; 1822–43 Batavia, Java; 1826 toured Chinese settlements on Java coast; 1835 voyage of *Huron* up China coast; 1843 Shanghai, interpreter-adviser to Br. consul G. Balfour (qv); 1845 inland journey in disguise; 1848 victim of 'Qingpu (Tsingpu) Outrage', Shanghai; translator, Delegates' Committee, 1852 Chinese Bible; doyen of Br. community.

MEDHURST, Sir Walter Henry, son of W. H. Medhurst DD; HBM consul, and ambassador, Peking.

MELBOURNE, Viscount, Prime Minister, 1835–41; chief adviser to Queen Victoria.

MENGKU KHAN, Mongol ruler, grandson of Genghis Khan; tolerant of all religions, attended Nestorian worship.

MÉRITENS, Baron de, with Abbé Delamarre (qv) interpreter to Baron Gros (qv) 1860.

MEZZABARBA, 1720 papal legate after Mgr de Tournon; concessions on Chinese rites repudiated by Rome.

MILNE, William, DD; (1785–1822); 1813 Macao; 1815–22 Malacca; 1818 Anglo-Chinese College, Malacca; Hon. DD Glasgow; 1819 baptised Liang A-fa (qv); 1822 completed OT translation with R. Morrison.

MILNE, William C., son of William and Rachel Milne; 1842

Chusan Is.; 1842–43 Ningbo; 1846 Shanghai; 1857 travelling sec., Chinese Evang. Soc.

MONTE CORVINO, John of, first RC priest to China; dep. 1289, arr. 1294; 1307 archbishop of Cambalac (Peking); d. *c* 1328–33.

MORGAN, R. C., editor, *The Revival* (*The Christian*); director, Marshall, Morgan & Scott; co-founder, Foreign Evangelist Soc.

MORRISON, Robert, DD, FRS; (1782–1834); LMS; 1807 Macao, Canton; 1813 completed Chinese NT; 1814 first convert; 1816 interpreter-negotiator to Lord Amherst embassy; 1817 Hon. DD Glas.; 1819 completed OT with Milne (qv); 1822 completed Chinese dictionary; 1824 FRS etc.; 1834 interpreter to Lord Napier; d. Aug. 1.

MORRISON, John Robert, (1814–43); son of R. Morrison; aged 16 official translator, East India Co.; Canton; 1842 interpreter-negotiator to Sir H. Pottinger, Treaty of Nanking; 1843 Chinese Sec. to Gov. of Hong Kong; chairman, first LMS and General Missions Conferences, Hong Kong.

MOSELEY, William, LL D; Congregational Minister; 1798 found in British Museum MS of RC Chinese translation of NT books; urged translation of whole NT; introduced R. Morrison to LMS and to Dr Bogue (qv).

MOULE, Arthur Evans, CMS; 1861 Ningbo; 1876 Hangzhou (Hangchow); archdeacon.

MOULE, George Evans, CMS; 1858 Ningbo; 1864 Hangzhou (Hangchow); 1880 bishop in Mid-China.

MOULY, Mgr Joseph Martial, Lazarist; 1841 vicar-apostolic, Mongolia &c; sent Abbé Huc and Gabet on Tibet journey; 1853 deported; 1856 vicar-apostolic N. Zhili (Chihli) (Peking); 1861 obtained territorial concessions for RC church.

MUIRHEAD, William, DD; (1822–1900); LMS; evangelist, renowned preacher, translator; 1846–90 (53 years) at Shanghai; 1848 victim of 'Qingpu (Tsingpu) Outrage', Shanghai.

MÜLLER, George, (1805–98); German-born; married sister of A. N. Groves (qv); 1832 read biography of A. H. Francke; 1835 founded Orphan Homes, Bristol, 2,000 children, financed 'by faith in God'.

NAPIER, Lord, 1834, William IV's envoy to China; Chief Supt. of Br. Trade; d. 1834.

NEATBY, Thomas, FRCS; boyhood friend of J.H.T.; assistant

to James Taylor and Robert Hardey (qv); surgeon, St Bartholomew's hospital; biblical expositor.

NESTORIUS, bishop of Constantinople until Council of Ephesus, AD 431; d. 451; Nestorianism extended to Syria, Persia, India; AD 635 to China (see A-lo-pen); Nestorian monument erected 781, discovered 1625 near Xi'an (Sian).

NEUMANN, Robert, Berlin Miss. Soc. for China; colleague of Gutzlaff; 1850–54 Hong Kong, Guangdong (Kwangtung).

NEVIUS, John Livingston, (1832–93); Am. Presby. Mission; 1854 Ningbo; 1859 Hangzhou (Hangchow); 1860 Japan; 1861 Shandong (Shantung); Bible translator, author; 1890 Korea, exponent of 'indigenous church' policy.

NOMMENSEN, Ludwig Ingwer, Rhenish (Barmen) Mission; 1862 pioneer of Bataks, Sumatra.

NORRIS, Sir William, Chief Justice, High Court, Straits Settlements; friend of Dyers (qv).

NOTMAN, Jean, recruit sent by J.H.T. to Ningbo, 1864; assistant to Mrs Bausum (qv).

OLYPHANT, D. W. C., Am. Presby. merchant ship-owner, partner of C. W. King (qv); 1826 Canton, donated press and office for Chinese Repository; donated 51 trans-Pacific passages for missionaries; d. 1851.

PALMERSTON, Viscount, (1784–1865); Tory, Whig statesman, 1808–65; 1830–51 periodically Foreign Sec.; 1855, 1859–65 Prime Minister.

PARKER, H. M., Am. Episc.; Shangdong (Shantung); 1861 martyred Yantai (Chefoo).

PARKER, Dr John, brother of Dr Wm. Parker; 1863 Ningbo, independent; 1865 United Presby. Ch. of Scotland, Ningbo.

PARKER, Dr Peter, MD; (1804–88); Am. Board (ABCFM); 1834 Canton; first medical missionary in China (not first western physician); 1835 Ophthalmic Hospital; 1838 formed 'Medical Missionary Soc. in China'; 1843–44, semi-skilled interpreter-negotiator for US treaty; 1850 General Hosp., Canton; several times US chargé d'affaires and minister.

PARKER, Dr William, CES 1854–63; Shanghai, Ningbo.

PARKES, Sir Henry (Harry) S., c 1850 HBM interpreter (consular cadet); 1860, hero of Tientsin-Peking campaign; 1856 vice-consul, Canton; knighthood; HBM minister, Peking.

PEARCY, George, Am. Southern Bapt., Shanghai; cholera at Shanghai, nursed by J.H.T.

PEARSE, George, London stockbroker; CES foreign sec.; co-founder Foreign Evangelist Soc.; friend and adviser of J.H.T.; later missionary to N. Africa, initiated N. Africa Mission.

PENNEFATHER, William, vicar, Christ Church, Barnet; later Mildmay, N. London; convener, Barnet and Mildmay conferences; hymn-writer, friend of J.H.T.

PERRY, Commodore, 1853–54 Am. treaty with Japan.

PIERCY, George, 1850 to China at own expense; 1851 Canton; 1853 adopted by Wesleyan Meth. Miss. Soc.; joined by Josiah Cox (qv).

POLO, Nicolo and Matteo, 1260 to China; 1267 welcomed by Kublai Khan; 1269 arr. Venice with Khan's request to Pope for 100 wise men; 1271 to China with Marco (qv).

POLO, Marco, (1245–1324); son of Nicolo; 1275 Peking, served Kublai Khan; 1275 (aged 30) gov. of Yangzhou (Yangchow); official journeys to S.W. China, Burma, Indo-China, India; 1292 with Nicolo and Matteo escorted royal princess by sea to Persian Gulf and N. Persia; to Venice via Black Sea; 1298 commanded ship in war with Genoa, imprisoned with a writer, dictated travels.

POTT, F. L. Hawks, DD; Am. Prot. Episc.; president, St John's Univ., Shanghai; historian of Shanghai.

POTTIER, François, founder 1756, West China mission of Soc. des Missions Étrangères de Paris.

POTTINGER, Sir Henry, 1841 HBM plenipotentiary, Supt. of Trade, succeeded Capt. Charles Elliot; concluded first opium war; 1842 'diplomatic honeymoon' with Qi Ying (qv), negotiated Nanking Treaty.

QIAN LONG, (Ch'ien Lung) (1736–96); 4th emperor, Qing (Ch'ing) dynasty.

QI SHAN, (Ch'i Shan) 1840 gov. of Zhili (Chihli); viceroy of Canton after Lin Ze-xu (qv); cashiered, exiled, after Convention of Chuanbi (Ch'üanpi).

QI YING, 1842 succeeded Qi Shan; initiated 'diplomatic honeymoon', negotiated Nanking Treaty; gov. of Canton; issued edict of toleration.

QIU A-GONG, (Ch'iu A-kung; Kew A-gang); Christian printer, Malacca, with Liang A-fa (qv).

QUARTERMAN, J. W., Am. Presby.; 1847–57 Ningbo; smallpox, nursed by J.H.T.; d. 1857.

RADCLIFFE, Reginald, solicitor, gentleman-evangelist of second evangelical awakening; friend of J.H.T.

RADSTOCK, Lord, evangelical Anglican evangelist in aristocratic Russian, E. European society; closely associated with Brethren; friend of J.H.T.

RAFFLES, Sir Thomas Stamford, (1781–1826); 1805 Penang; 1811–16 lieut-gov., Java; 1817 knighted; 1817 *et seq* gov. of Sumatra; 1819 founded Singapore; 1820–24 gov. Singapore and Bencoolen, Sumatra.

RANKIN, Henry V., Am. Presby.; 1847 Ningbo; co-translator of Ningbo vernacular NT.

REED, Hon. W. B., US ambassador, Peking, 1858–60.

RICCI, Matteo/Matthew, (1552–1610); Soc. of Jesus; 1582 Macao; 1585–89 Zhaoqing, Zhaozhou (Chaoch'ing, Chaochow); 1601 Peking; by 1605 had converts at Court and Hanlin Academy, 200 neophytes; enjoyed confidence of Kang Xi (K'ang Hsi); policies repudiated by papacy.

ROBERTS, Issachar Jacocks, (not R.J.R. as in some sources); Am. Bapt.; 1833–67 Canton, Shanghai; 1837 Canton, taught Hong Xiu-quan (qv), Taiping leader; 1842 first missionary in Hong Kong, with J. L. Shuck.

RUSSELL, William Armstrong, CMS; 1847 Ningbo; 1872–79 first bishop of N. China; d. 1879.

SCHALL von BELL, Johann Adam, (1591–1666); Soc. of Jesus; astronomer; 1622 Peking; 1645 president, Imperial Board of Astronomers; chaplain to imperial palace.

SCHERESCHEWSKY, Samuel Isaac Joseph, (1831–1906); converted rabbi; Am. Prot. Episc.; 1839 Shanghai; 1862 Peking; 1877 bishop; 1881 paralysed; for next 25 years China's greatest Bible translator.

SCHMIDT, Charles, 1. 1860 missionary in Suzhou (Soochow); friend of J.H.T.; 2. 1864 officer of Ever-Victorious Army converted through James Meadows; became missionary in Suzhou (see Notes).

SEYMOUR, Admiral Sir Michael, commander-in-chief, East Asia; 1856 blockaded, bombarded, occupied Canton; deported viceroy, Ye Ming-sheng (qv).

SHEPHERD, William, one of Wesley's first seven travelling preachers; daughter (? grand-daughter) m. John Taylor, J.H.T.'s grandfather.

SHUCK, J. Lewis, first Am. Baptist in China proper; 1836 Macao; with I. J. Roberts (qv), first missionary in Hong Kong; member of Delegates' Committee, 1852 Bible.

SHUN ZHI, (Shun Chih) first Qing (Ch'ing) dynasty emperor, 1644–61.

SISSONS, Elizabeth, rejected J.H.T.'s proposals.

SKINNER, Anne, fiancée of George Crombie (qv); 1865 Ningbo.

SMITH, George, CMS; China survey, 1844; 1846 returned with T. McClatchie (qv); 1849–64 first bishop of Victoria, Hong Kong.

SOONG, (conventional, for Song) Methodist minister, m. descendant of Paul Xu (Hsü) daughters m. Sun Yat-sen, Chiang Kai-shek, H. H. Kung.

SOOTHILL, W. E., United Methodist Free Church, Ningbo, Wenzhou (Wenchow); educationalist, author, translator; 1920–35 Prof. of Chinese, Oxford.

STACEY, Miss, one-time Quaker, member of Brook Street chapel, Tottenham; long a friend of J.H.T.

STALLYBRASS, Thomas, Mongolian-speaking son of Edward Stallybrass, LMS missionary to Buriat Mongols, 1817–44; offered to CES.

STAUNTON, Sir George Thomas, Bart., aged 15 to China; 1793 interpreter, East India Co. and Lord Macartney's embassy; Chief of East India Co., Canton; 1816 First Commissioner on Lord Amherst's embassy.

STAVELEY, Sir Charles, 1862 commander, British land forces, China.

STEVENS, Edwin, Am. Seamen's Friend Soc. and Am. Board (ABCFM); 1832–36 Canton; d. 1836.

STEVENSON, John Whiteford, (1844–1918); son of laird of Thriepwood, Renfrewshire; with G. Stott (qv) first of CIM after Crombie (qv); Oct. 1865 dep. UK; 1866–74 Ningbo, Shaoxing (Shaohsing); 1875–80 Burma; 1880 crossed China W. to E. 1,900 miles; 1885–1916 deputy-director, CIM.

STOCK, Eugene, CMS Gen. Sec. after H. Venn; historian.

STOTT, George, Aberdeenshire schoolmaster, one-legged; Oct. 1865 dep. UK; 1866 Ningbo; 1869–89 Wenzhou (Wenchow); d. 1889.

STRONACH, John, LMS, 1838–76, 30 years without furlough; 1838–44 Singapore; 1846 Amoy; Bible translator, Delegates' Committee, 1852; S. Dyer's friend.

STRONACH, Alexander, LMS; 1838–39 Singapore; 1839–44 Penang; 1844–46 Singapore; 1846 Amoy.

SUN YAT-SEN, (1867–1925); 1891 first medical graduate, Hong Kong; 1905 founded China Revolutionary League, in Europe, Japan; 1911–12 founder and first president Republic of China; m. descendant of Paul Xu (see Soong).

TAMERLANE, (Timur-i-leng) (1335–1405); descendant of founder of Mogul dynasty, India; conquered Turkestan, Persia, Syria; a scourge; died preparing to invade China.

TAO KUANG, (*see* Dao Guang).

TARN, William, brother of Samuel Dyer's wife; director, Religious Tract Soc.; guardian of Burella and Maria Dyer.

TAYLOR, Amelia, (1808–81); first daughter of Benjamin Brook Hudson; J.H.T.'s mother.

TAYLOR, Amelia Hudson, (1835–1918); J.H.T.'s sister.

TAYLOR, Arthur, CES missionary, Hong Kong; 1853–55.

TAYLOR, James Sr. (1749–95); host to J. Wesley.

TAYLOR, John, (1778–1834); 1799 m. Mary Shepherd (*see* Wm. Shepherd).

TAYLOR, James Jr, (1807–81); J.H.T.'s father.

TAYLOR, James Hudson (21 May 1832–3 June 1905); 1853 dep. UK; 1 Mar. 1854 arr. Shanghai; 20 Jan. 1858 m. Maria Jane Dyer; 1857 with J. Jones (qv) began Ningbo Mission; 1865 founded China Inland Mission; 28 Nov. 1871 m. Jane E. Faulding; 3 June 1905 d. Changsha, Hunan.

TAYLOR, Maria Jane, née Dyer, (1837–70) daughter of Samuel Dyer (qv); wife of J.H.T.; mother of Grace, Herbert Hudson, Frederick Howard, Samuel, Jane, Maria, Charles, Noel.

TIDMAN, Dr Arthur, Foreign Sec., LMS; member CES Gen. Committee.

TOMLIN, Jacob, LMS; 1827 Malaya; 1828 Bangkok with Gutzlaff.

TOURNON, (*see* de Tournon).

TRUELOVE, Richard, 1865 recruit for Ningbo, failed to go.

TSENG KUO-FAN, (*see* Zeng); TZ'U HSI, (*see* Ci Xi).

UNDERHILL, C. B., Sec. BMS; friend of J.H.T., nominated him for FRGS.

VALENTINE, Jarvis D., CMS recruit taught by J.H.T.; 1864 Ningbo.

VALIGNANO, Allesandri, (1537–1606); 1579 Jesuit Visitor to Japan.

van SOMMER, J., member, Hackney Brethren circle with W. T. Berger (brother-in-law) and Philip H. Gosse; editor, *The Missionary Reporter*.

VAUGHAN, Marianne, first fiancée of J.H.T.

VENIAMINOV, John (Innokenty), (1797–1879); Russian Orthodox pioneer, Aleutians, Kuriles, N. Siberia, Manchuria,

Japan; Metropolitan of Moscow; founded Orthodox Missionary Soc.

VENN, Henry, Sr and Jr, secretaries of CMS.

VENN, John, member of Eclectic Society (Clapham Sect); father of Henry, Sr.

VERBIEST, Ferdinand, (1617–88) Jesuit astronomer, Peking.

VIGEON, Mr and Mrs, 1865 recruits for Ningbo, prevented from going.

VOGEL, Karl, Kassel Miss. Assoc.; 1847 Hong Kong, Guangdong (Kwangtung); Gutzlaff's recruit.

WADE, Lieut Thomas Francis, British forces, Ningbo, 1841; vice-consul Shanghai under Alcock; Battle of Muddy Flat; became Sinologue, HBM minister, Peking.

WANG LAE-DJÜN, (Wang Li-jun); Ningbo Mission convert; with J.H.T. London, 1860–64; pastor, Hangzhou (Hangchow).

WARD, Col. Frederick Townsend, Am. commander, Ever-Victorious Army; 1862 mortally wounded at Cixi (Tzeki), Ningbo.

WARD, Hon. John E. 1859 US plenipotentiary; 1860 at capture and Convention of Peking.

WAY, R. Q., Am. Presby.; 1844 Ningbo; brother-in-law of J. W. Quarterman (qv).

WELLS WILLIAMS, Samuel, DD; (1812–84); Am. Board, printer, scholar; 1833 Canton; 1847 author *The Middle Kingdom*; 1851 succeeded E. C. Bridgman (qv) editor, *Chinese Repository*; interpreter to US legation, Peking; chargé d'affaires to 1876; Prof. of Chinese, Yale Univ.

WELTON, Dr, CMS; first medical, Fuzhou (Foochow).

WHITEFIELD, George, (1714–70); at Oxford with J. and C. Wesley; Methodist until 1741, then independent; d. in America.

WILLIAMSON, Alexander, LL D; (1829–90); 1855 LMS Shanghai; 1863 National Bible Soc. of Scotland, Shandong, Yantai; 1865 Peking, Mongolia, Manchuria; 1887 founded Christian Literature Soc.

WINNES, Ph., Basel Mission; 1852 joined Theodore Hamberg (qv), Guangdong (Kwangtung) after R. Lechler died.

WYLIE, Alexander, (1815–87); LMS; 1847 Shanghai, printer, Delegates' version of Bible; 1863 Bible Soc. (BFBS); one of the greatest Sinologues.

XAVIER, Francis, (1506–52); Basque co-founder with Ignatius Loyola of Jesuit order; 1542 India; 1549 Japan; 1552 d. Shangchuan (Shangch'üan) Is., near Macao.

XI LIAO-ZHU, (Hsi Liao-chu, Hsi Sheng-mo) (1835–96);

graduate (Xiu-cai) of Shanxi (Shansi); 1879 converted through David Hill; hymnwriter, well-known as 'Pastor Hsi'.

XIAN FENG, (Hsien Feng) (1851–61); 7th Qing (Ch'ing) dynasty emperor.

XU GUANG-QI, (Hsü Kuang-ch'i, Paul Hsü); Ming dynasty official; convert of Matthew Ricci before 1610; 1850 his family home Xu Jia Wei (Siccawei) became Jesuit headquarters, near Shanghai.

YE MING-SHENG, (Yeh Ming-shen) imperial commissioner and viceroy, Canton; 1856–57 'Arrow' incident and Br. attack on Canton, captured, d. Calcutta.

YEHONALA, *see* Ci Xi.

YONG SAM-TEK, Chinese mandarin in London, 1805; taught Chinese to Morrison; later helped him in Canton.

ZENG GUO-FAN, (Tseng Kuo-fan) (1811–72) scholar, provincial governor; 1854 defeated Taipings; viceroy of the 'Two Jiangs' (Jiangxi, Jiangsu), Zhili.

ZHONG WANG, (Chung Wang) Taiping 'Loyal Prince'; military strategist, commander in final successes, 1863–64 before defeat ending rebellion.

ZHU JIU-DAO, (Chu Chiu-tao) Taiping rebel leader; planned anti-Manchu, pro-Ming revolt; joined Hong Xiu-quan (qv) to wage Taiping rebellion.

BIBLIOGRAPHY
(for Books One to Three)

British
Library ref.

BALL, Richard, *Handbook of China*, 1854,
OMFA 11

B & FB Society, *Monthly Reporter*, Vols 1 & 2,   London III,
1858–88   pp. 926.f

BENTLEY-TAYLOR, David, *Java Saga:
Christian Progress in Muslim Java (The
Weathercock's Reward)*, CIM/OMF Books
1967/1975

BERESFORD, C. W. D., *The Break-up of China*,   8022.dd.32
1899

BOONE, M. Muriel *The Seed of the Church in
China*, St Andrew Press, Edinburgh

BREDON, Juliet *Sir Robert Hart* Hutchinson &   010817.de.10
Co 1909

BRIDGMAN, Mrs E. J. G. *The Life and Labors
of Elijah Coleman Bridgman* 1864

BRIDGMAN, Elijah C. & Eliza J. G. *The*   4985.aaa.27
Pioneer of American Missions in China 1864

BRINE, Lindesay *The Taeping Rebellion* 1862   9056.b.10

BROOMHALL, Marshall *Heirs Together: A*   4908.e.6
Memoir of Benjamin & Amelia Broomhall
Morgan & Scott/CIM 1918

   John W. Stevenson: One of Christ's Stalwarts   4956.aa.33
Morgan & Scott/CIM 1919

   Hudson Taylor: The Man who Dared   4907.aa.34
Religious Tract Society/CIM

   Hudson Taylor: The Man who Believed God   4907.dd.21
Hodder & Stoughton 1929

   Robert Morrison: A Master-builder CIM 1924   4908.ee.24

   The Jubilee Story of the China Inland Mission   4763.g.4
Morgan & Scott/CIM 1915

   Hudson Taylor's Legacy Hodder &   10823.a.16
Stoughton 1931

By Love Compelled: The Call of the China Inland Mission CIM 1947 (H & S 1936)   4768.a.34

The Chinese Empire: A General & Missionary Survey Morgan & Scott/CIM 1907   4767.eeee.4

BRYANT, Sir Arthur *A Thousand Years of the British Monarchy* Collins

CARY-ELWES, Columba *China and the Cross* Longmans, Green & Co 1957   4768.ccc.21

CHINA MAIL (Hong Kong)   British Library, Colindale

CHINA'S MILLIONS Magazine of the China Inland Mission 1875–1951

Chinese Evangelization Society REPORT 1853 OMFA (Archives of OMF)

CHINESE RECORDER AND MISSIONARY JOURNAL: Vol 1 1868 et seq OMFA

CHINESE REPOSITORY, *The*, Canton 1832–42

CMS *Gleaner, Intelligencer, Register, Reports* Church Missionary Society

COLE, R. A. *The Gospel according to St Mark*: Tyndale Commentary, The Tyndale Press 1961

COLLIER, Richard *William Booth: The General Next to God* Collins 1965   X.100.1629

COLLIS, Maurice Stewart *Foreign Mud* 1946   9059.df.15

CLARK-KENNEDY, A. E. *'The London' (Hospital)* 2 vols

CORDIER, Henri *The Life of Alexander Wylie* 1887   10803.cc.4/6

DAVIES, Evan *China and her Spiritual Claims* John Snow 1845   1369.b.24

Memoir of the Reverend Samuel Dyer John Snow 1846   1372.c.20

DU BUSE, H. C. *The Dragon Image and Demon: The Three Religions of China* A. C. Armstrong (USA) 1887

DYSON, Verne *A Hong Kong Governor: Sir John Bowring* Macao 1930   010822.df.39

EAMES, James Bromby *The English in China* 1909   09008.f.19

FAIRBANK, John King *Trade and Diplomacy on*   Ac.2692.10
the China Coast 2 vols. 1953 Edn. Cambridge,
Massachusetts

FORBES, Archibald *Chinese Gordon* George
Routledge & Sons 1884

FOREIGN OFFICE LIBRARY China FO/17
Public Records Office

FOSTER, John *The Nestorian Tablet and Hymns*
SPCK

GLEANER, CES *The Gleaner in the Missionary Field*
The Chinese & General Missionary Gleaner
The Chinese Missionary Gleaner Chinese Evangelization
Society 1850–60 OMFA

GUTZLAFF, Charles *A Journal of Three*   1046.c.16
Voyages along the Coast of China in 1831, 1832
& 1833 with notices of Siam, Corea and the
Loochoo Islands 1833

    Report of Proceedings on a Voyage to the   1046.c.15
Northern Ports of China (*see* LINDSAY, H. H)
1833

HACKNEY GAZETTE *North London:*
Historical Associations 1928

HALDANE, Charlotte *The Last Great Empress*
of China Constable 1965

HALL, Capt. Basil, RN *Narrative of a Voyage to*   982.i.16
Java, China and the Great Loochoo Island
Edward Moxen 1818

    1840 edn.   G.15729

HART, Sir Robert *These from the Land of Sinim*   8022.cc.48/
                                                 010817.d.10

HAWKS, POTT, F. L. *A Short History of*   010056.aaa.46
Shanghai Kelly & Walsh 1928

HOLT, Edgar C. *The Opium Wars in China* 1964   X.709-581
edn.

HOOK, Brian *China's Three Thousand Years*: The Modern
History of China THE TIMES Newspaper (publishers)

HUGGETT, Frank E. *Victorian England as seen*
by PUNCH Sidgwick & Johnson 1978

HUC, Evariste Régis *Christianity in China,*   2208.bb.8
Tartary and Thibet 1857

    Life and Travel in Tartary, Thibet and China   10057.aa.39
1867

INGLIS, Brian *The Opium War* Hodder &   09059.pp.30
Stoughton 1976

LATOURETTE, Kenneth Scott *A History of*   4763.g.4
Christian Missions in China SPCK 1929

    A History of the Expansion of Christianity   4533.ff.22
1800–1914 Eyre and Spottiswoode

    These Sought a Country: Tipple Lectures   4807.e.25
1950 edn. Harper & Brothers

LEGGE, Helen E. *James Legge (1815–97)*   04429.1.37
Religious Tract Society 1905

LEGGE, James *The Famine in China* 1878 edn.   11102.b.20

    The Nestorian Monument (Oxford   4532.ee.13/14
University Lecture) 1888 edn.

LINDSAY, H. H. *Report to the Hon. East India*
Company on a Voyage to the Northern Ports of
China 1832 (voyage of the Lord Amherst)

LINTON, E. Lynn *A Night in a Hospital* (from
magazine *Belgravia*) 1879

LOCKHART, William *The Medical Missionary in*   10058.d.16
China 1861 edn.

MacGILLIVRAY, Donald *A Century of*   4764.ff.11
Protestant Missions in China (Centennial
Conference Historical Volume) Shanghai 1907

McGILVARY, Daniel *A Half-Century among the*
Siamese and the Lao Fleming, Revell & Co.
1912

McNEUR, George Hunter *Liang A-fa* Oxford
University Press China Agency 1934

MARTIN, W. A. P. *A Cycle of Cathay* 1896   010056.g.7

MEDHURST, W. H., Sr *China: Its State and*   571.g.10
Prospects John Snow 1838

    A Glance at the Interior of China in 1845   10055.c.25
Shanghai Mission Press 1849

MEDHURST, Sir Walter H. *Curiosities of Street*   10057.aaa.16
Literature in China 1871

    The Foreigner in Far Cathay Edward Stanton   010058.ee.35
1872

MICHIE, Alexander *Missionaries in China*   4767.ccc.10
Edward Stanford, Ldn. 1891

    The Englishman in China: as illustrated in the   09057.d.3
Career of Sir Rutherford Alcock Wm.

Blackwood & Sons, Edin. 1900 2 vols.

MORRIS, E. W. *The London Hospital* Edward
Arnold 1910

MORRISON, Mrs Robert *Memoirs of. . . Robert
Morrison* Longmans 2 vols 1839

MORSE, Hosea Ballou *The International*   2386.c.17
Relations of the Chinese Empire (9 vols) vols
1–3 1910

MOULE, Arthur E. *The Story of the Cheh-Kiang
Mission* CMS 1879

MÜLLER, George (ed. G. F. Bergin)
Autobiography: Narrative J. Nisbet & Co. Ltd.
1905

NEATBY, Mrs Thomas *The Life and Ministry of
Thomas Neatby* Pickering & Inglis

NEILL, Rt Rev Stephen C. *A History of Christian
Missions* (Pelican History of the Church)
Penguin Books 1964

NEVIUS, Helen S. C. *The Life of John Livingston*   4985.eee.5
Nevius Revell 1895

NORTH CHINA HERALD (newspaper) 1854 et
seq British Library, Colindale

PADWICK, Constance E. *Henry Martyn:
Confessor of the Faith* Inter-Varsity Fellowship
1922

PARLEY, Peter *China and the Chinese* Simpkin   10058.a.26
Marshall 1843

PARLIAMENTARY PAPERS 1831–32 Vols VII,
X, XI, XXXVI, XLI (*see* Foreign Office
1840–60 opium wars) 1857 XLIII relating to the
opium trade with China

PIERSON, A. T. *George Müller of Bristol* Jas.
Nisbet & Co. Ltd. 1905

POLLOCK, John C. *Hudson Taylor & Maria*
Hodder & Stoughton

POLO, Marco *The Book of Ser Marco Polo, The
Venetian,* 1298 First printed edition 1477 (*see*
YULE)

PUNCH *PUNCH Panorama 1845–65* (*see*
HUGGETT, F. E.)

SELLMAN, R. R. *An Outline Atlas of Eastern
History* Edward Arnold Ltd.

Sianfu: The Nestorian Tablet   WP. 4683.49

SMITH, Arthur H. *The Uplift of China* The Young People's Missionary Movement of America 1909

STOCK, Eugene *A History of the Church*   4765.cc.28 *Missionary Society* Vols I–III 1899–1916

TAYLOR, Dr & Mrs Howard, *Hudson Taylor in Early Years: The Growth of a Soul* CIM and RTS, 1911

     Hudson Taylor and the China Inland Mission: The Growth of a Work of God, CIM and RTS, 1918

     Hudson Taylor's Spiritual Secret, CIM, 1932

TAYLOR, Mrs Howard (M. Geraldine Guinness), *The Story of the China Inland Mission*, 2 vols, 1892, Morgan & Scott

     Behind the Ranges: A Biography of J. O. Fraser, CIM

TAYLOR, J. Hudson, *China: Its Spiritual Need and Claims*, 1st–6th edns. 1865 et seq, CIM

     China's Spiritual Need and Claims, 7th edn. 1887, CIM 8th edn. 1890, CIM

     A Retrospect, 1875, CIM

     After Thirty Years, 1895, Morgan & Scott and CIM

WALEY, Arthur David, *The Opium War through*   09059. pp. 30 *Chinese Eyes*, London, 1958

WANG, Mary, *The Chinese Church that will not Die*, Hodder & Stoughton

WOODCOCK, George, *The British in the Far East*, Weidenfeld & Nicholson, 1969 (A Social History of the British Overseas)

WURTZBURG, C. E., *Raffles of the Eastern Isles*, Hodder & Stoughton, 1954

YULE, Sir Henry, *The Book of Ser Marco Polo the Venetian*, 1878, 2 vols.

INDEX

417